MW00788526

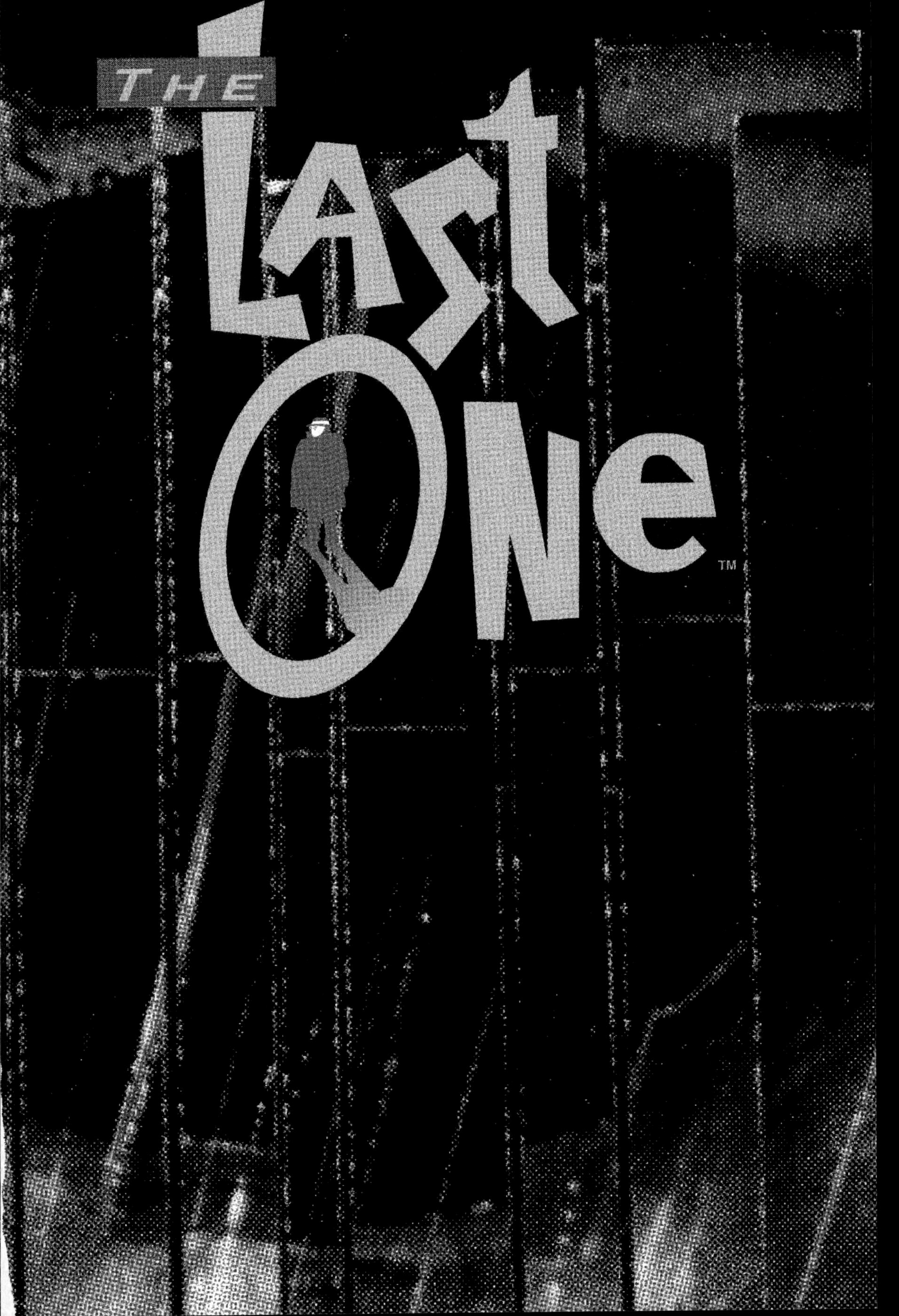
THE
Last
One™

Become our fan on Facebook **facebook.com/idwpublishing**
Follow us on Twitter **@idwpublishing**
Subscribe to us on YouTube **youtube.com/idwpublishing**
See what's new on Tumblr **tumblr.idwpublishing.com**
Check us out on Instagram **instagram.com/idwpublsing**

ISBN: 978-1-63140-685-0   19 18 17 16   1 2 3 4

Originally published by Vertigo as THE LAST ONE issues #1–6.

Ted Adams, CEO & Publisher
Greg Goldstein, President & COO
Robbie Robbins, EVP/Sr. Graphic Artist
Chris Ryall, Chief Creative Officer/Editor-in-Chief
Matthew Ruzicka, CPA, Chief Financial Officer
Dirk Wood, VP of Marketing
Lorelei Bunjes, VP of Digital Services
Jeff Webber, VP of Licensing, Digital and Subsidiary Rights
Jerry Bennington, VP of New Product Development

J.M. DeMatteis
Writer

Dan Sweetman
Artist

Todd Klein
Letterer

Karen Berger
Original Series Editor

Shelly Bond
Original Series
Assistant Editor

Justin Eisinger and
Alonzo Simon
Collection Editors

Ron Estevez
Collection Designer

Ted Adams
Publisher

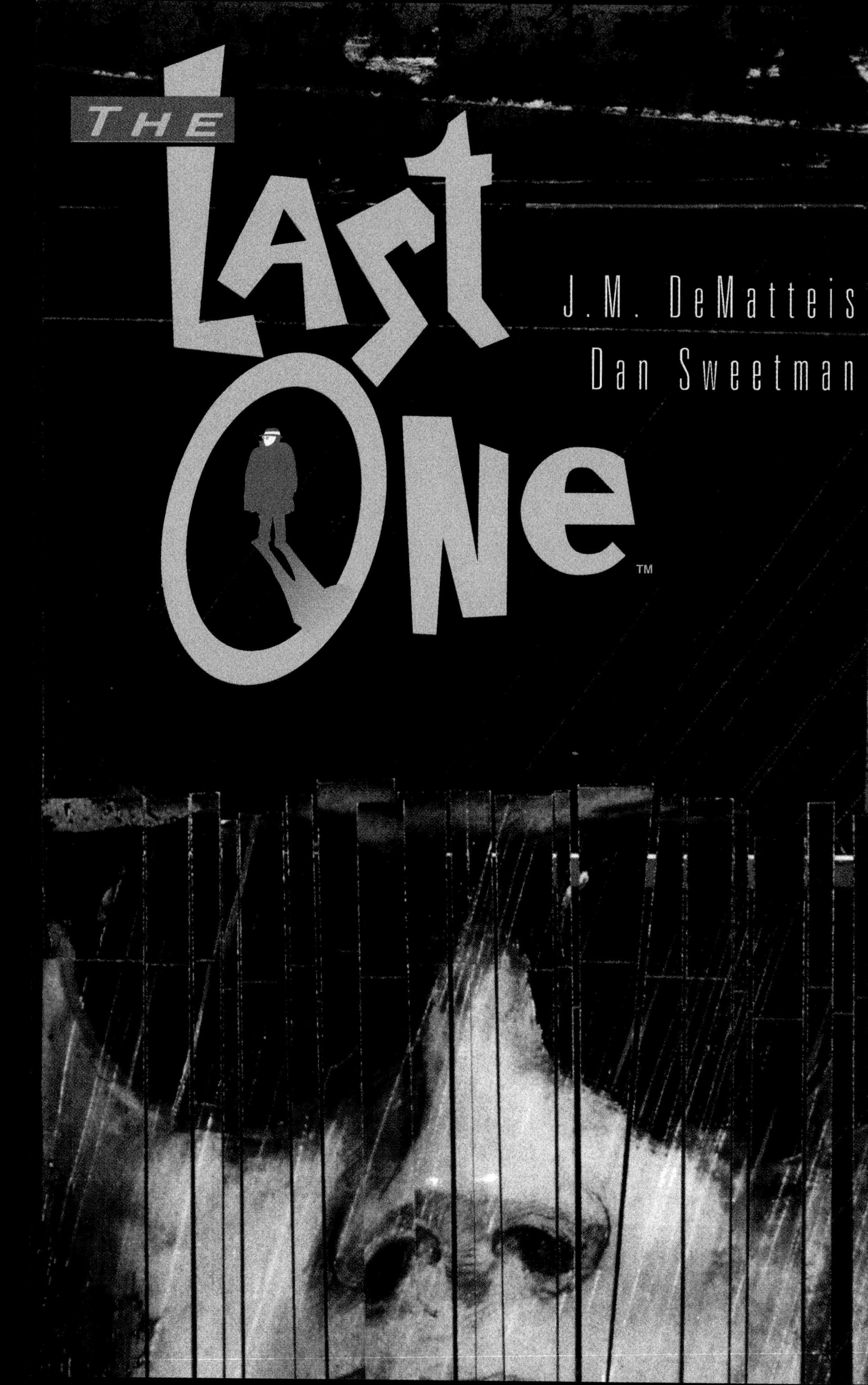
THE
Last One
TM
J.M. DeMatteis
Dan Sweetman

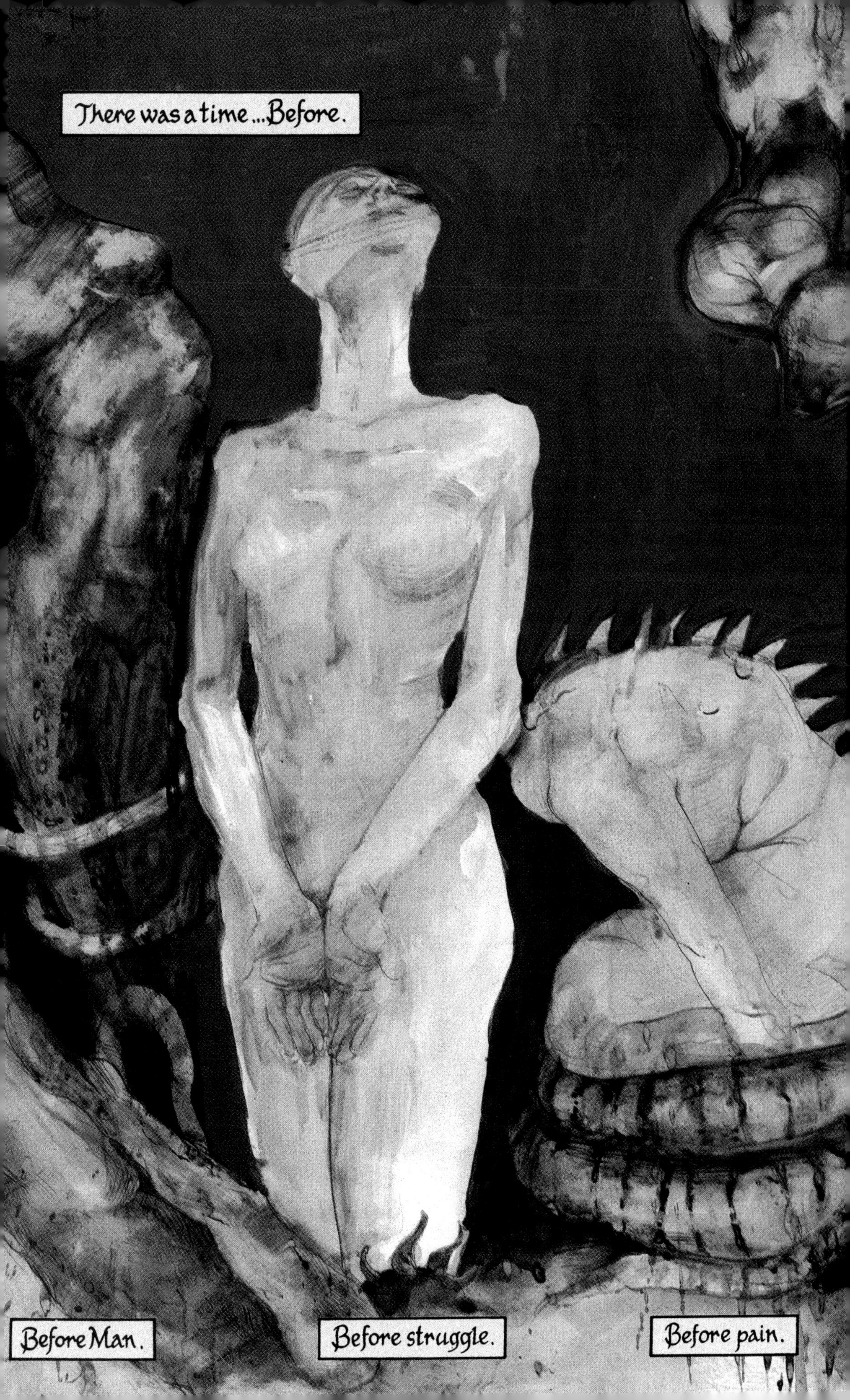
There was a time ... Before.
Before Man.
Before struggle.
Before pain.

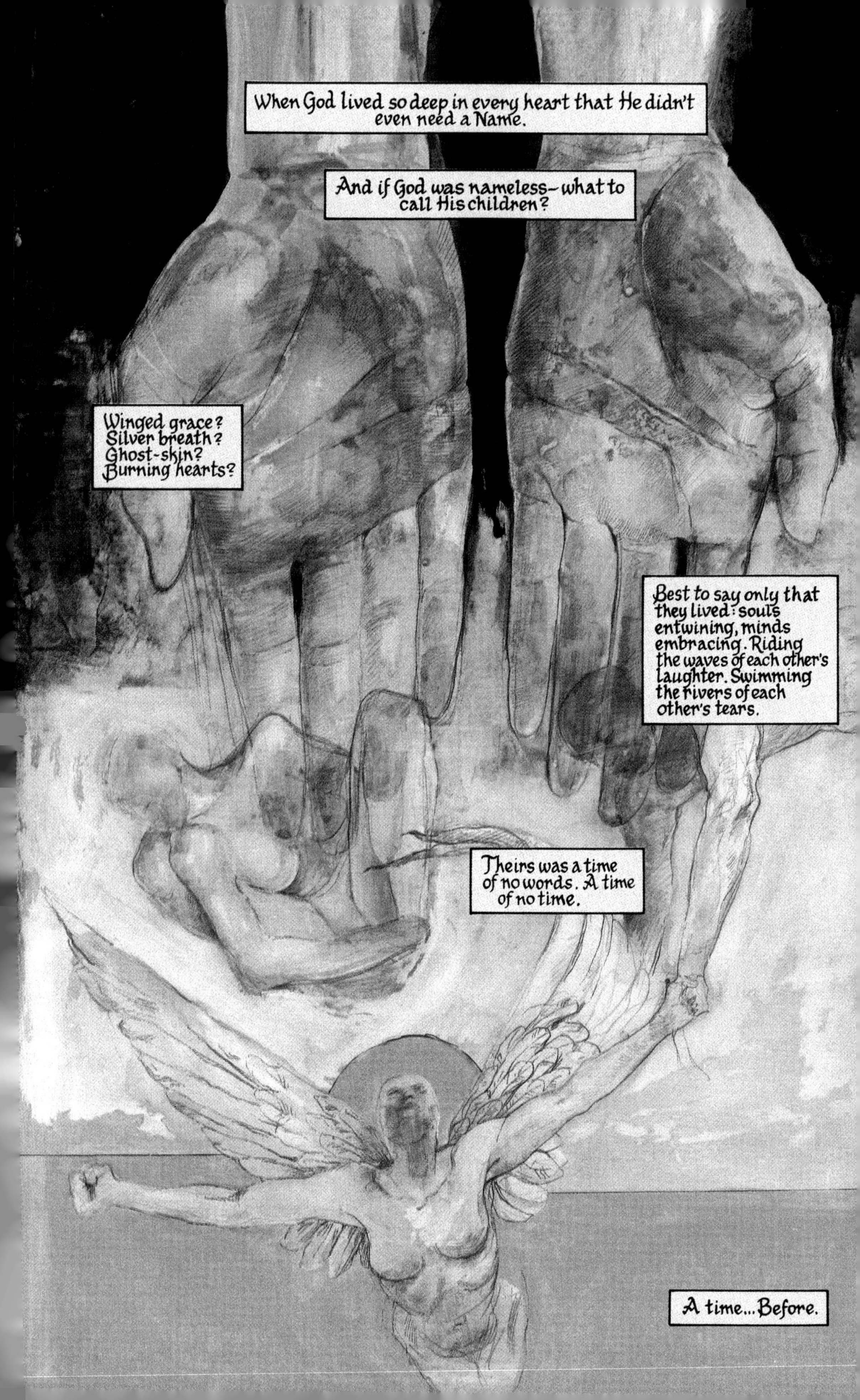
When God lived so deep in every heart that He didn't even need a Name.
And if God was nameless— what to call His children?
Winged grace? Silver breath? Ghost-skin? Burning hearts?
Best to say only that they lived: souls entwining, minds embracing. Riding the waves of each other's laughter. Swimming the rivers of each other's tears.
Theirs was a time of no words. A time of no time.
A time... Before.

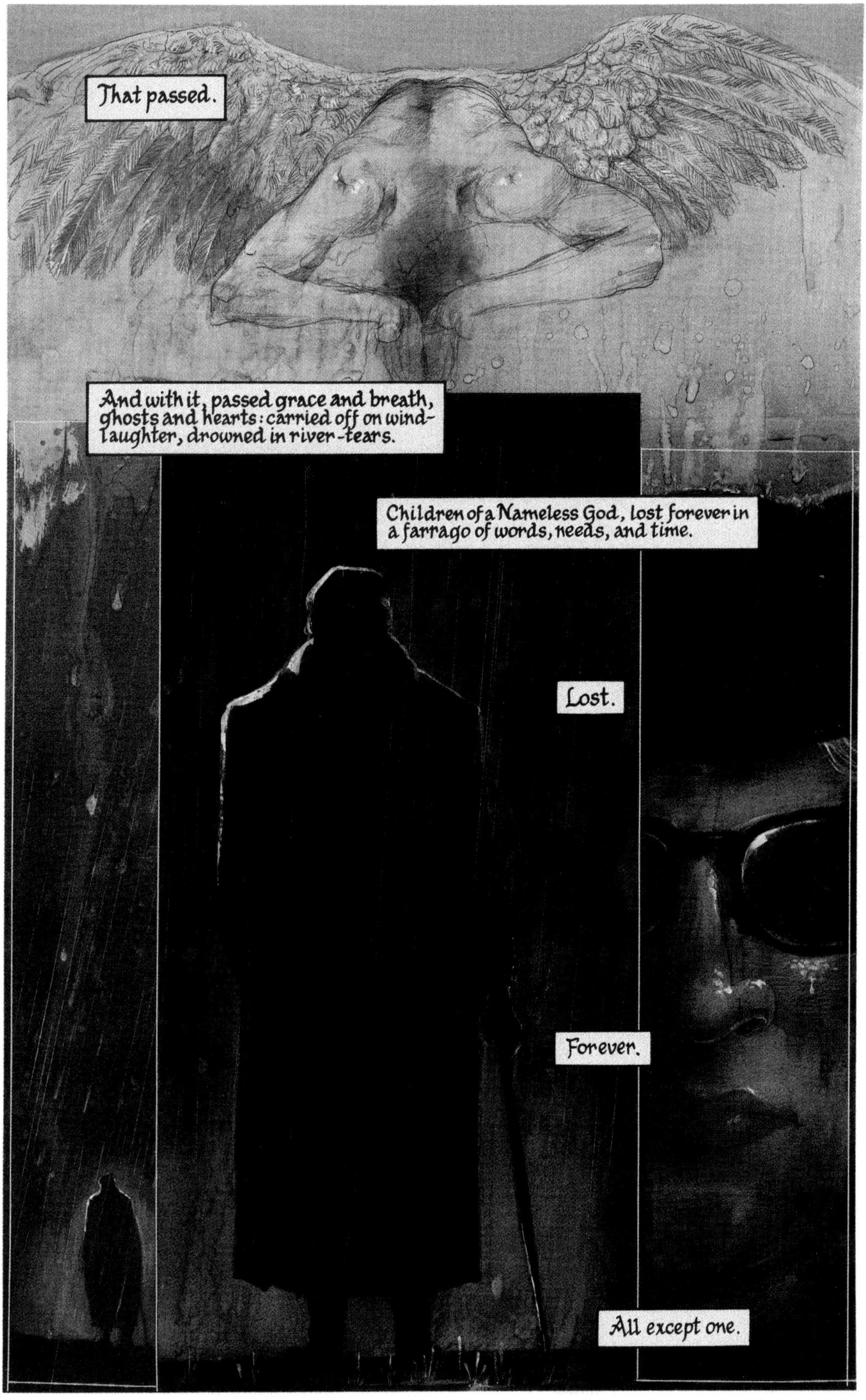
That passed.
And with it, passed grace and breath, ghosts and hearts: carried off on wind-laughter, drowned in river-tears.
Children of a Nameless God, lost forever in a farrago of words, needs, and time.
Lost.
Forever.
All except one.

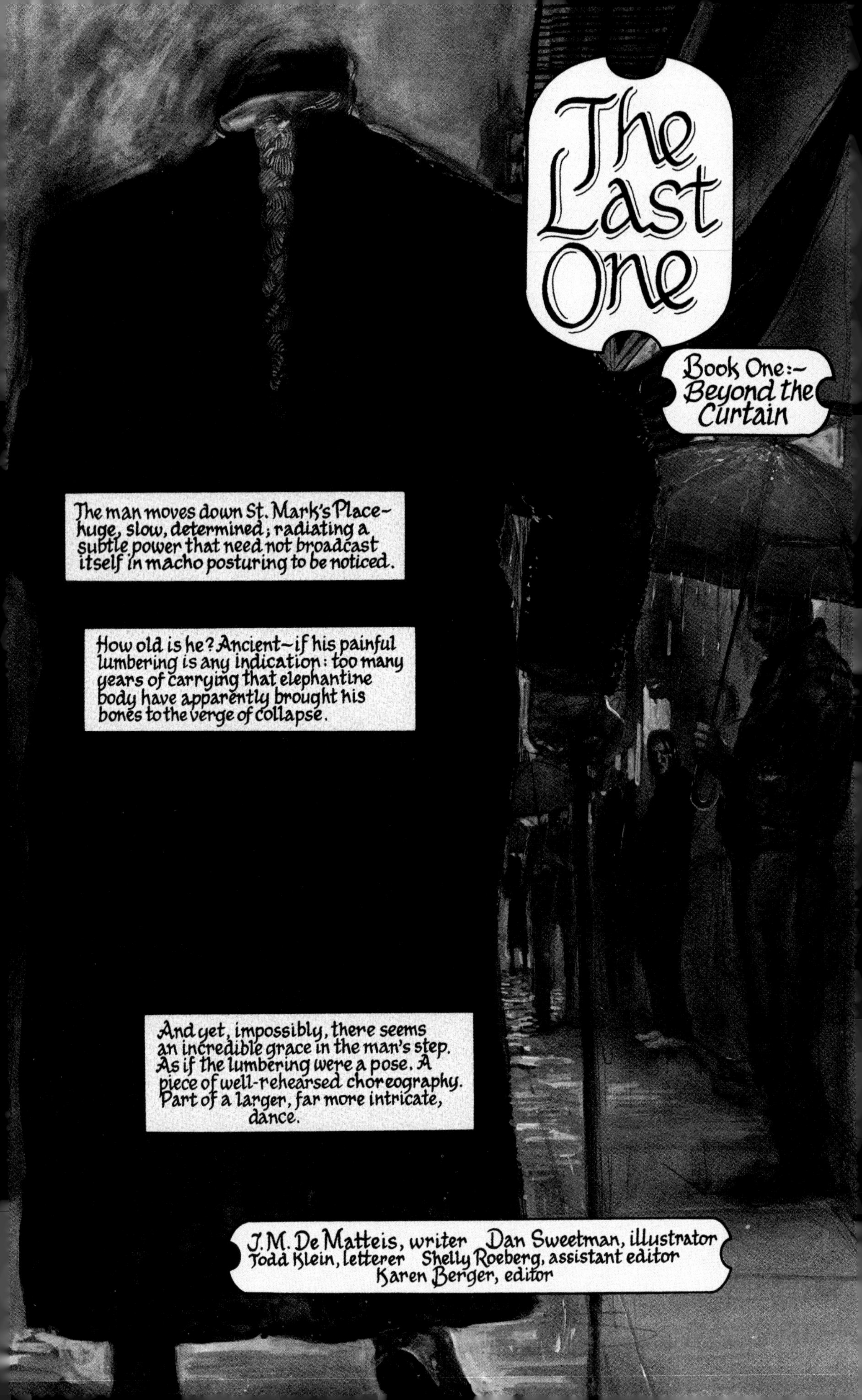
The Last One
Book One:- Beyond the Curtain
The man moves down St. Mark's Place- huge, slow, determined; radiating a subtle power that need not broadcast itself in macho posturing to be noticed.
How old is he? Ancient- if his painful lumbering is any indication: too many years of carrying that elephantine body have apparently brought his bones to the verge of collapse.
And yet, impossibly, there seems an incredible grace in the man's step. As if the lumbering were a pose. A piece of well-rehearsed choreography. Part of a larger, far more intricate, dance.
J.M. De Matteis, writer Dan Sweetman, illustrator Todd Klein, letterer Shelly Roeberg, assistant editor Karen Berger, editor

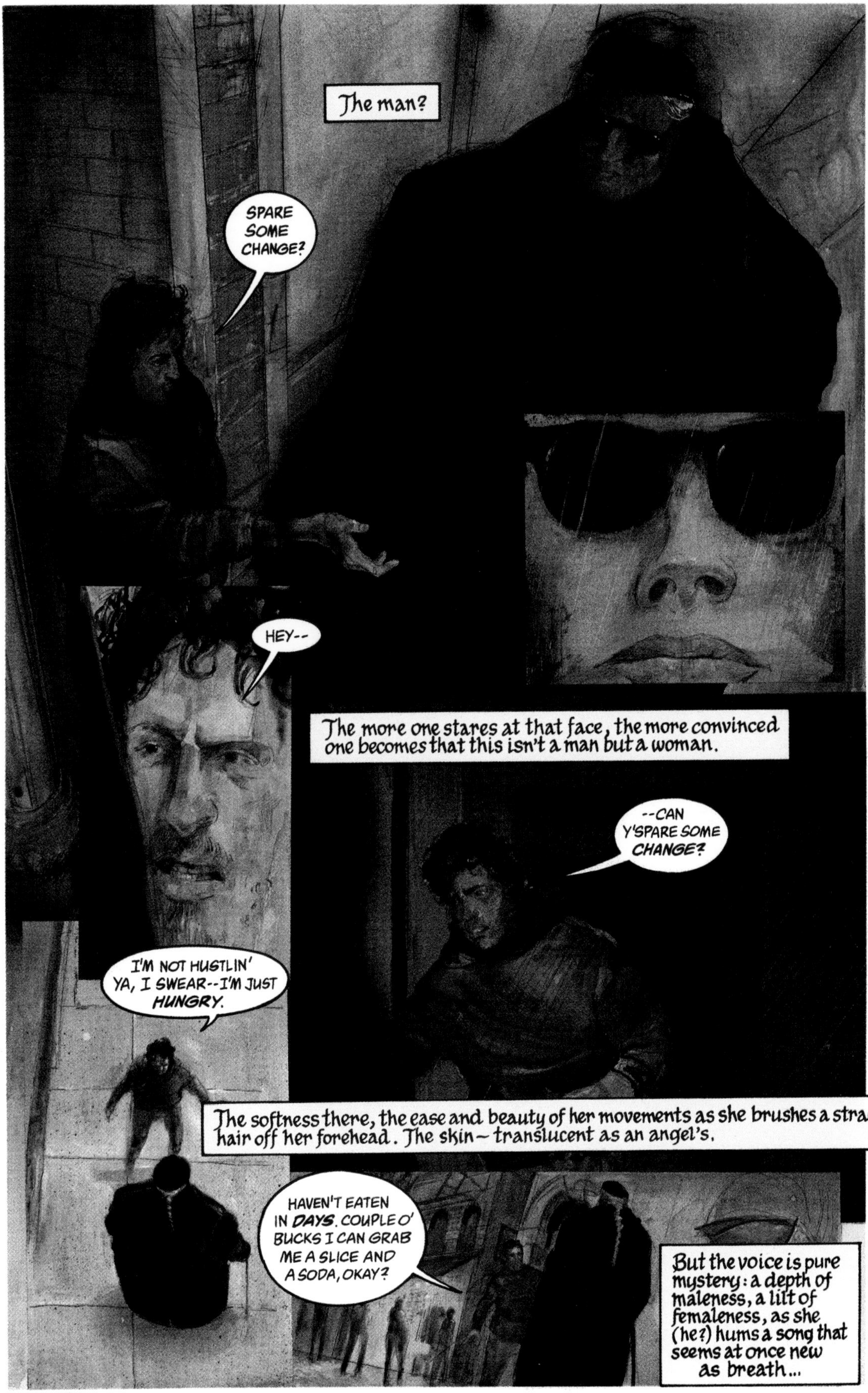
The man?
SPARE SOME CHANGE?
HEY--
The more one stares at that face, the more convinced one becomes that this isn't a man but a woman.
--CAN Y'SPARE SOME CHANGE?
I'M NOT HUSTLIN' YA, I SWEAR--I'M JUST HUNGRY.
The softness there, the ease and beauty of her movements as she brushes a stray hair off her forehead. The skin ~ translucent as an angel's.
HAVEN'T EATEN IN DAYS. COUPLE O' BUCKS I CAN GRAB ME A SLICE AND A SODA, OKAY?
But the voice is pure mystery: a depth of maleness, a lilt of femaleness, as she (he?) hums a song that seems at once new as breath...

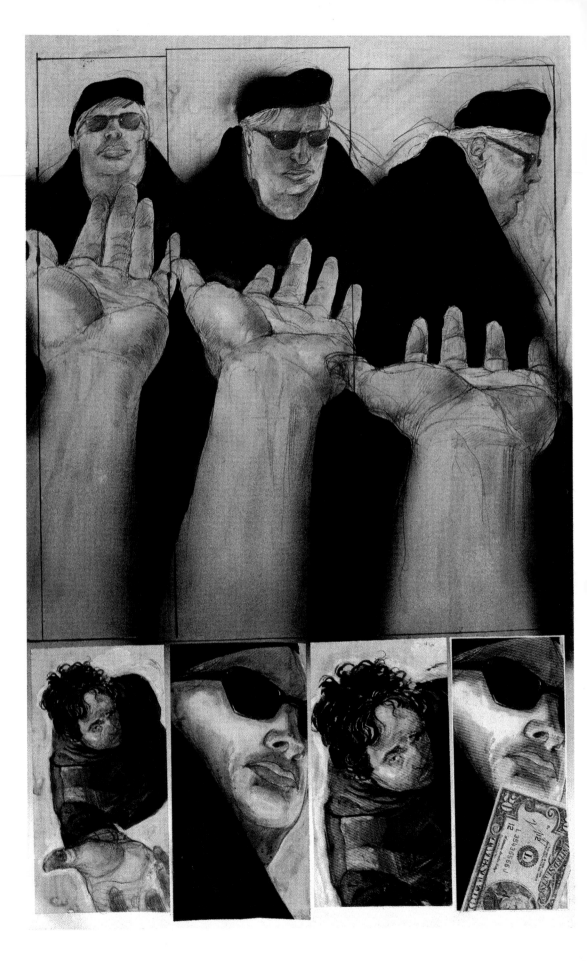

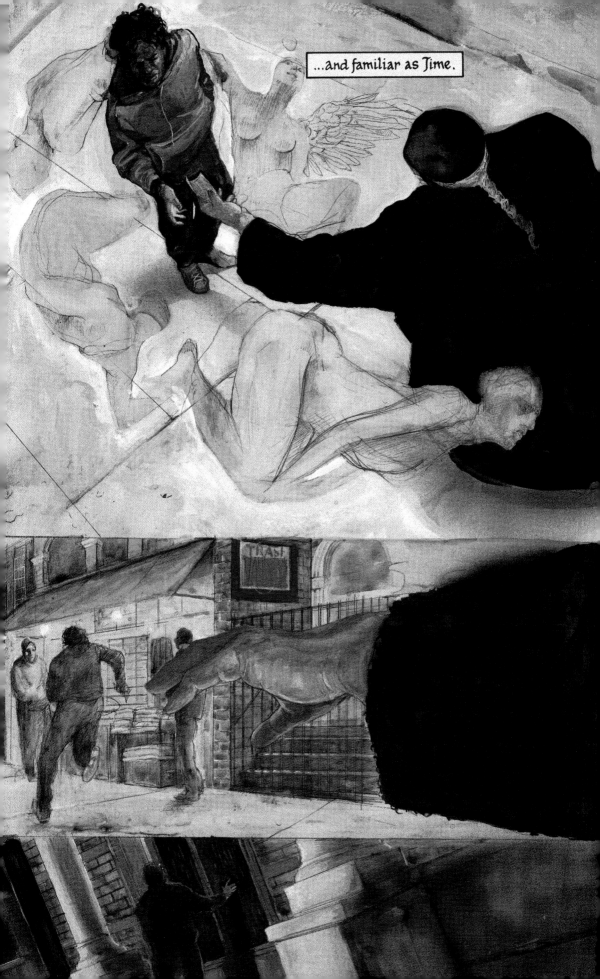

...and familiar as Time.

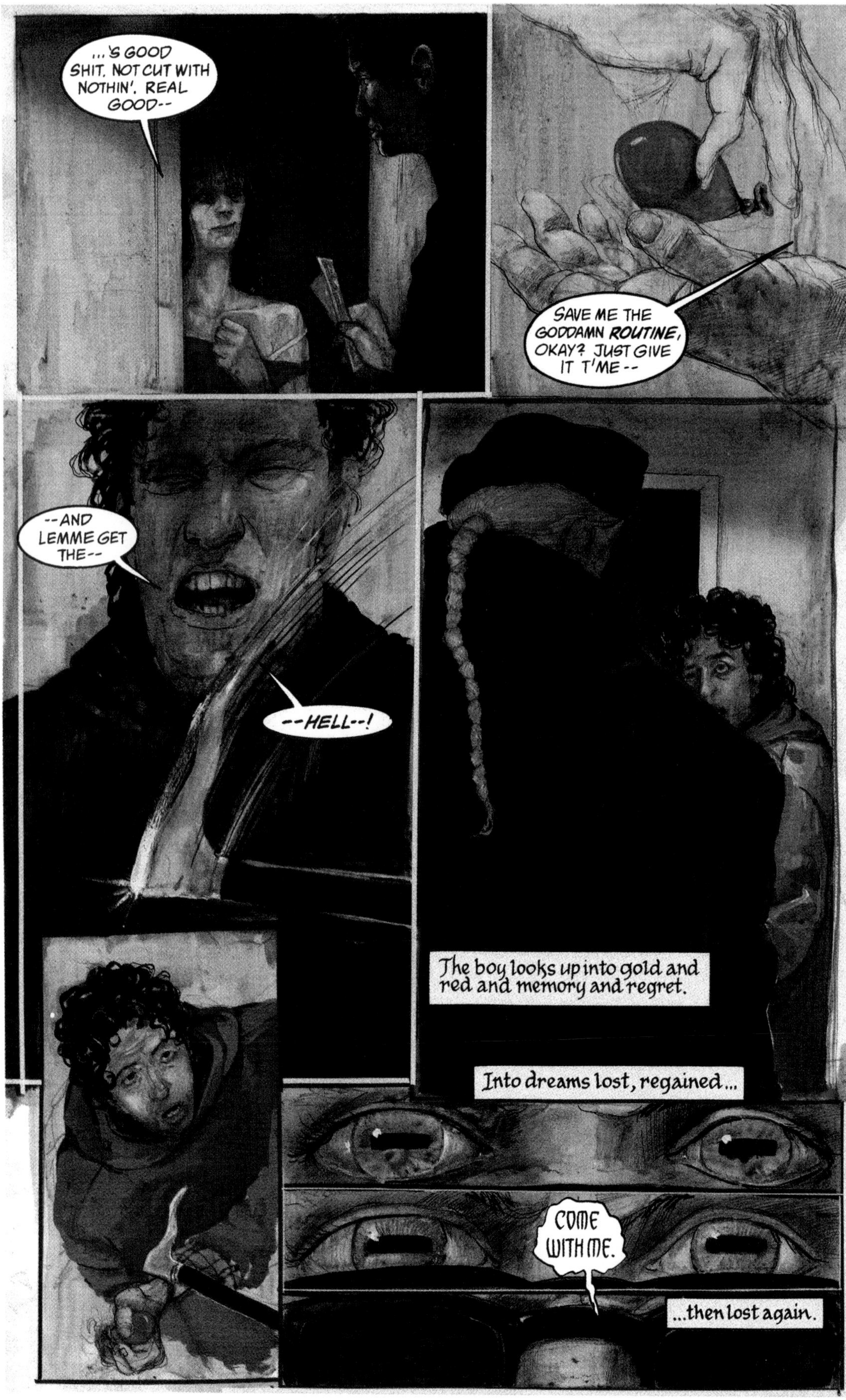
...'S GOOD SHIT. NOT CUT WITH NOTHIN'. REAL GOOD--
SAVE ME THE GODDAMN ROUTINE, OKAY? JUST GIVE IT T'ME--
--AND LEMME GET THE--
--HELL--!
The boy looks up into gold and red and memory and regret.
Into dreams lost, regained...
COME WITH ME.
...then lost again.

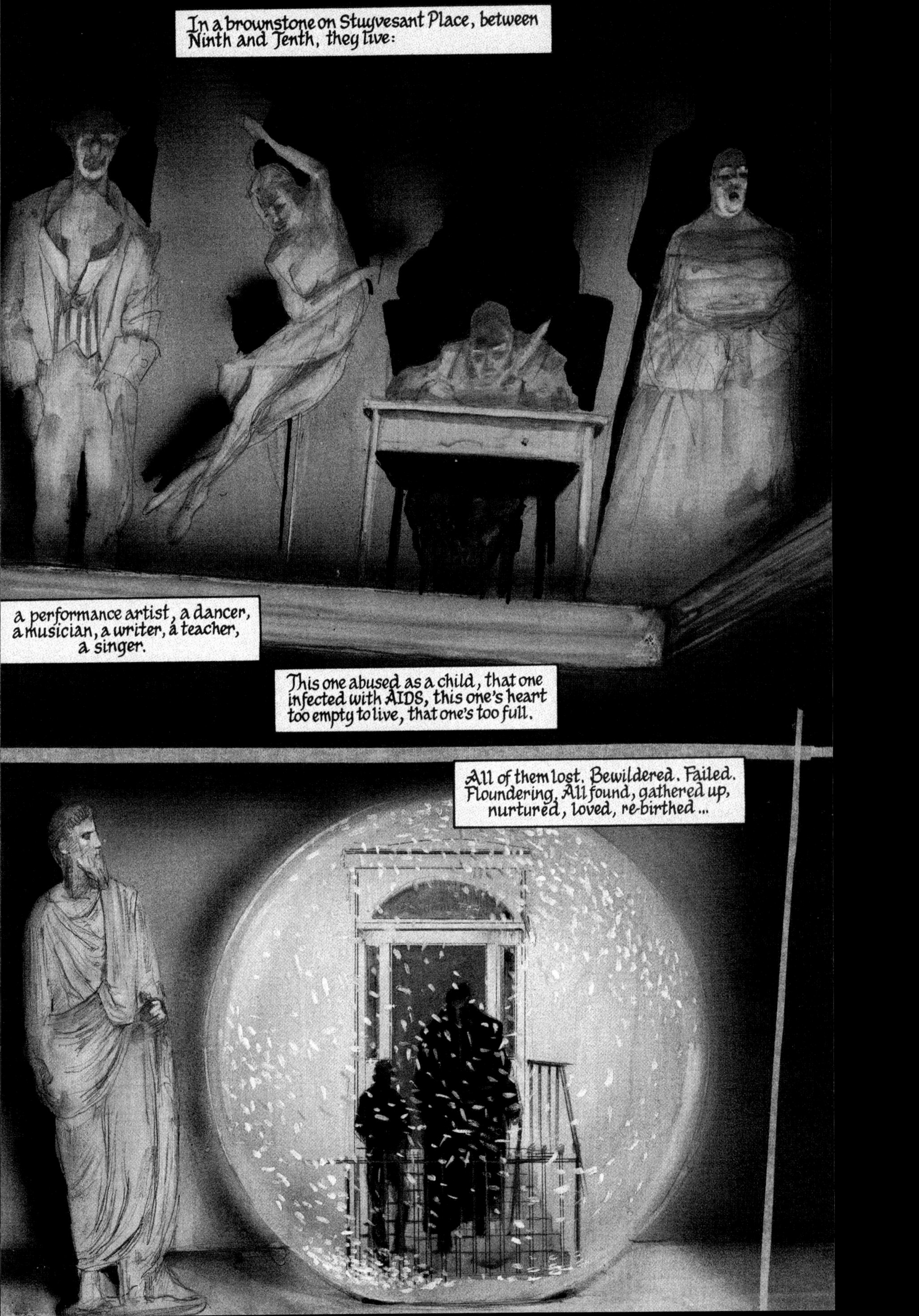
In a brownstone on Stuyvesant Place, between Ninth and Tenth, they live:
a performance artist, a dancer, a musician, a writer, a teacher, a singer.
This one abused as a child, that one infected with AIDS, this one's heart too empty to live, that one's too full.
All of them lost. Bewildered. Failed. Floundering. All found, gathered up, nurtured, loved, re-birthed ...

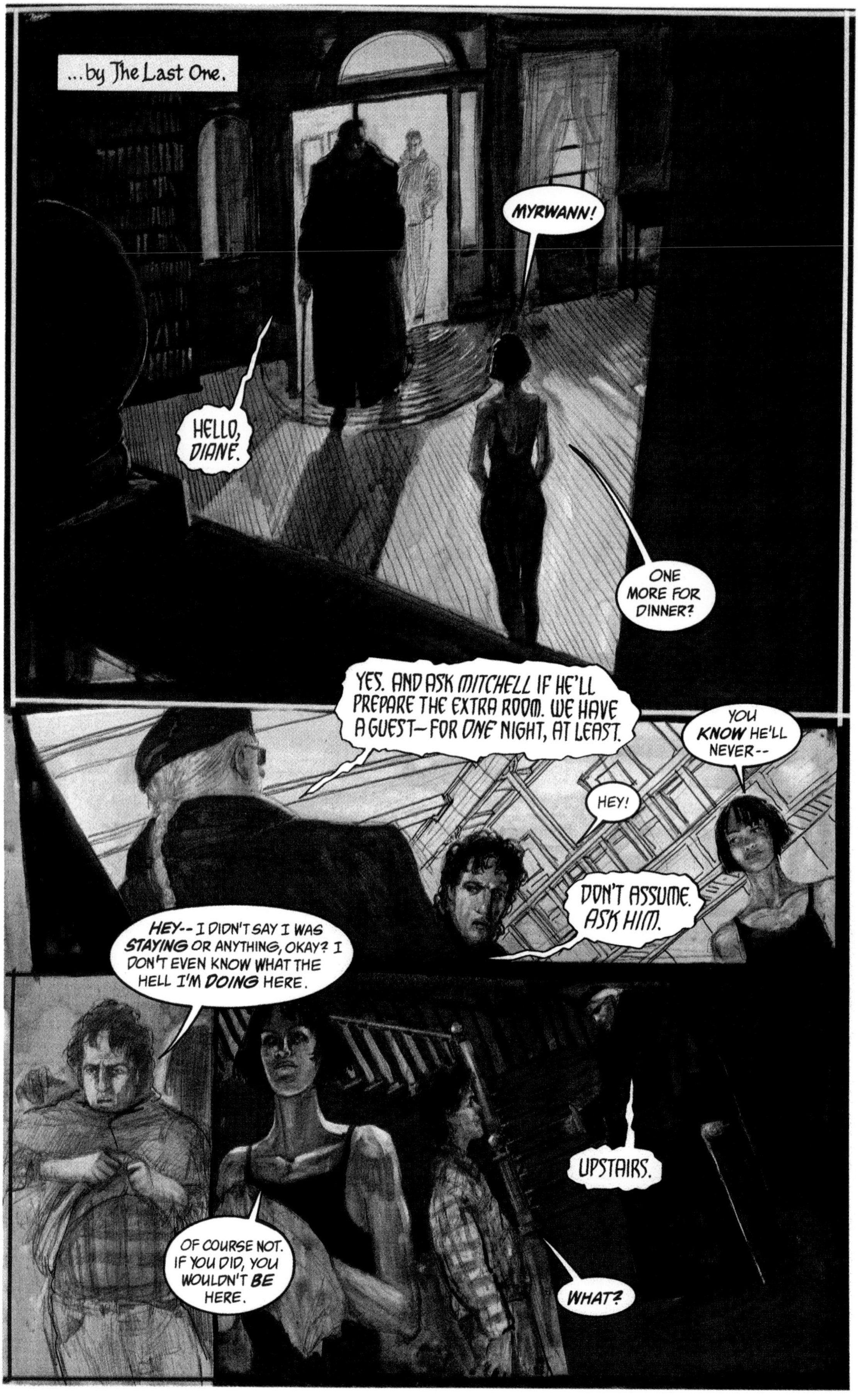
...by The Last One.
MYRWANN!
HELLO, DIANE.
ONE MORE FOR DINNER?
YES. AND ASK MITCHELL IF HE'LL PREPARE THE EXTRA ROOM. WE HAVE A GUEST-- FOR ONE NIGHT, AT LEAST.
YOU KNOW HE'LL NEVER--
HEY!
DON'T ASSUME. ASK HIM.
HEY-- I DIDN'T SAY I WAS STAYING OR ANYTHING, OKAY? I DON'T EVEN KNOW WHAT THE HELL I'M DOING HERE.
OF COURSE NOT. IF YOU DID, YOU WOULDN'T BE HERE.
UPSTAIRS.
WHAT?

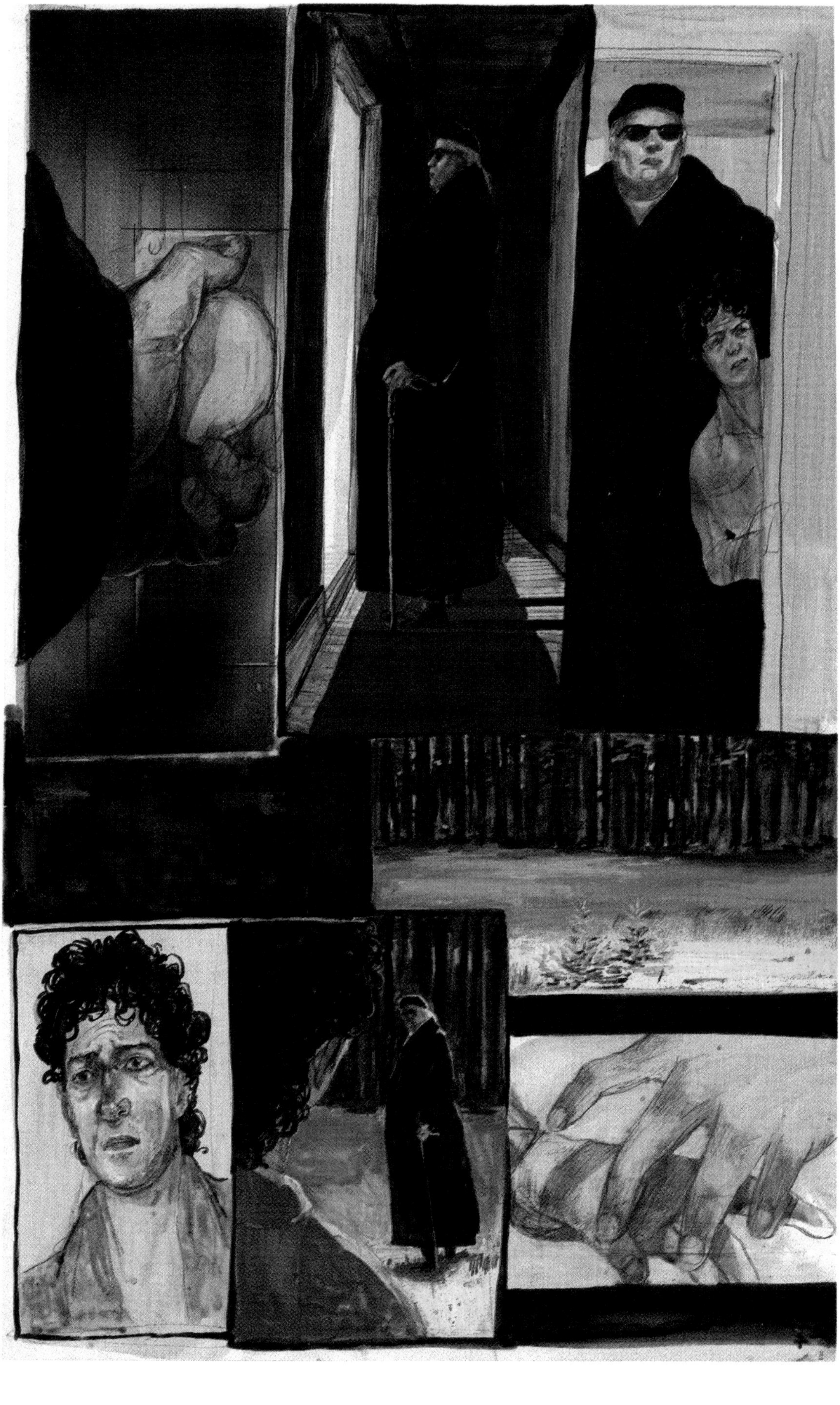

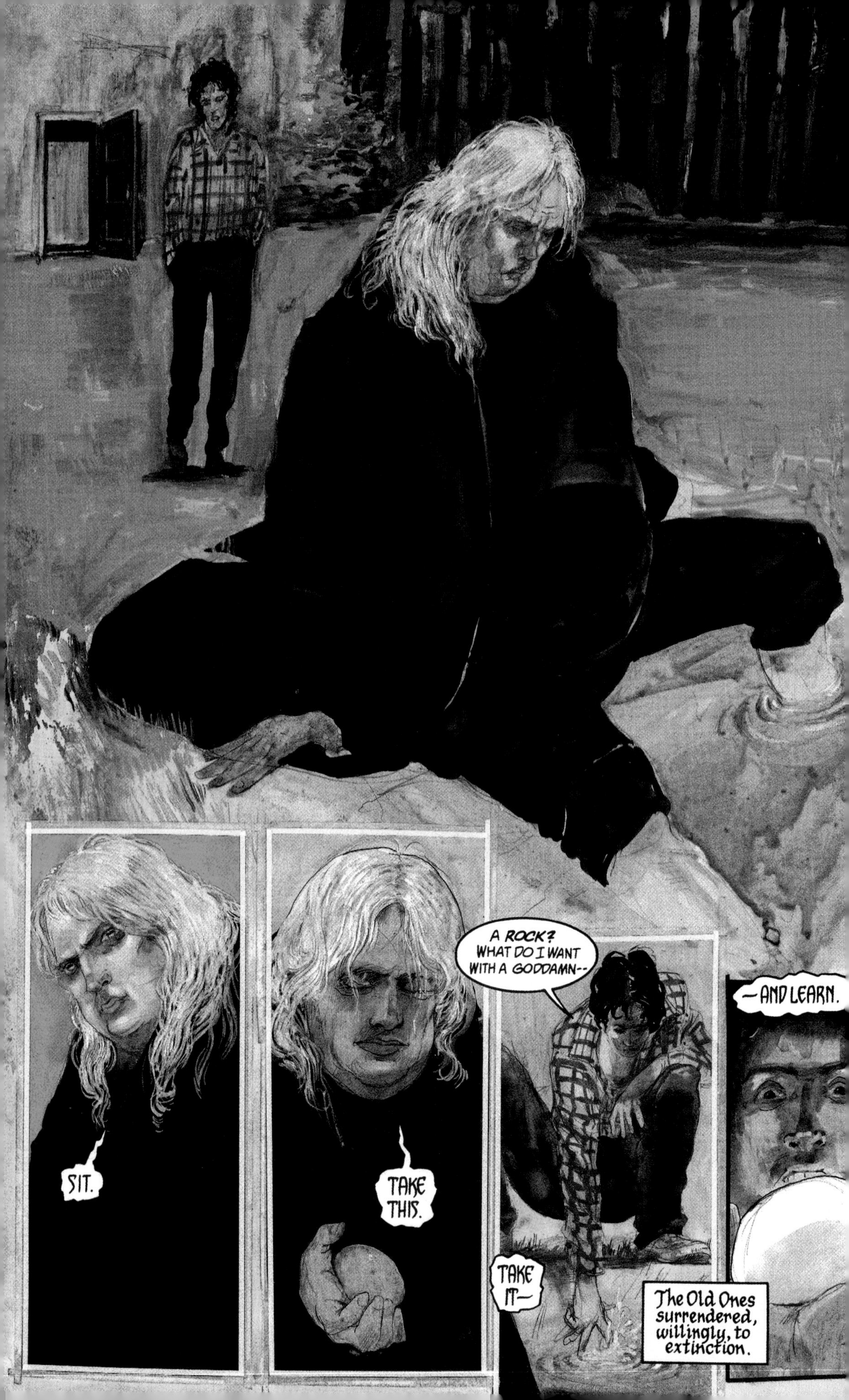
SIT.
TAKE THIS.
A ROCK? WHAT DO I WANT WITH A GODDAMN--
TAKE IT—
—AND LEARN.
The Old Ones surrendered, willingly, to extinction.

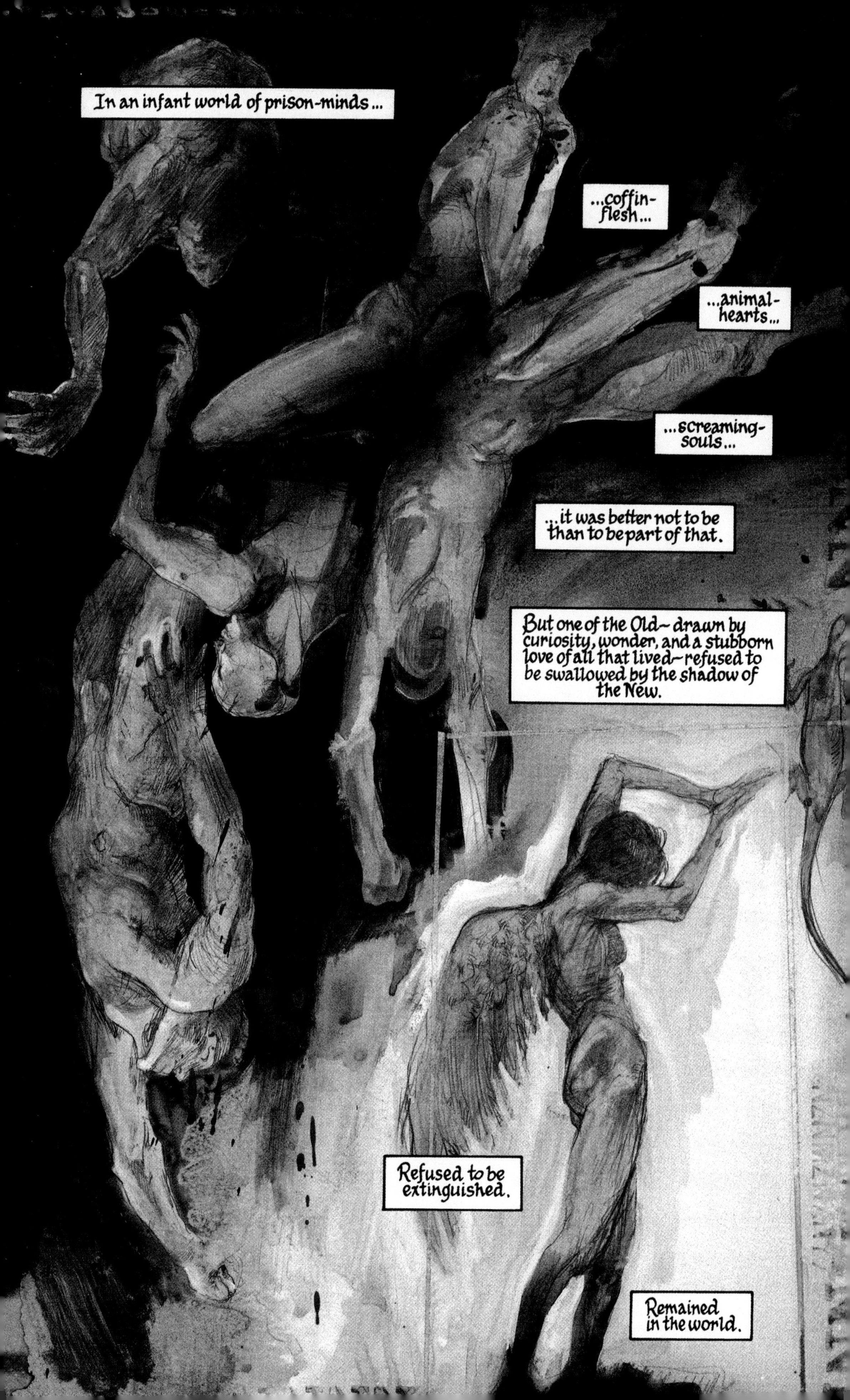
In an infant world of prison-minds...
...coffin-flesh...
...animal-hearts...
...screaming-souls...
...it was better not to be than to be part of that.
But one of the Old~ drawn by curiosity, wonder, and a stubborn love of all that lived~ refused to be swallowed by the shadow of the New.
Refused to be extinguished.
Remained in the world.

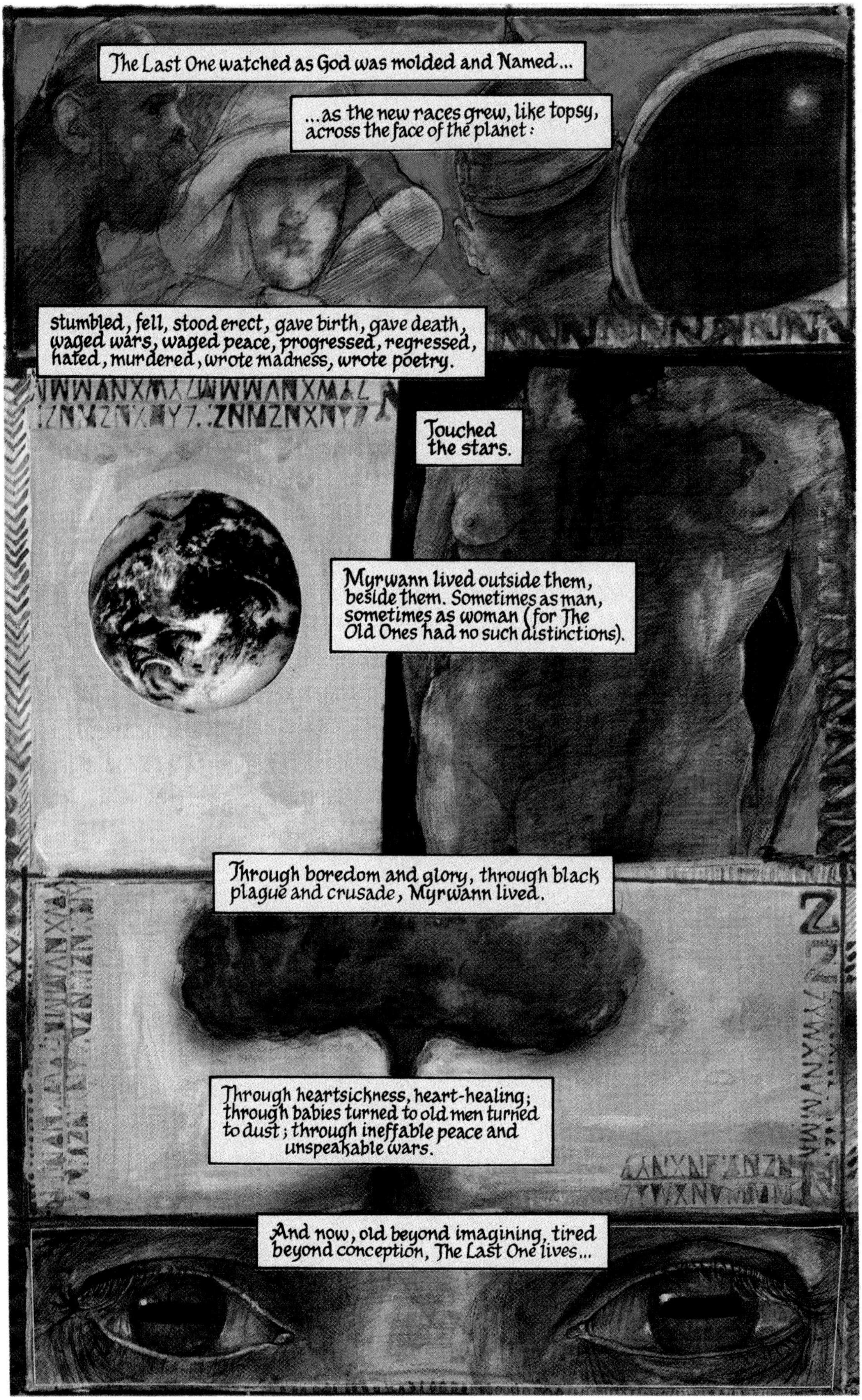
The Last One watched as God was molded and Named...
...as the new races grew, like topsy, across the face of the planet:
stumbled, fell, stood erect, gave birth, gave death, waged wars, waged peace, progressed, regressed, hated, murdered, wrote madness, wrote poetry.
Touched the stars.
Myrwann lived outside them, beside them. Sometimes as man, sometimes as woman (for The Old Ones had no such distinctions).
Through boredom and glory, through black plague and crusade, Myrwann lived.
Through heartsickness, heart-healing; through babies turned to old men turned to dust; through ineffable peace and unspeakable wars.
And now, old beyond imagining, tired beyond conception, The Last One lives...

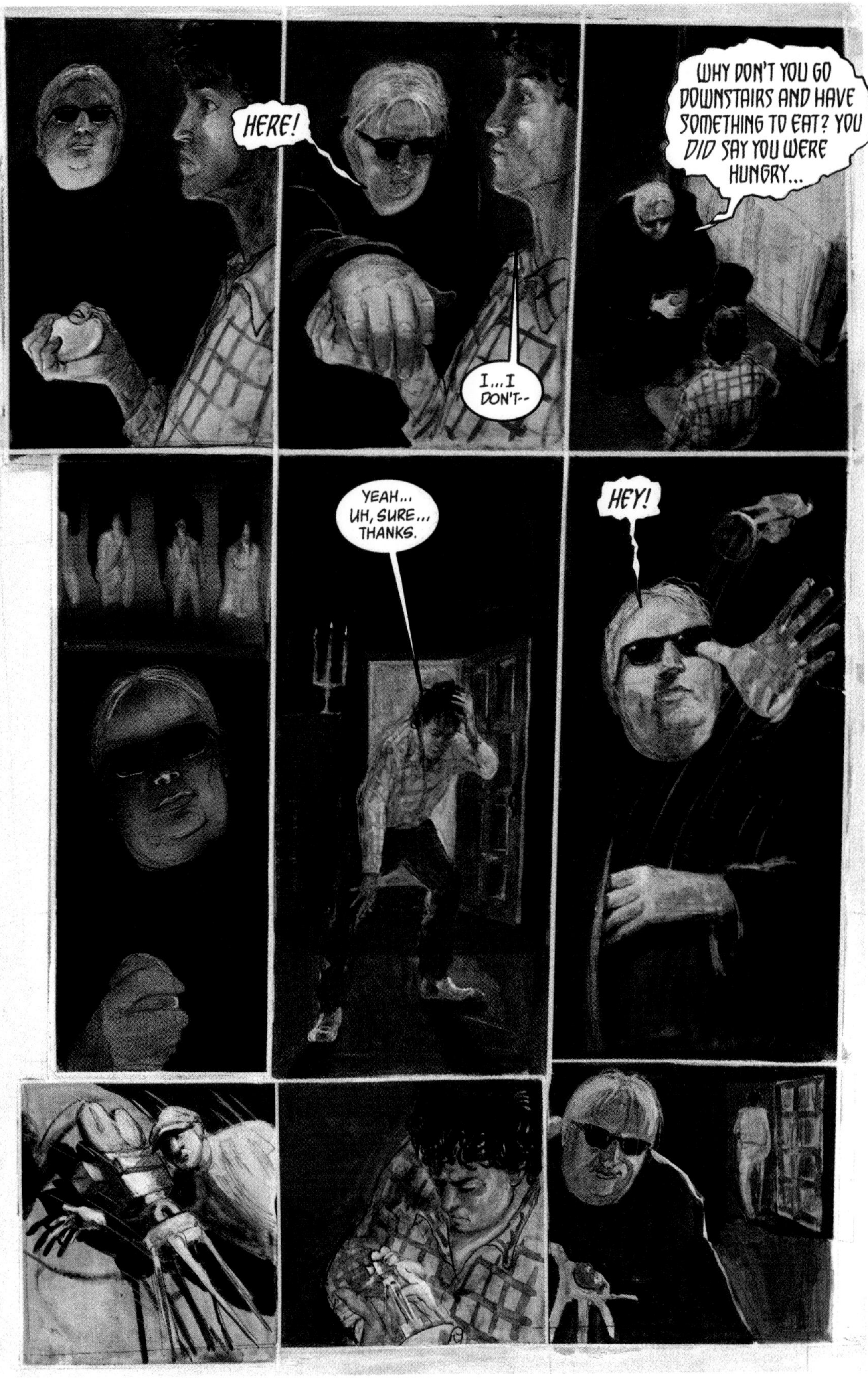
HERE!
I...I DON'T--
WHY DON'T YOU GO DOWNSTAIRS AND HAVE SOMETHING TO EAT? YOU *DID* SAY YOU WERE HUNGRY...
YEAH... UH, SURE... THANKS.
HEY!

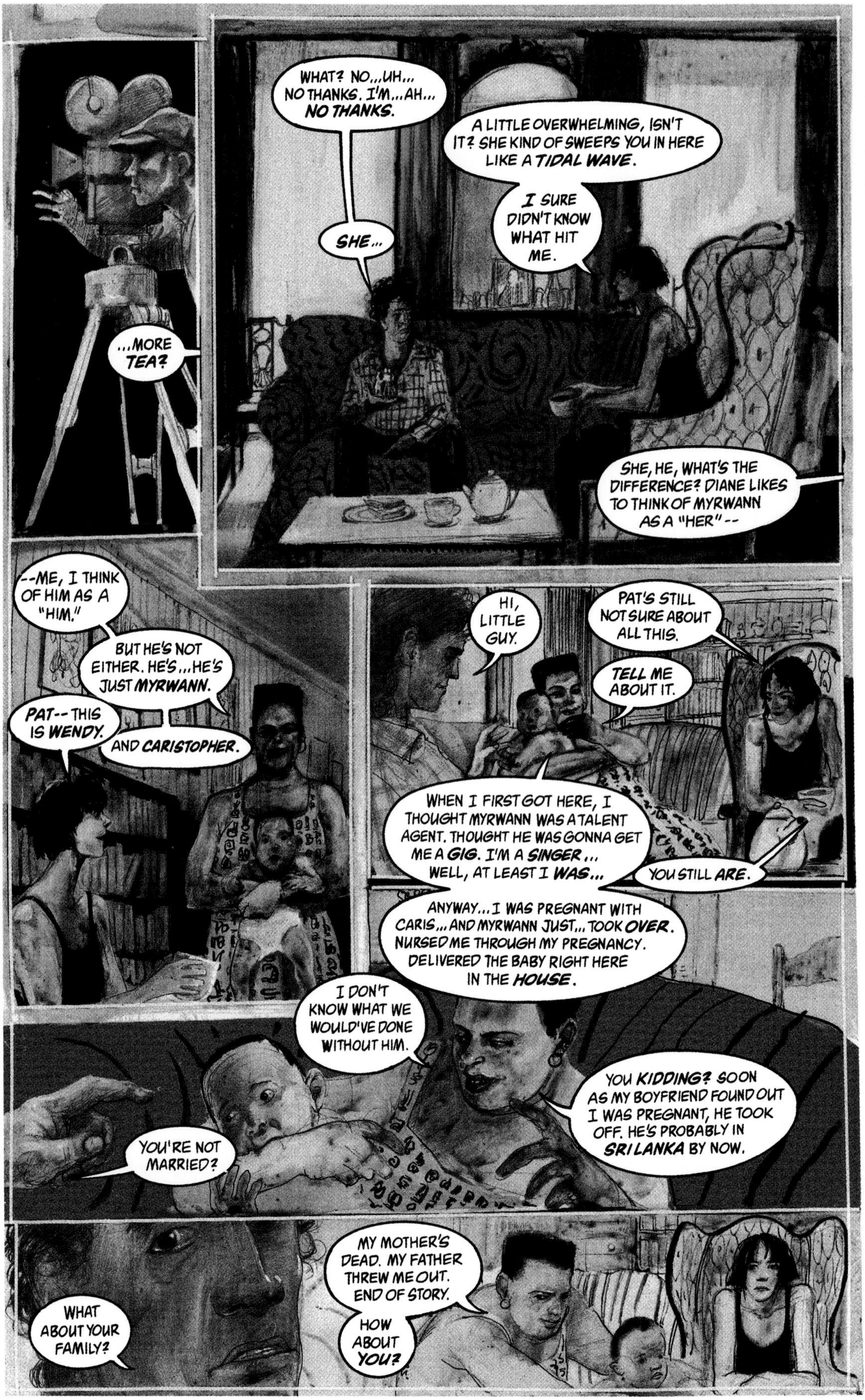
...MORE TEA?
WHAT? NO...UH... NO THANKS. I'M...AH... NO THANKS.
SHE...
A LITTLE OVERWHELMING, ISN'T IT? SHE KIND OF SWEEPS YOU IN HERE LIKE A TIDAL WAVE.
I SURE DIDN'T KNOW WHAT HIT ME.
SHE, HE, WHAT'S THE DIFFERENCE? DIANE LIKES TO THINK OF MYRWANN AS A "HER" --
--ME, I THINK OF HIM AS A "HIM."
BUT HE'S NOT EITHER. HE'S...HE'S JUST MYRWANN.
PAT-- THIS IS WENDY.
AND CARISTOPHER.
HI, LITTLE GUY.
PAT'S STILL NOT SURE ABOUT ALL THIS.
TELL ME ABOUT IT.
WHEN I FIRST GOT HERE, I THOUGHT MYRWANN WAS A TALENT AGENT. THOUGHT HE WAS GONNA GET ME A GIG. I'M A SINGER... WELL, AT LEAST I WAS...
YOU STILL ARE.
ANYWAY... I WAS PREGNANT WITH CARIS... AND MYRWANN JUST... TOOK OVER. NURSED ME THROUGH MY PREGNANCY. DELIVERED THE BABY RIGHT HERE IN THE HOUSE.
I DON'T KNOW WHAT WE WOULD'VE DONE WITHOUT HIM.
YOU'RE NOT MARRIED?
YOU KIDDING? SOON AS MY BOYFRIEND FOUND OUT I WAS PREGNANT, HE TOOK OFF. HE'S PROBABLY IN SRI LANKA BY NOW.
WHAT ABOUT YOUR FAMILY?
MY MOTHER'S DEAD. MY FATHER THREW ME OUT. END OF STORY.
HOW ABOUT YOU?

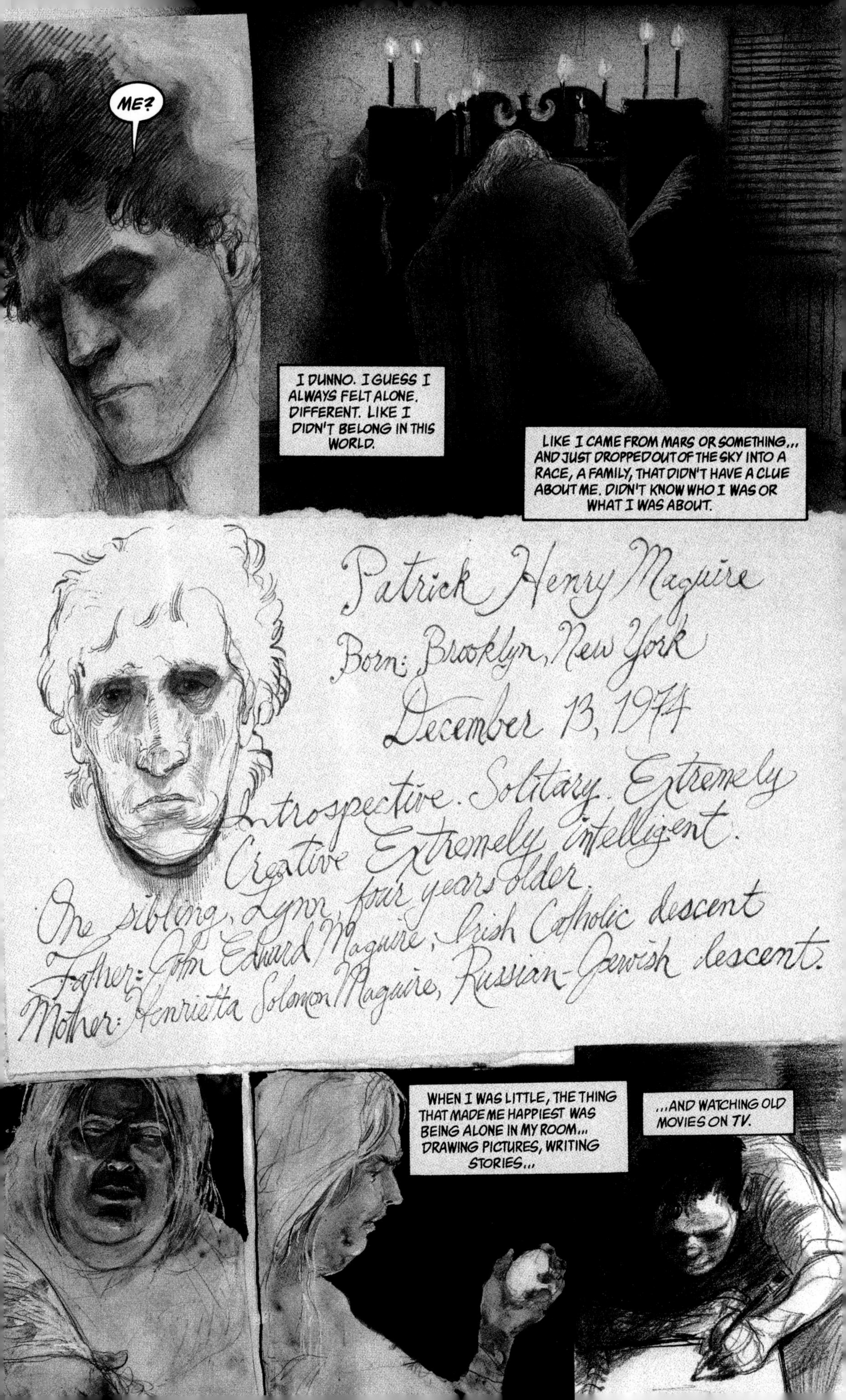
ME?
I DUNNO. I GUESS I ALWAYS FELT ALONE. DIFFERENT. LIKE I DIDN'T BELONG IN THIS WORLD.
LIKE I CAME FROM MARS OR SOMETHING... AND JUST DROPPED OUT OF THE SKY INTO A RACE, A FAMILY, THAT DIDN'T HAVE A CLUE ABOUT ME. DIDN'T KNOW WHO I WAS OR WHAT I WAS ABOUT.
Patrick Henry Maguire
Born: Brooklyn, New York
December 13, 1974
Introspective. Solitary. Extremely Creative Extremely intelligent.
One sibling, Lynn, four years older
Father: John Edward Maguire, Irish Catholic descent
Mother: Henrietta Solomon Maguire, Russian-Jewish descent.
WHEN I WAS LITTLE, THE THING THAT MADE ME HAPPIEST WAS BEING ALONE IN MY ROOM... DRAWING PICTURES, WRITING STORIES...
...AND WATCHING OLD MOVIES ON TV.

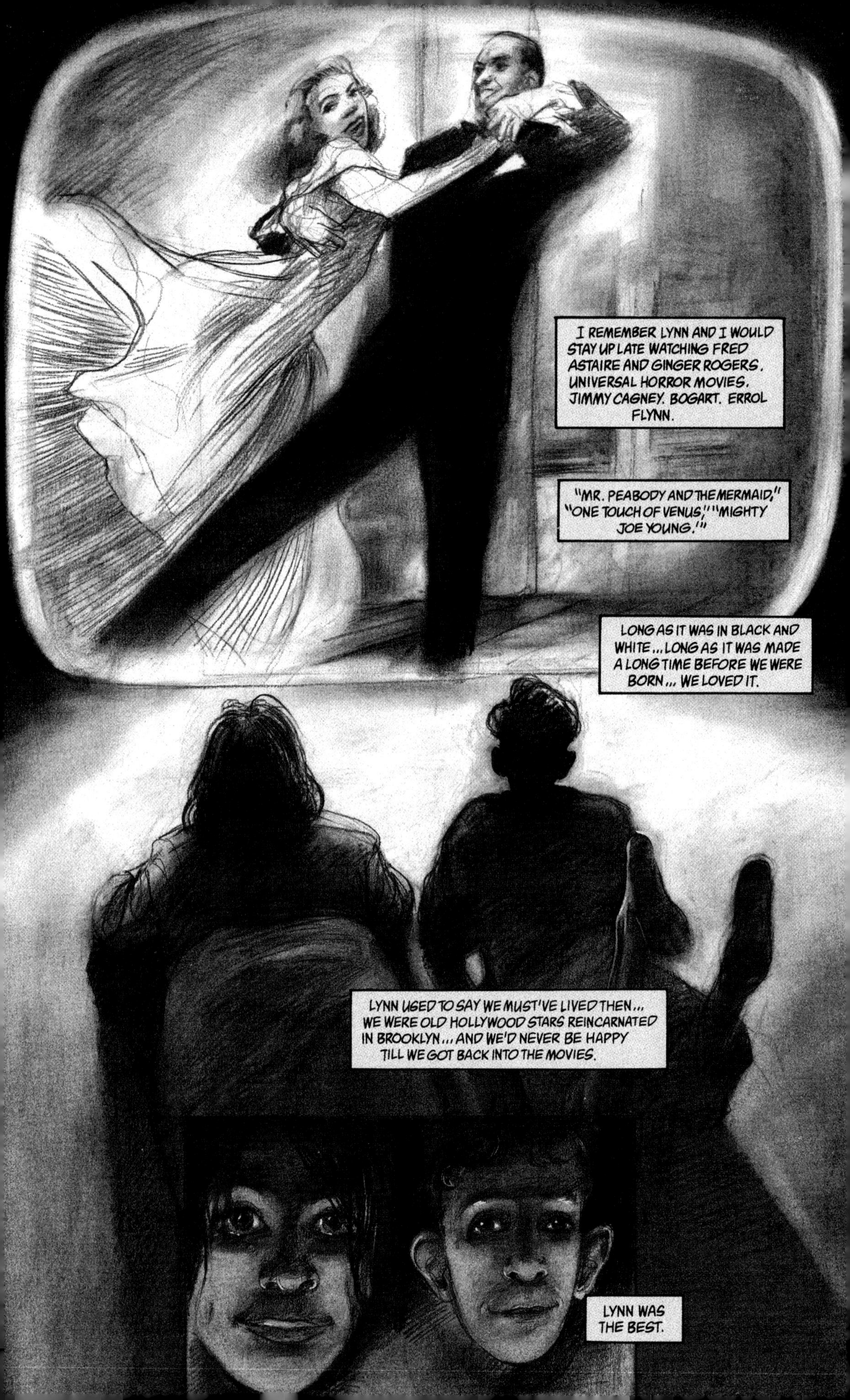
I REMEMBER LYNN AND I WOULD STAY UP LATE WATCHING FRED ASTAIRE AND GINGER ROGERS. UNIVERSAL HORROR MOVIES. JIMMY CAGNEY. BOGART. ERROL FLYNN.
"MR. PEABODY AND THE MERMAID," "ONE TOUCH OF VENUS," "MIGHTY JOE YOUNG."
LONG AS IT WAS IN BLACK AND WHITE... LONG AS IT WAS MADE A LONG TIME BEFORE WE WERE BORN... WE LOVED IT.
LYNN USED TO SAY WE MUST'VE LIVED THEN... WE WERE OLD HOLLYWOOD STARS REINCARNATED IN BROOKLYN... AND WE'D NEVER BE HAPPY TILL WE GOT BACK INTO THE MOVIES.
LYNN WAS THE BEST.

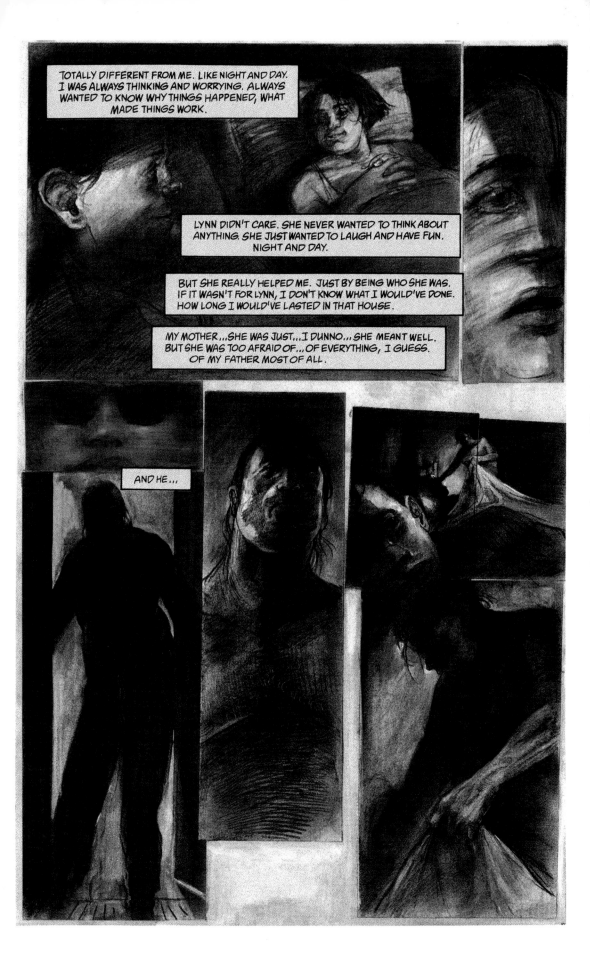

TOTALLY DIFFERENT FROM ME. LIKE NIGHT AND DAY. I WAS ALWAYS THINKING AND WORRYING. ALWAYS WANTED TO KNOW WHY THINGS HAPPENED, WHAT MADE THINGS WORK.

LYNN DIDN'T CARE. SHE NEVER WANTED TO THINK ABOUT ANYTHING. SHE JUST WANTED TO LAUGH AND HAVE FUN. NIGHT AND DAY.

BUT SHE REALLY HELPED ME. JUST BY BEING WHO SHE WAS. IF IT WASN'T FOR LYNN, I DON'T KNOW WHAT I WOULD'VE DONE. HOW LONG I WOULD'VE LASTED IN THAT HOUSE.

MY MOTHER...SHE WAS JUST...I DUNNO...SHE MEANT WELL. BUT SHE WAS TOO AFRAID OF...OF EVERYTHING, I GUESS. OF MY FATHER MOST OF ALL.

AND HE...

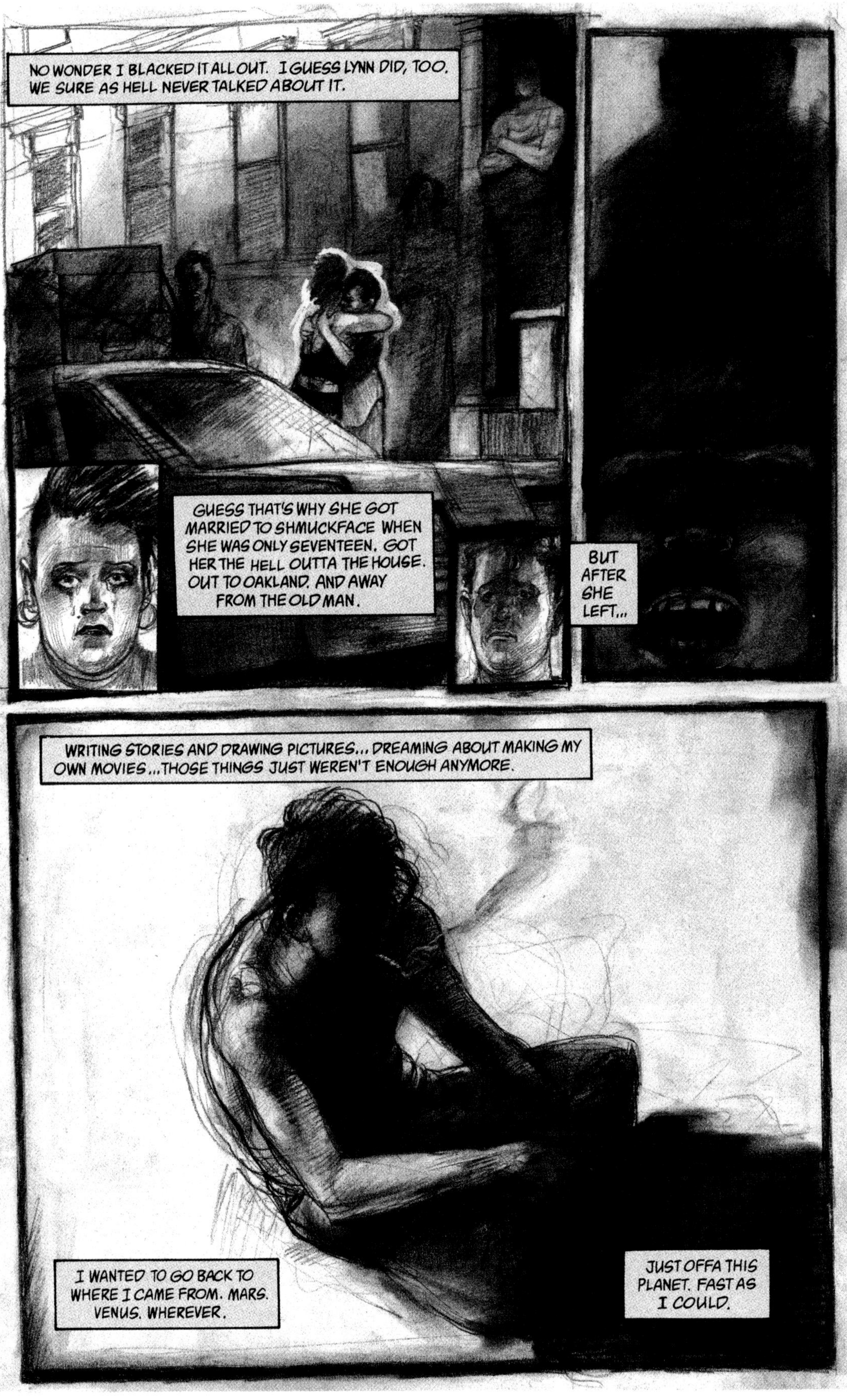
NO WONDER I BLACKED IT ALL OUT. I GUESS LYNN DID, TOO. WE SURE AS HELL NEVER TALKED ABOUT IT.
GUESS THAT'S WHY SHE GOT MARRIED TO SHMUCKFACE WHEN SHE WAS ONLY SEVENTEEN. GOT HER THE HELL OUTTA THE HOUSE. OUT TO OAKLAND. AND AWAY FROM THE OLD MAN.
BUT AFTER SHE LEFT...
WRITING STORIES AND DRAWING PICTURES... DREAMING ABOUT MAKING MY OWN MOVIES... THOSE THINGS JUST WEREN'T ENOUGH ANYMORE.
I WANTED TO GO BACK TO WHERE I CAME FROM. MARS. VENUS. WHEREVER.
JUST OFFA THIS PLANET. FAST AS I COULD.

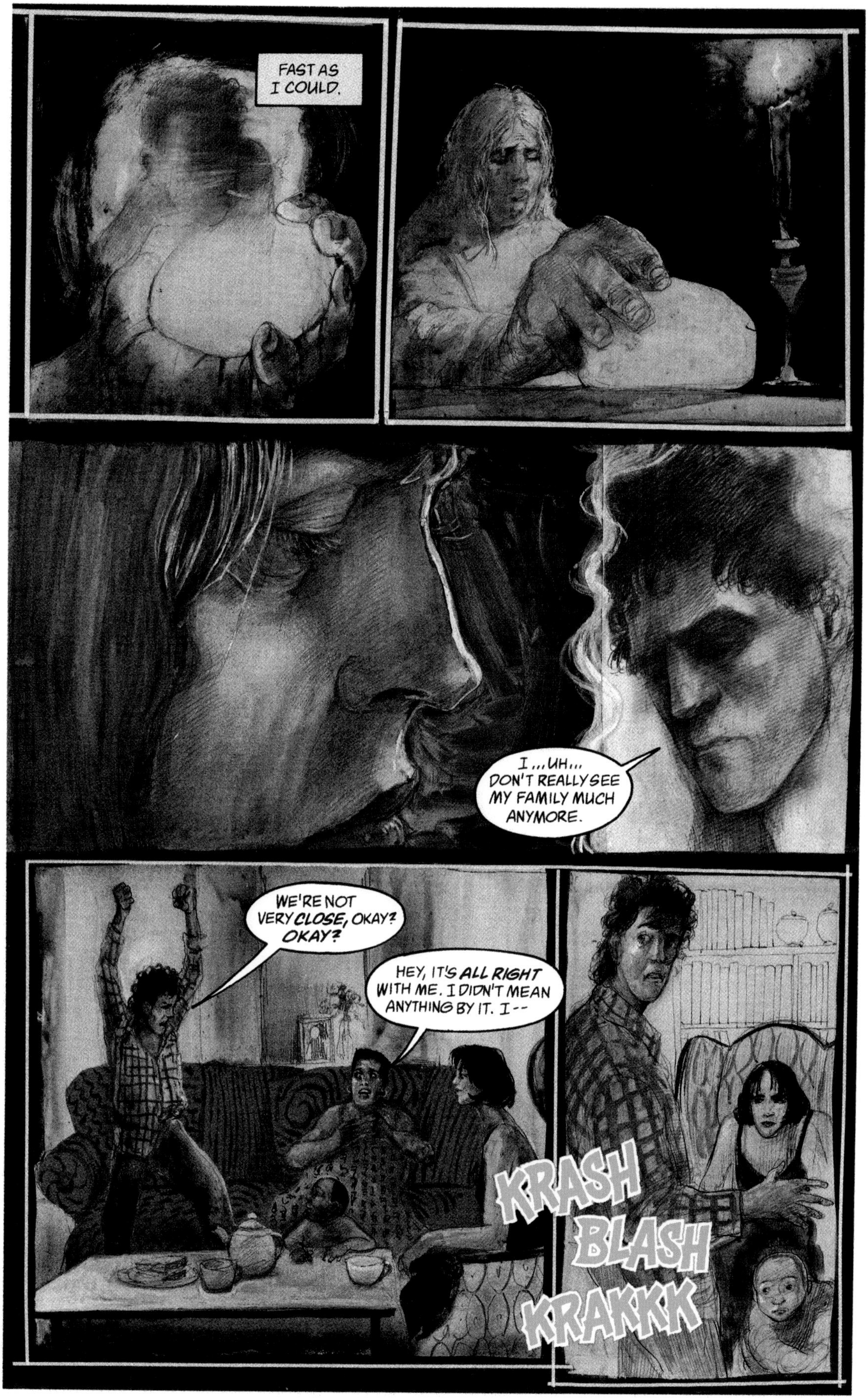
FAST AS I COULD.
I ... UH... DON'T REALLY SEE MY FAMILY MUCH ANYMORE.
WE'RE NOT VERY **CLOSE**, OKAY? **OKAY?**
HEY, IT'S **ALL RIGHT** WITH ME. I DIDN'T MEAN ANYTHING BY IT. I --
KRASH
BLASH
KRAKKK

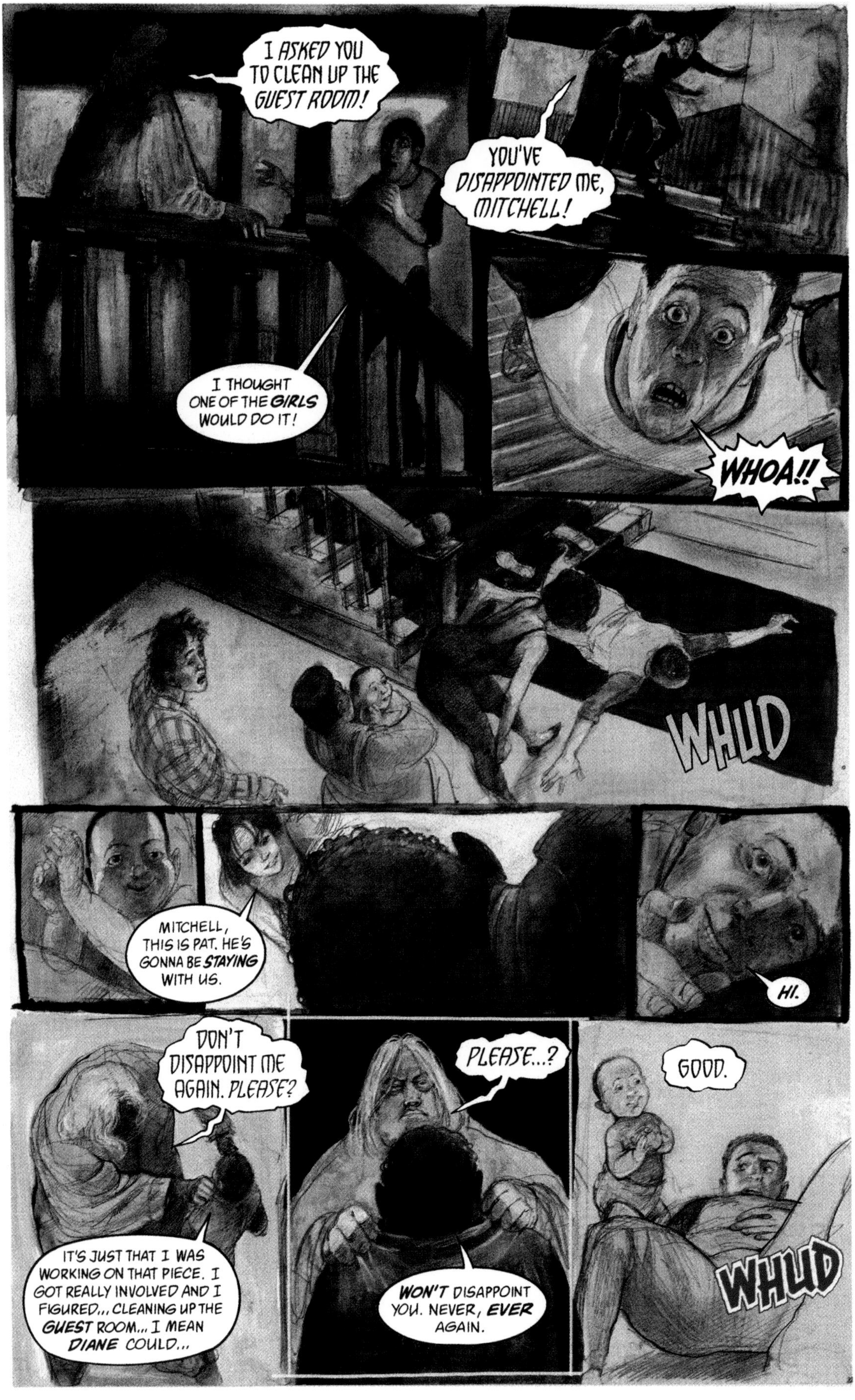
I ASKED YOU TO CLEAN UP THE GUEST ROOM!
YOU'VE DISAPPOINTED ME, MITCHELL!
I THOUGHT ONE OF THE GIRLS WOULD DO IT!
WHOA!!
WHUD
MITCHELL, THIS IS PAT. HE'S GONNA BE STAYING WITH US.
HI.
DON'T DISAPPOINT ME AGAIN. PLEASE?
IT'S JUST THAT I WAS WORKING ON THAT PIECE. I GOT REALLY INVOLVED AND I FIGURED... CLEANING UP THE GUEST ROOM... I MEAN DIANE COULD...
PLEASE...?
WON'T DISAPPOINT YOU. NEVER, EVER AGAIN.
GOOD.
WHUD

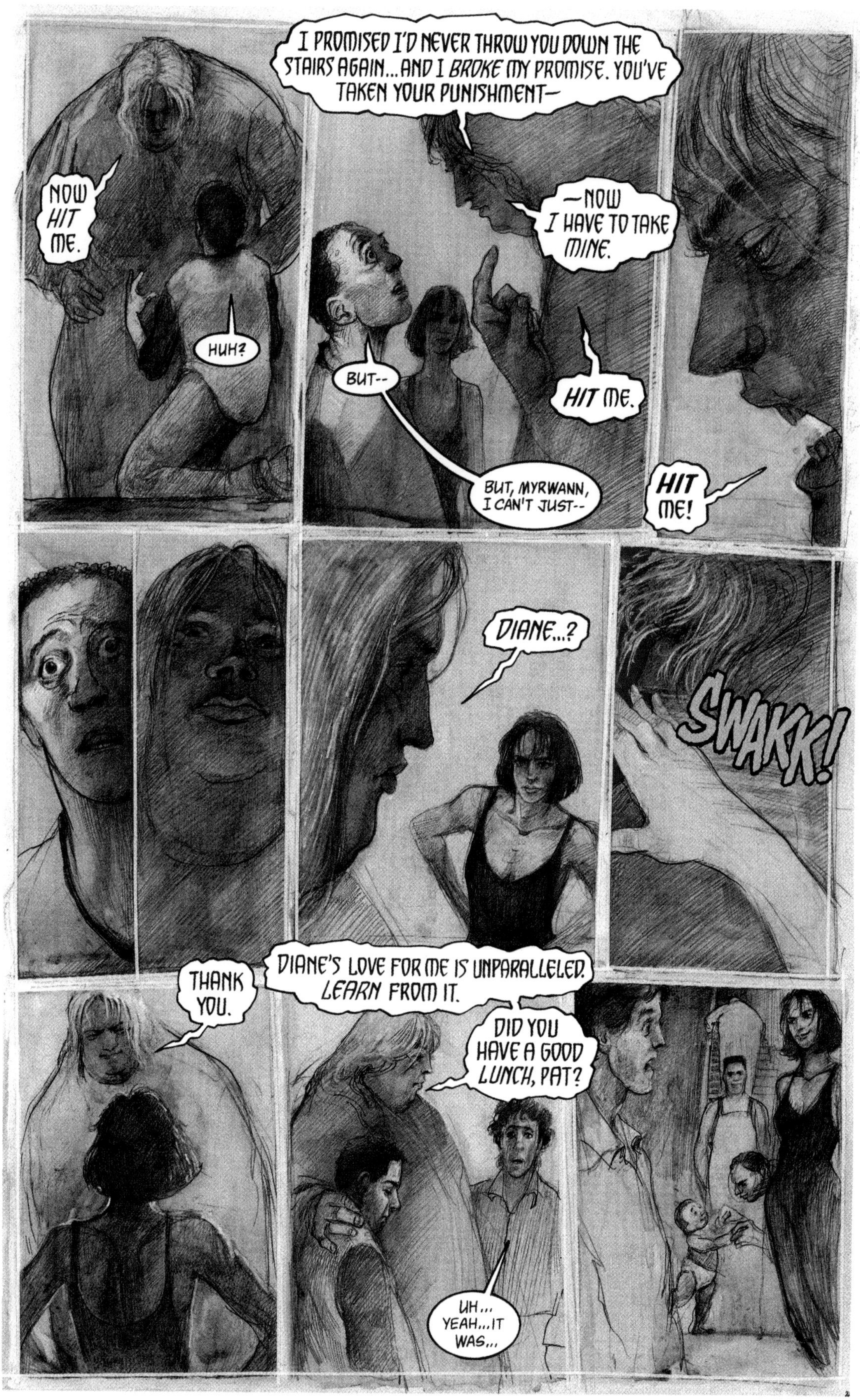

NOW HIT ME.
HUH?
I PROMISED I'D NEVER THROW YOU DOWN THE STAIRS AGAIN...AND I BROKE MY PROMISE. YOU'VE TAKEN YOUR PUNISHMENT—
—NOW I HAVE TO TAKE MINE.
BUT--
HIT ME.
BUT, MYRWANN, I CAN'T JUST--
HIT ME!
DIANE...?
SWAKK!
THANK YOU.
DIANE'S LOVE FOR ME IS UNPARALLELED. LEARN FROM IT.
DID YOU HAVE A GOOD LUNCH, PAT?
UH... YEAH...IT WAS...

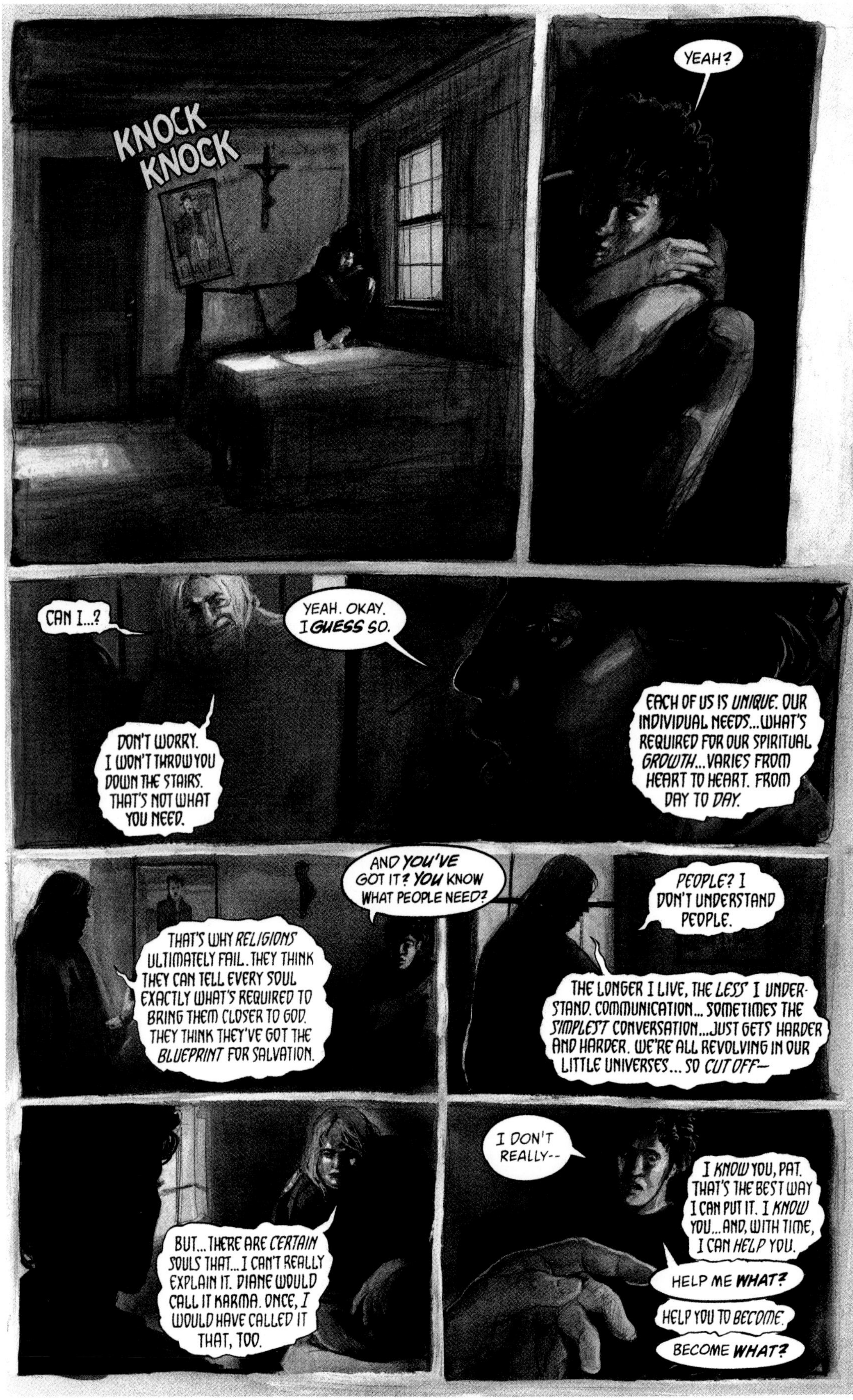
KNOCK KNOCK
YEAH?
CAN I...?
YEAH. OKAY. I GUESS SO.
DON'T WORRY. I WON'T THROW YOU DOWN THE STAIRS. THAT'S NOT WHAT YOU NEED.
EACH OF US IS UNIQUE. OUR INDIVIDUAL NEEDS...WHAT'S REQUIRED FOR OUR SPIRITUAL GROWTH...VARIES FROM HEART TO HEART. FROM DAY TO DAY.
THAT'S WHY RELIGIONS ULTIMATELY FAIL. THEY THINK THEY CAN TELL EVERY SOUL EXACTLY WHAT'S REQUIRED TO BRING THEM CLOSER TO GOD. THEY THINK THEY'VE GOT THE BLUEPRINT FOR SALVATION.
AND YOU'VE GOT IT? YOU KNOW WHAT PEOPLE NEED?
PEOPLE? I DON'T UNDERSTAND PEOPLE.
THE LONGER I LIVE, THE LESS I UNDERSTAND. COMMUNICATION... SOMETIMES THE SIMPLEST CONVERSATION...JUST GETS HARDER AND HARDER. WE'RE ALL REVOLVING IN OUR LITTLE UNIVERSES... SO CUT OFF—
BUT... THERE ARE CERTAIN SOULS THAT... I CAN'T REALLY EXPLAIN IT. DIANE WOULD CALL IT KARMA. ONCE, I WOULD HAVE CALLED IT THAT, TOO.
I DON'T REALLY--
I KNOW YOU, PAT. THAT'S THE BEST WAY I CAN PUT IT. I KNOW YOU...AND, WITH TIME, I CAN HELP YOU.
HELP ME WHAT?
HELP YOU TO BECOME.
BECOME WHAT?

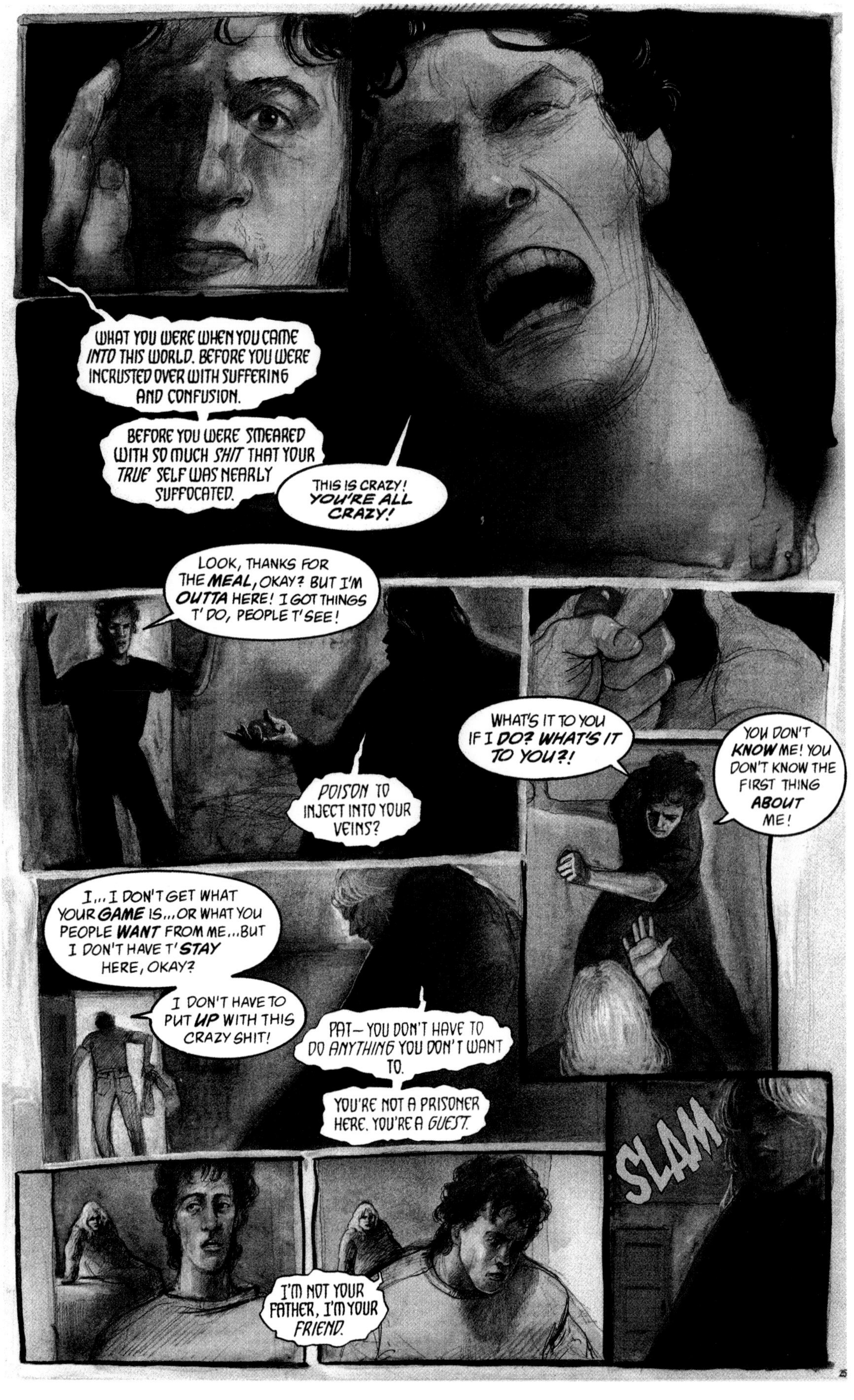
WHAT YOU WERE WHEN YOU CAME INTO THIS WORLD. BEFORE YOU WERE INCRUSTED OVER WITH SUFFERING AND CONFUSION.
BEFORE YOU WERE SMEARED WITH SO MUCH SHIT THAT YOUR TRUE SELF WAS NEARLY SUFFOCATED.
THIS IS CRAZY! YOU'RE ALL CRAZY!
LOOK, THANKS FOR THE MEAL, OKAY? BUT I'M OUTTA HERE! I GOT THINGS T' DO, PEOPLE T' SEE!
POISON TO INJECT INTO YOUR VEINS?
WHAT'S IT TO YOU IF I DO? WHAT'S IT TO YOU?!
YOU DON'T KNOW ME! YOU DON'T KNOW THE FIRST THING ABOUT ME!
I... I DON'T GET WHAT YOUR GAME IS... OR WHAT YOU PEOPLE WANT FROM ME... BUT I DON'T HAVE T' STAY HERE, OKAY?
I DON'T HAVE TO PUT UP WITH THIS CRAZY SHIT!
PAT– YOU DON'T HAVE TO DO ANYTHING YOU DON'T WANT TO.
YOU'RE NOT A PRISONER HERE. YOU'RE A GUEST.
SLAM
I'M NOT YOUR FATHER, I'M YOUR FRIEND.

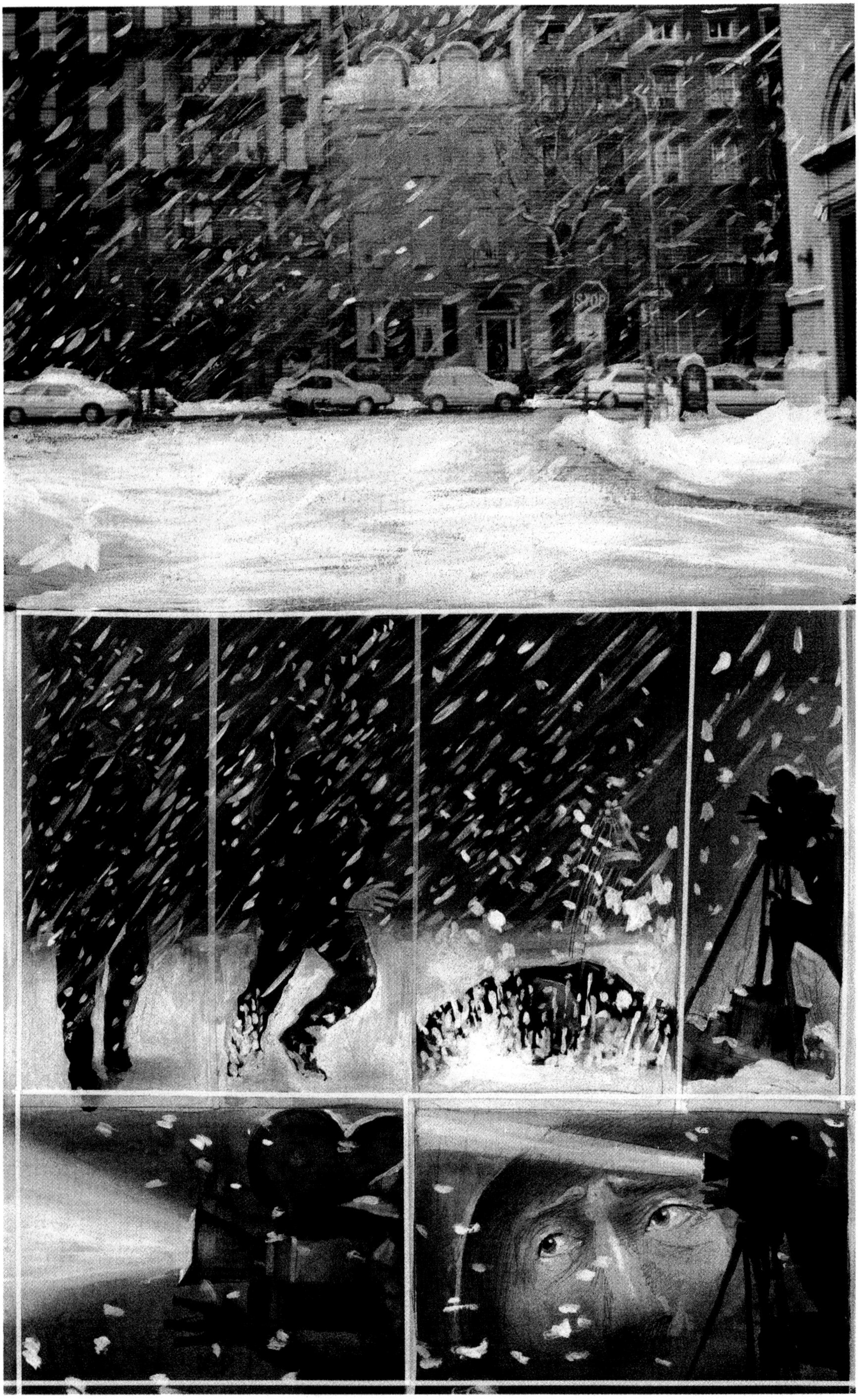
STOP

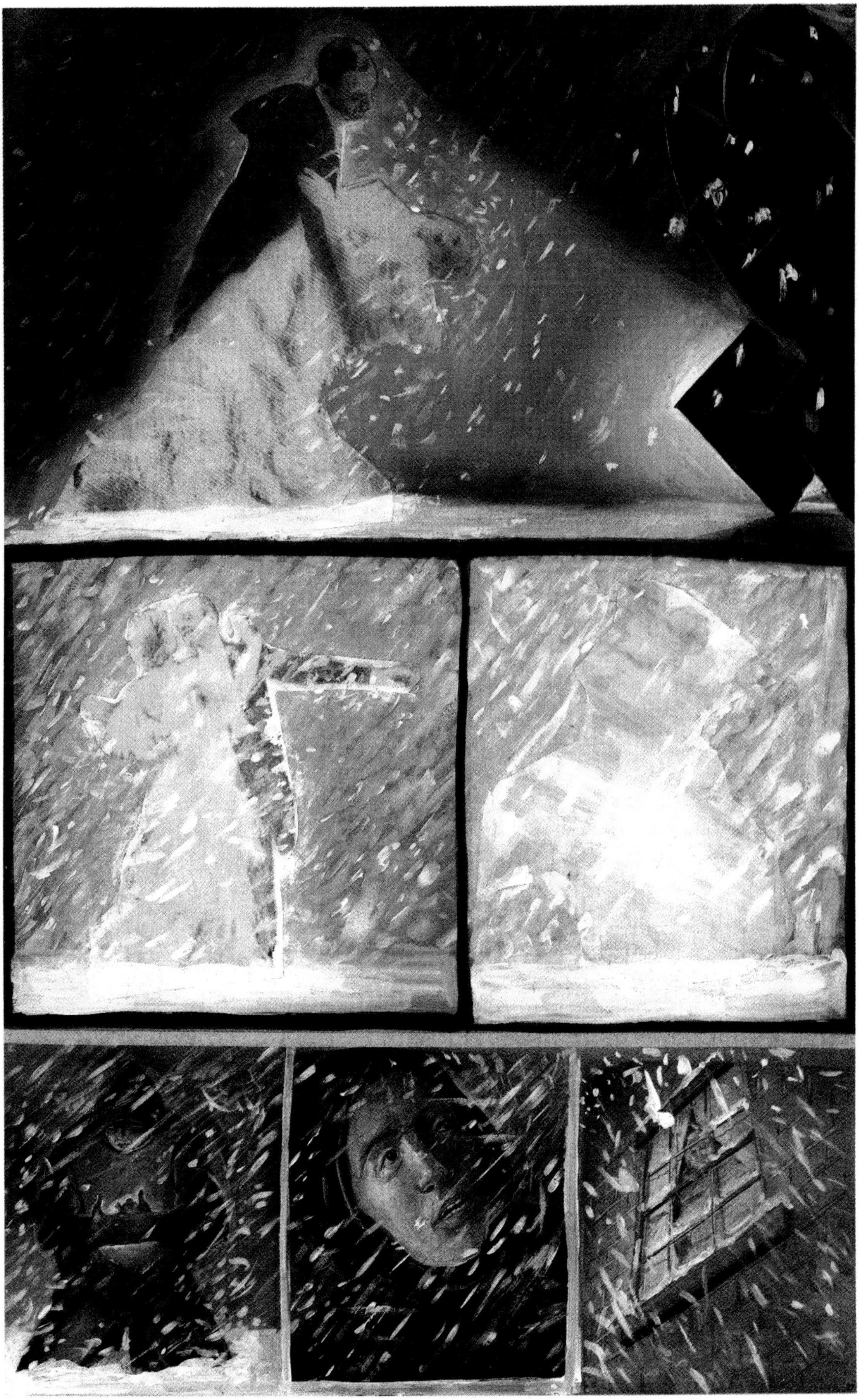

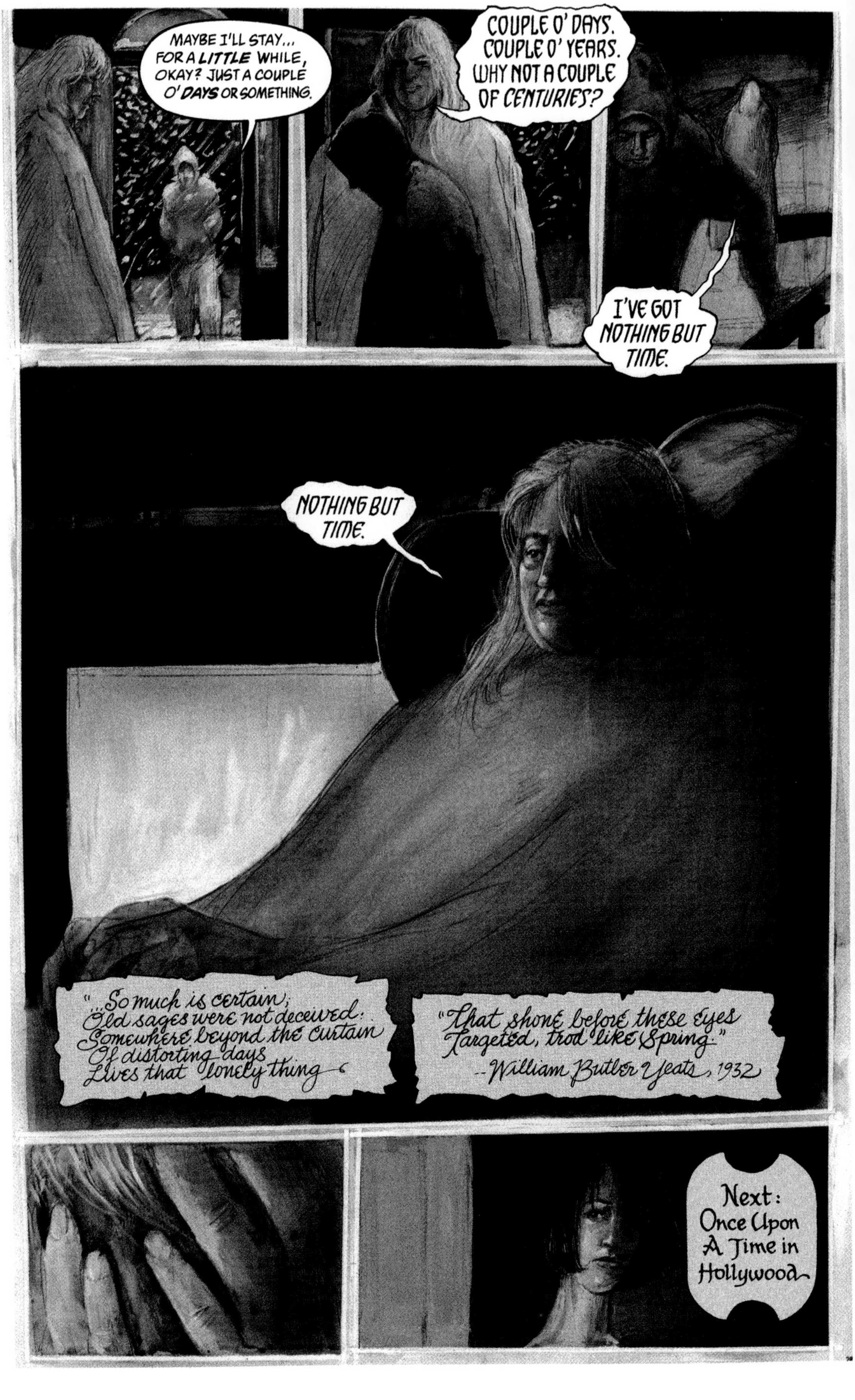
MAYBE I'LL STAY... FOR A LITTLE WHILE, OKAY? JUST A COUPLE O' DAYS OR SOMETHING.
COUPLE O' DAYS. COUPLE O' YEARS. WHY NOT A COUPLE OF CENTURIES?
I'VE GOT NOTHING BUT TIME.
NOTHING BUT TIME.
"...So much is certain; Old sages were not deceived: Somewhere beyond the curtain Of distorting days Lives that lonely thing
"That shone before these eyes Targeted, trod like Spring."
--William Butler Yeats, 1932
Next: Once Upon A Time in Hollywood

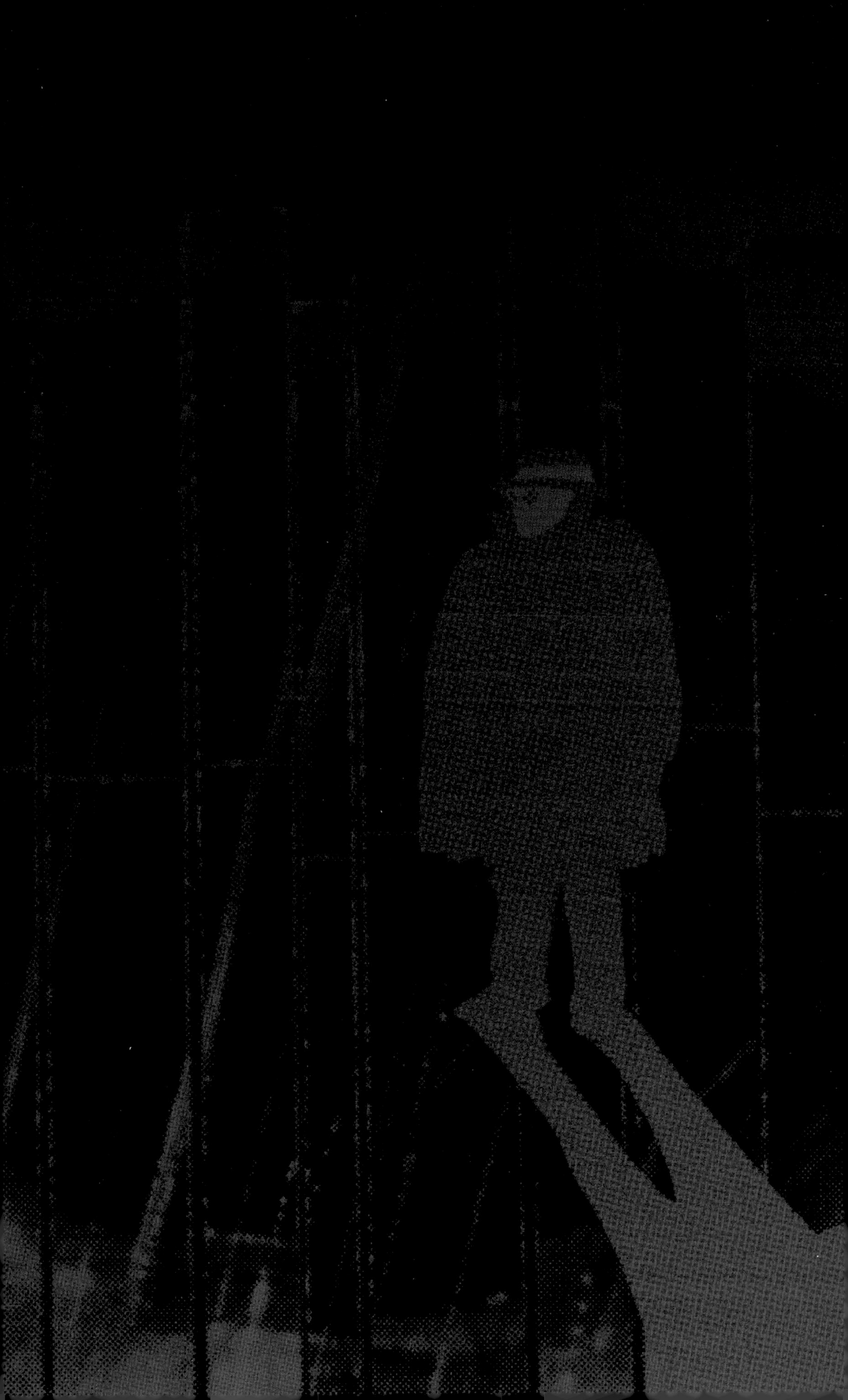

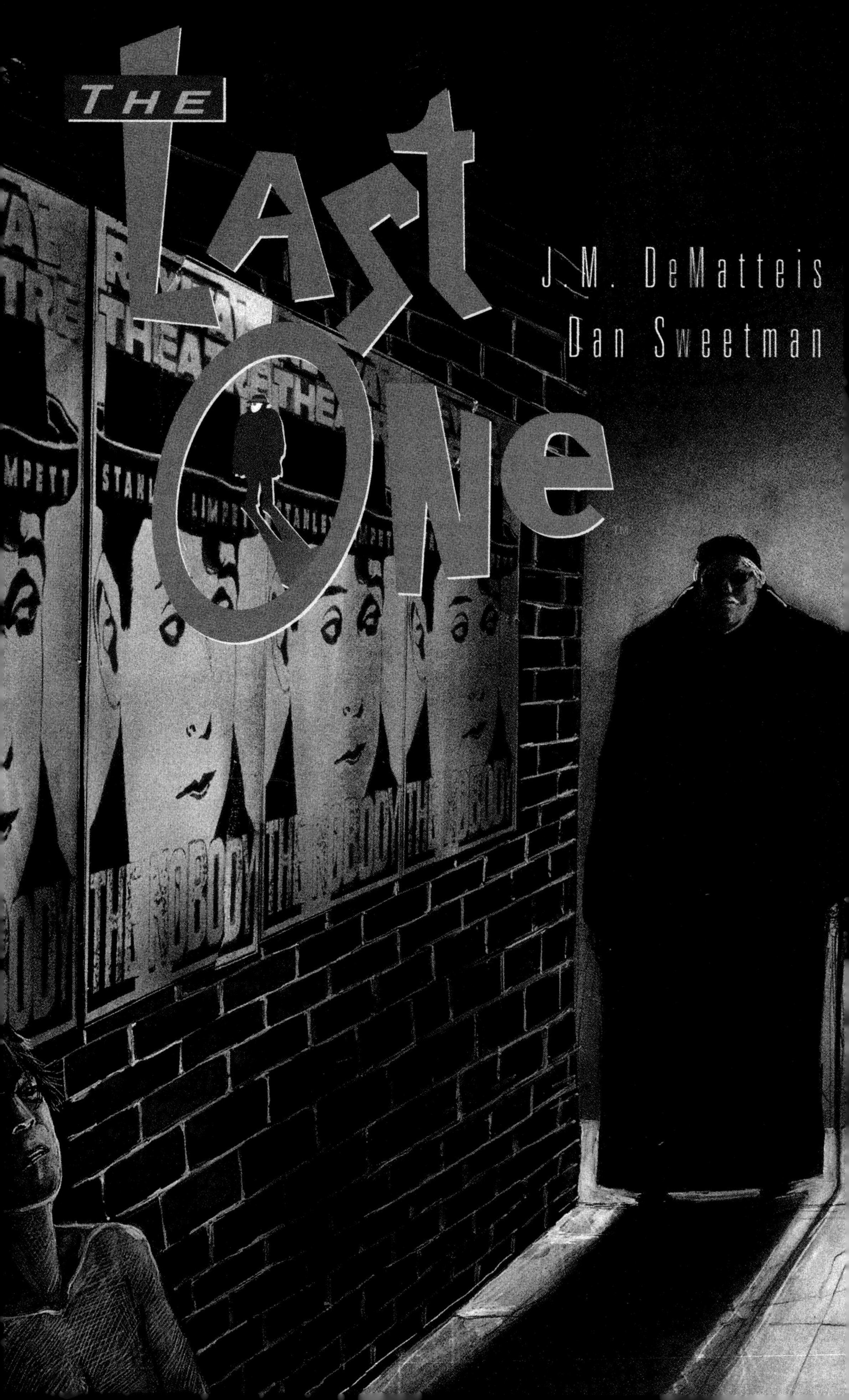
THE
Last
One
J.M. DeMatteis
Dan Sweetman

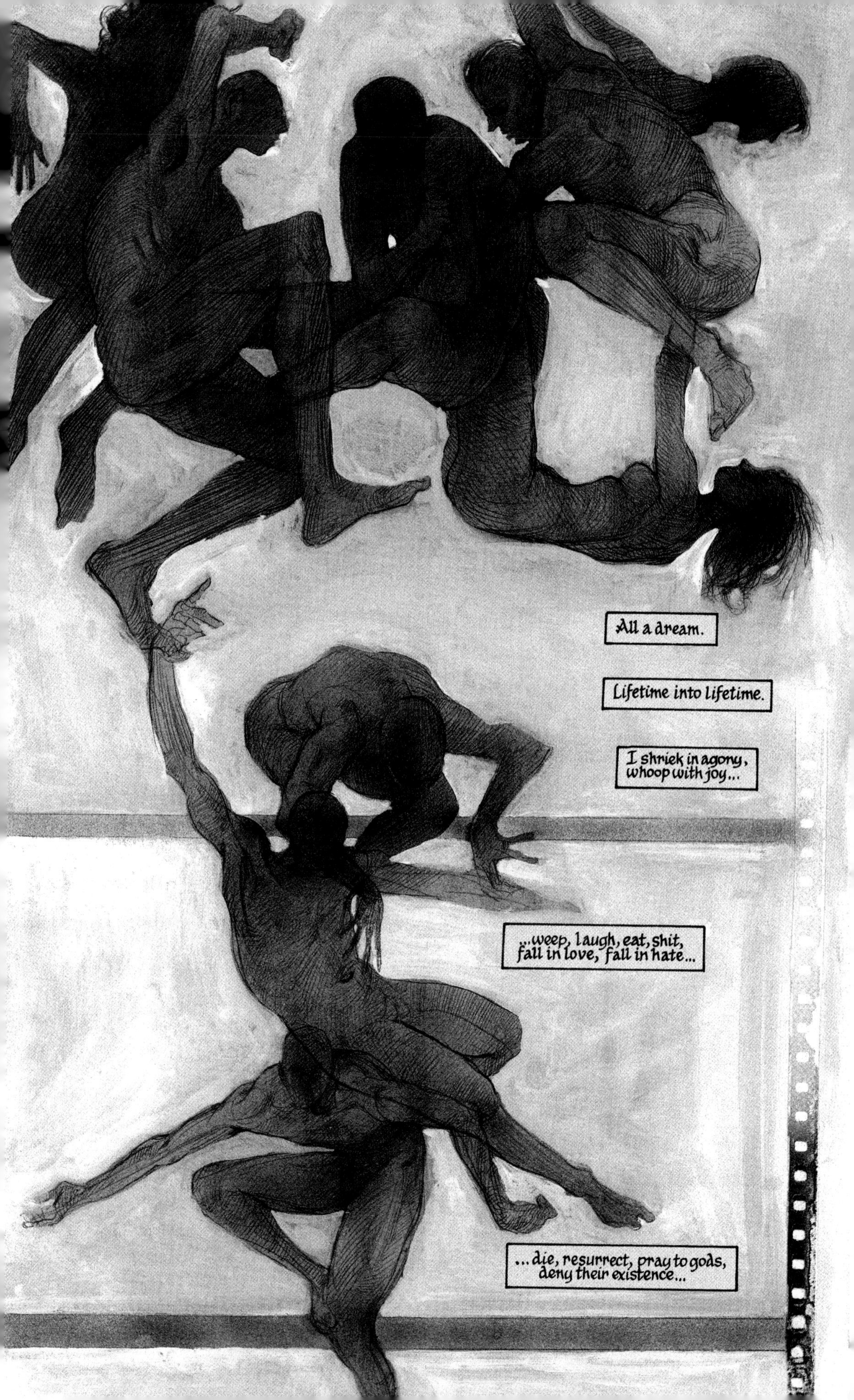
All a dream.
Lifetime into lifetime.
I shriek in agony, whoop with joy...
...weep, laugh, eat, shit, fall in love, fall in hate...
... die, resurrect, pray to gods, deny their existence...

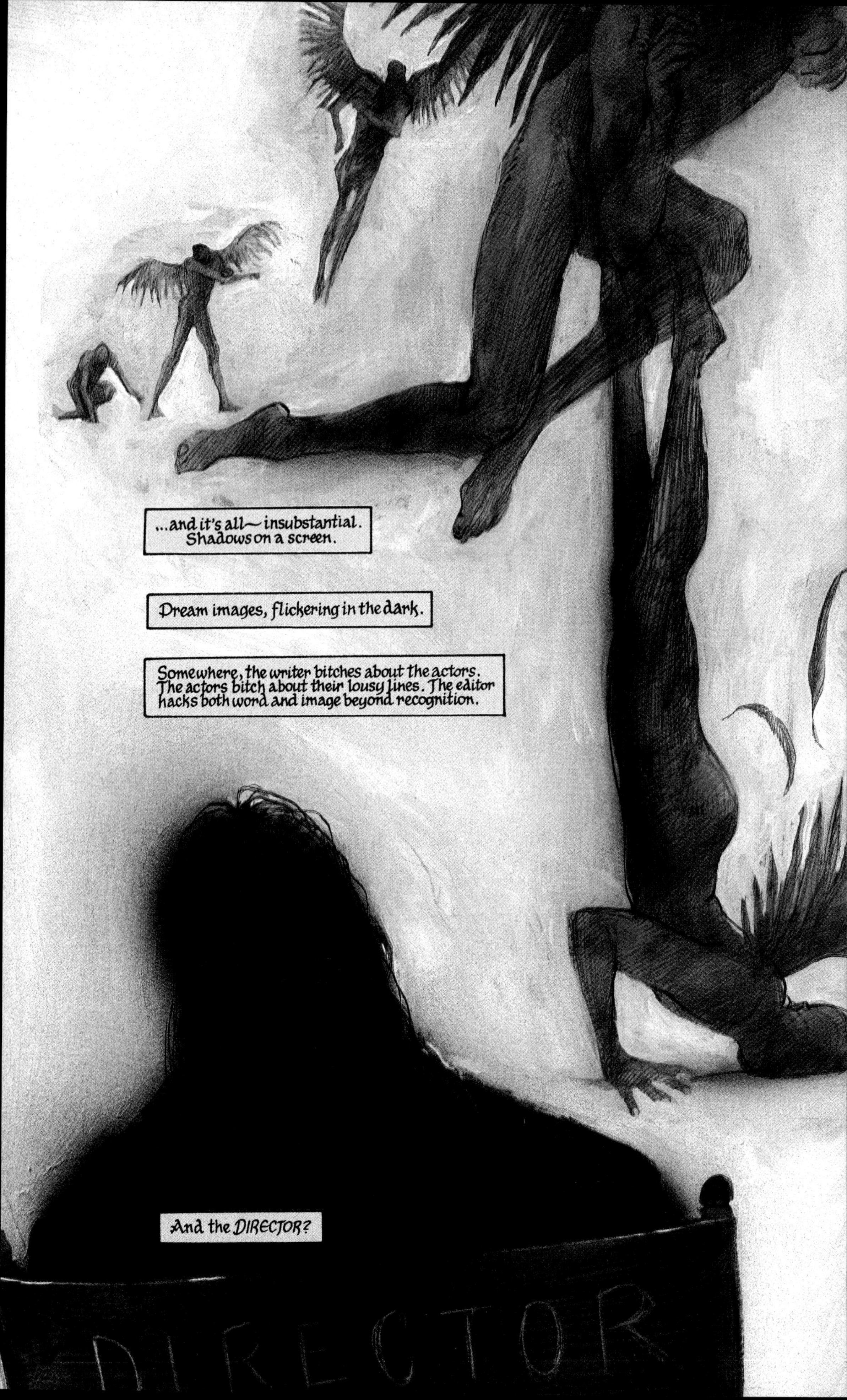
...and it's all— insubstantial. Shadows on a screen.
Dream images, flickering in the dark.
Somewhere, the writer bitches about the actors. The actors bitch about their lousy lines. The editor hacks both word and image beyond recognition.
And the DIRECTOR?
DIRECTOR

The Last One

BOOK TWO: A MEMORABLE ·FANCY·

J. M. De Matteis, writer
Dan Sweetman, illustrator
Todd Klein, letterer
Shelly Roeberg, asst. editor
Karen Berger, editor

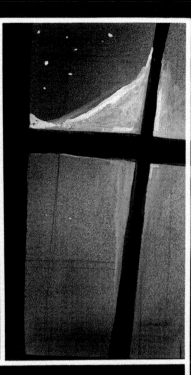

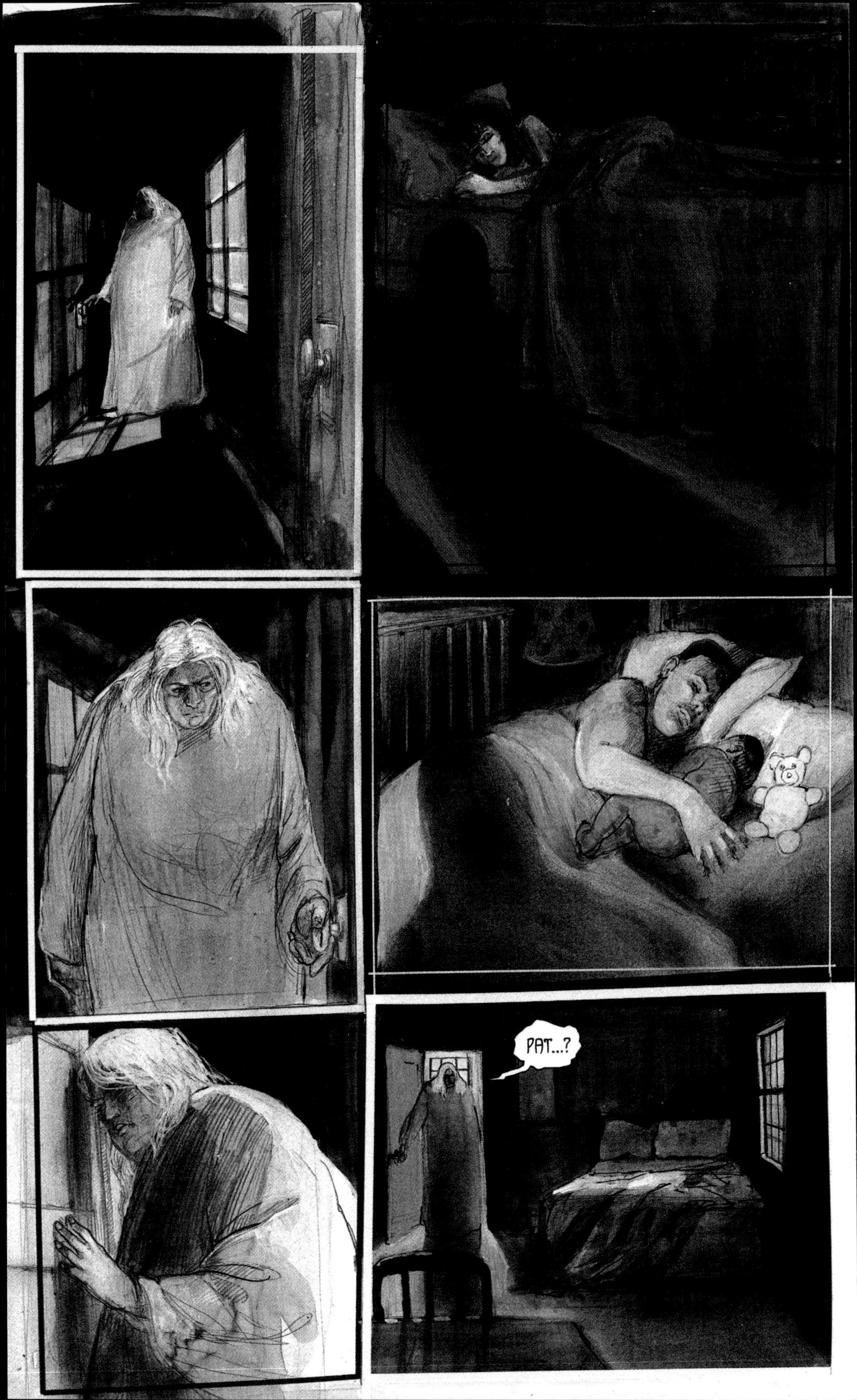
PAT...?

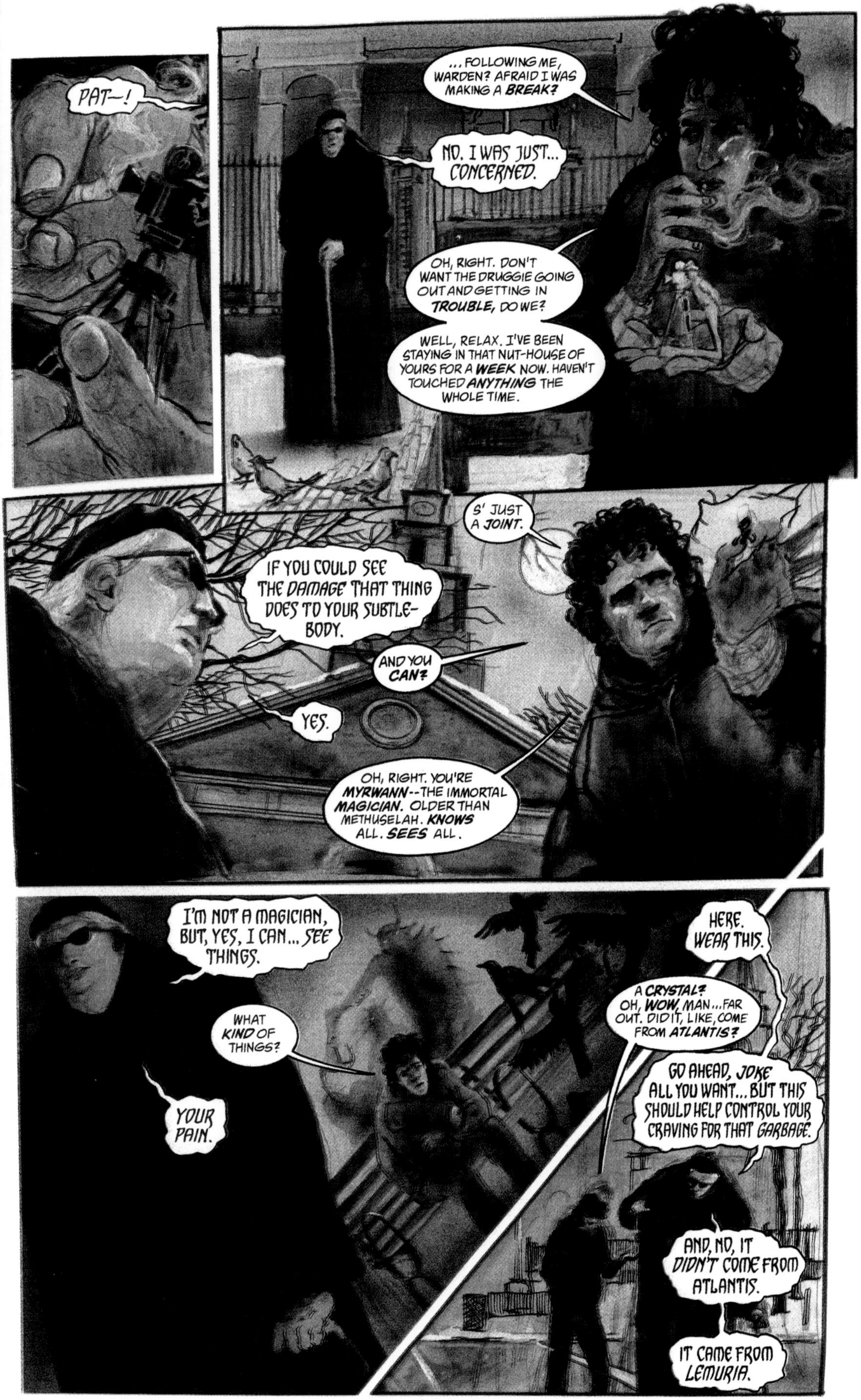
PAT--!
...FOLLOWING ME, WARDEN? AFRAID I WAS MAKING A BREAK?
NO. I WAS JUST... CONCERNED.
OH, RIGHT. DON'T WANT THE DRUGGIE GOING OUT AND GETTING IN TROUBLE, DO WE?
WELL, RELAX. I'VE BEEN STAYING IN THAT NUT-HOUSE OF YOURS FOR A WEEK NOW. HAVEN'T TOUCHED ANYTHING THE WHOLE TIME.
S' JUST A JOINT.
IF YOU COULD SEE THE DAMAGE THAT THING DOES TO YOUR SUBTLE-BODY.
AND YOU CAN?
YES.
OH, RIGHT. YOU'RE MYRWANN--THE IMMORTAL MAGICIAN. OLDER THAN METHUSELAH. KNOWS ALL. SEES ALL.
I'M NOT A MAGICIAN, BUT, YES, I CAN... SEE THINGS.
WHAT KIND OF THINGS?
YOUR PAIN.
HERE. WEAR THIS.
A CRYSTAL? OH, WOW, MAN...FAR OUT. DID IT, LIKE, COME FROM ATLANTIS?
GO AHEAD, JOKE ALL YOU WANT... BUT THIS SHOULD HELP CONTROL YOUR CRAVING FOR THAT GARBAGE.
AND, NO, IT DIDN'T COME FROM ATLANTIS.
IT CAME FROM LEMURIA.

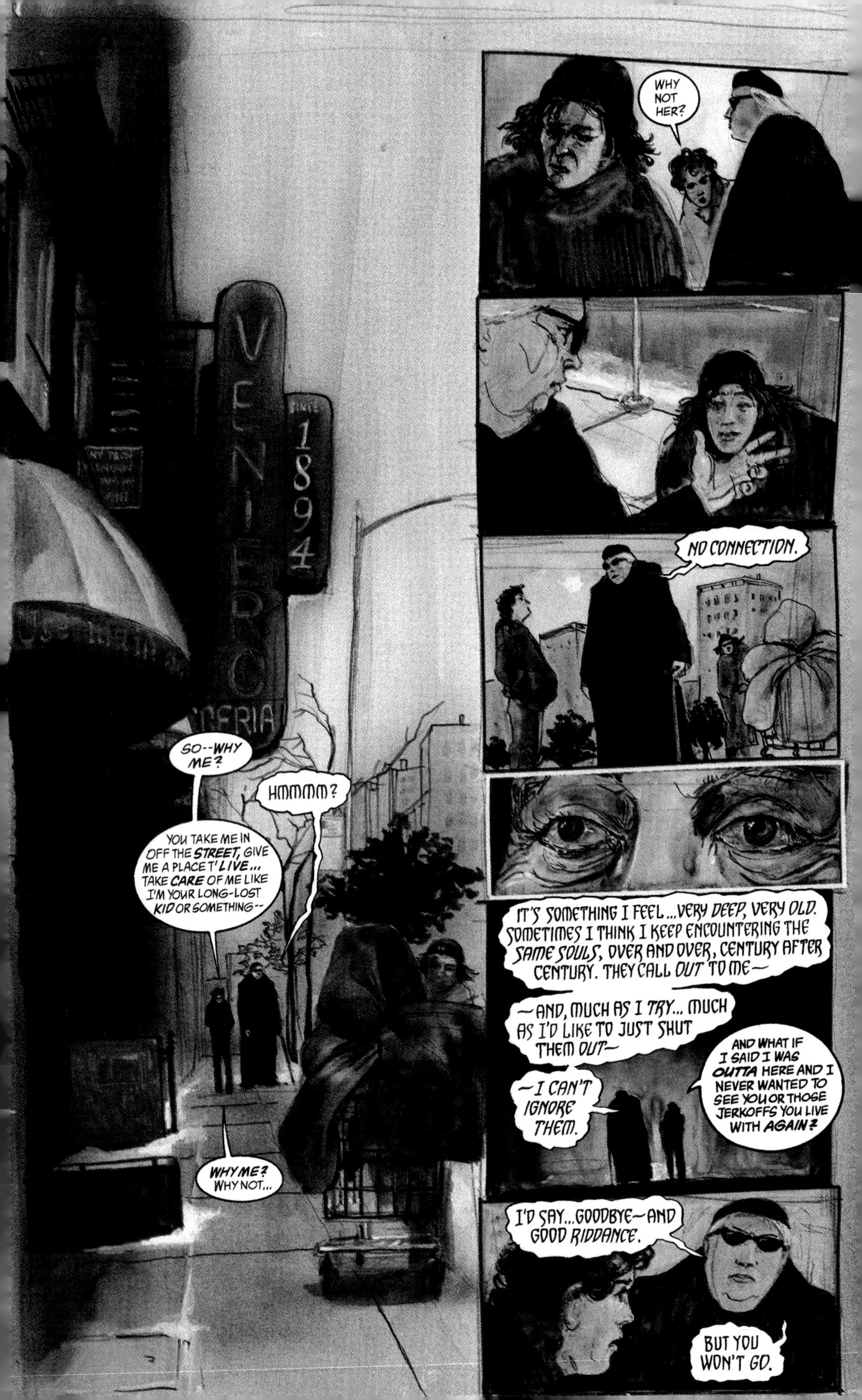
SO--WHY ME?
HMMMM?
YOU TAKE ME IN OFF THE STREET, GIVE ME A PLACE T' LIVE... TAKE CARE OF ME LIKE I'M YOUR LONG-LOST KID OR SOMETHING--
WHY ME? WHY NOT...
WHY NOT HER?
NO CONNECTION.
IT'S SOMETHING I FEEL... VERY DEEP, VERY OLD. SOMETIMES I THINK I KEEP ENCOUNTERING THE SAME SOULS, OVER AND OVER, CENTURY AFTER CENTURY. THEY CALL OUT TO ME—
—AND, MUCH AS I TRY... MUCH AS I'D LIKE TO JUST SHUT THEM OUT—
—I CAN'T IGNORE THEM.
AND WHAT IF I SAID I WAS OUTTA HERE AND I NEVER WANTED TO SEE YOU OR THOSE JERKOFFS YOU LIVE WITH AGAIN?
I'D SAY... GOODBYE—AND GOOD RIDDANCE.
BUT YOU WON'T GO.

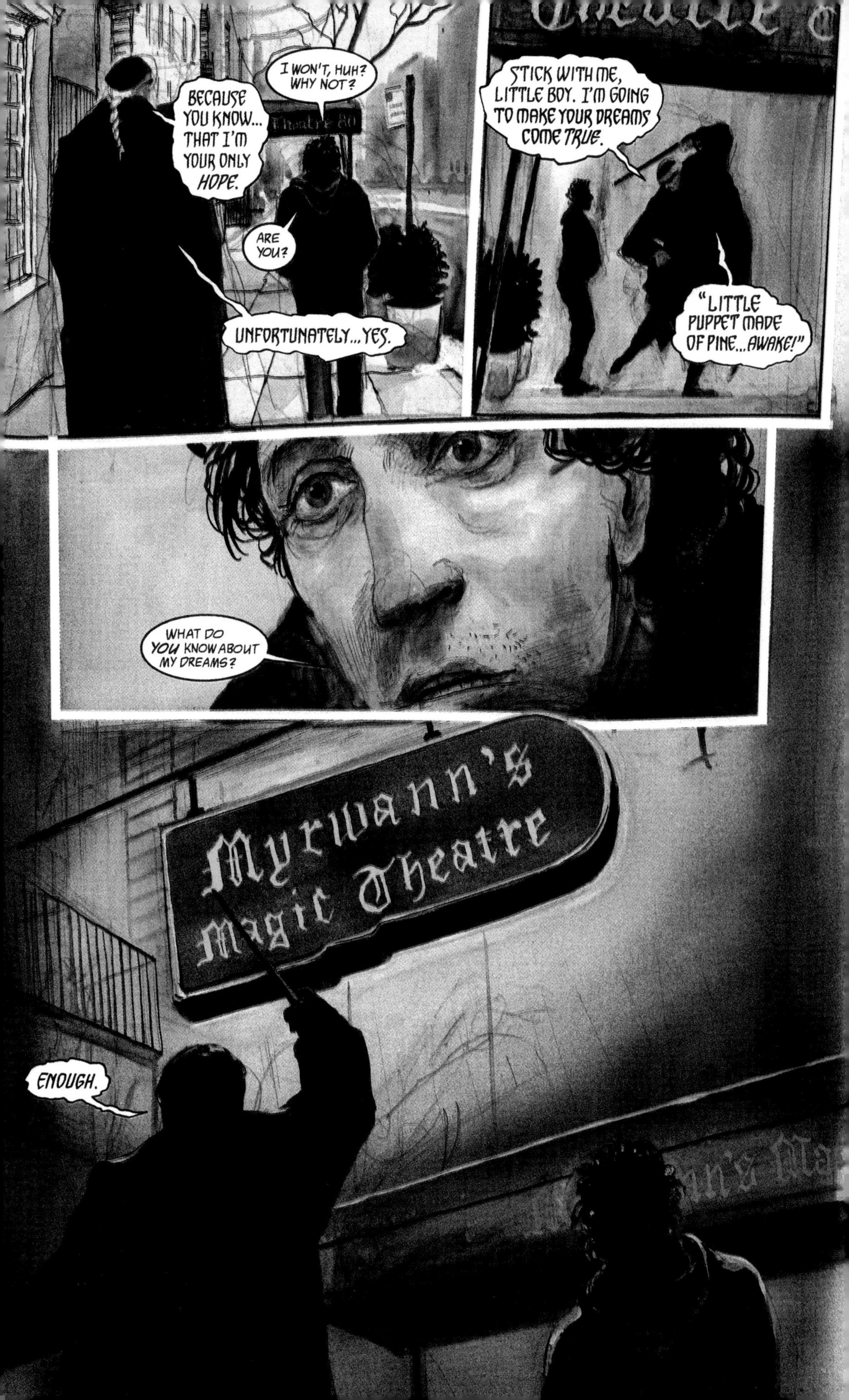
BECAUSE YOU KNOW... THAT I'M YOUR ONLY HOPE.
I WON'T, HUH? WHY NOT?
ARE YOU?
UNFORTUNATELY... YES.
STICK WITH ME, LITTLE BOY. I'M GOING TO MAKE YOUR DREAMS COME TRUE.
"LITTLE PUPPET MADE OF PINE... AWAKE!"
WHAT DO YOU KNOW ABOUT MY DREAMS?
Myrwann's Magic Theatre
ENOUGH.

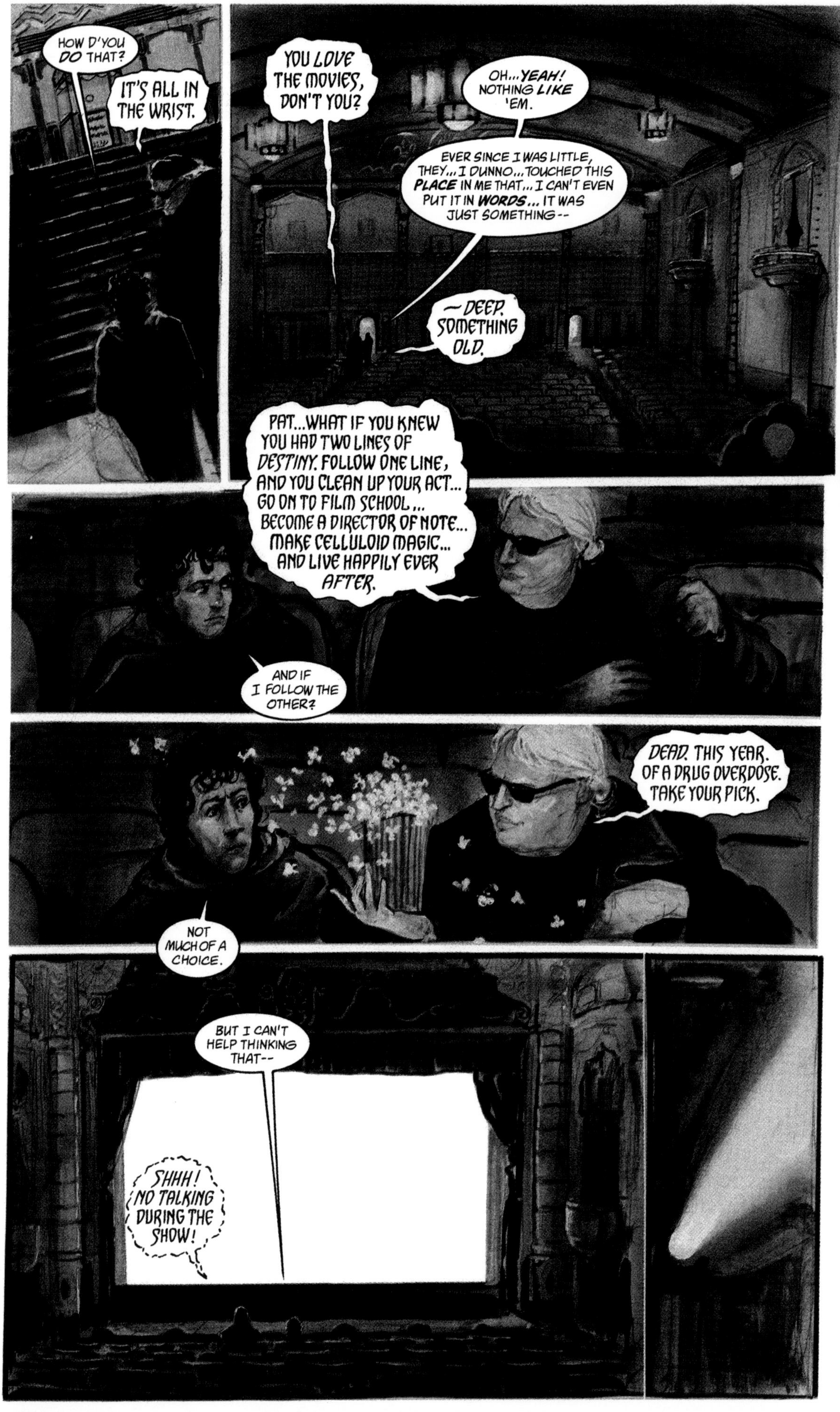
HOW D'YOU DO THAT?
IT'S ALL IN THE WRIST.
YOU LOVE THE MOVIES, DON'T YOU?
OH... YEAH! NOTHING LIKE 'EM.
EVER SINCE I WAS LITTLE, THEY... I DUNNO... TOUCHED THIS PLACE IN ME THAT... I CAN'T EVEN PUT IT IN WORDS... IT WAS JUST SOMETHING--
--DEEP. SOMETHING OLD.
PAT... WHAT IF YOU KNEW YOU HAD TWO LINES OF DESTINY. FOLLOW ONE LINE, AND YOU CLEAN UP YOUR ACT... GO ON TO FILM SCHOOL... BECOME A DIRECTOR OF NOTE... MAKE CELLULOID MAGIC... AND LIVE HAPPILY EVER AFTER.
AND IF I FOLLOW THE OTHER?
DEAD. THIS YEAR. OF A DRUG OVERDOSE. TAKE YOUR PICK.
NOT MUCH OF A CHOICE.
BUT I CAN'T HELP THINKING THAT--
SHHH! NO TALKING DURING THE SHOW!

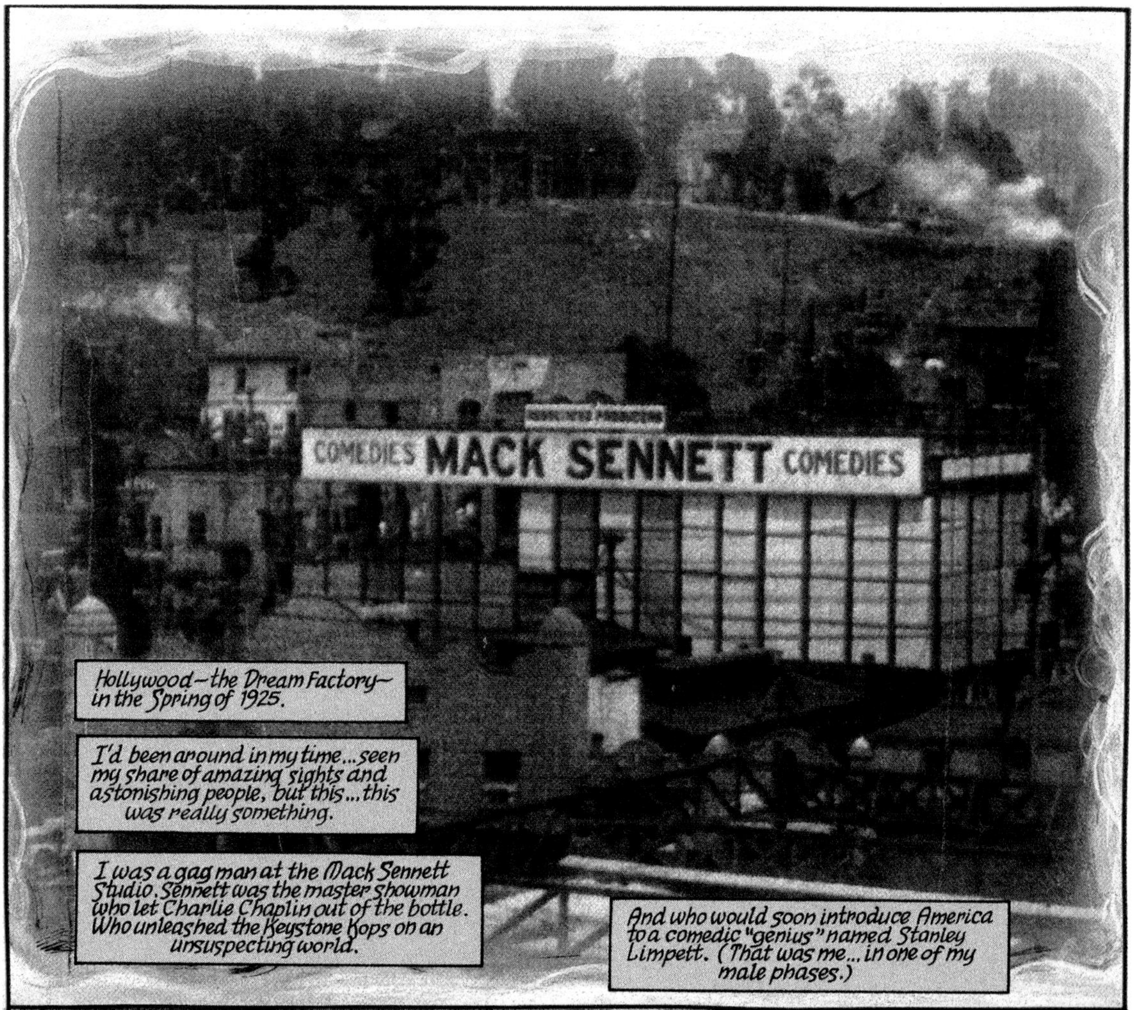
MACK SENNETT
COMEDIES
COMEDIES
Hollywood—the Dream Factory—in the Spring of 1925.
I'd been around in my time... seen my share of amazing sights and astonishing people, but this... this was really something.
I was a gag man at the Mack Sennett Studio. Sennett was the master showman who let Charlie Chaplin out of the bottle. Who unleashed the Keystone Kops on an unsuspecting world.
And who would soon introduce America to a comedic "genius" named Stanley Limpett. (That was me... in one of my male phases.)

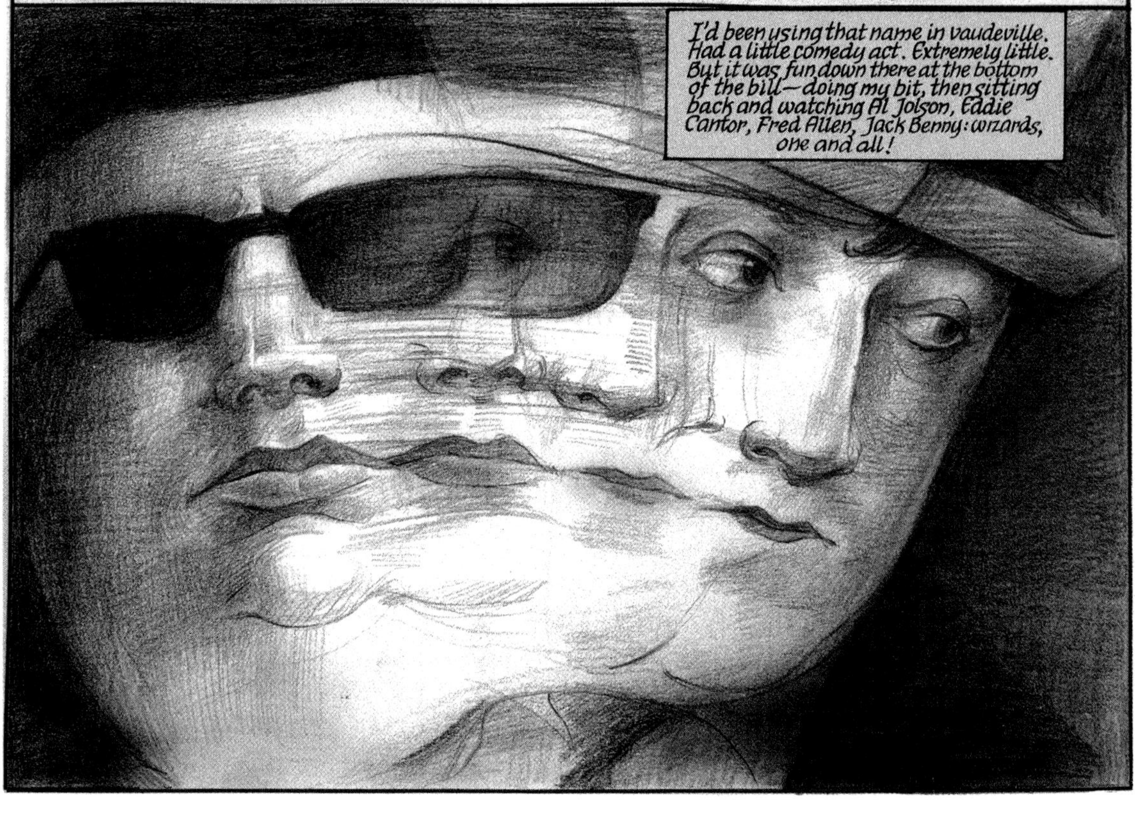
I'd been using that name in vaudeville. Had a little comedy act. Extremely little. But it was fun down there at the bottom of the bill—doing my bit, then sitting back and watching Al Jolson, Eddie Cantor, Fred Allen, Jack Benny: wizards, one and all!

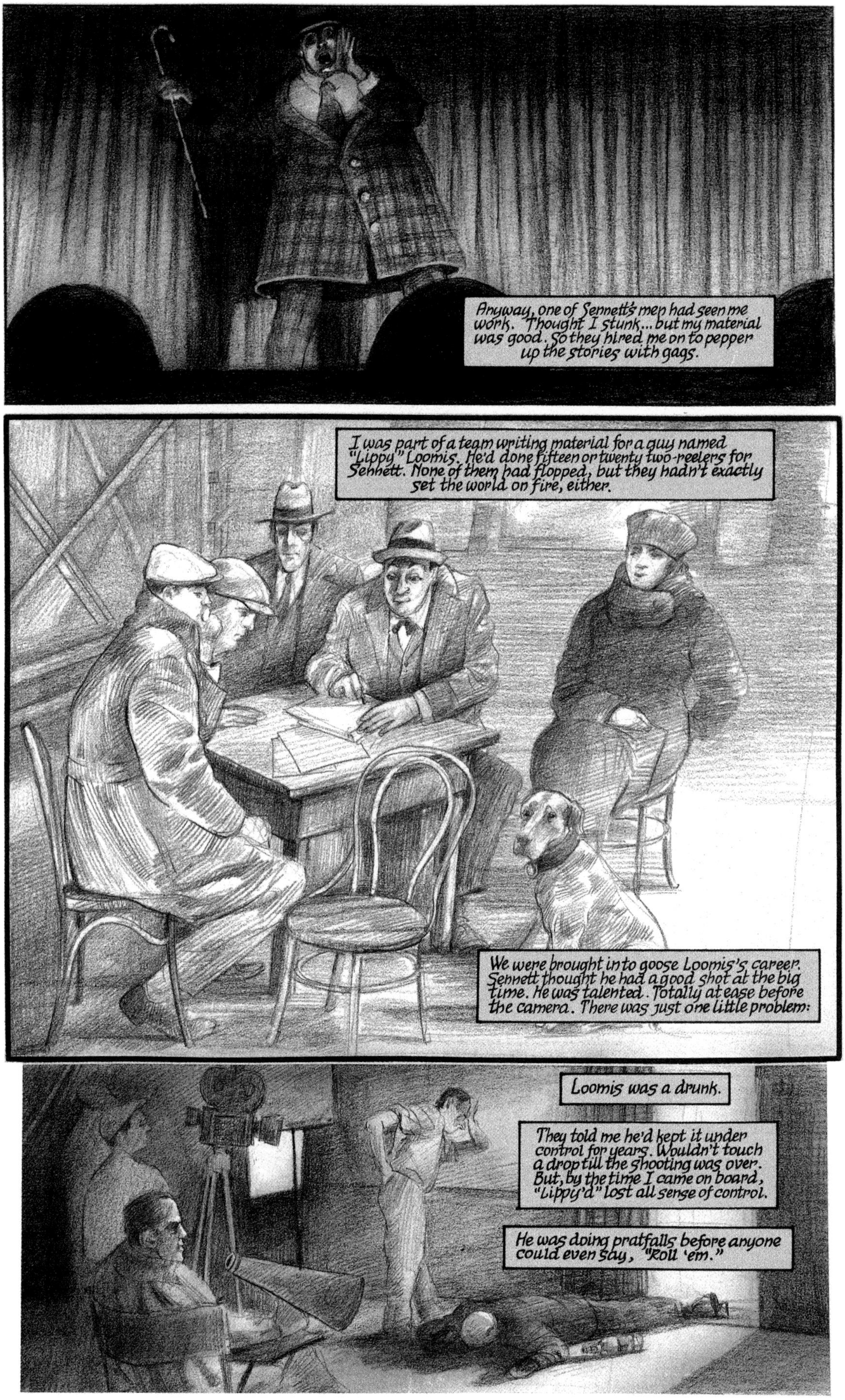
Anyway, one of Sennett's men had seen me work. Thought I stunk... but my material was good. So they hired me on to pepper up the stories with gags.
I was part of a team writing material for a guy named "Lippy" Loomis. He'd done fifteen or twenty two-reelers for Sennett. None of them had flopped, but they hadn't exactly set the world on fire, either.
We were brought in to goose Loomis's career. Sennett thought he had a good shot at the big time. He was talented. Totally at ease before the camera. There was just one little problem:
Loomis was a drunk.
They told me he'd kept it under control for years. Wouldn't touch a drop till the shooting was over. But, by the time I came on board, "Lippy'd" lost all sense of control.
He was doing pratfalls before anyone could even say, "Roll 'em."

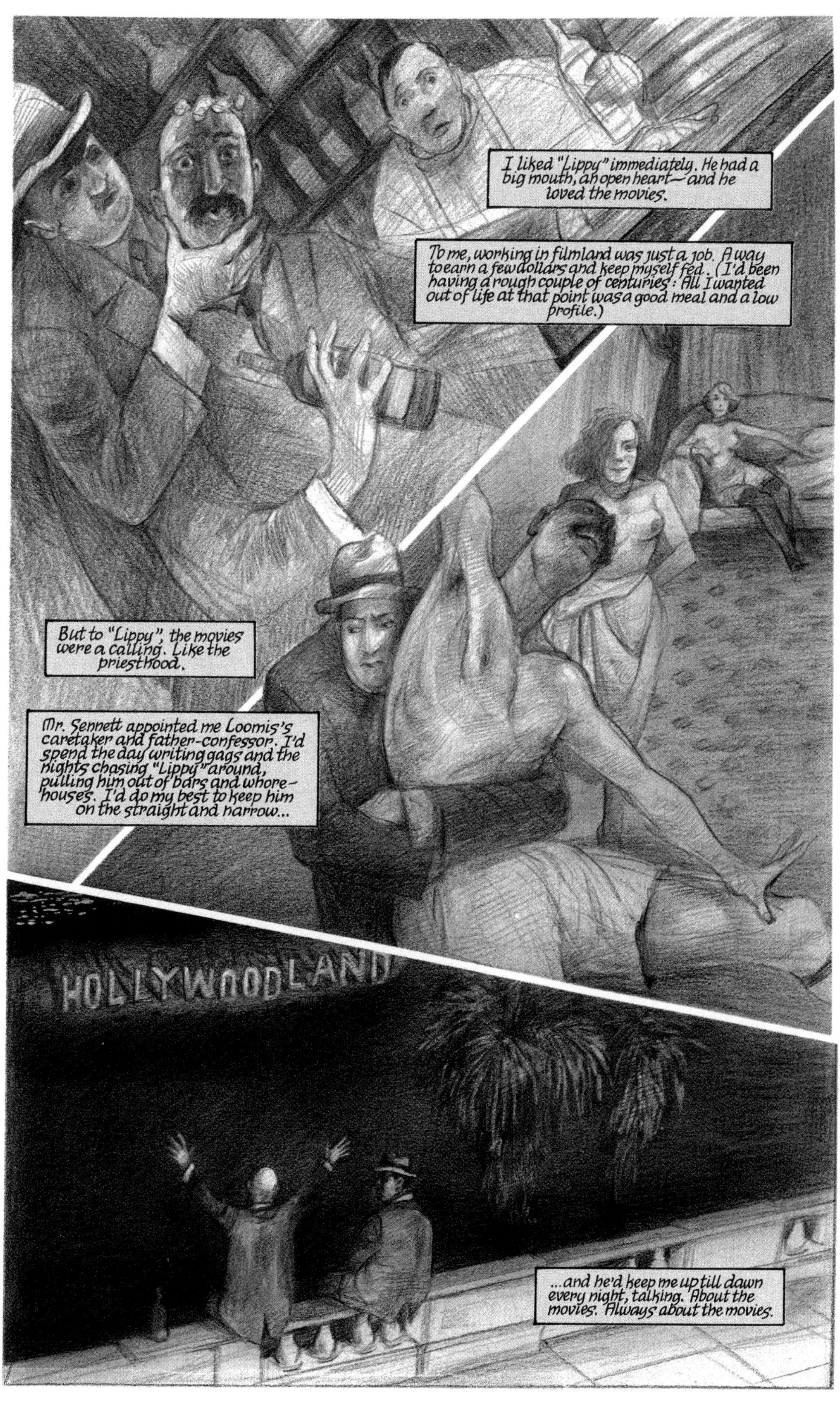
I liked "Lippy" immediately. He had a big mouth, an open heart— and he loved the movies.
To me, working in filmland was just a job. A way to earn a few dollars and keep myself fed. (I'd been having a rough couple of centuries: All I wanted out of life at that point was a good meal and a low profile.)
But to "Lippy", the movies were a calling. Like the priesthood.
Mr. Sennett appointed me Loomis's caretaker and father-confessor. I'd spend the day writing gags and the nights chasing "Lippy" around, pulling him out of bars and whore-houses. I'd do my best to keep him on the straight and narrow...
HOLLYWOODLAND
...and he'd keep me up till dawn every night, talking. About the movies. Always about the movies.

To "Lippy" film was God's greatest gift since the Ten Commandments. He thought it would end war, famine, pestilence and disease.

ALL OVER THE *WORLD*--

—he'd say—

--PEOPLE ARE LOOKIN' AT CHAPLIN, FAIRBANKS, PICKFORD... AND THEY'RE LAUGHING THEIR *ASSES* OFF! THEY'RE BAWLING THEIR *EYES* OUT!

THEY'RE STANDING ON THEIR SEATS AND *CHEERING!*

ONCE PEOPLE REALIZE THAT *WE'RE* ALL TOUCHED BY THE SAME THINGS...IT'S GONNA CHANGE THE WHOLE *HUMAN RACE,* STAN!

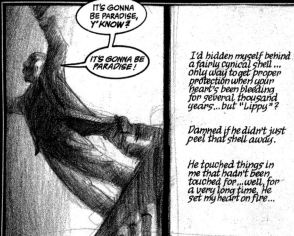

IT'S GONNA BE PARADISE, Y'KNOW?

IT'S GONNA BE PARADISE!

I'd hidden myself behind a fairly cynical shell... only way to get proper protection when your heart's been bleeding for several thousand years...but "Lippy"?

Damned if he didn't just peel that shell away.

He touched things in me that hadn't been touched for...well, for a very long time. He set my heart on fire...

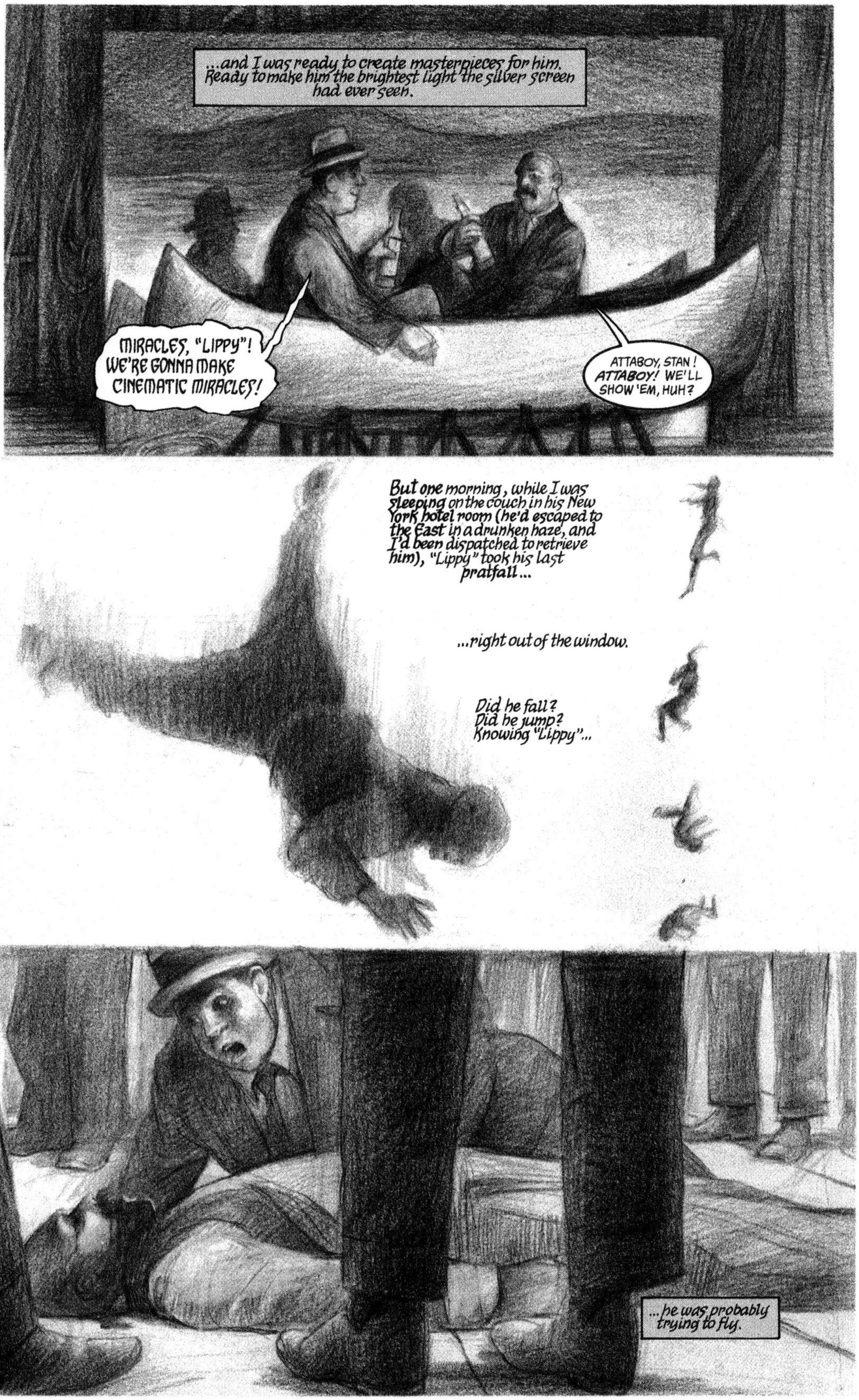
...and I was ready to create masterpieces for him. Ready to make him the brightest light the silver screen had ever seen.
MIRACLES, "LIPPY"! WE'RE GONNA MAKE CINEMATIC MIRACLES!
ATTABOY, STAN! ATTABOY! WE'LL SHOW 'EM, HUH?
But one morning, while I was sleeping on the couch in his New York hotel room (he'd escaped to the East in a drunken haze, and I'd been dispatched to retrieve him), "Lippy" took his last pratfall...
...right out of the window.
Did he fall? Did he jump? Knowing "Lippy"...
...he was probably trying to fly.

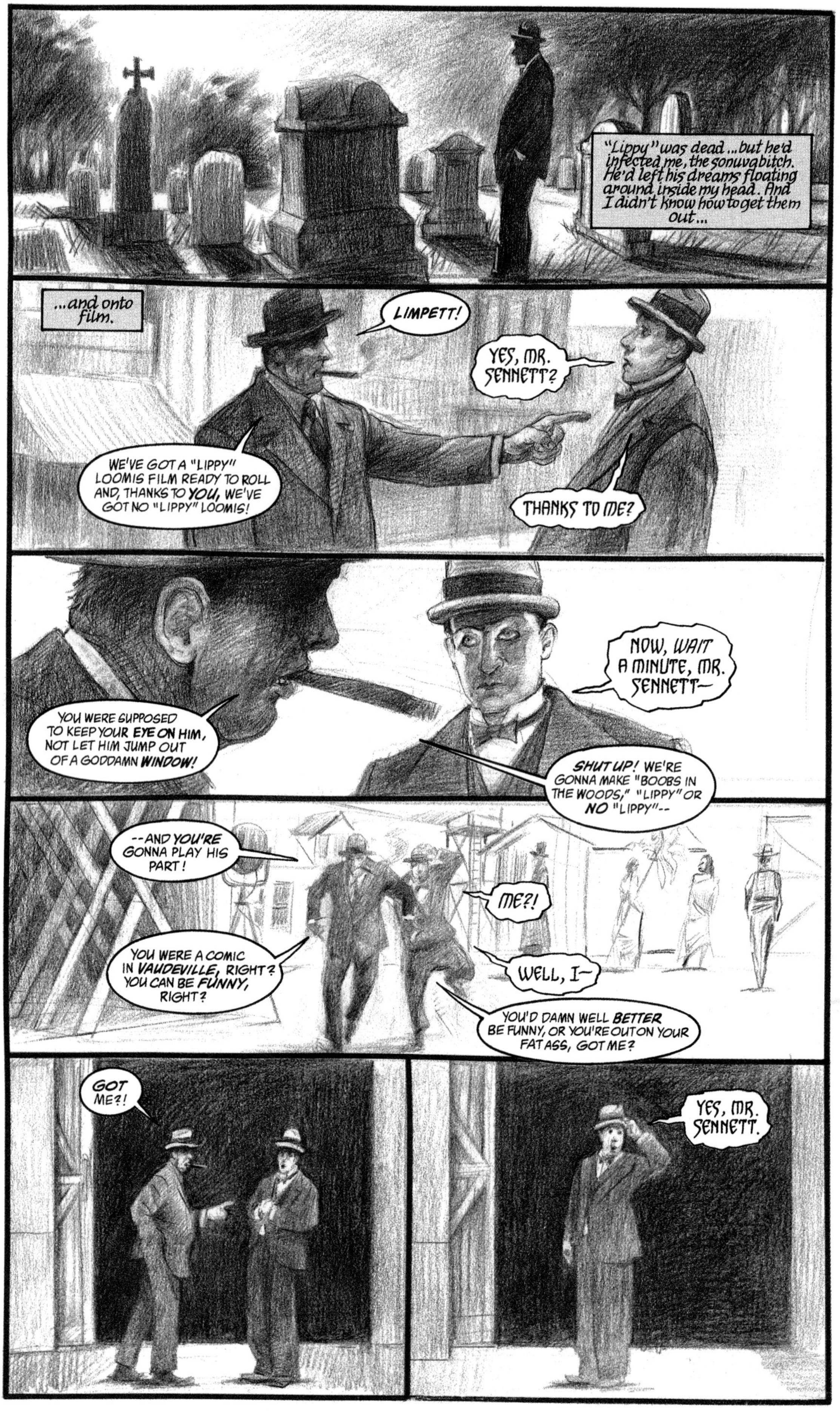
"Lippy" was dead... but he'd infected me, the sonuvabitch. He'd left his dreams floating around inside my head. And I didn't know how to get them out...
...and onto film.
LIMPETT!
YES, MR. SENNETT?
WE'VE GOT A "LIPPY" LOOMIS FILM READY TO ROLL AND, THANKS TO YOU, WE'VE GOT NO "LIPPY" LOOMIS!
THANKS TO ME?
NOW, WAIT A MINUTE, MR. SENNETT—
YOU WERE SUPPOSED TO KEEP YOUR EYE ON HIM, NOT LET HIM JUMP OUT OF A GODDAMN WINDOW!
SHUT UP! WE'RE GONNA MAKE "BOOBS IN THE WOODS," "LIPPY" OR NO "LIPPY"--
--AND YOU'RE GONNA PLAY HIS PART!
ME?!
YOU WERE A COMIC IN VAUDEVILLE, RIGHT? YOU CAN BE FUNNY, RIGHT?
WELL, I—
YOU'D DAMN WELL BETTER BE FUNNY, OR YOU'RE OUT ON YOUR FAT ASS, GOT ME?
GOT ME?!
YES, MR. SENNETT.

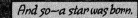

And so—a star was born.

Sort of.

Okay, "Boobs in the Woods" wasn't exactly high art. And my reviews were hardly enthusiastic. But it was funny. And it made money. Enough to merit another Stanley Limpett two-reeler.

And another.

And another.

The whole premise of the "Lippy" Loomis character was that he was a total innocent. Absolutely trusting. Never suspicious of a soul.

The entire universe would be collapsing all around him and he'd sail sweetly along, not even aware that anything was wrong.

His innocence was his protection. His guarantee that he'd never be harmed. That invisible angels would always be there to save him.

MACK SENNETT PRESENTS

BOOBS IN THE WOODS

STARRING THAT NEW COMEDY SENSATION

STANLEY LIMPETT

A COMEDY

PATHÉ
DISTRIBUTORS

Thing was, people didn't buy it from "Lippy." Maybe it was too hard to reconcile the innocent on the screen with all the stories about booze and sex they were reading in "Photoplay." Or maybe it was just fate.

But what they wouldn't buy from Loomis, they bought from Limpett. Bought it? Hell...

...they ate it up.

I don't know. Maybe they could sense that, underneath the makeup and silly hats, I really was an outsider blundering through a world that was totally alien to me. Maybe an innocence I thought I'd lost hundreds of years before was somehow being captured by the camera.

Or maybe they just liked the way I dropped my drawers.

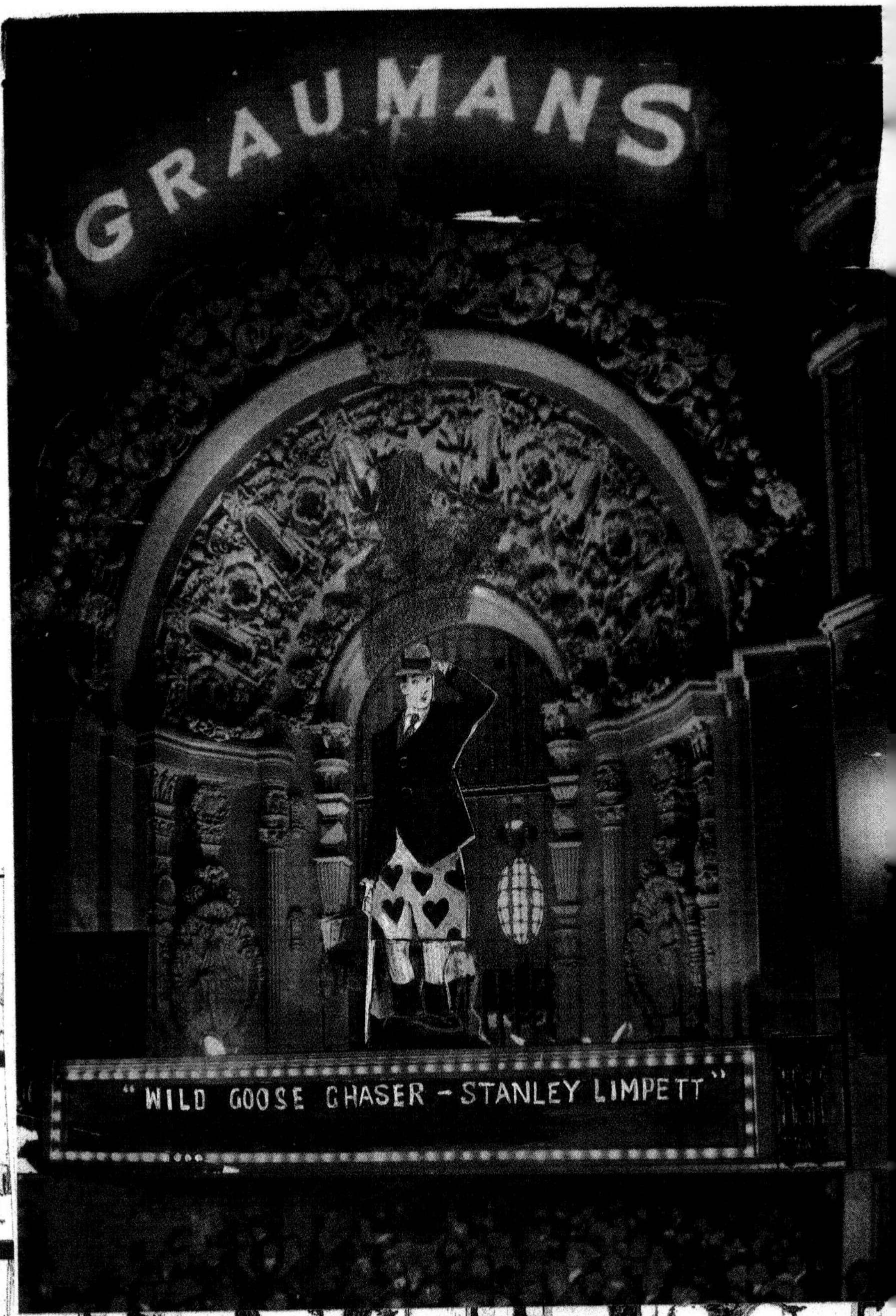
GRAUMANS
"WILD GOOSE CHASER - STANLEY LIMPETT"

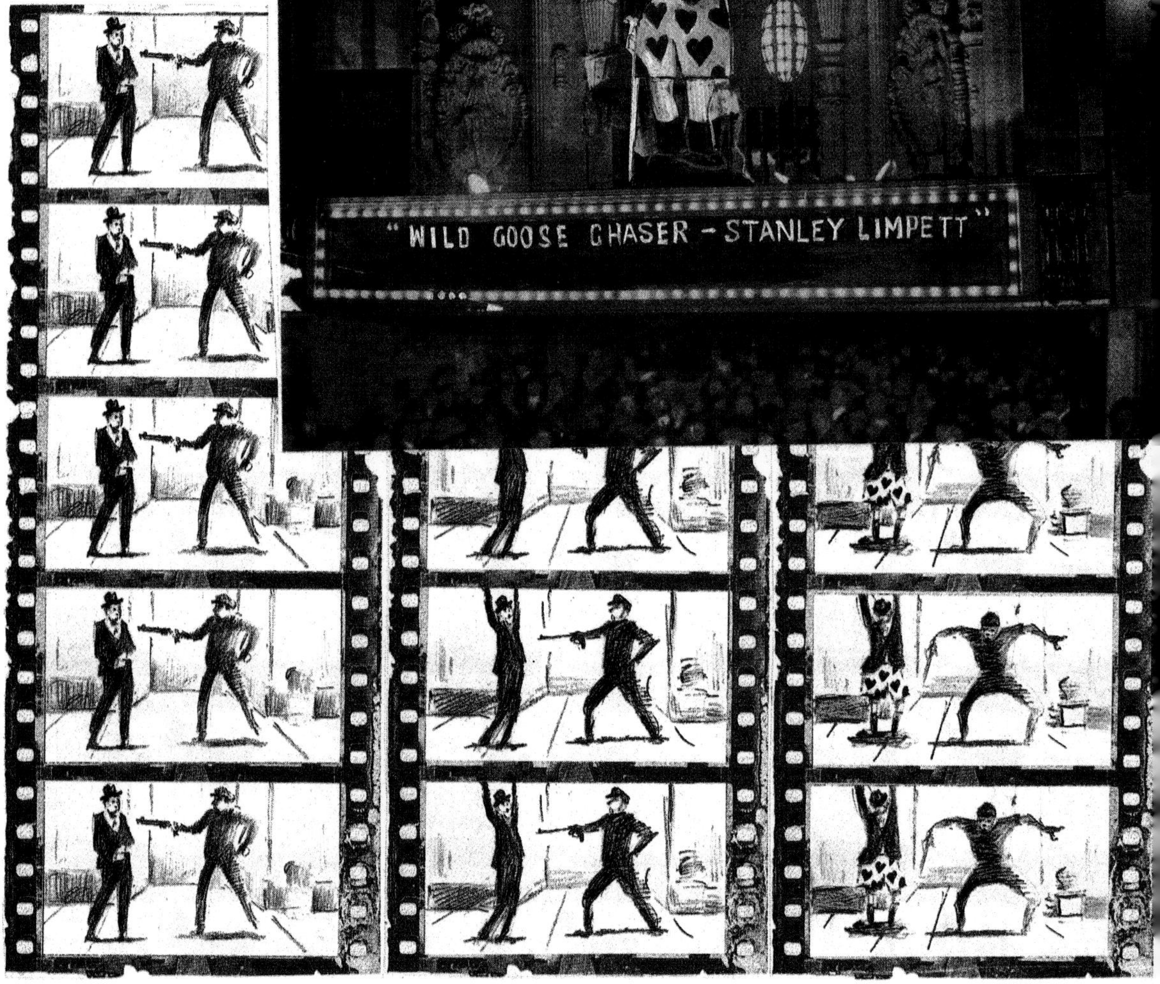

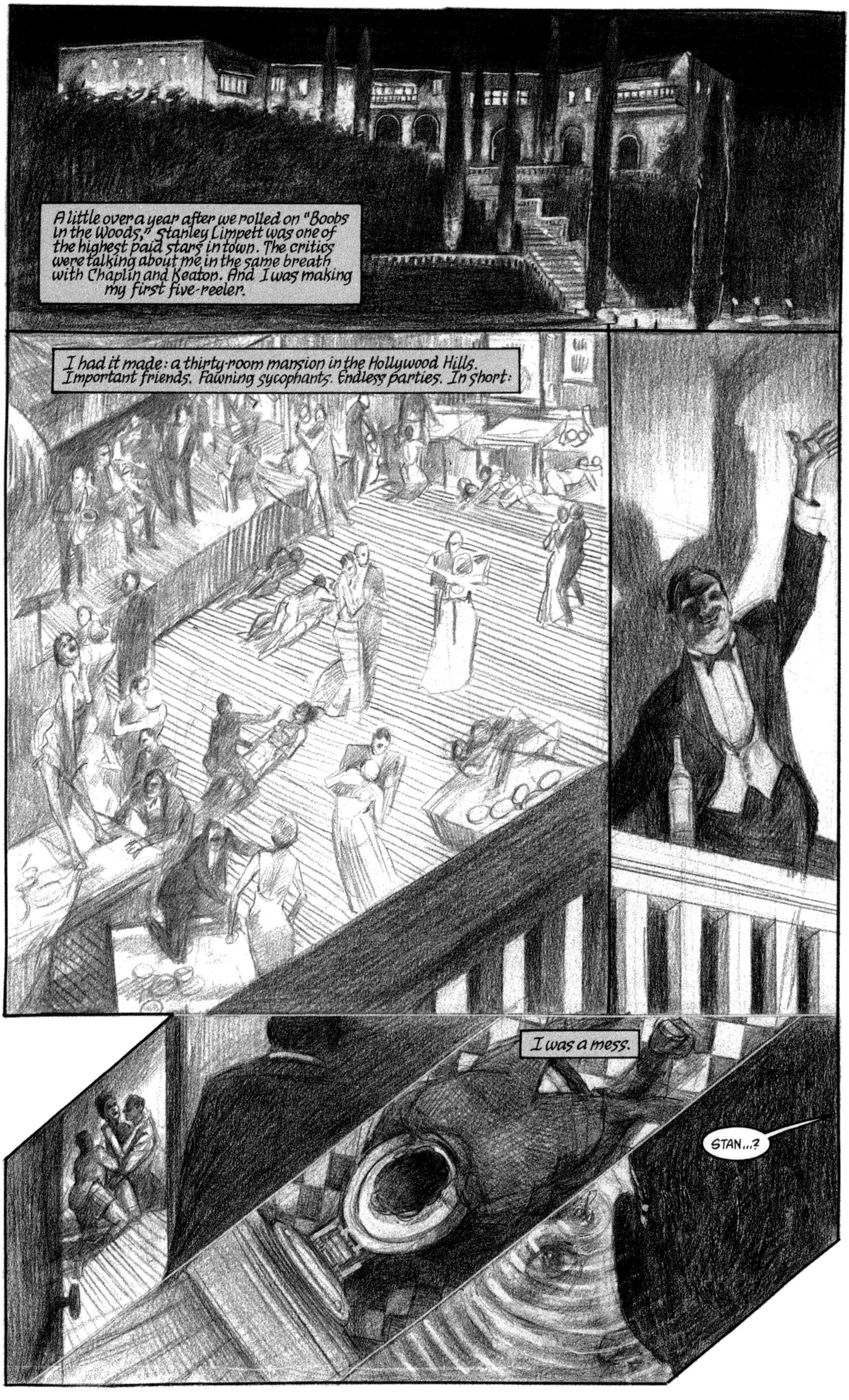
A little over a year after we rolled on "Boobs in the Woods," Stanley Limpett was one of the highest paid stars in town. The critics were talking about me in the same breath with Chaplin and Keaton. And I was making my first five-reeler.
I had it made: a thirty-room mansion in the Hollywood Hills. Important friends. Fawning sycophants. Endless parties. In short:
I was a mess.
STAN...?

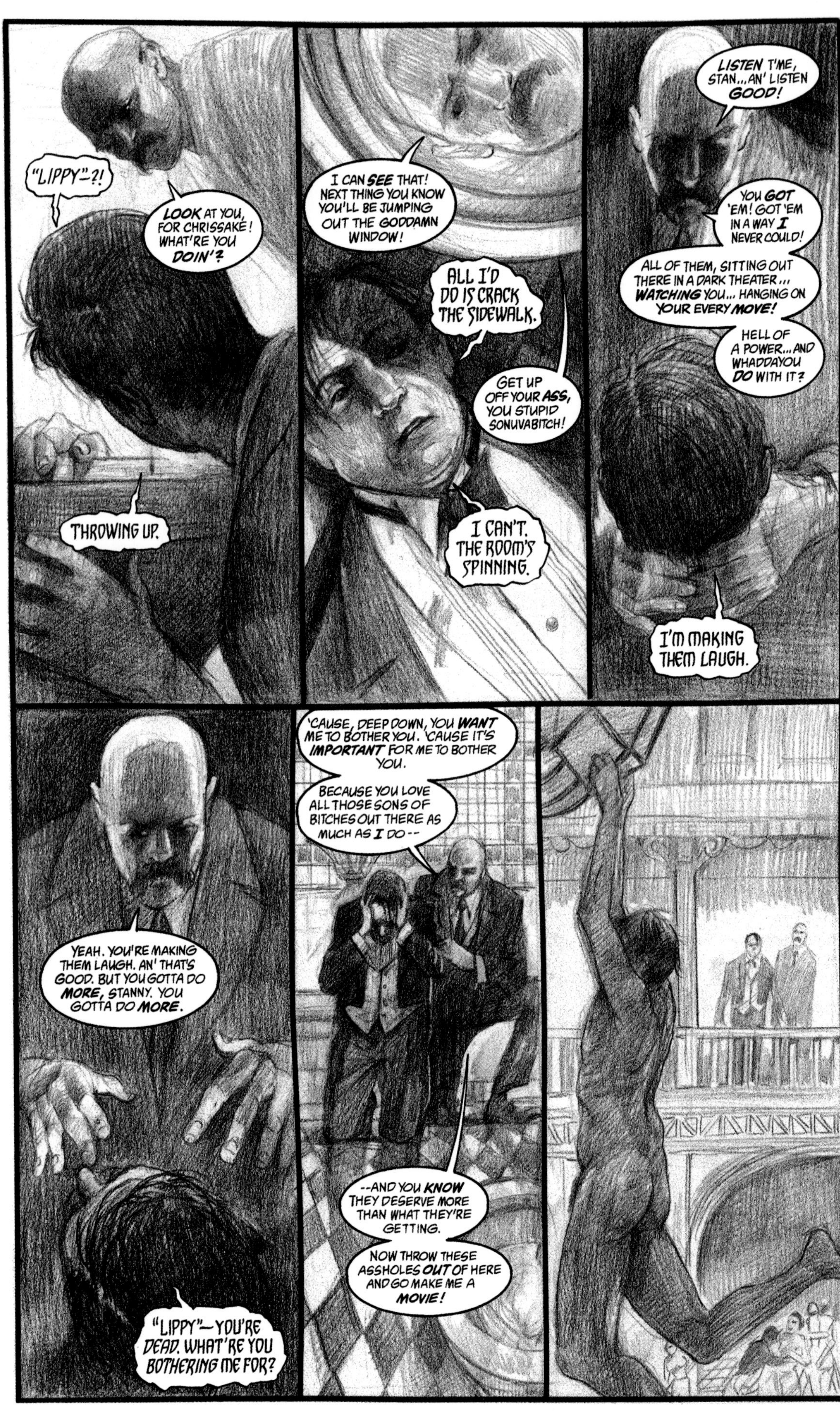
"LIPPY"--?!
LOOK AT YOU, FOR CHRISSAKE! WHAT'RE YOU DOIN'?
THROWING UP.
I CAN SEE THAT! NEXT THING YOU KNOW YOU'LL BE JUMPING OUT THE GODDAMN WINDOW!
ALL I'D DO IS CRACK THE SIDEWALK.
GET UP OFF YOUR ASS, YOU STUPID SONUVABITCH!
I CAN'T. THE ROOM'S SPINNING.
LISTEN T'ME, STAN... AN' LISTEN GOOD!
YOU GOT 'EM! GOT 'EM IN A WAY I NEVER COULD!
ALL OF THEM, SITTING OUT THERE IN A DARK THEATER... WATCHING YOU... HANGING ON YOUR EVERY MOVE!
HELL OF A POWER... AND WHADDAYOU DO WITH IT?
I'M MAKING THEM LAUGH.
YEAH. YOU'RE MAKING THEM LAUGH. AN' THAT'S GOOD. BUT YOU GOTTA DO MORE, STANNY. YOU GOTTA DO MORE.
"LIPPY"--YOU'RE DEAD. WHAT'RE YOU BOTHERING ME FOR?
'CAUSE, DEEP DOWN, YOU WANT ME TO BOTHER YOU. 'CAUSE IT'S IMPORTANT FOR ME TO BOTHER YOU.
BECAUSE YOU LOVE ALL THOSE SONS OF BITCHES OUT THERE AS MUCH AS I DO--
--AND YOU KNOW THEY DESERVE MORE THAN WHAT THEY'RE GETTING.
NOW THROW THESE ASSHOLES OUT OF HERE AND GO MAKE ME A MOVIE!

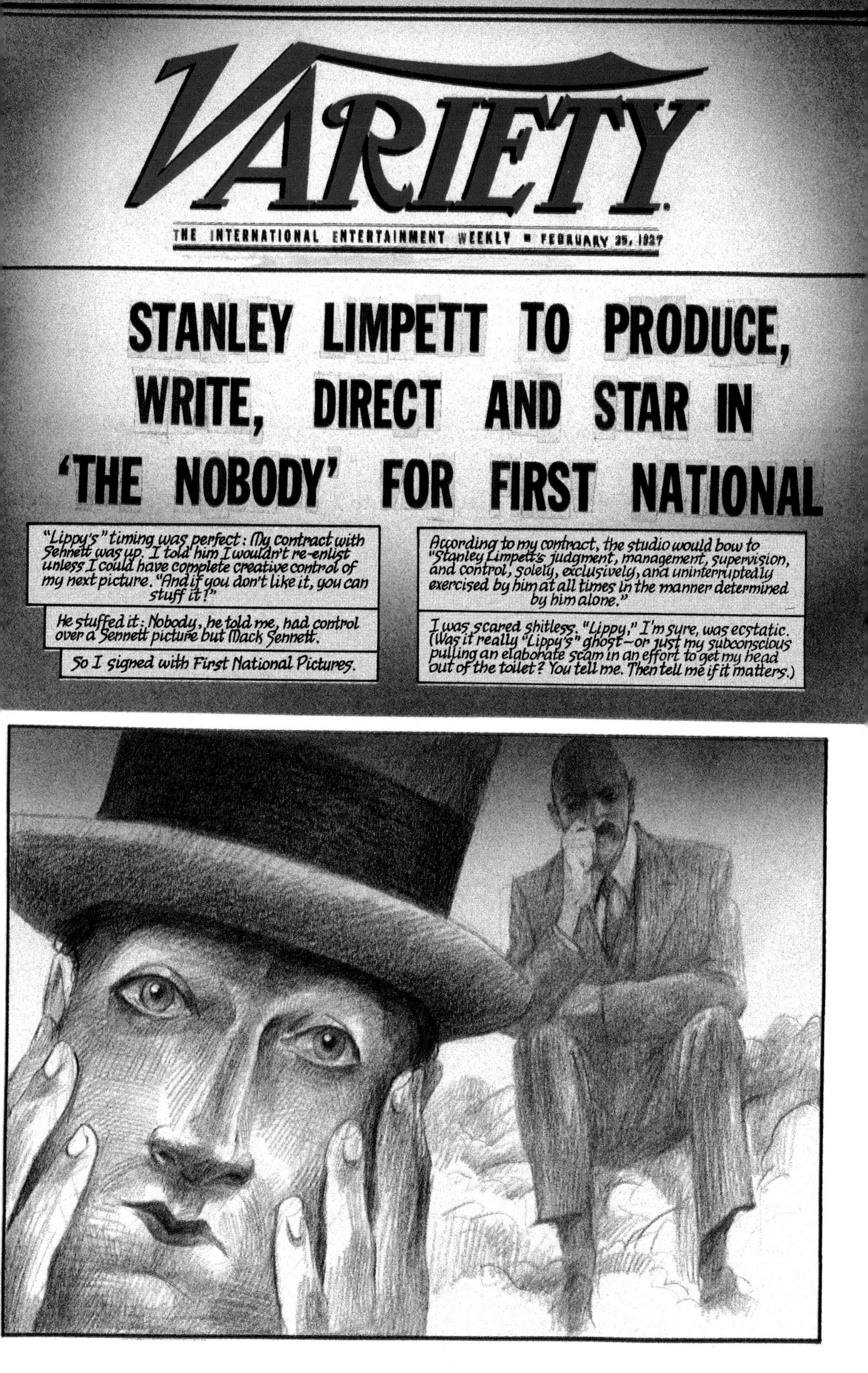
VARIETY
THE INTERNATIONAL ENTERTAINMENT WEEKLY ■ FEBRUARY 25, 1927
STANLEY LIMPETT TO PRODUCE, WRITE, DIRECT AND STAR IN 'THE NOBODY' FOR FIRST NATIONAL
"Lippy's" timing was perfect: My contract with Sennett was up. I told him I wouldn't re-enlist unless I could have complete creative control of my next picture. "And if you don't like it, you can stuff it!"
He stuffed it: Nobody, he told me, had control over a Sennett picture but Mack Sennett.
So I signed with First National Pictures.
According to my contract, the studio would bow to "Stanley Limpett's judgment, management, supervision, and control, solely, exclusively, and uninterruptedly exercised by him at all times in the manner determined by him alone."
I was scared shitless. "Lippy," I'm sure, was ecstatic. (Was it really "Lippy's" ghost—or just my subconscious pulling an elaborate scam in an effort to get my head out of the toilet? You tell me. Then tell me if it matters.)

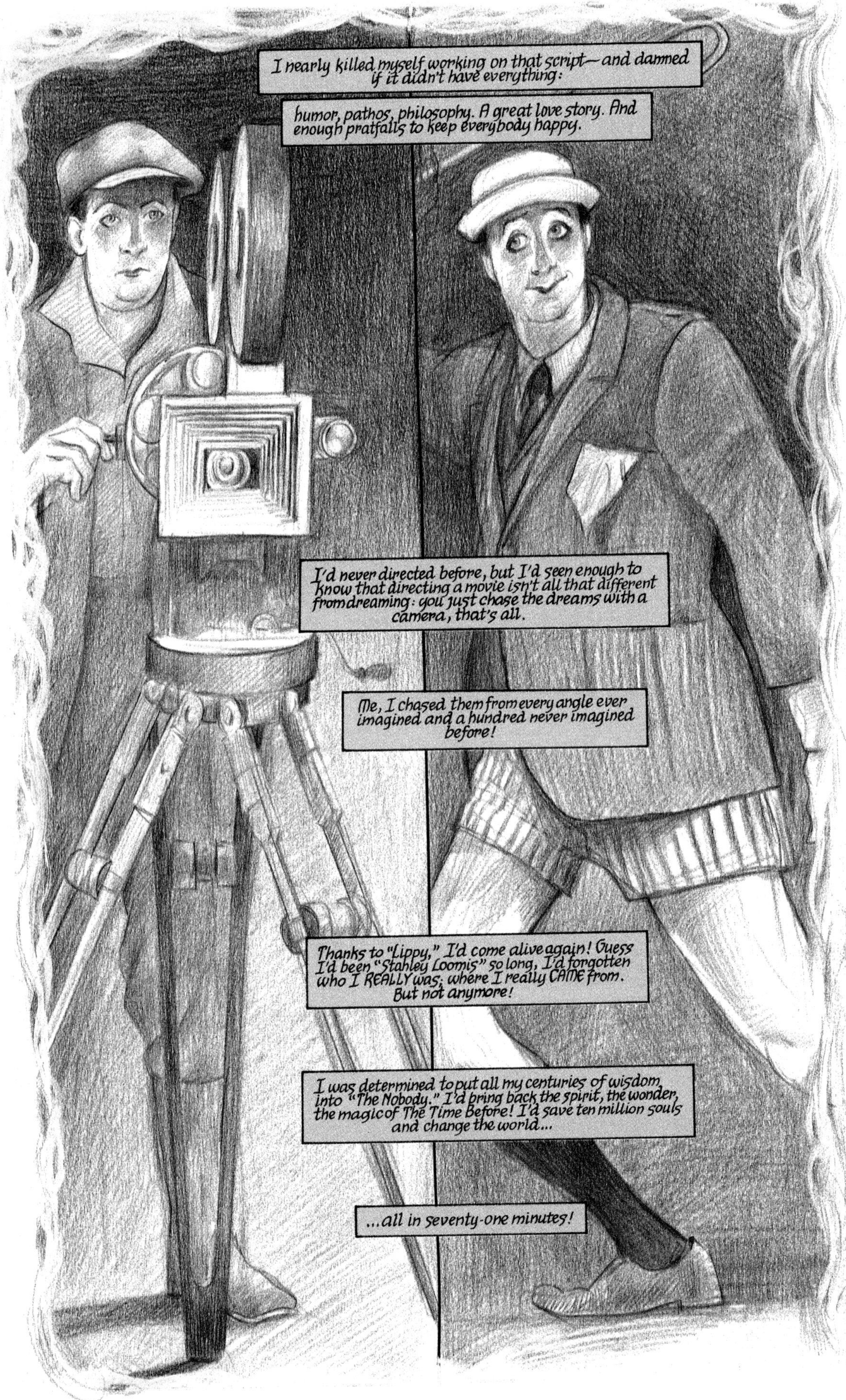
I nearly killed myself working on that script— and damned if it didn't have everything:
humor, pathos, philosophy. A great love story. And enough pratfalls to keep everybody happy.
I'd never directed before, but I'd seen enough to know that directing a movie isn't all that different from dreaming: you just chase the dreams with a camera, that's all.
Me, I chased them from every angle ever imagined and a hundred never imagined before!
Thanks to "Lippy," I'd come alive again! Guess I'd been "Stanley Loomis" so long, I'd forgotten who I REALLY was, where I really CAME from. But not anymore!
I was determined to put all my centuries of wisdom into "The Nobody." I'd bring back the spirit, the wonder, the magic of The Time Before! I'd save ten million souls and change the world...
...all in seventy-one minutes!

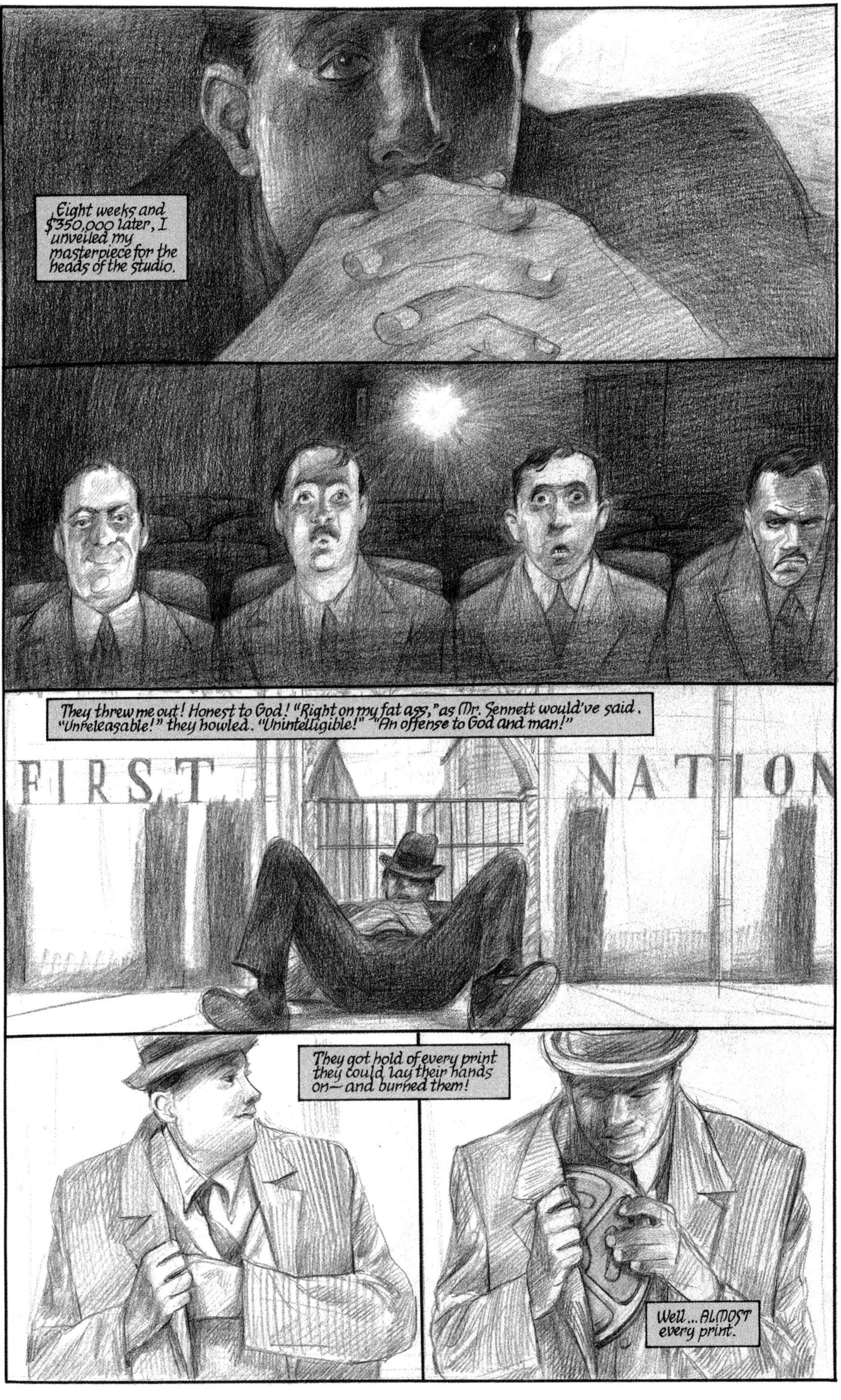
Eight weeks and $350,000 later, I unveiled my masterpiece for the heads of the studio.
They threw me out! Honest to God! "Right on my fat ass," as Mr. Sennett would've said. "Unreleasable!" they howled. "Unintelligible!" "An offense to God and man!"
FIRST
NATION
They got hold of every print they could lay their hands on— and burned them!
Well ... ALMOST every print.

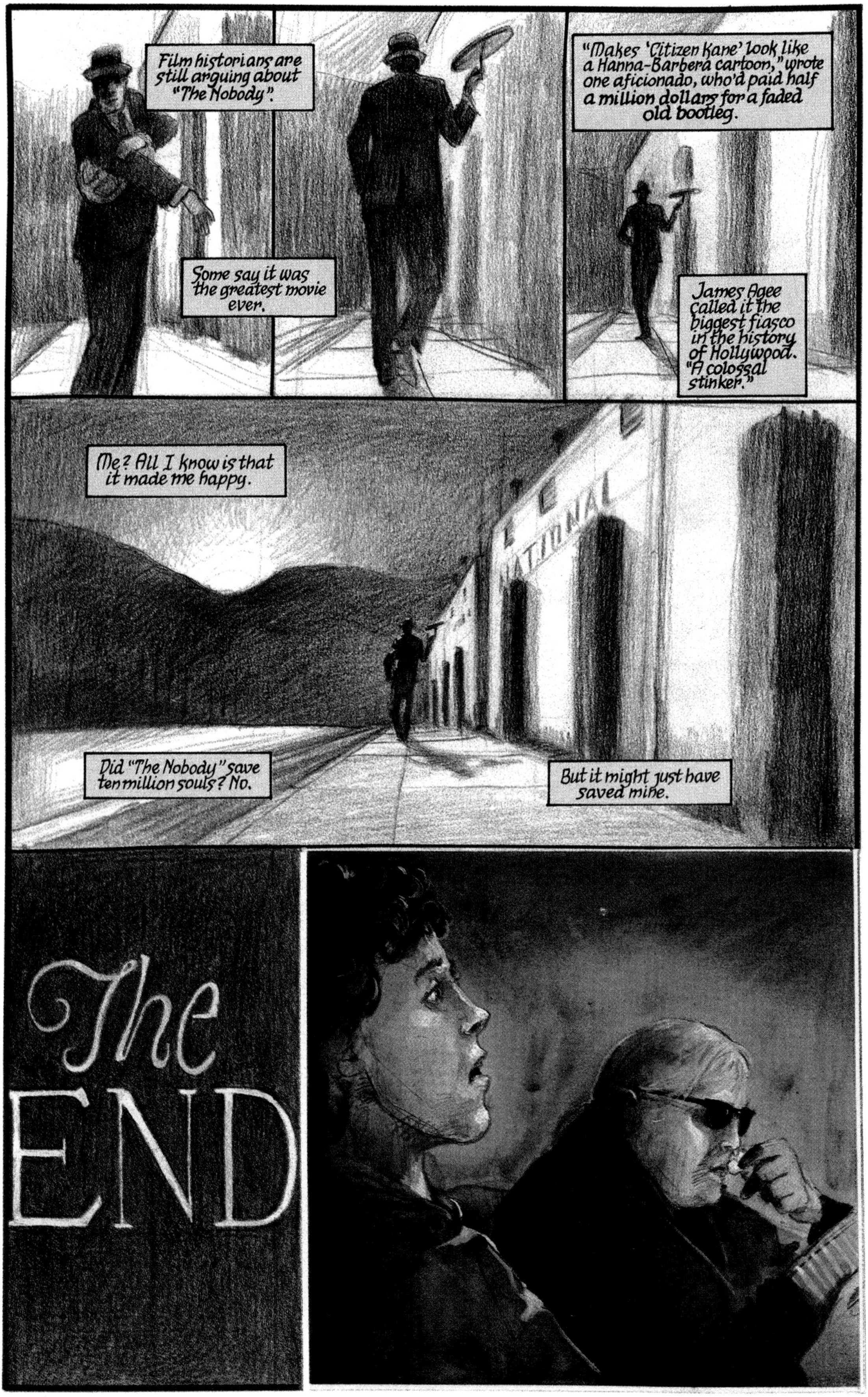
Film historians are still arguing about "The Nobody".
Some say it was the greatest movie ever.
"Makes 'Citizen Kane' look like a Hanna-Barbera cartoon," wrote one aficionado, who'd paid half a million dollars for a faded old bootleg.
James Agee called it the biggest fiasco in the history of Hollywood. "A colossal stinker."
Me? All I know is that it made me happy.
Did "The Nobody" save ten million souls? No.
But it might just have saved mine.
The END

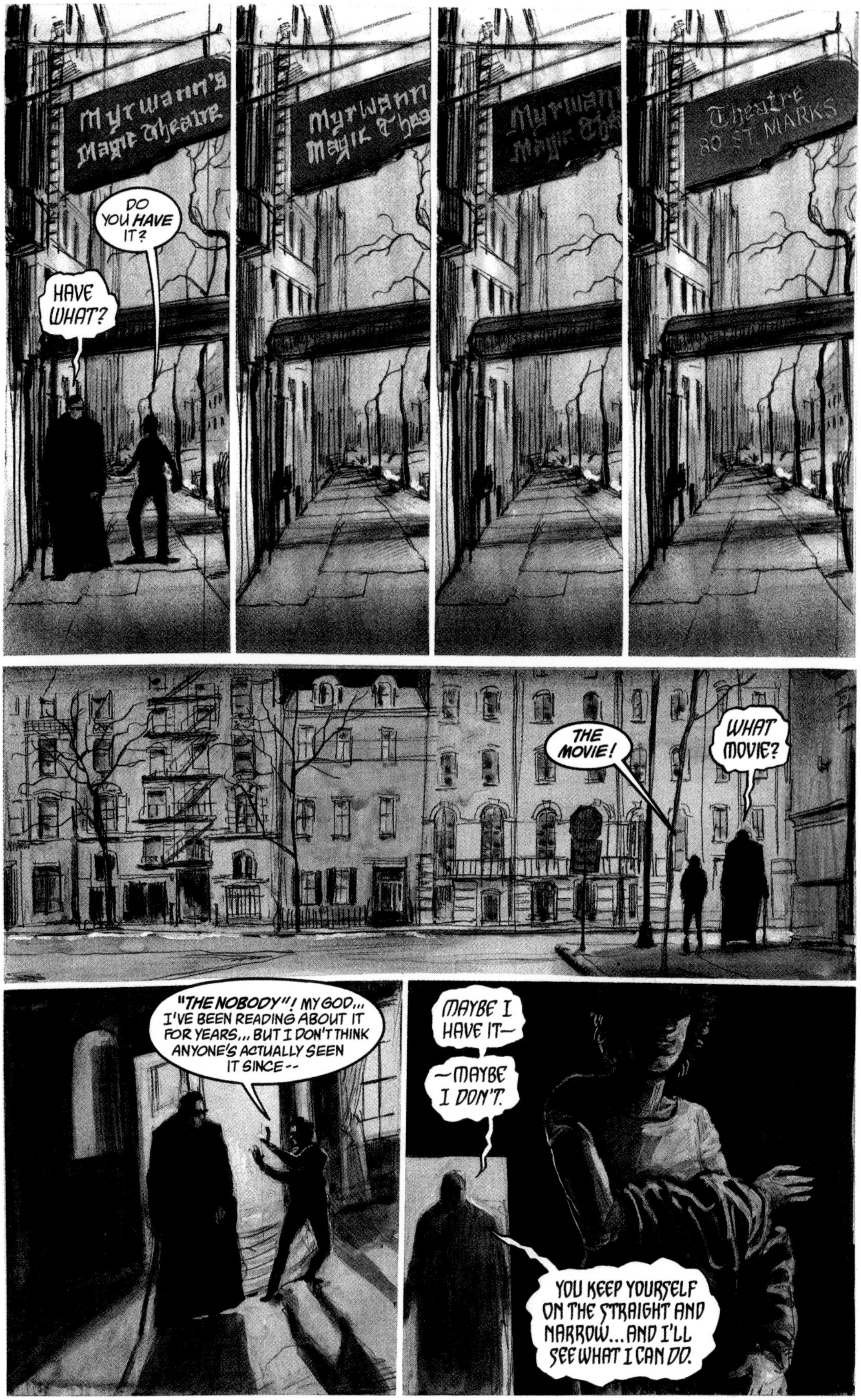
Myrwann's Magic Theatre
DO YOU HAVE IT?
HAVE WHAT?
Theatre 80 ST. MARKS
THE MOVIE!
WHAT MOVIE?
"THE NOBODY"! MY GOD... I'VE BEEN READING ABOUT IT FOR YEARS... BUT I DON'T THINK ANYONE'S ACTUALLY SEEN IT SINCE--
MAYBE I HAVE IT—
—MAYBE I DON'T.
YOU KEEP YOURSELF ON THE STRAIGHT AND NARROW... AND I'LL SEE WHAT I CAN DO.

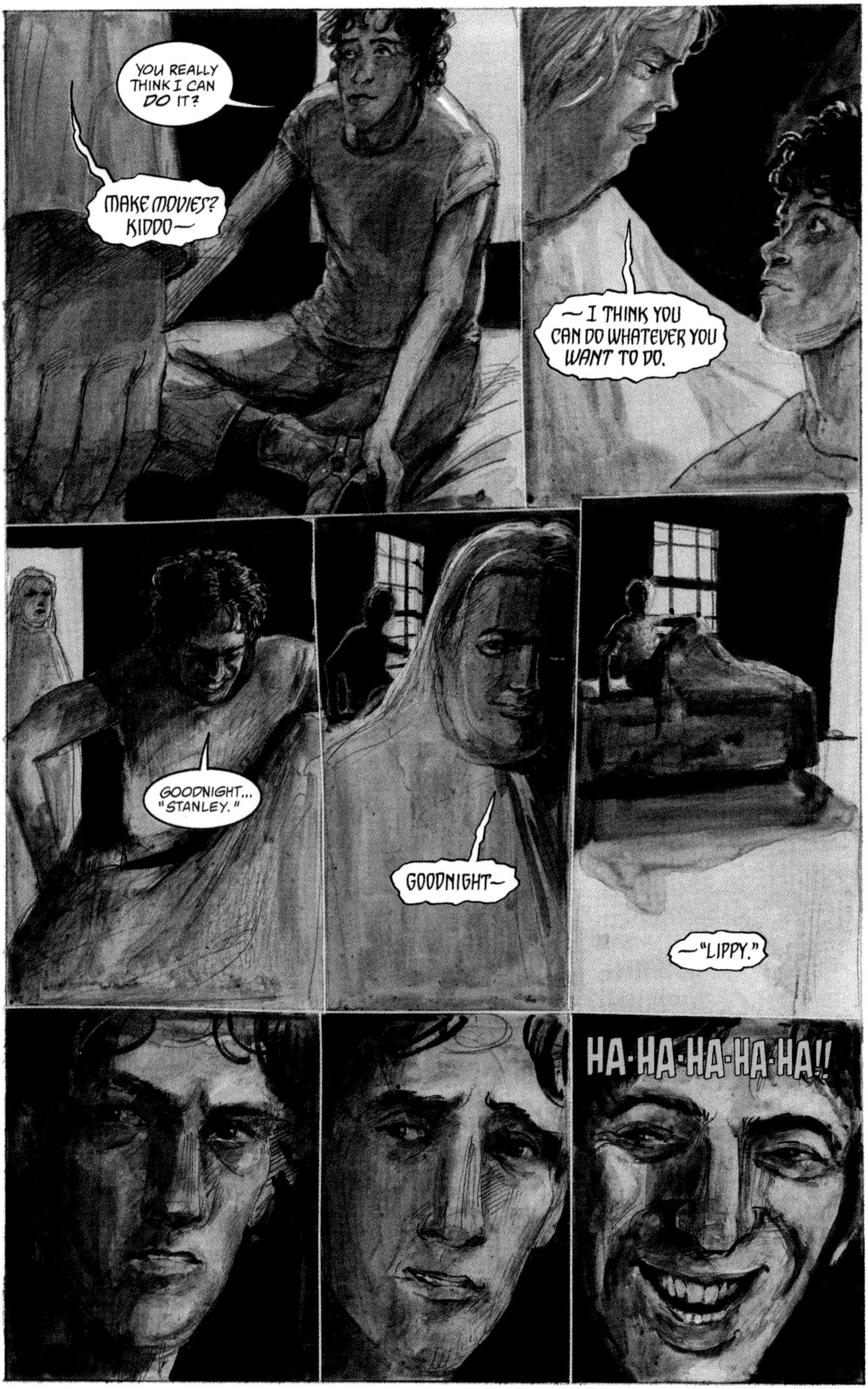

YOU REALLY THINK I CAN DO IT?
MAKE MOVIES? KIDDO—
—I THINK YOU CAN DO WHATEVER YOU WANT TO DO.
GOODNIGHT... "STANLEY."
GOODNIGHT—
—"LIPPY."
HA-HA-HA-HA-HA!!

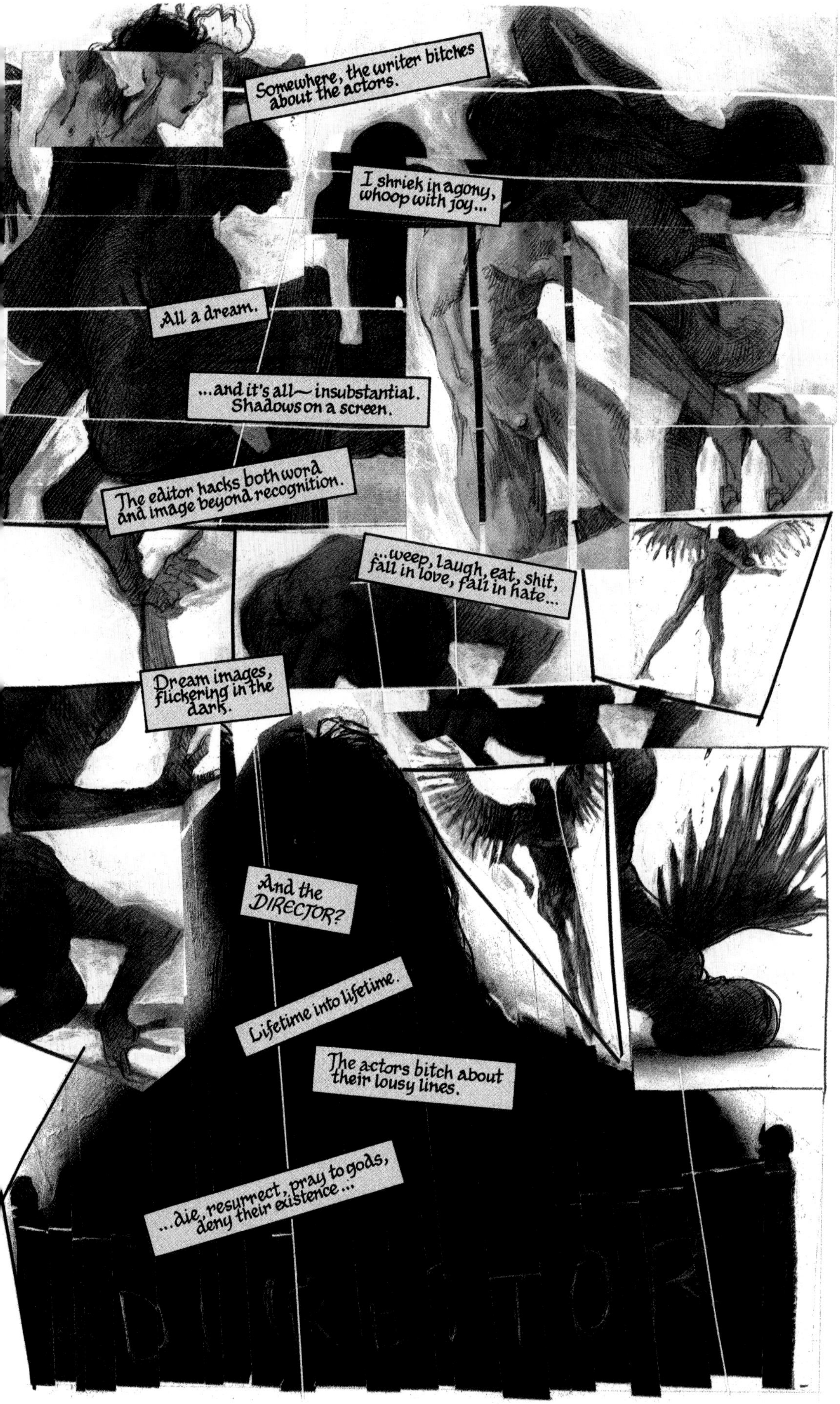
Somewhere, the writer bitches about the actors.
I shriek in agony, whoop with joy...
All a dream.
...and it's all— insubstantial. Shadows on a screen.
The editor hacks both word and image beyond recognition.
...weep, laugh, eat, shit, fall in love, fall in hate...
Dream images, flickering in the dark.
And the DIRECTOR?
Lifetime into lifetime.
The actors bitch about their lousy lines.
...die, resurrect, pray to gods, deny their existence...

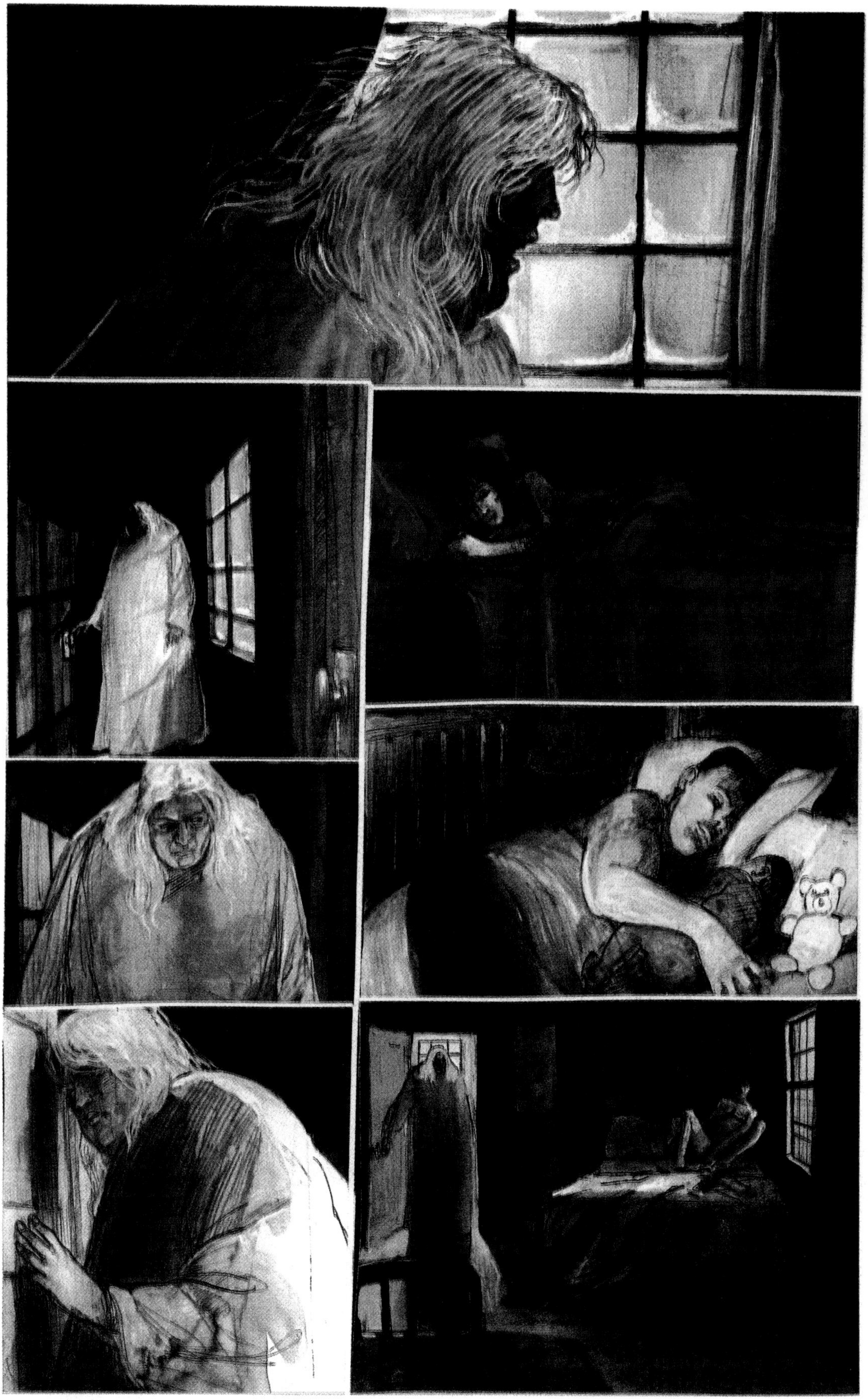

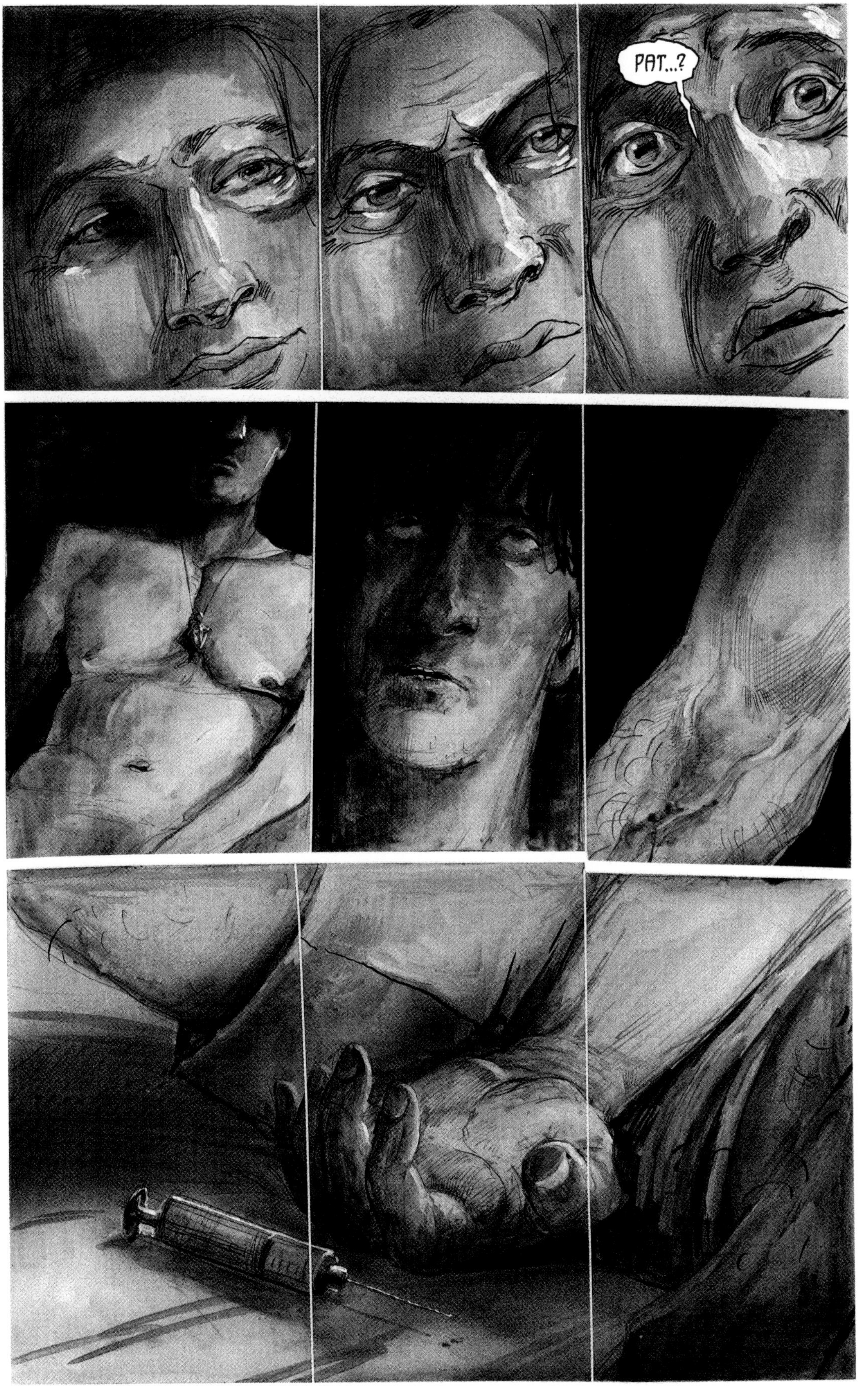
PAT...?

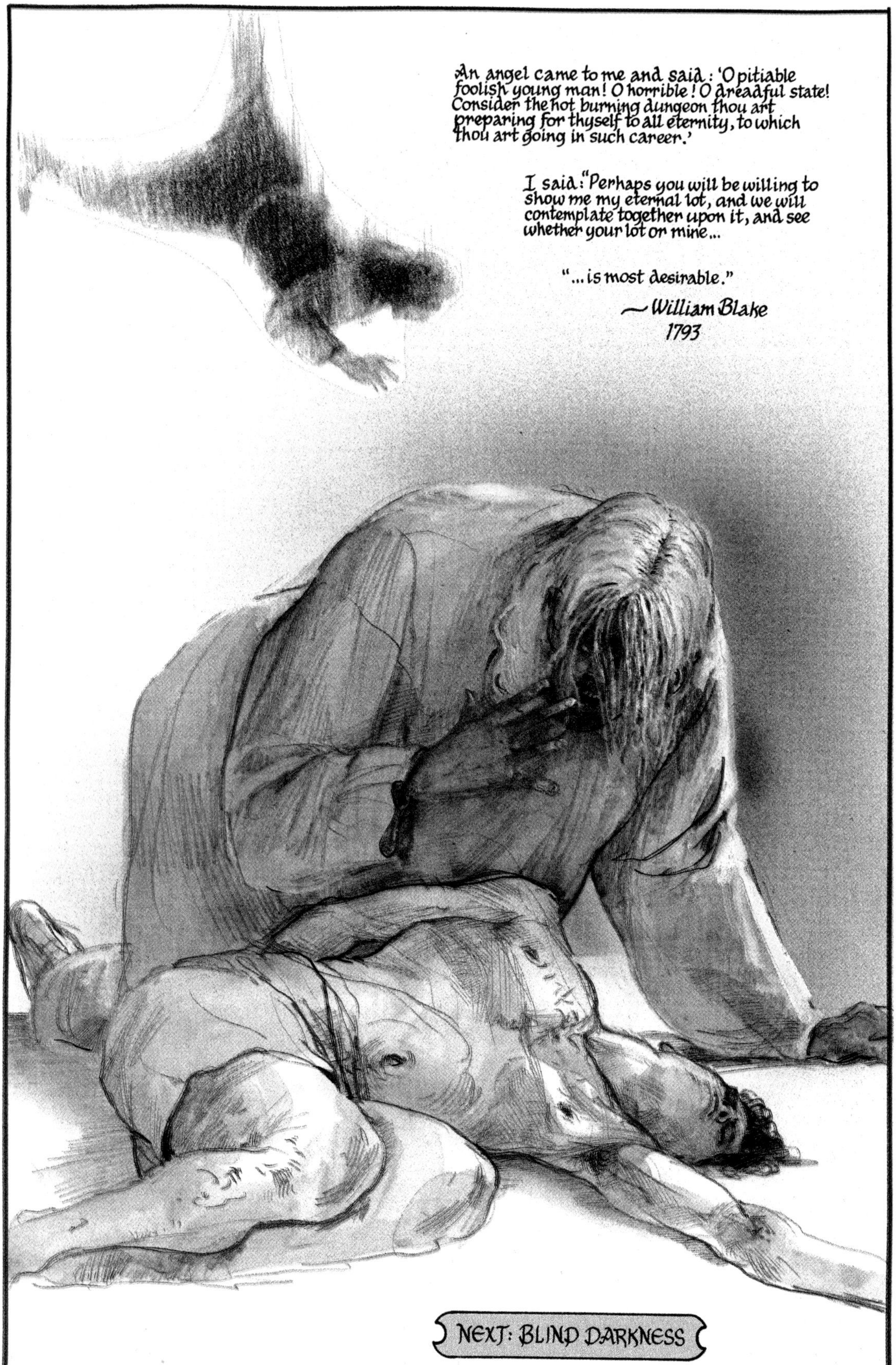
An angel came to me and said: 'O pitiable foolish young man! O horrible! O dreadful state! Consider the hot burning dungeon thou art preparing for thyself to all eternity, to which thou art going in such career.'
I said: "Perhaps you will be willing to show me my eternal lot, and we will contemplate together upon it, and see whether your lot or mine...
"...is most desirable."
—William Blake
1793
NEXT: BLIND DARKNESS

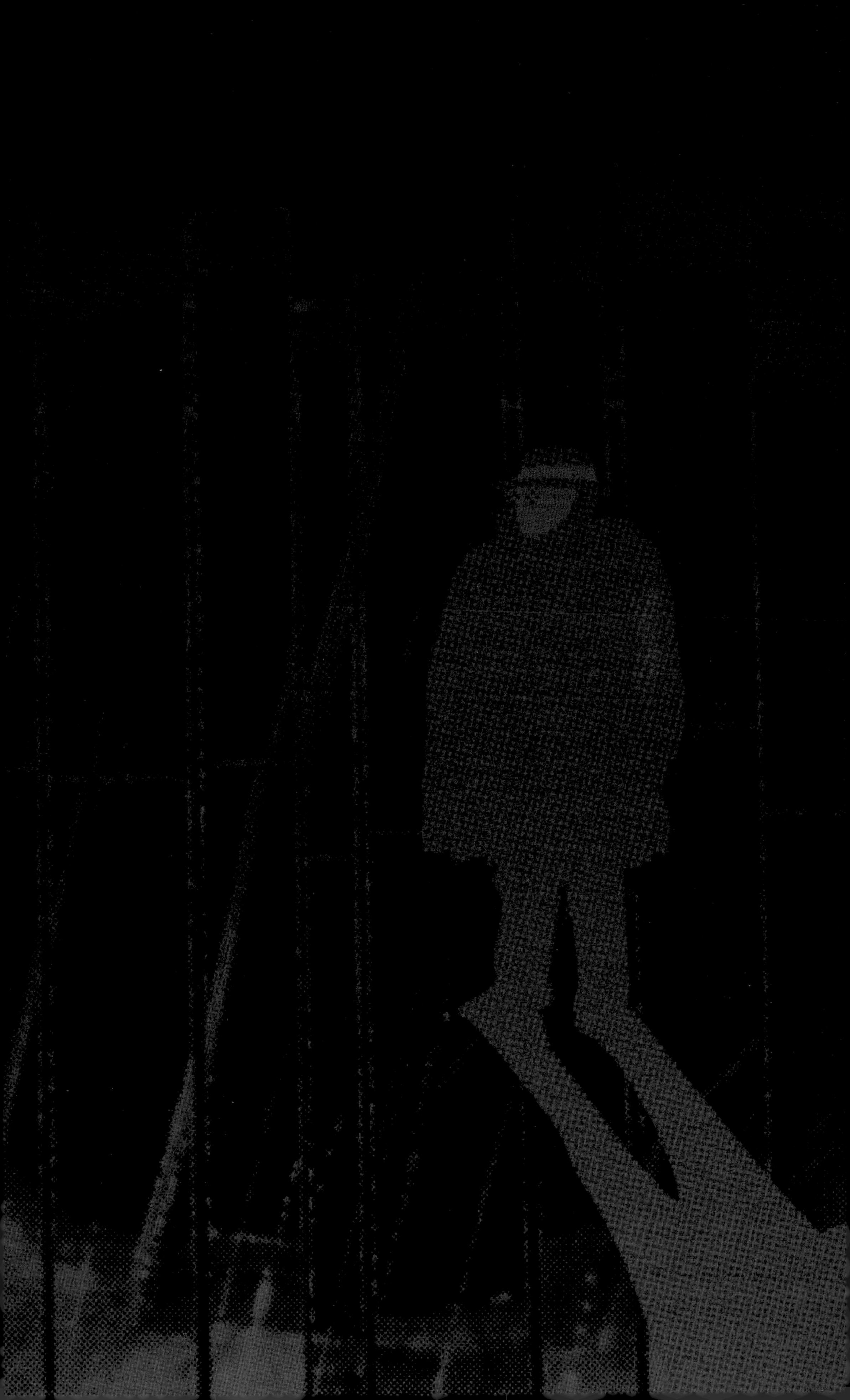

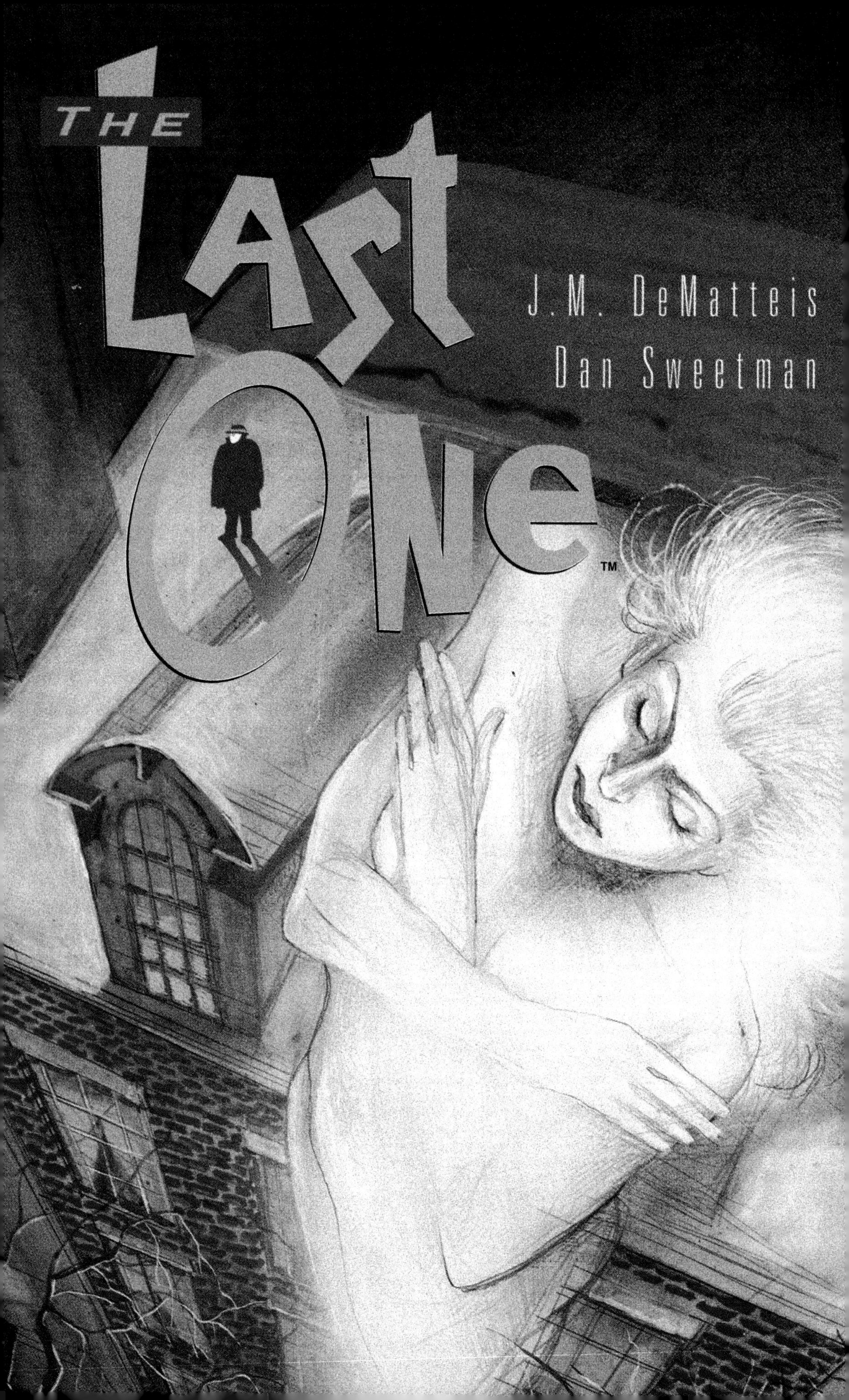
THE
LAST
ONE™
J.M. DeMatteis
Dan Sweetman

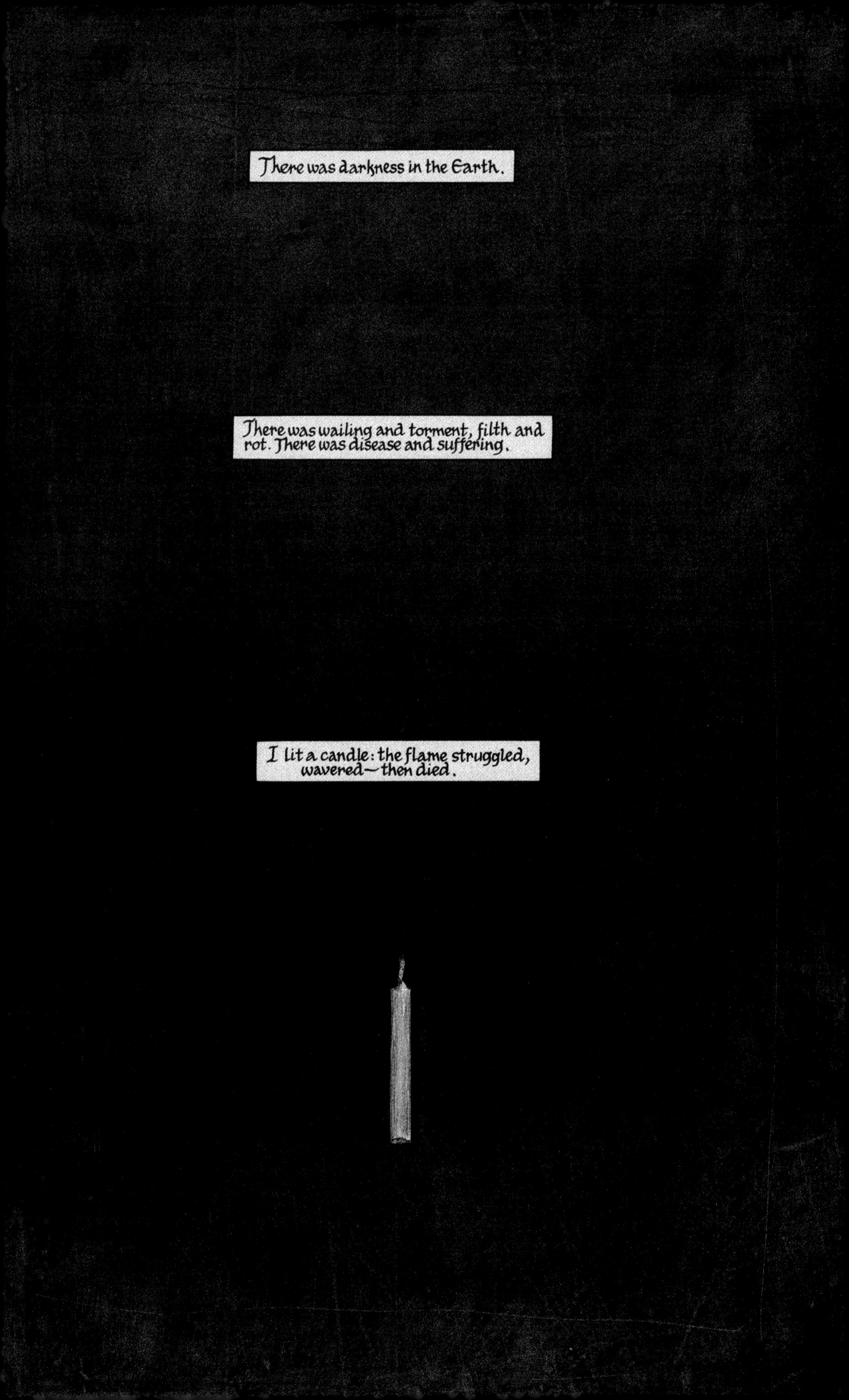
There was darkness in the Earth.
There was wailing and torment, filth and rot. There was disease and suffering.
I lit a candle: the flame struggled, wavered—then died.

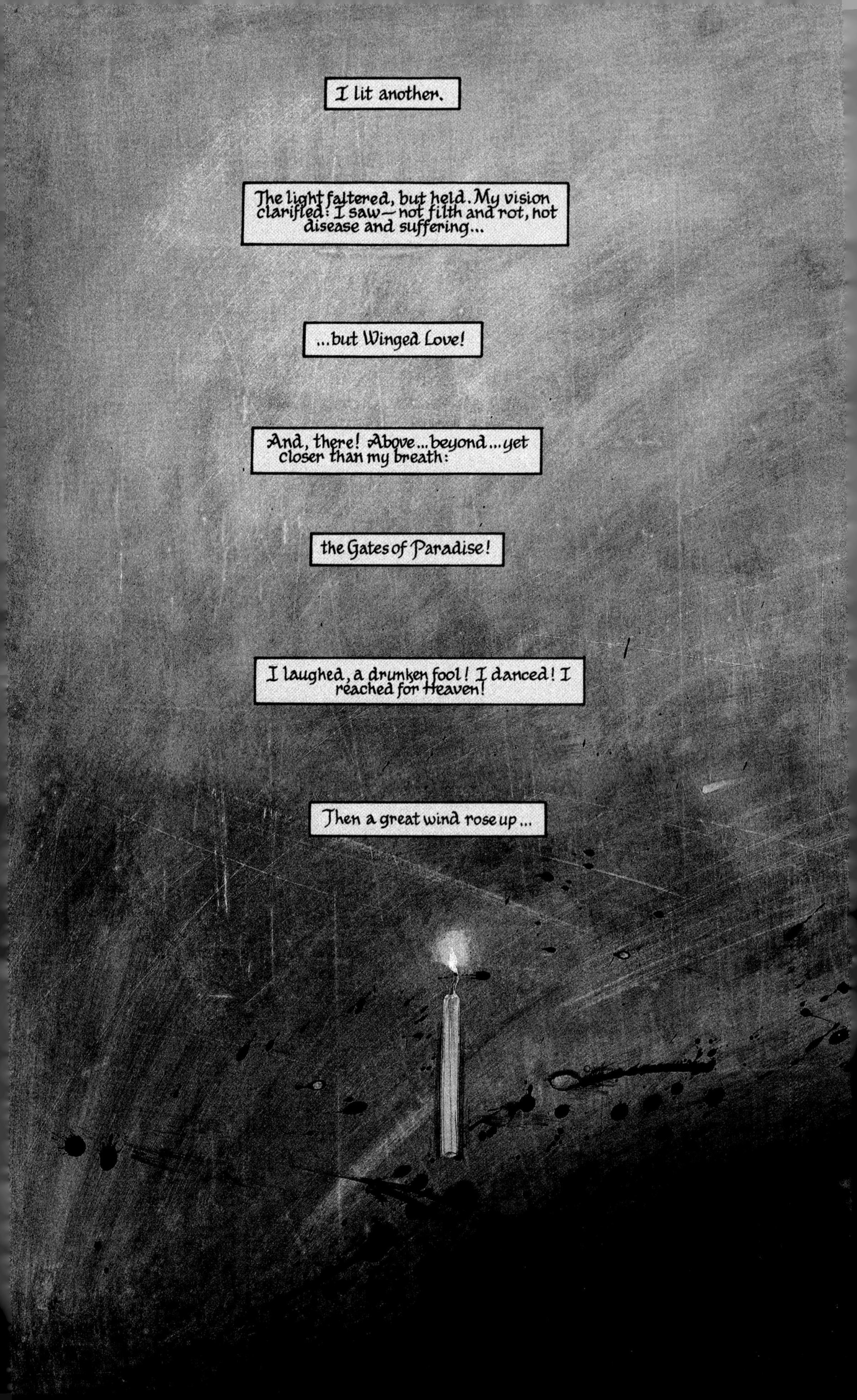
I lit another.
The light faltered, but held. My vision clarified: I saw— not filth and rot, not disease and suffering...
...but Winged Love!
And, there! Above... beyond... yet closer than my breath:
the Gates of Paradise!
I laughed, a drunken fool! I danced! I reached for Heaven!
Then a great wind rose up...

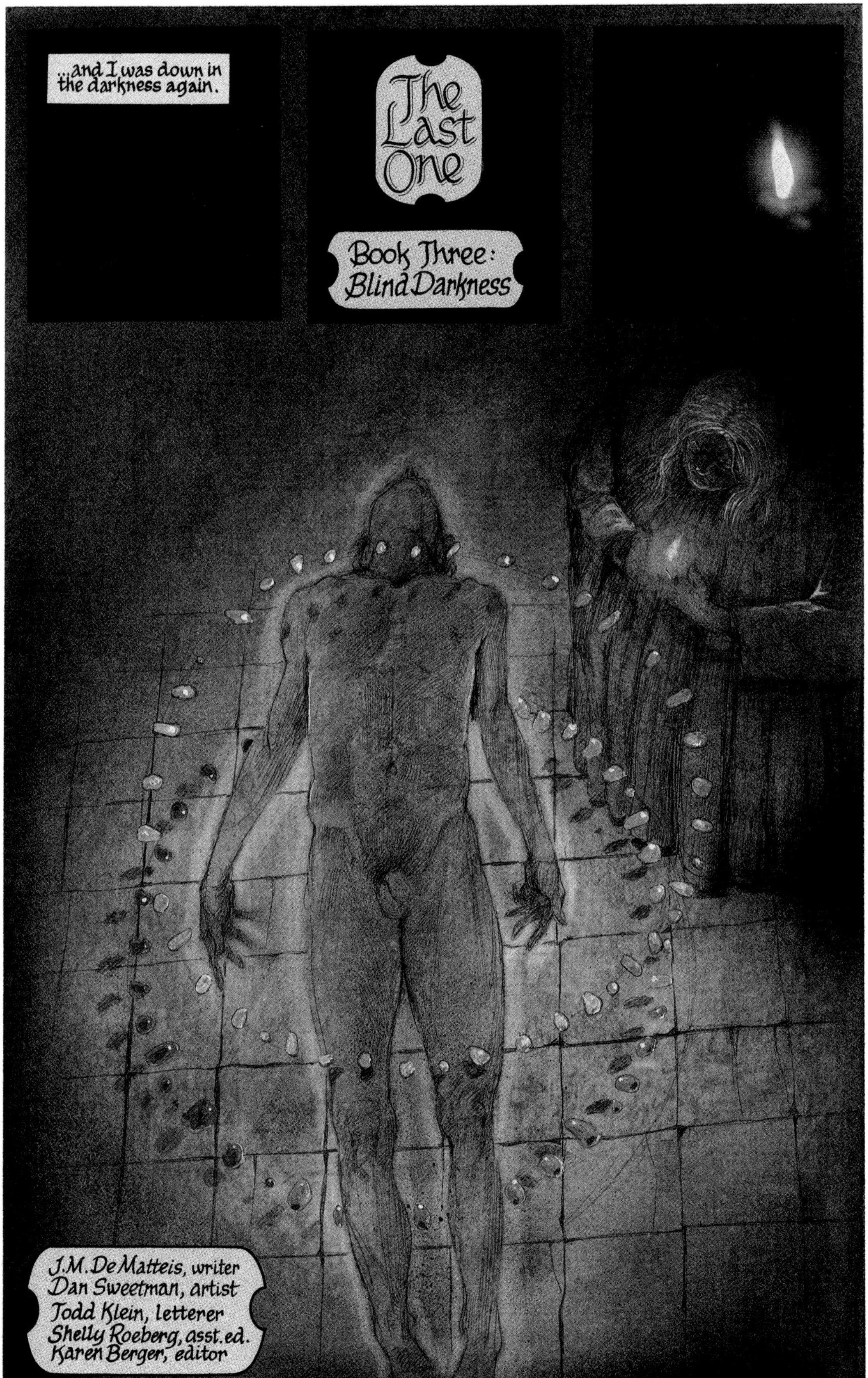

...and I was down in the darkness again.
The Last One
Book Three: Blind Darkness
J.M. DeMatteis, writer
Dan Sweetman, artist
Todd Klein, letterer
Shelly Roeberg, asst.ed.
Karen Berger, editor

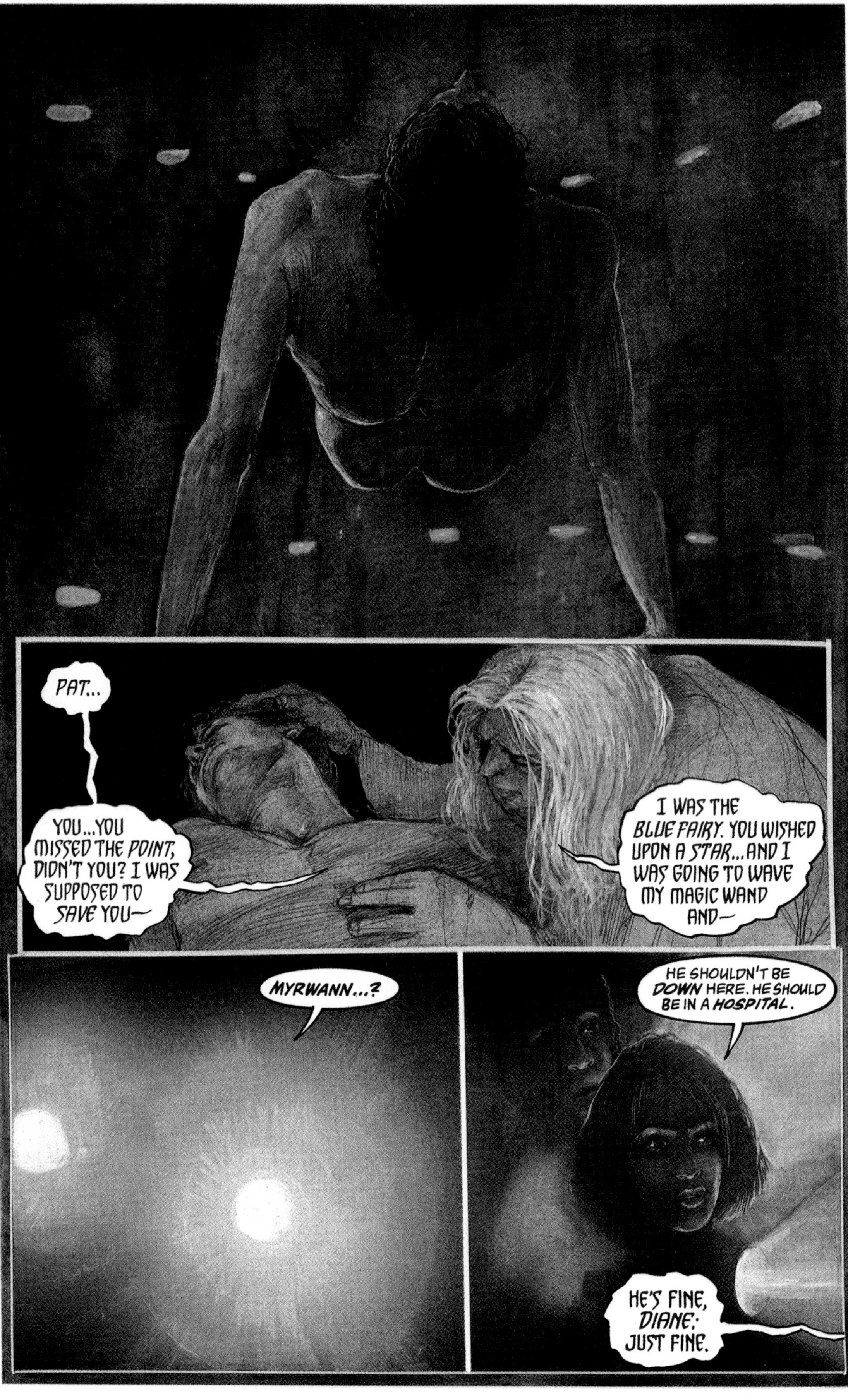
PAT...
YOU...YOU MISSED THE POINT, DIDN'T YOU? I WAS SUPPOSED TO SAVE YOU—
I WAS THE BLUE FAIRY. YOU WISHED UPON A STAR...AND I WAS GOING TO WAVE MY MAGIC WAND AND—
MYRWANN...?
HE SHOULDN'T BE DOWN HERE. HE SHOULD BE IN A HOSPITAL.
HE'S FINE, DIANE; JUST FINE.

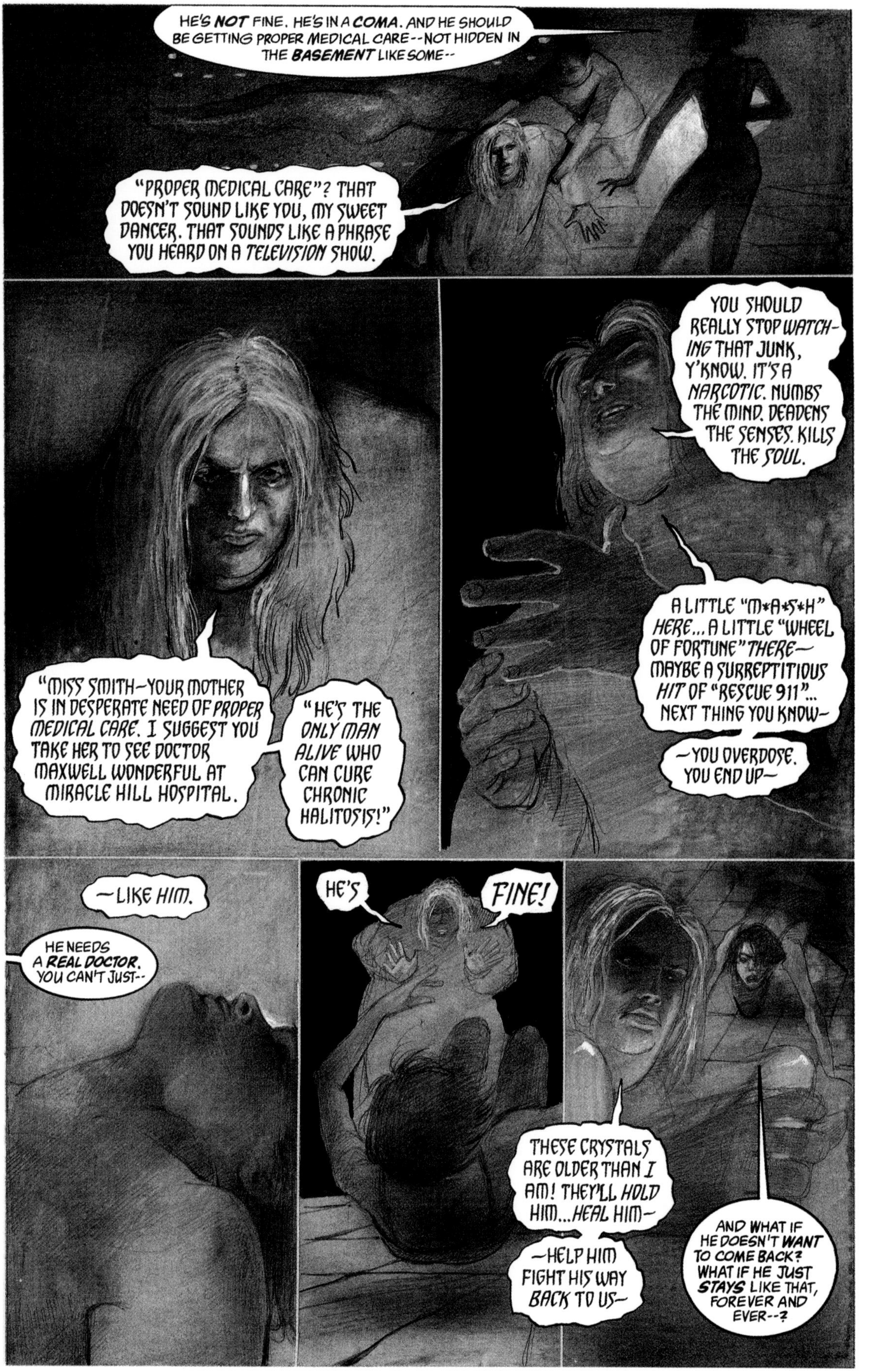
HE'S NOT FINE. HE'S IN A COMA. AND HE SHOULD BE GETTING PROPER MEDICAL CARE--NOT HIDDEN IN THE BASEMENT LIKE SOME--
"PROPER MEDICAL CARE"? THAT DOESN'T SOUND LIKE YOU, MY SWEET DANCER. THAT SOUNDS LIKE A PHRASE YOU HEARD ON A TELEVISION SHOW.
"MISS SMITH—YOUR MOTHER IS IN DESPERATE NEED OF PROPER MEDICAL CARE. I SUGGEST YOU TAKE HER TO SEE DOCTOR MAXWELL WONDERFUL AT MIRACLE HILL HOSPITAL.
"HE'S THE ONLY MAN ALIVE WHO CAN CURE CHRONIC HALITOSIS!"
YOU SHOULD REALLY STOP WATCHING THAT JUNK, Y'KNOW. IT'S A NARCOTIC. NUMBS THE MIND. DEADENS THE SENSES. KILLS THE SOUL.
A LITTLE "M*A*S*H" HERE... A LITTLE "WHEEL OF FORTUNE" THERE— MAYBE A SURREPTITIOUS HIT OF "RESCUE 911"... NEXT THING YOU KNOW—
—YOU OVERDOSE. YOU END UP—
—LIKE HIM.
HE NEEDS A REAL DOCTOR. YOU CAN'T JUST--
HE'S
FINE!
THESE CRYSTALS ARE OLDER THAN I AM! THEY'LL HOLD HIM... HEAL HIM—
—HELP HIM FIGHT HIS WAY BACK TO US—
AND WHAT IF HE DOESN'T WANT TO COME BACK? WHAT IF HE JUST STAYS LIKE THAT, FOREVER AND EVER--?

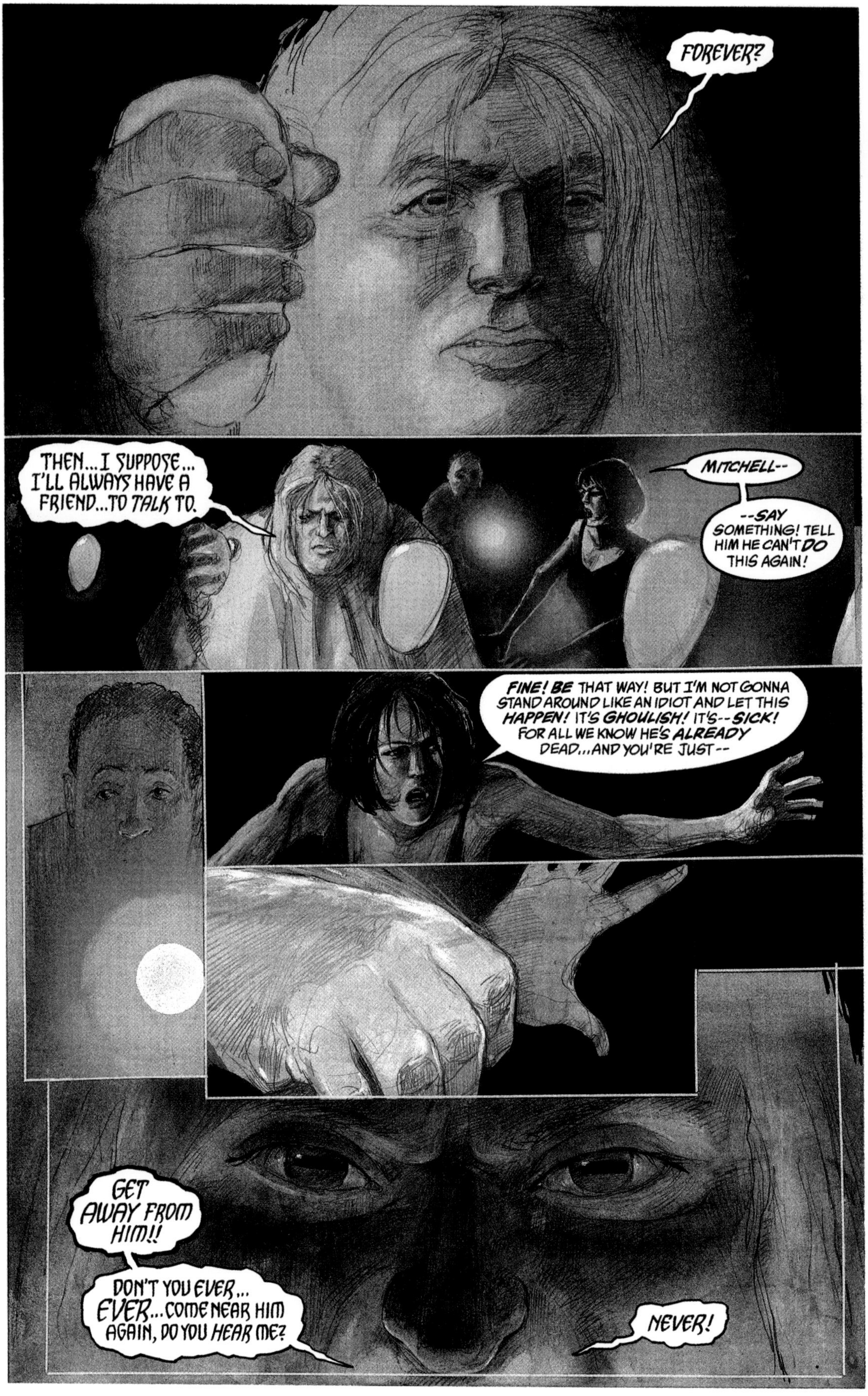
FOREVER?
THEN...I SUPPOSE... I'LL ALWAYS HAVE A FRIEND...TO TALK TO.
MITCHELL--
--SAY SOMETHING! TELL HIM HE CAN'T DO THIS AGAIN!
FINE! BE THAT WAY! BUT I'M NOT GONNA STAND AROUND LIKE AN IDIOT AND LET THIS HAPPEN! IT'S GHOULISH! IT'S--SICK! FOR ALL WE KNOW HE'S ALREADY DEAD...AND YOU'RE JUST--
GET AWAY FROM HIM!!
DON'T YOU EVER... EVER...COME NEAR HIM AGAIN, DO YOU HEAR ME?
NEVER!

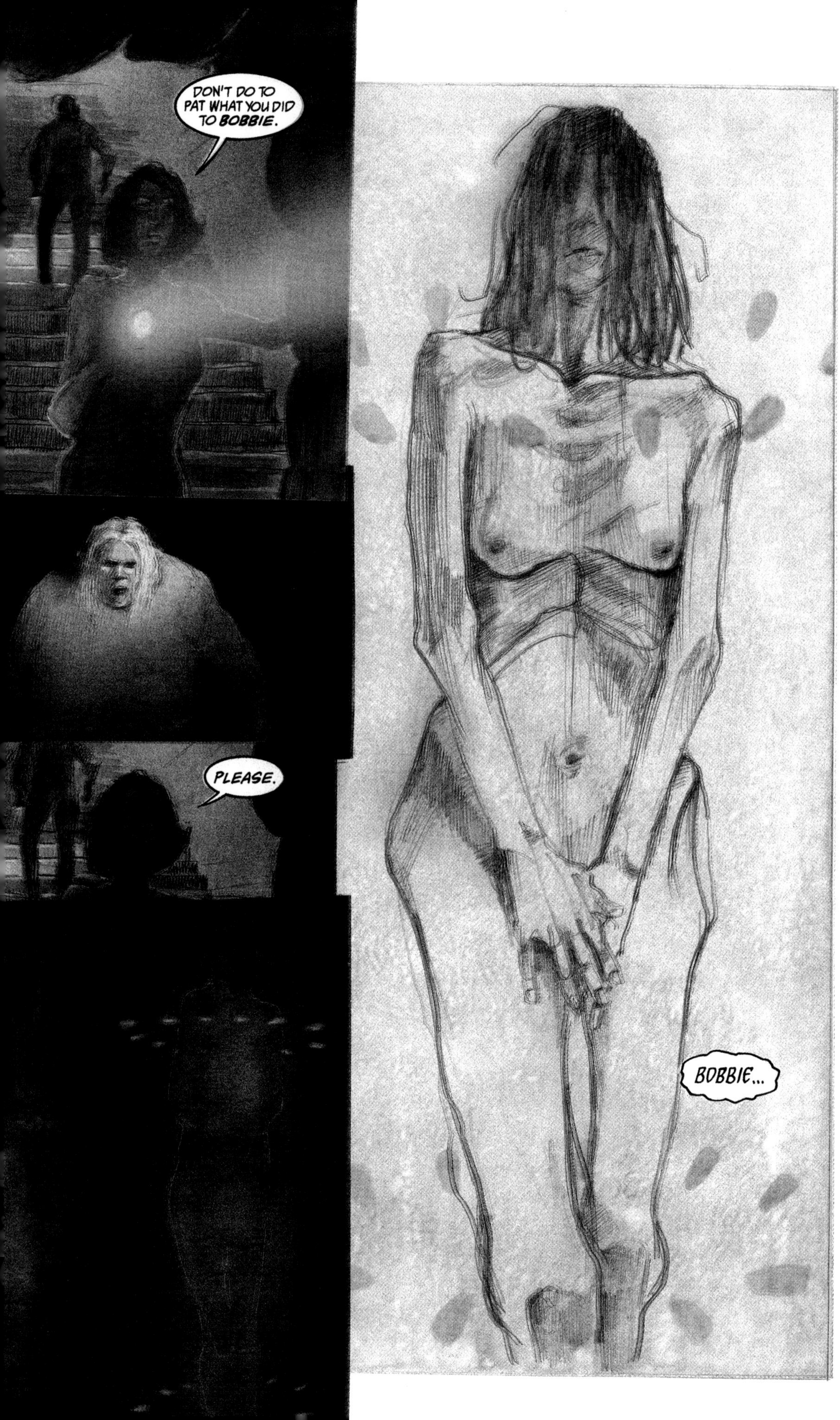
DON'T DO TO PAT WHAT YOU DID TO BOBBIE.
PLEASE.
BOBBIE...

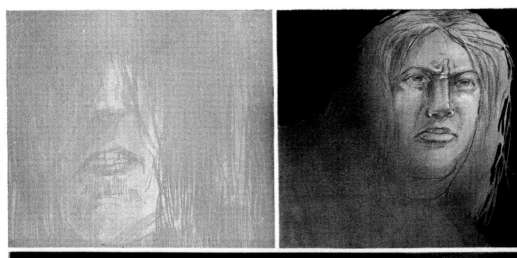

DO YOU MIND IF I—?

WHAT?

IS ANYONE SITTING HERE?

WELL, FRANKLY, YES.

"YES" SOMEONE'S SITTING HERE?

"YES"... I MIND.

TOO BAD.

SHE TOLD ME LATER THAT SHE KNEW I HAD THE DISEASE THE SECOND SHE SET EYES ON ME. "IS THAT WHY YOU STOPPED?" I ASKED HER. "BECAUSE YOU TOOK PITY ON ME?"

SHE TOLD ME SHE HAD NO PITY LEFT. "I STOPPED," SHE SAID...

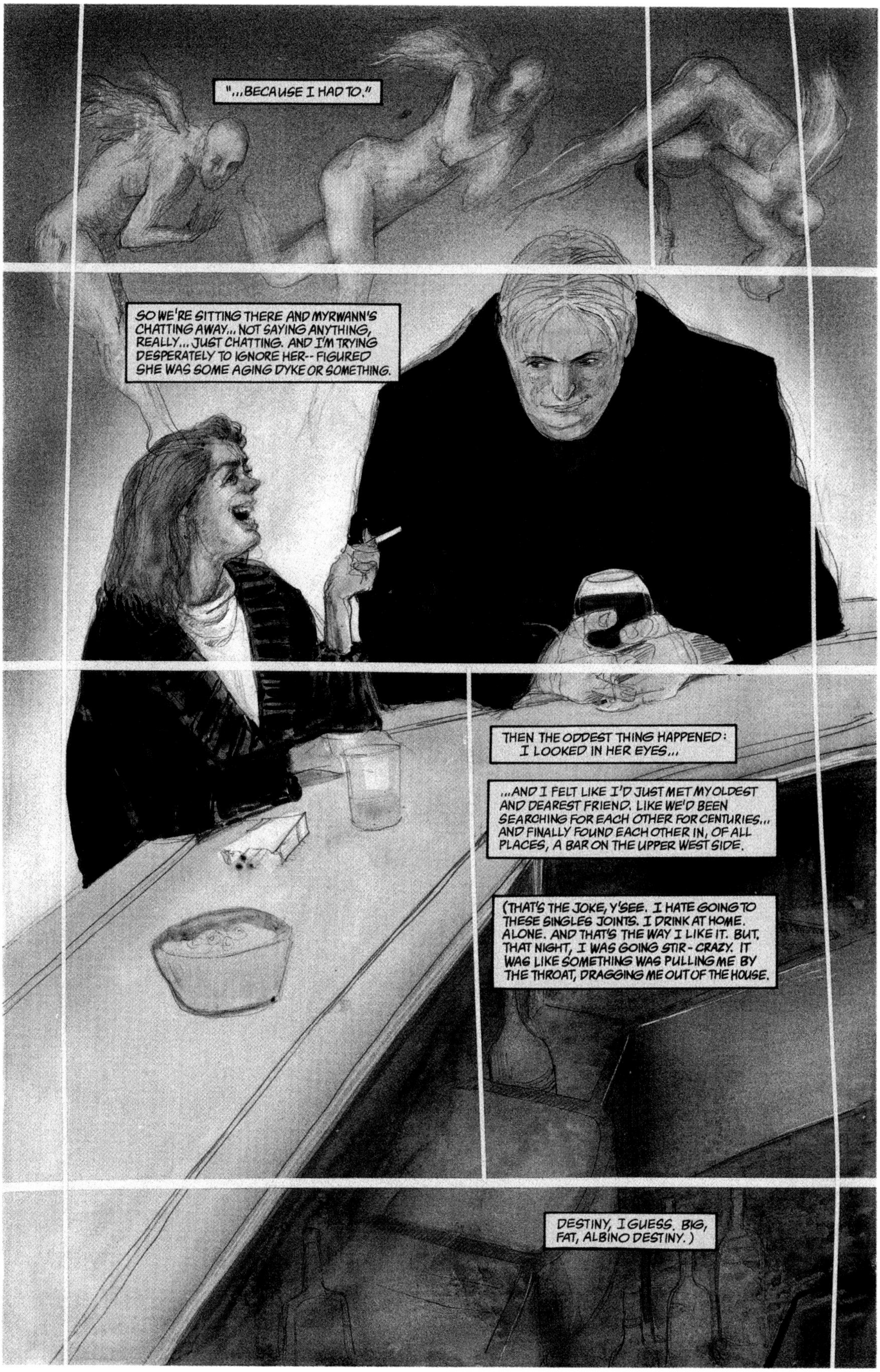
"...BECAUSE I HAD TO."
SO WE'RE SITTING THERE AND MYRWANN'S CHATTING AWAY... NOT SAYING ANYTHING, REALLY... JUST CHATTING. AND I'M TRYING DESPERATELY TO IGNORE HER-- FIGURED SHE WAS SOME AGING DYKE OR SOMETHING.
THEN THE ODDEST THING HAPPENED: I LOOKED IN HER EYES...
...AND I FELT LIKE I'D JUST MET MY OLDEST AND DEAREST FRIEND. LIKE WE'D BEEN SEARCHING FOR EACH OTHER FOR CENTURIES... AND FINALLY FOUND EACH OTHER IN, OF ALL PLACES, A BAR ON THE UPPER WEST SIDE.
(THAT'S THE JOKE, Y'SEE. I HATE GOING TO THESE SINGLES JOINTS. I DRINK AT HOME. ALONE. AND THAT'S THE WAY I LIKE IT. BUT, THAT NIGHT, I WAS GOING STIR-CRAZY. IT WAS LIKE SOMETHING WAS PULLING ME BY THE THROAT, DRAGGING ME OUT OF THE HOUSE.
DESTINY, I GUESS. BIG, FAT, ALBINO DESTINY.)

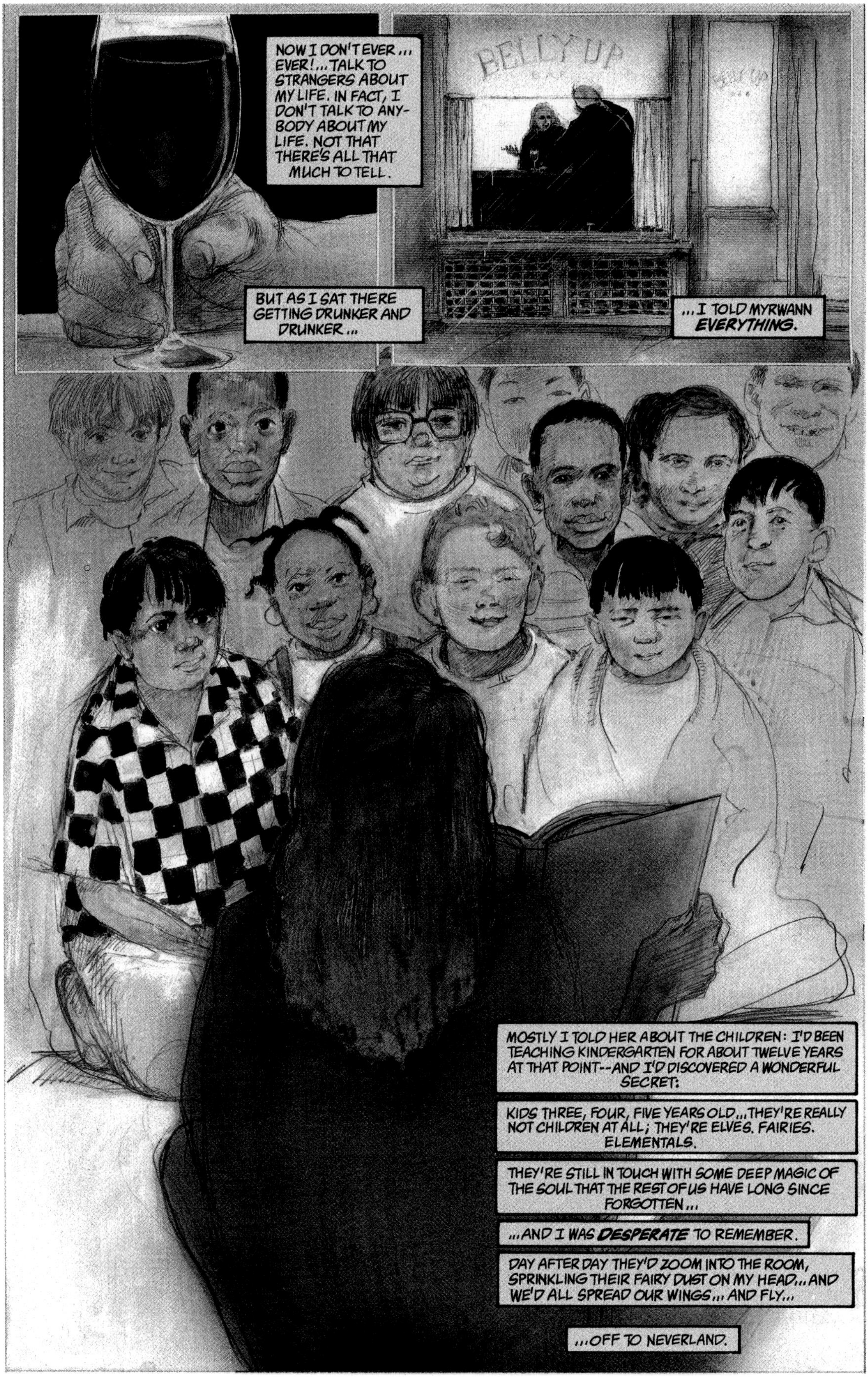
NOW I DON'T EVER... EVER!... TALK TO STRANGERS ABOUT MY LIFE. IN FACT, I DON'T TALK TO ANYBODY ABOUT MY LIFE. NOT THAT THERE'S ALL THAT MUCH TO TELL.
BUT AS I SAT THERE GETTING DRUNKER AND DRUNKER...
BELLY UP
...I TOLD MYRWANN **EVERYTHING.**
MOSTLY I TOLD HER ABOUT THE CHILDREN: I'D BEEN TEACHING KINDERGARTEN FOR ABOUT TWELVE YEARS AT THAT POINT--AND I'D DISCOVERED A WONDERFUL SECRET:
KIDS THREE, FOUR, FIVE YEARS OLD... THEY'RE REALLY NOT CHILDREN AT ALL; THEY'RE ELVES. FAIRIES. ELEMENTALS.
THEY'RE STILL IN TOUCH WITH SOME DEEP MAGIC OF THE SOUL THAT THE REST OF US HAVE LONG SINCE FORGOTTEN...
...AND I WAS ***DESPERATE*** TO REMEMBER.
DAY AFTER DAY THEY'D ZOOM INTO THE ROOM, SPRINKLING THEIR FAIRY DUST ON MY HEAD... AND WE'D ALL SPREAD OUR WINGS... AND FLY...
...OFF TO NEVERLAND.

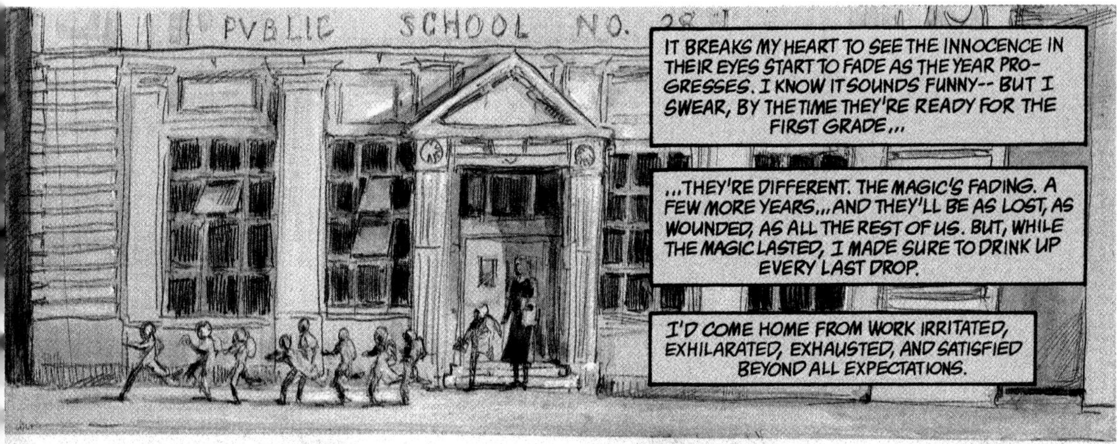
PUBLIC SCHOOL NO. 28
IT BREAKS MY HEART TO SEE THE INNOCENCE IN THEIR EYES START TO FADE AS THE YEAR PROGRESSES. I KNOW IT SOUNDS FUNNY-- BUT I SWEAR, BY THE TIME THEY'RE READY FOR THE FIRST GRADE...
...THEY'RE DIFFERENT. THE MAGIC'S FADING. A FEW MORE YEARS... AND THEY'LL BE AS LOST, AS WOUNDED, AS ALL THE REST OF US. BUT, WHILE THE MAGIC LASTED, I MADE SURE TO DRINK UP EVERY LAST DROP.
I'D COME HOME FROM WORK IRRITATED, EXHILARATED, EXHAUSTED, AND SATISFIED BEYOND ALL EXPECTATIONS.

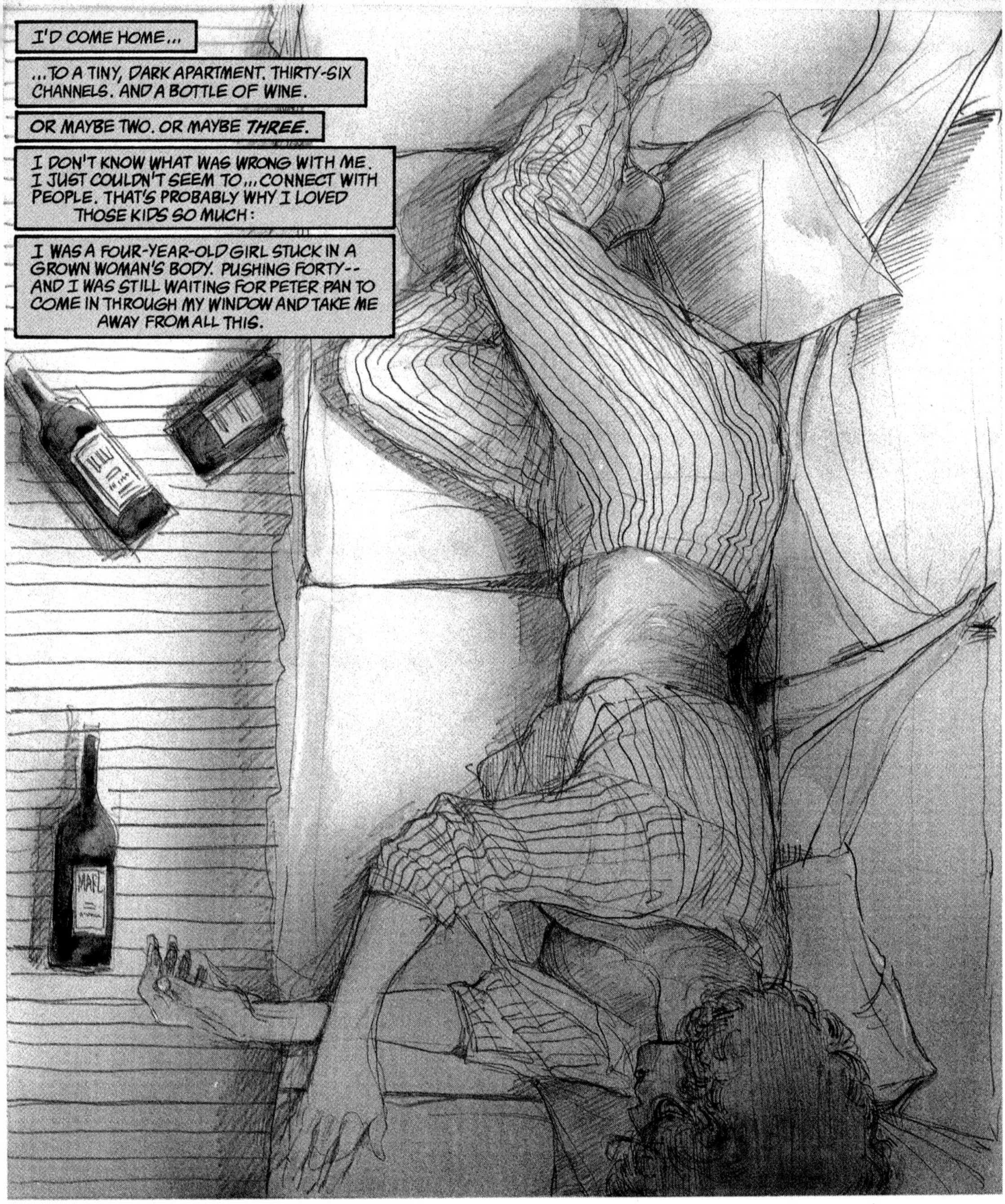
I'D COME HOME...
...TO A TINY, DARK APARTMENT. THIRTY-SIX CHANNELS. AND A BOTTLE OF WINE.
OR MAYBE TWO. OR MAYBE THREE.
I DON'T KNOW WHAT WAS WRONG WITH ME. I JUST COULDN'T SEEM TO... CONNECT WITH PEOPLE. THAT'S PROBABLY WHY I LOVED THOSE KIDS SO MUCH:
I WAS A FOUR-YEAR-OLD GIRL STUCK IN A GROWN WOMAN'S BODY. PUSHING FORTY-- AND I WAS STILL WAITING FOR PETER PAN TO COME IN THROUGH MY WINDOW AND TAKE ME AWAY FROM ALL THIS.

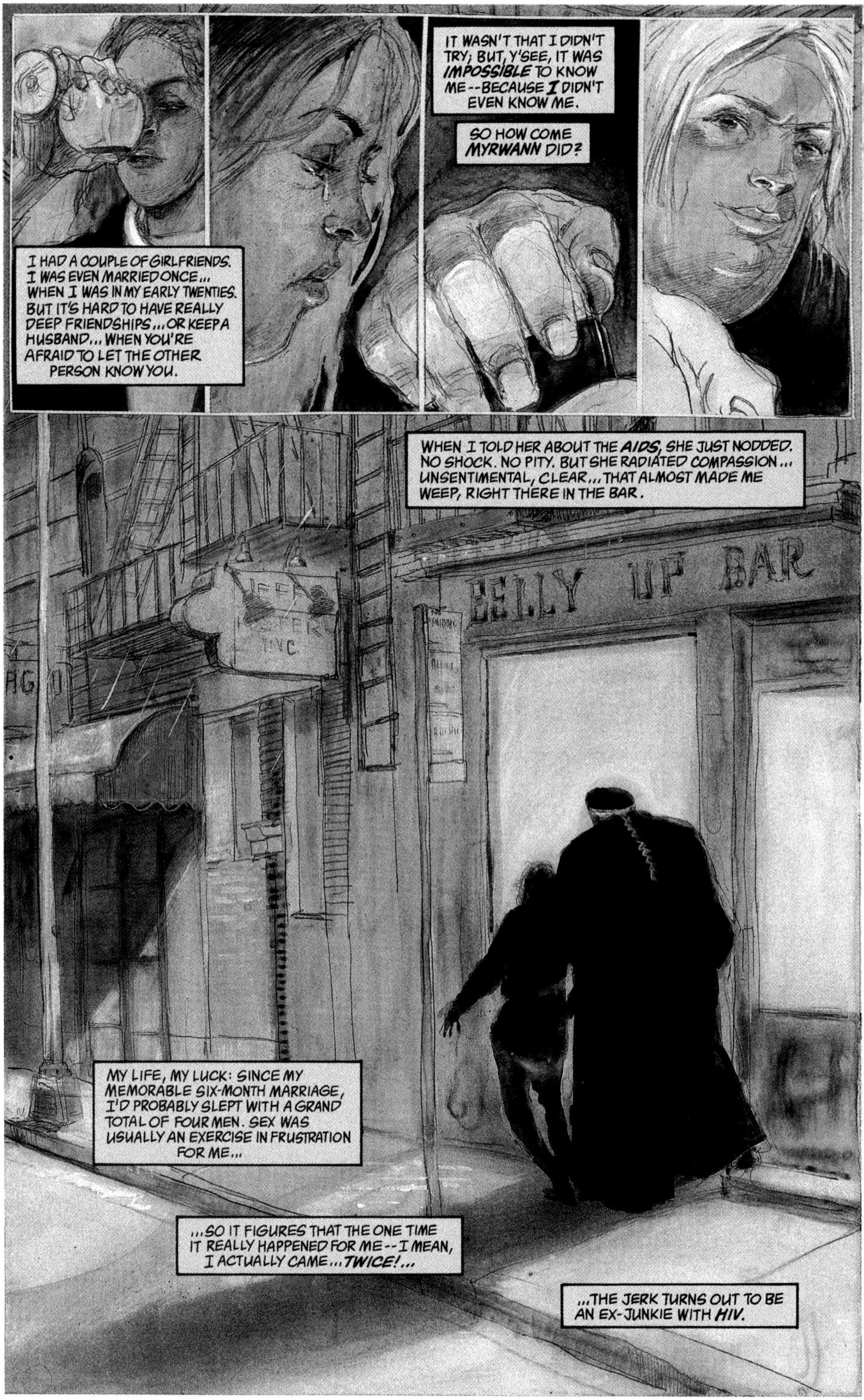
I HAD A COUPLE OF GIRLFRIENDS. I WAS EVEN MARRIED ONCE... WHEN I WAS IN MY EARLY TWENTIES. BUT IT'S HARD TO HAVE REALLY DEEP FRIENDSHIPS... OR KEEP A HUSBAND... WHEN YOU'RE AFRAID TO LET THE OTHER PERSON KNOW YOU.
IT WASN'T THAT I DIDN'T TRY; BUT, Y'SEE, IT WAS IMPOSSIBLE TO KNOW ME--BECAUSE I DIDN'T EVEN KNOW ME.
SO HOW COME MYRWANN DID?
WHEN I TOLD HER ABOUT THE AIDS, SHE JUST NODDED. NO SHOCK. NO PITY. BUT SHE RADIATED COMPASSION... UNSENTIMENTAL, CLEAR... THAT ALMOST MADE ME WEEP, RIGHT THERE IN THE BAR.
BELLY UP BAR
MY LIFE, MY LUCK: SINCE MY MEMORABLE SIX-MONTH MARRIAGE, I'D PROBABLY SLEPT WITH A GRAND TOTAL OF FOUR MEN. SEX WAS USUALLY AN EXERCISE IN FRUSTRATION FOR ME...
...SO IT FIGURES THAT THE ONE TIME IT REALLY HAPPENED FOR ME--I MEAN, I ACTUALLY CAME... TWICE!...
...THE JERK TURNS OUT TO BE AN EX-JUNKIE WITH HIV.

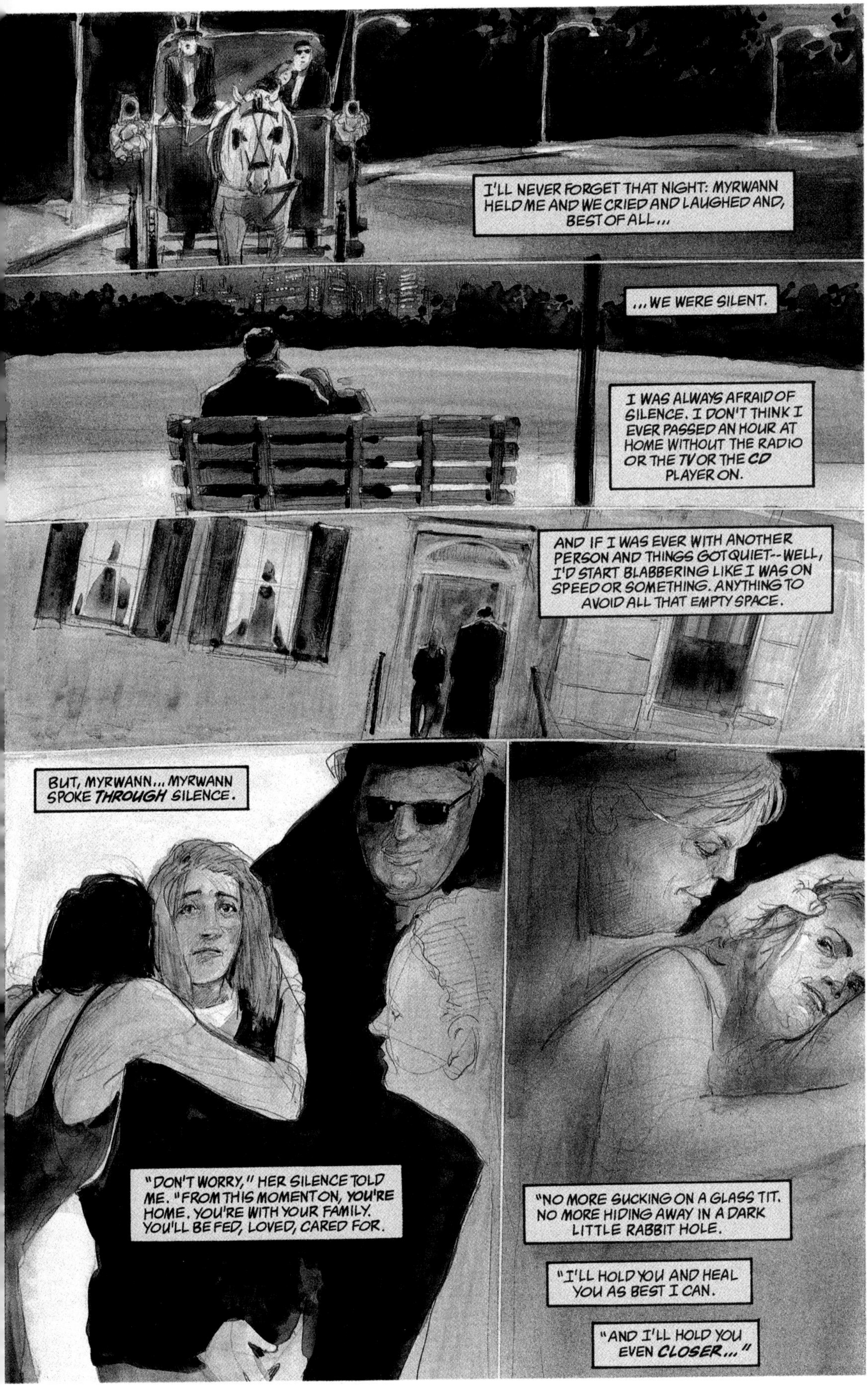
I'LL NEVER FORGET THAT NIGHT: MYRWANN HELD ME AND WE CRIED AND LAUGHED AND, BEST OF ALL...
...WE WERE SILENT.
I WAS ALWAYS AFRAID OF SILENCE. I DON'T THINK I EVER PASSED AN HOUR AT HOME WITHOUT THE RADIO OR THE TV OR THE CD PLAYER ON.
AND IF I WAS EVER WITH ANOTHER PERSON AND THINGS GOT QUIET--WELL, I'D START BLABBERING LIKE I WAS ON SPEED OR SOMETHING. ANYTHING TO AVOID ALL THAT EMPTY SPACE.
BUT, MYRWANN... MYRWANN SPOKE THROUGH SILENCE.
"DON'T WORRY," HER SILENCE TOLD ME. "FROM THIS MOMENT ON, YOU'RE HOME. YOU'RE WITH YOUR FAMILY. YOU'LL BE FED, LOVED, CARED FOR.
"NO MORE SUCKING ON A GLASS TIT. NO MORE HIDING AWAY IN A DARK LITTLE RABBIT HOLE.
"I'LL HOLD YOU AND HEAL YOU AS BEST I CAN.
"AND I'LL HOLD YOU EVEN CLOSER..."

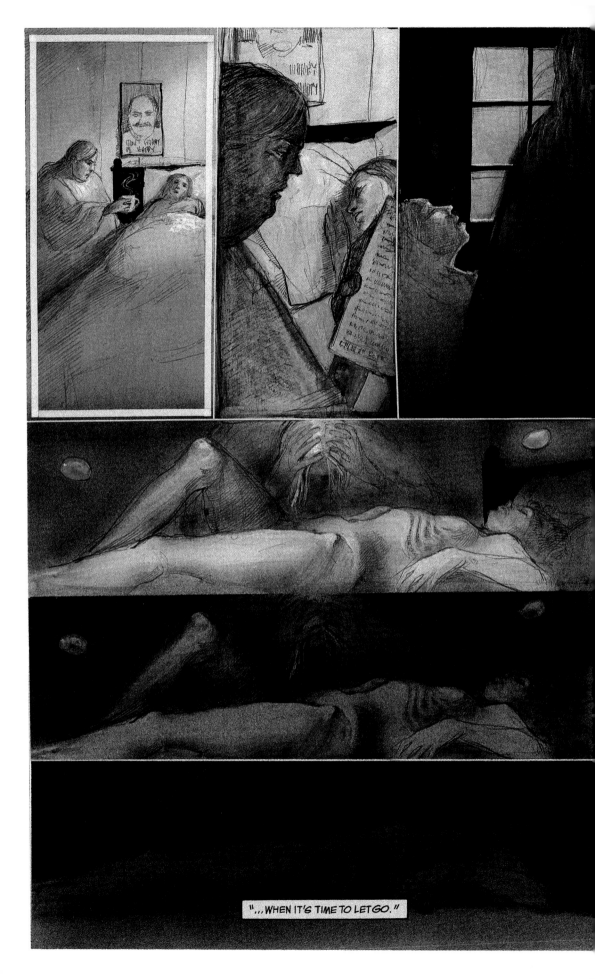

"...WHEN IT'S TIME TO LET GO."

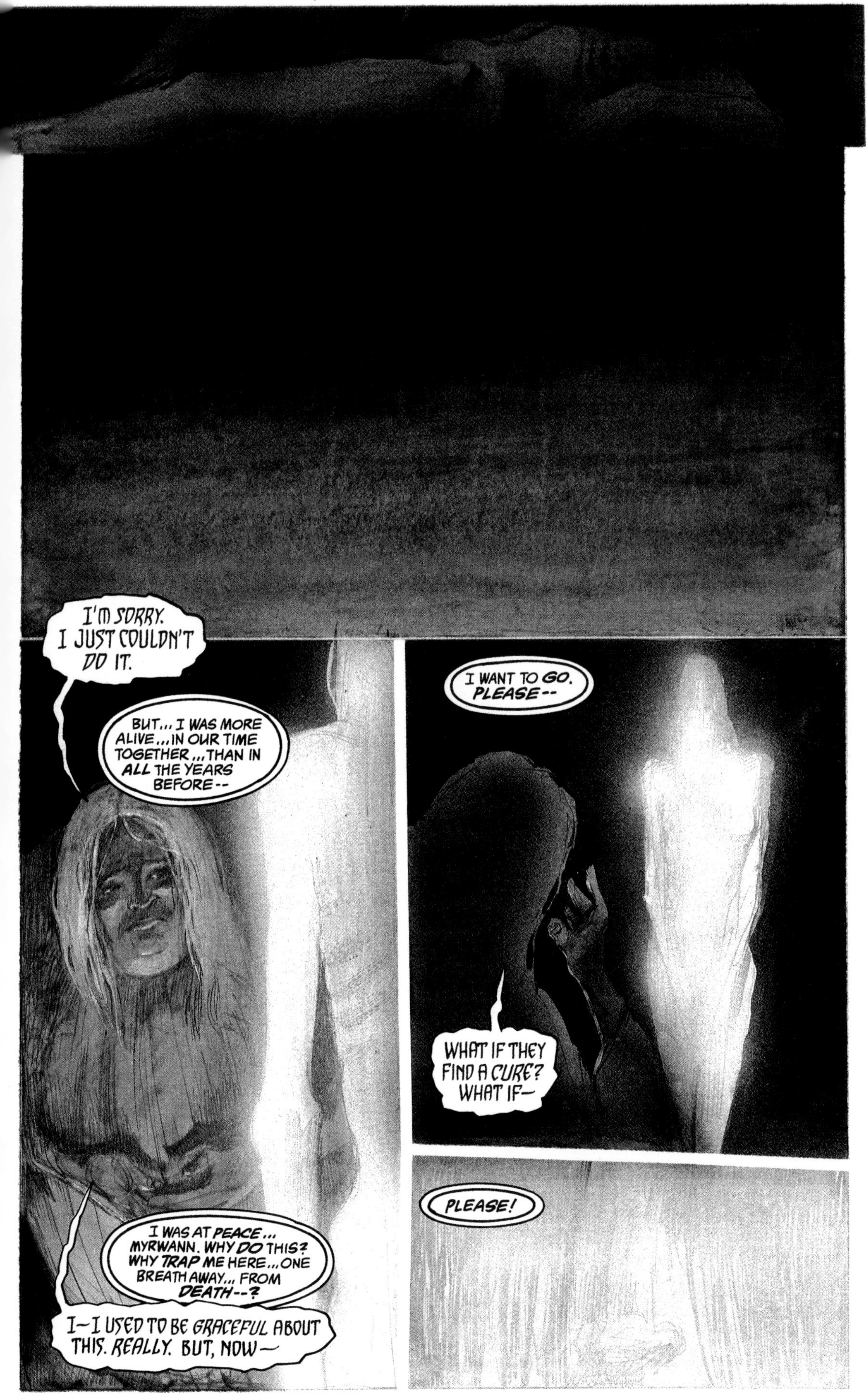
I'M SORRY. I JUST COULDN'T DO IT.
BUT... I WAS MORE ALIVE... IN OUR TIME TOGETHER... THAN IN ALL THE YEARS BEFORE--
I WAS AT PEACE... MYRWANN. WHY DO THIS? WHY TRAP ME HERE... ONE BREATH AWAY... FROM DEATH--?
I--I USED TO BE GRACEFUL ABOUT THIS. REALLY. BUT, NOW--
I WANT TO GO. PLEASE--
WHAT IF THEY FIND A CURE? WHAT IF--
PLEASE!

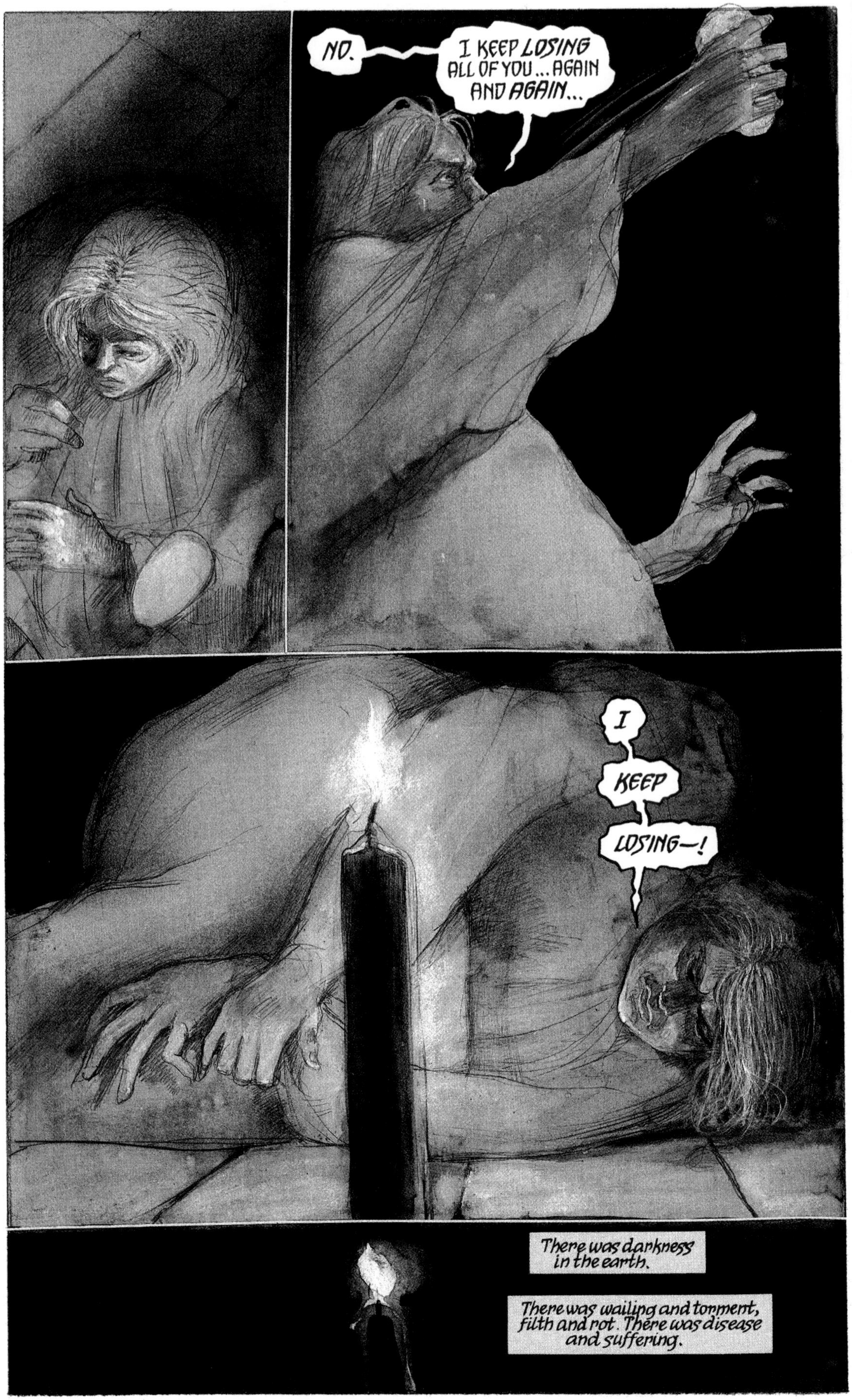
NO.
I KEEP LOSING ALL OF YOU... AGAIN AND AGAIN...
I
KEEP
LOSING—!
There was darkness in the earth.
There was wailing and torment, filth and rot. There was disease and suffering.

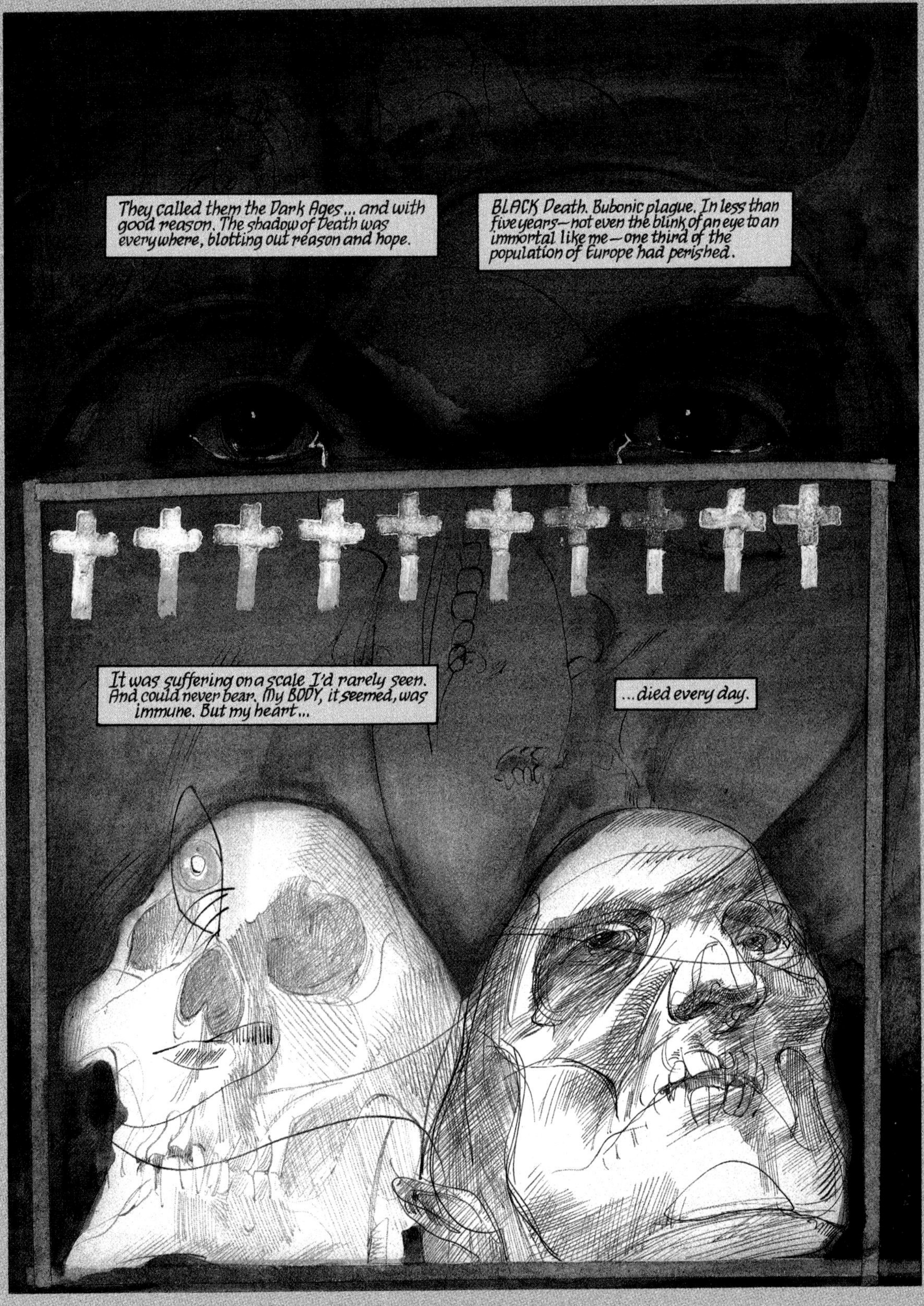
They called them the Dark Ages... and with good reason. The shadow of Death was everywhere, blotting out reason and hope.
BLACK Death. Bubonic plague. In less than five years—not even the blink of an eye to an immortal like me—one third of the population of Europe had perished.
It was suffering on a scale I'd rarely seen. And could never bear. My BODY, it seemed, was immune. But my heart...
...died every day.

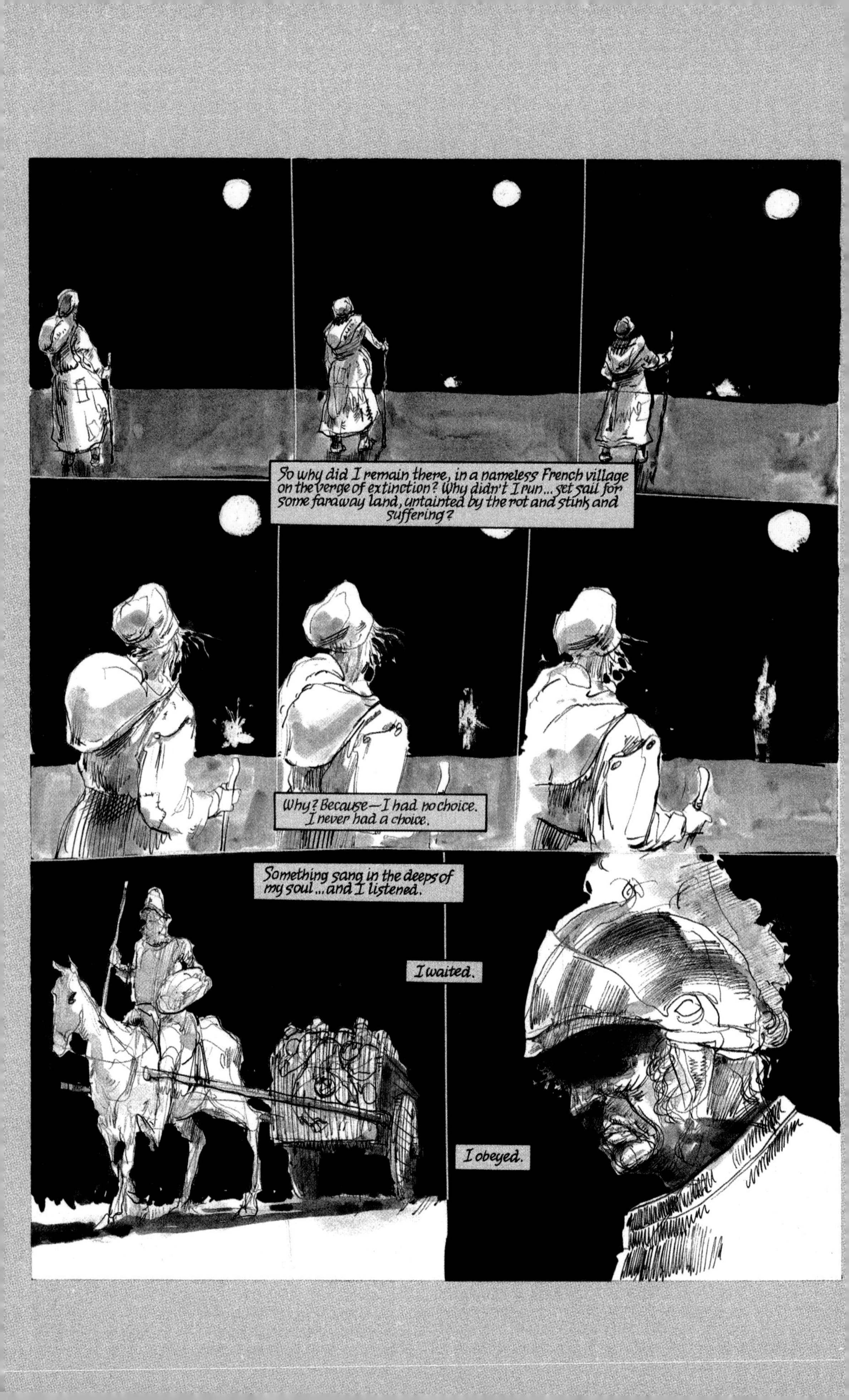
So why did I remain there, in a nameless French village on the verge of extinction? Why didn't I run... set sail for some faraway land, untainted by the rot and stink and suffering?
Why? Because—I had no choice. I never had a choice.
Something sang in the deeps of my soul... and I listened.
I waited.
I obeyed.

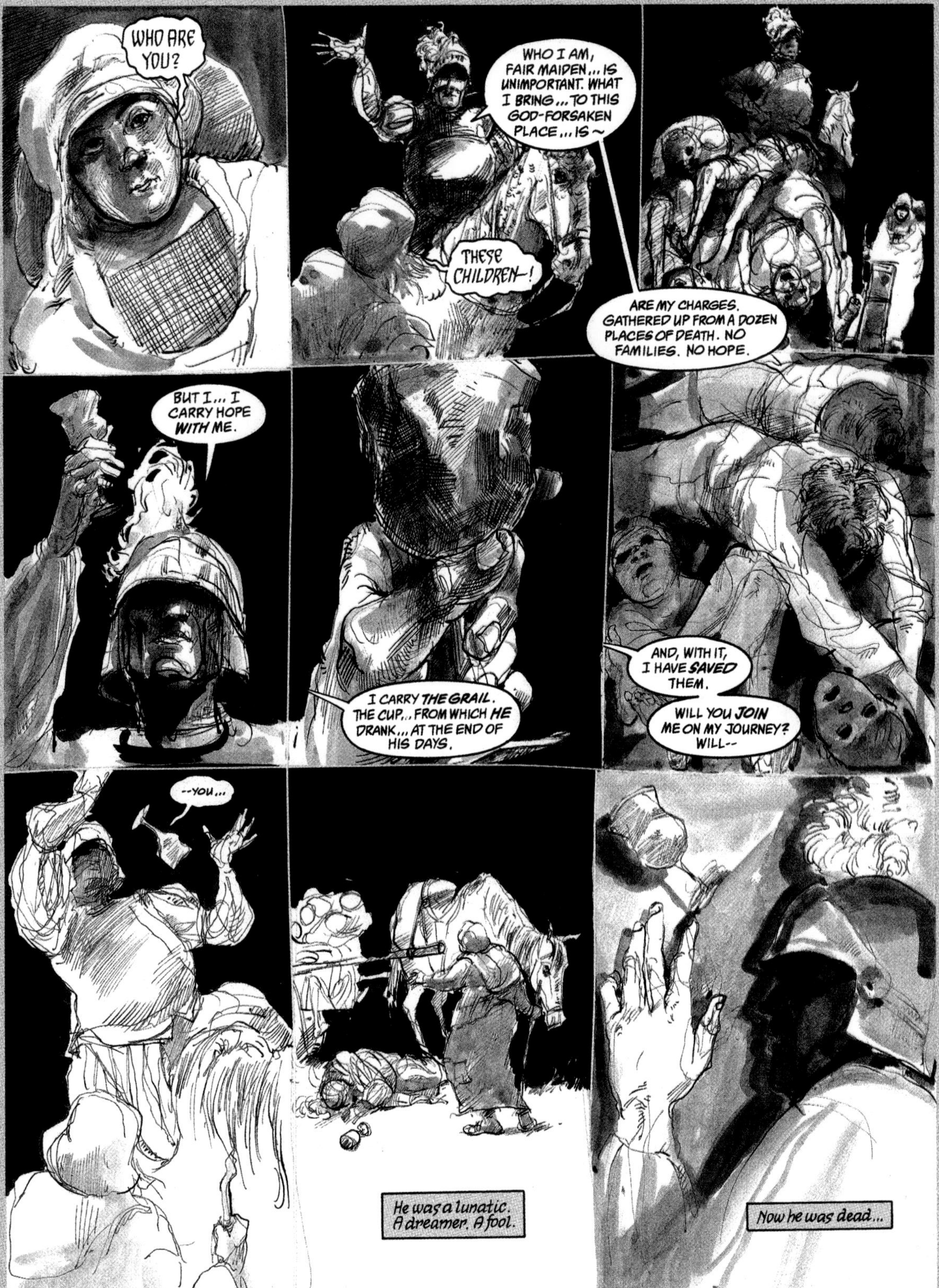
WHO ARE YOU?
WHO I AM, FAIR MAIDEN... IS UNIMPORTANT. WHAT I BRING... TO THIS GOD-FORSAKEN PLACE... IS ~
THESE CHILDREN--!
ARE MY CHARGES. GATHERED UP FROM A DOZEN PLACES OF DEATH. NO FAMILIES. NO HOPE.
BUT I... I CARRY HOPE WITH ME.
I CARRY THE GRAIL. THE CUP... FROM WHICH HE DRANK... AT THE END OF HIS DAYS.
AND, WITH IT, I HAVE SAVED THEM.
WILL YOU JOIN ME ON MY JOURNEY? WILL--
--YOU...
He was a lunatic. A dreamer. A fool.
Now he was dead...

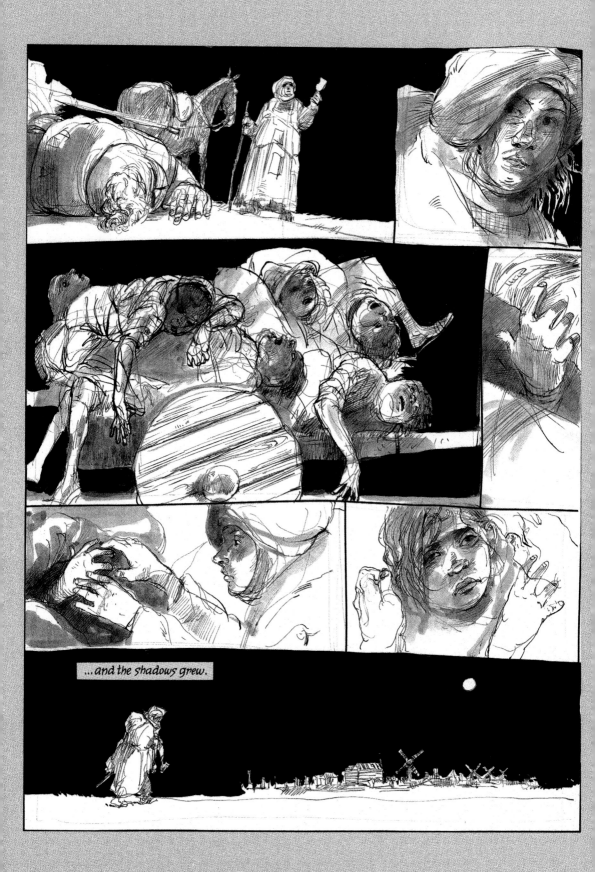

...and the shadows grew.

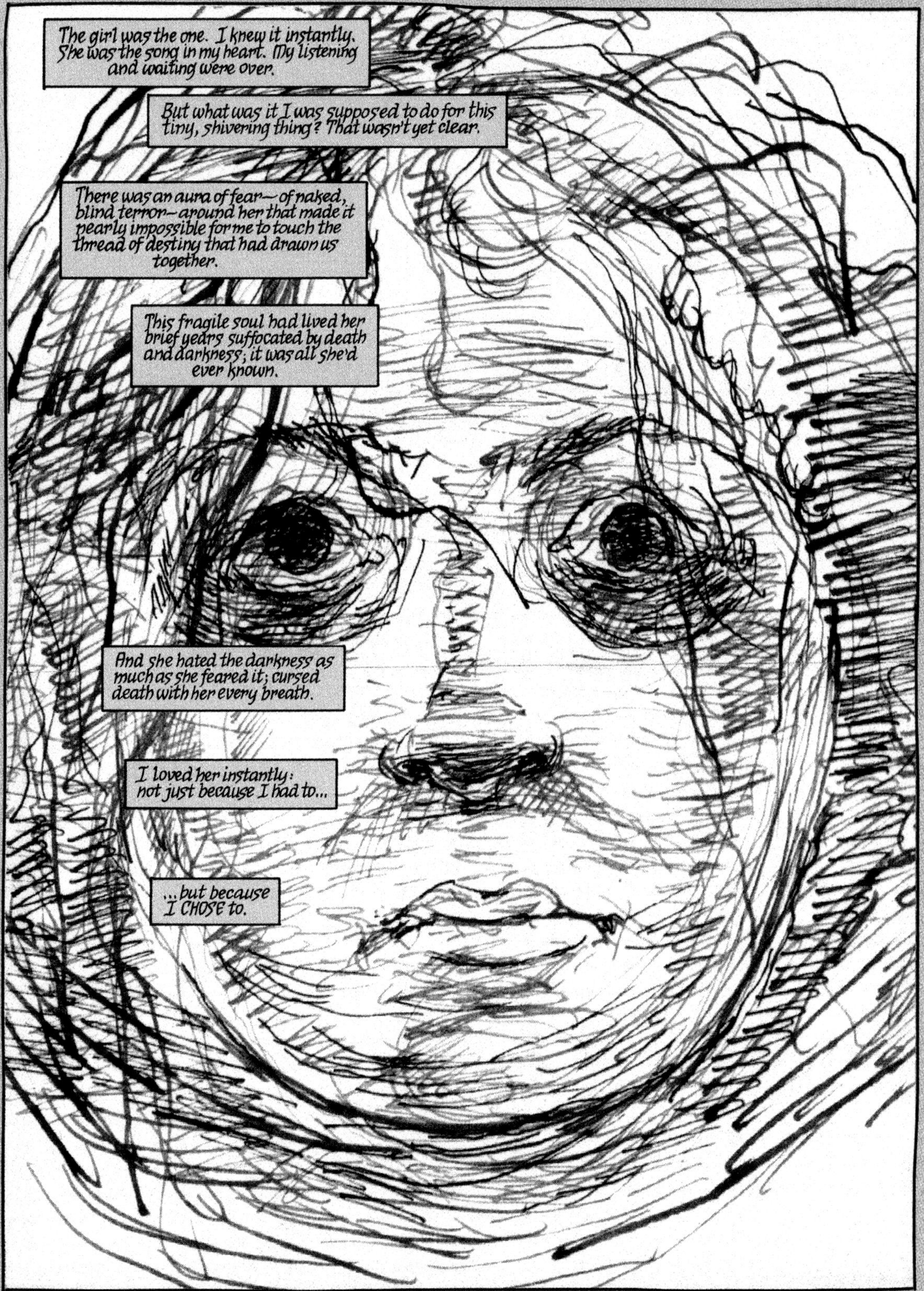
The girl was the one. I knew it instantly. She was the song in my heart. My listening and waiting were over.
But what was it I was supposed to do for this tiny, shivering thing? That wasn't yet clear.
There was an aura of fear— of naked, blind terror— around her that made it nearly impossible for me to touch the thread of destiny that had drawn us together.
This fragile soul had lived her brief years suffocated by death and darkness; it was all she'd ever known.
And she hated the darkness as much as she feared it; cursed death with her every breath.
I loved her instantly: not just because I had to...
...but because I CHOSE to.

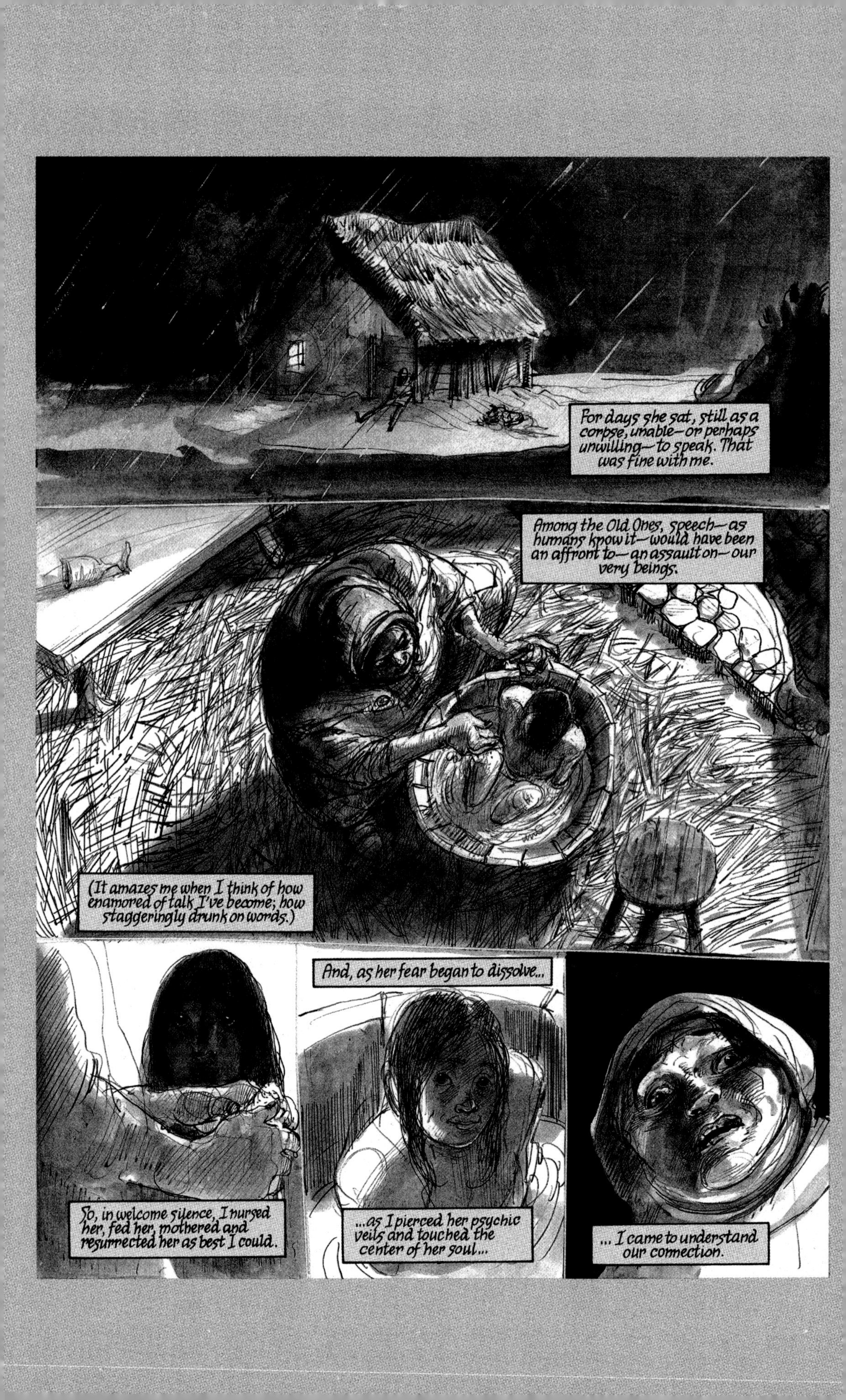
For days she sat, still as a corpse, unable—or perhaps unwilling—to speak. That was fine with me.
Among the Old Ones, speech—as humans know it—would have been an affront to—an assault on—our very beings.
(It amazes me when I think of how enamored of talk I've become; how staggeringly drunk on words.)
So, in welcome silence, I nursed her, fed her, mothered and resurrected her as best I could.
And, as her fear began to dissolve...
...as I pierced her psychic veils and touched the center of her soul...
... I came to understand our connection.

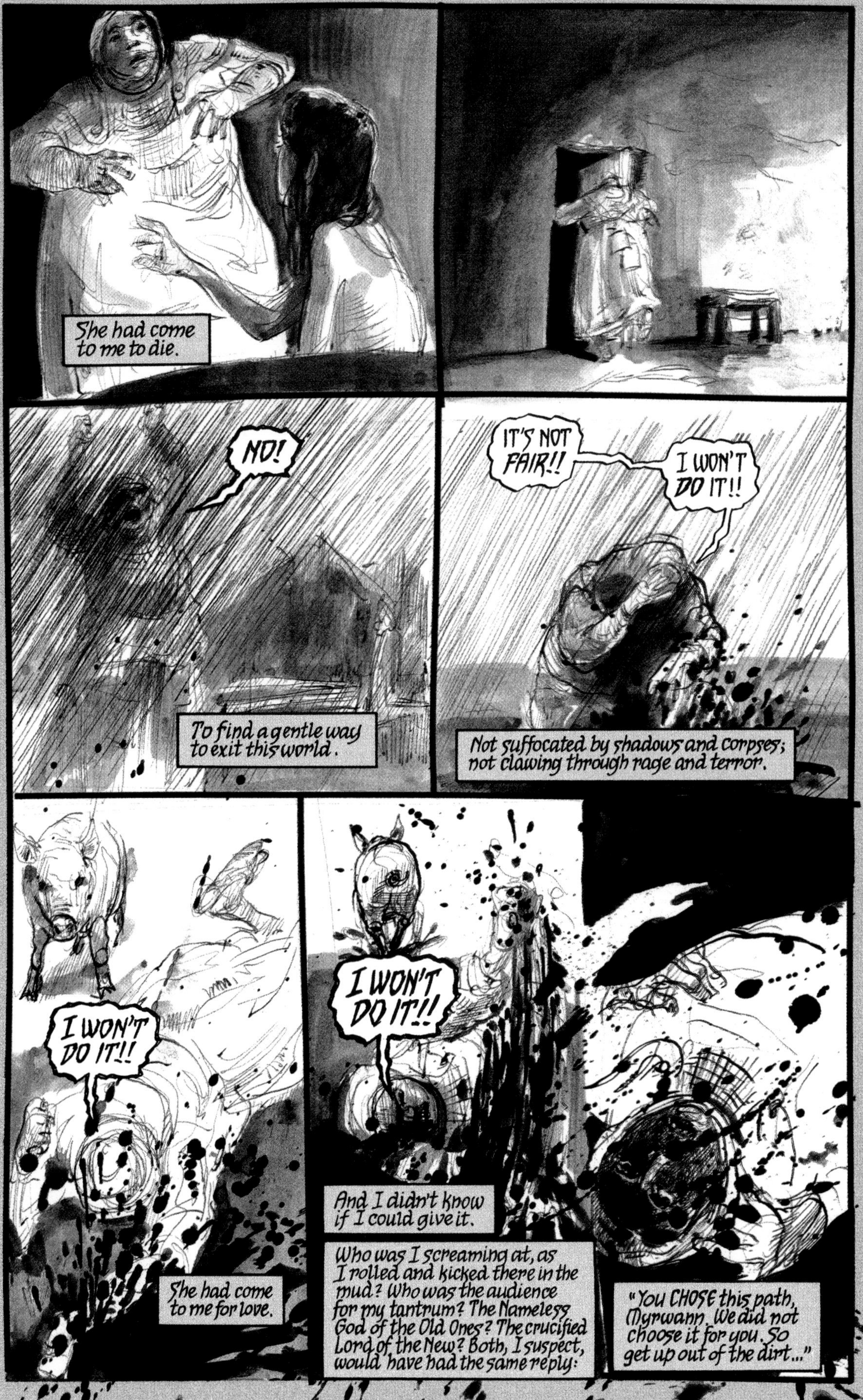
She had come to me to die.
NO!
To find a gentle way to exit this world.
IT'S NOT FAIR!!
I WON'T DO IT!!
Not suffocated by shadows and corpses; not clawing through rage and terror.
I WON'T DO IT!!
She had come to me for love.
I WON'T DO IT!!
And I didn't know if I could give it.
Who was I screaming at, as I rolled and kicked there in the mud? Who was the audience for my tantrum? The Nameless God of the Old Ones? The crucified Lord of the New? Both, I suspect, would have had the same reply:
"You CHOSE this path, Myrwann. We did not choose it for you. So get up out of the dirt..."

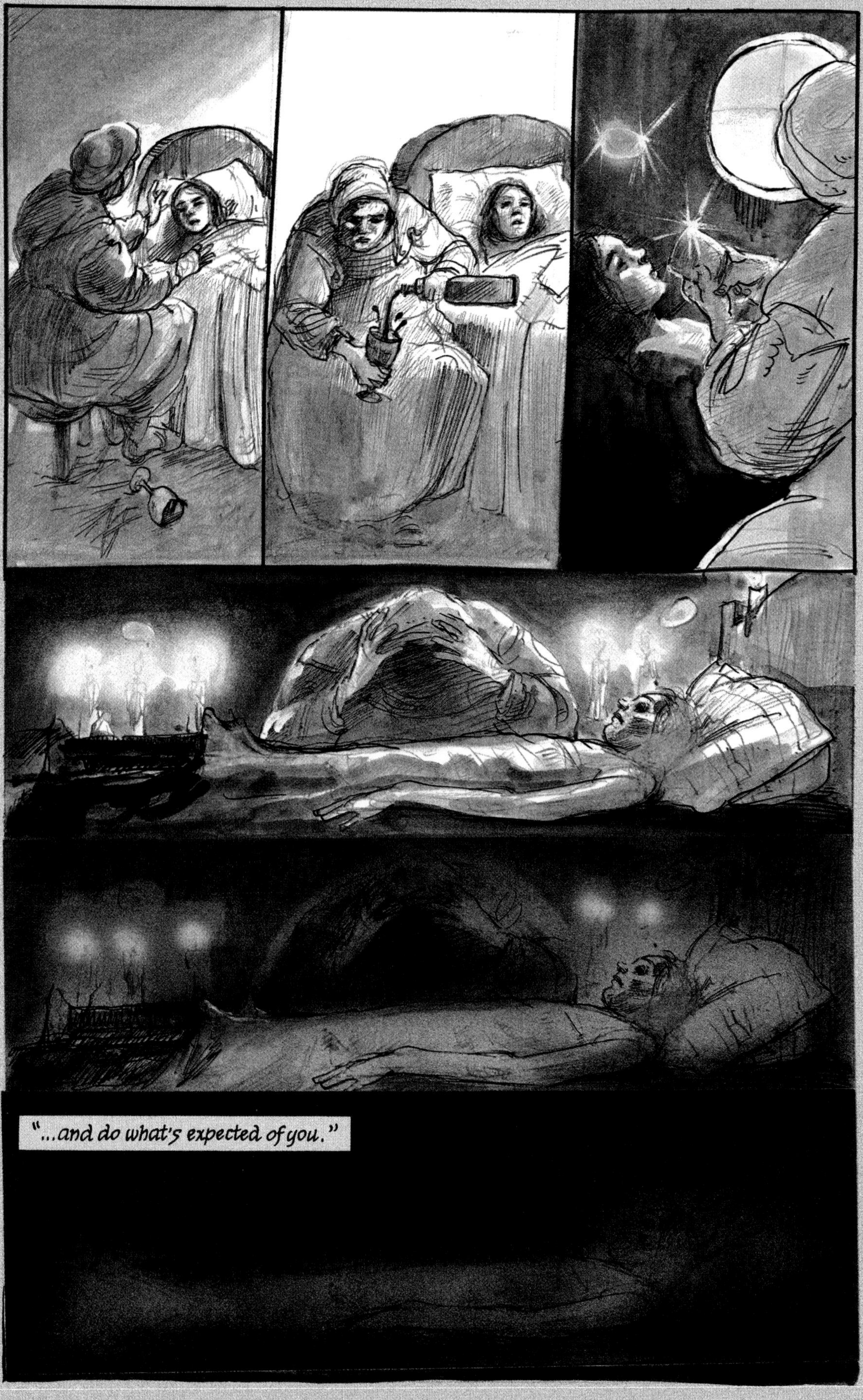
"...and do what's expected of you."

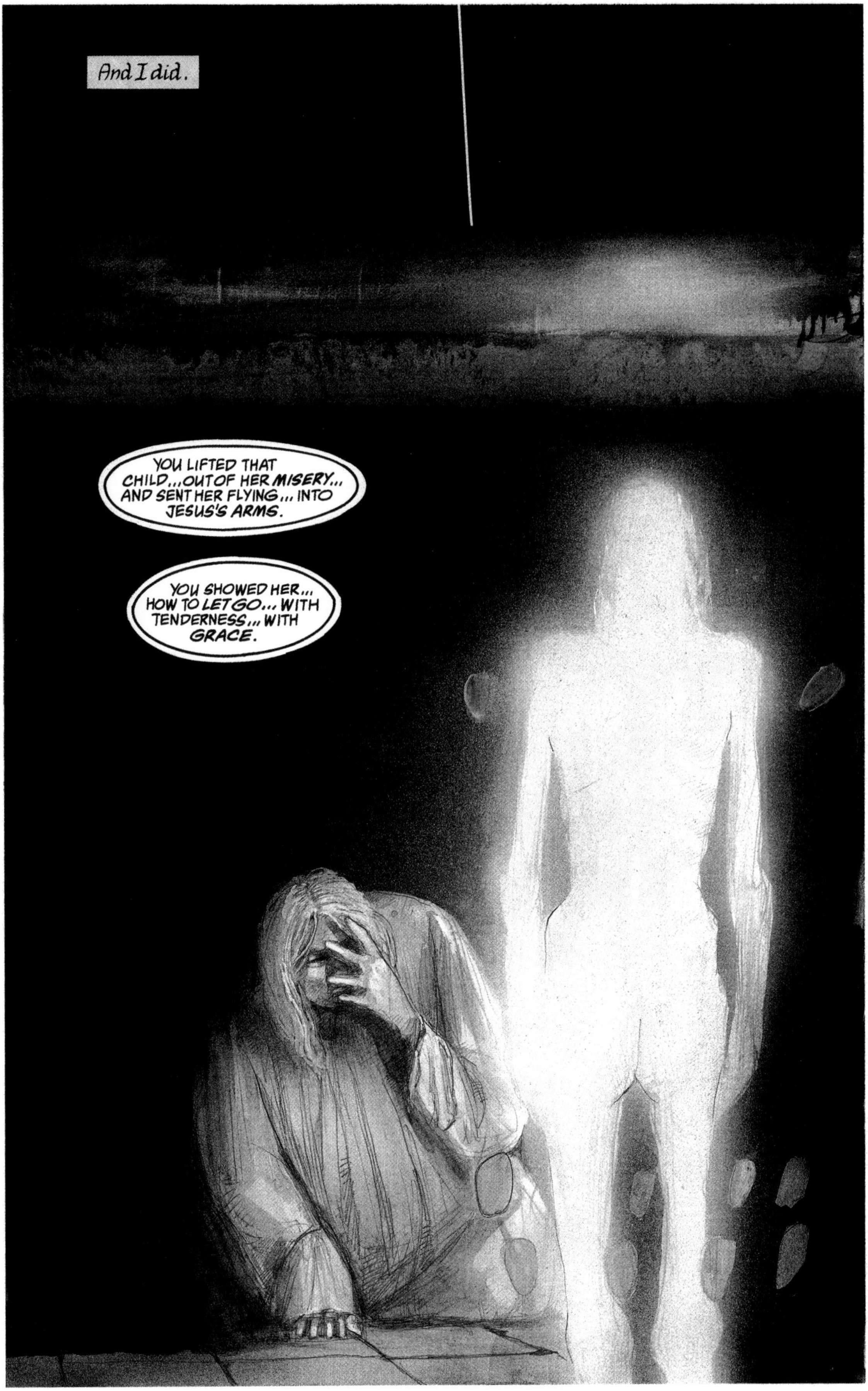
And I did.
YOU LIFTED THAT CHILD... OUT OF HER MISERY... AND SENT HER FLYING... INTO JESUS'S ARMS.
YOU SHOWED HER... HOW TO LET GO... WITH TENDERNESS... WITH GRACE.

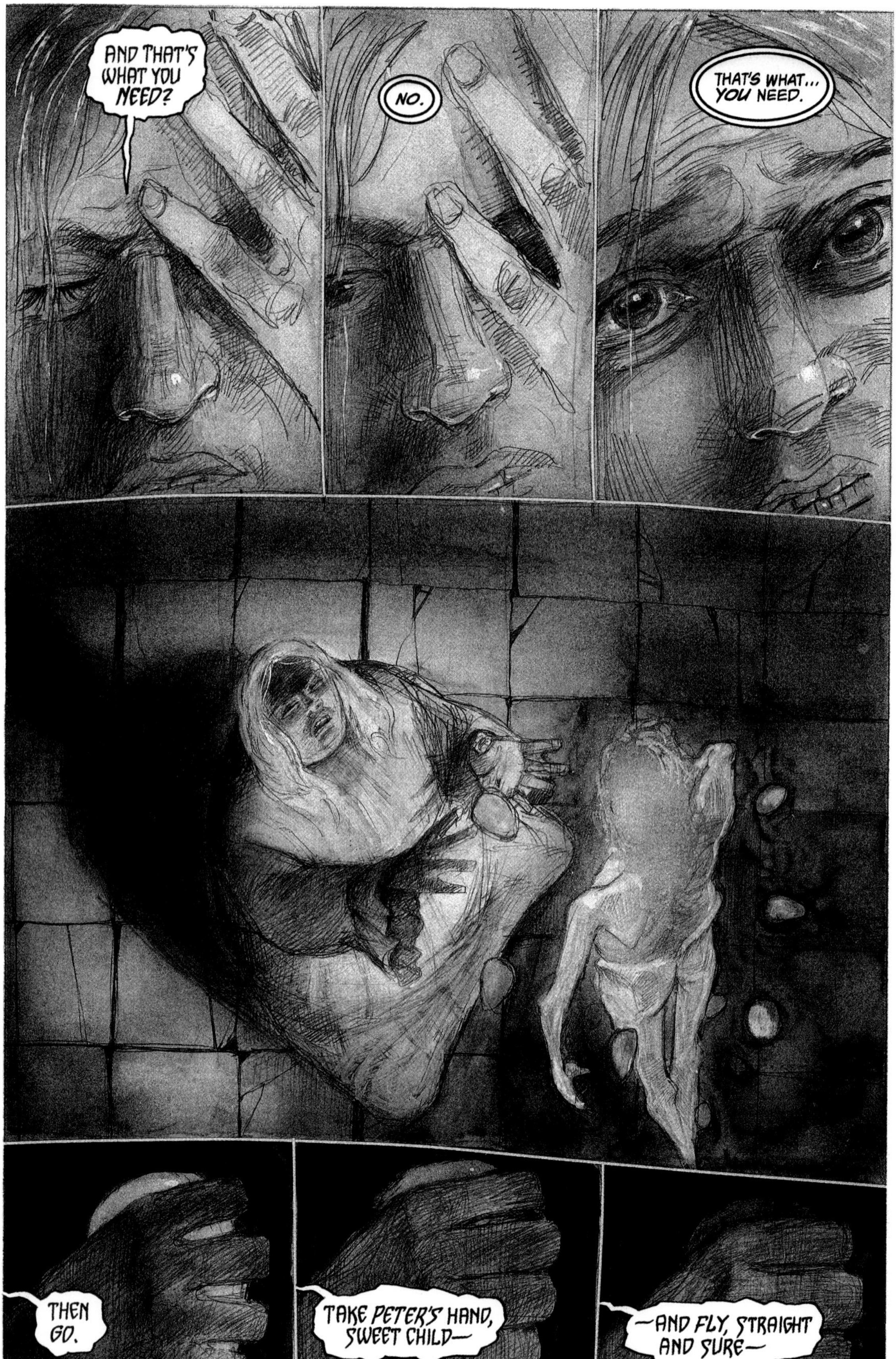
AND THAT'S WHAT YOU NEED?
NO.
THAT'S WHAT... YOU NEED.
THEN GO.
TAKE PETER'S HAND, SWEET CHILD—
—AND FLY, STRAIGHT AND SURE—

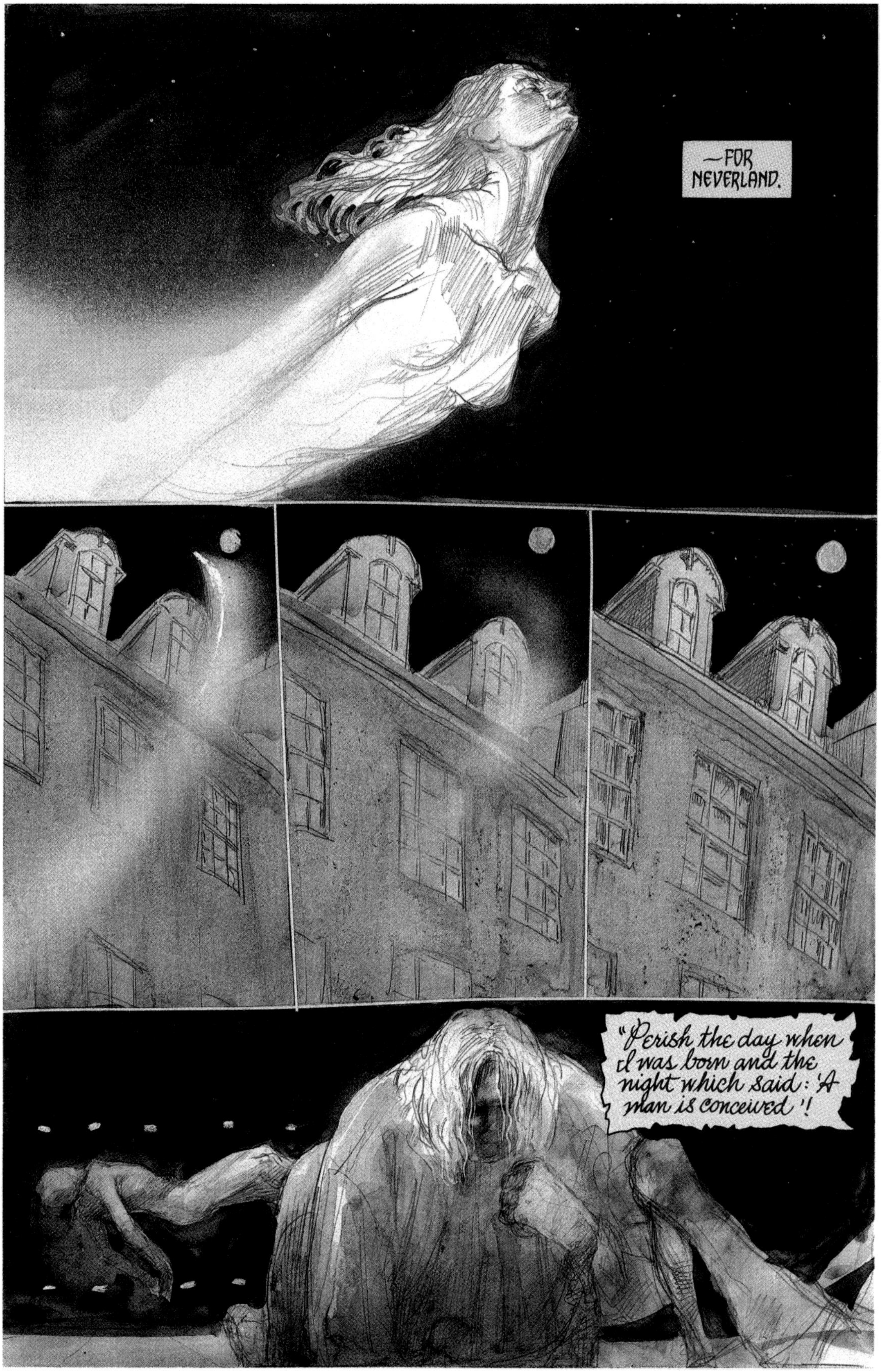
—FOR NEVERLAND.
"Perish the day when I was born and the night which said: 'A man is conceived'!

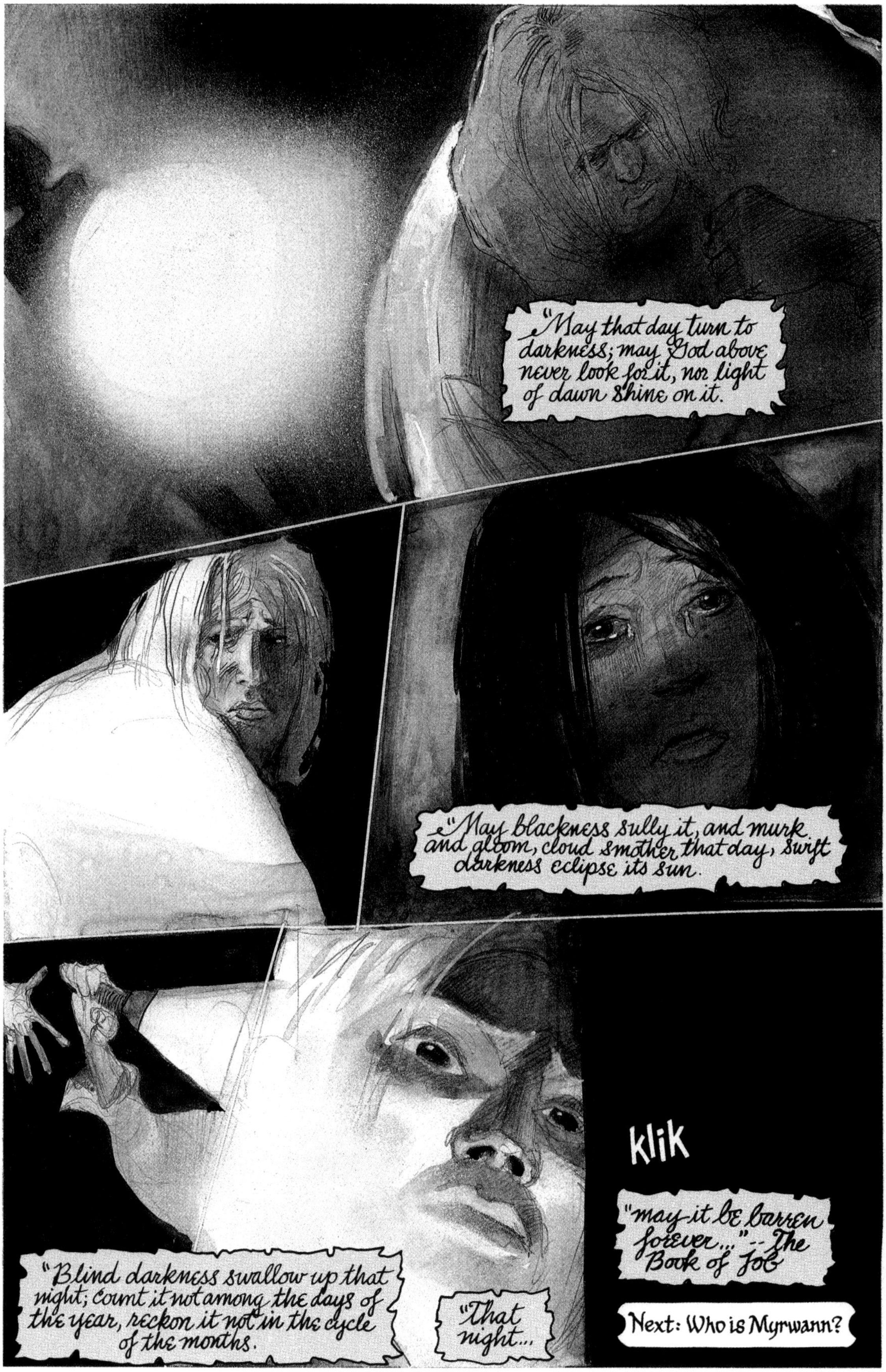
"May that day turn to darkness; may God above never look for it, nor light of dawn shine on it.
"May blackness sully it, and murk and gloom, cloud smother that day, swift darkness eclipse its sun.
"Blind darkness swallow up that night; count it not among the days of the year, reckon it not in the cycle of the months.
"That night...
klik
"may it be barren forever..." -- The Book of Job
Next: Who is Myrwann?

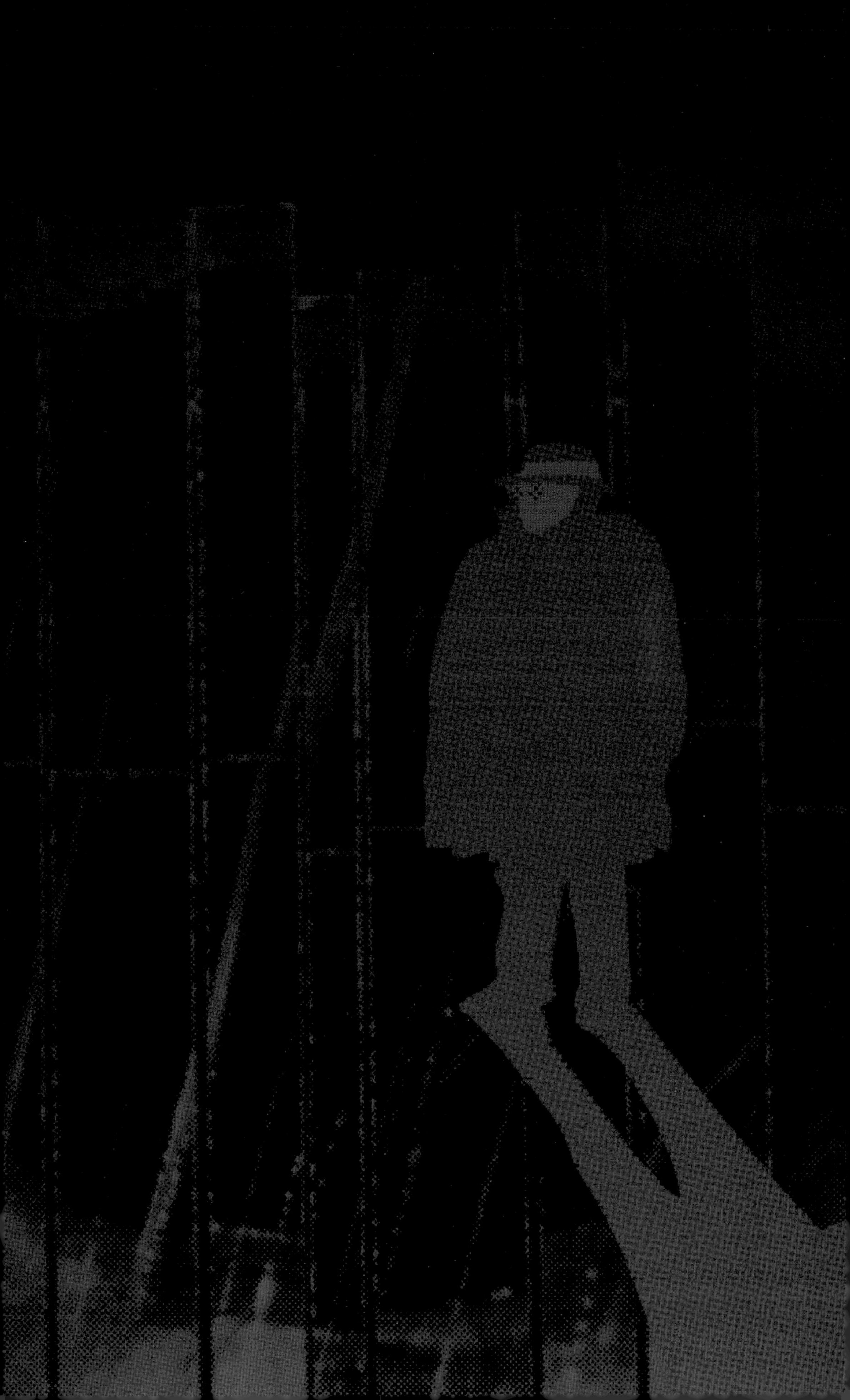

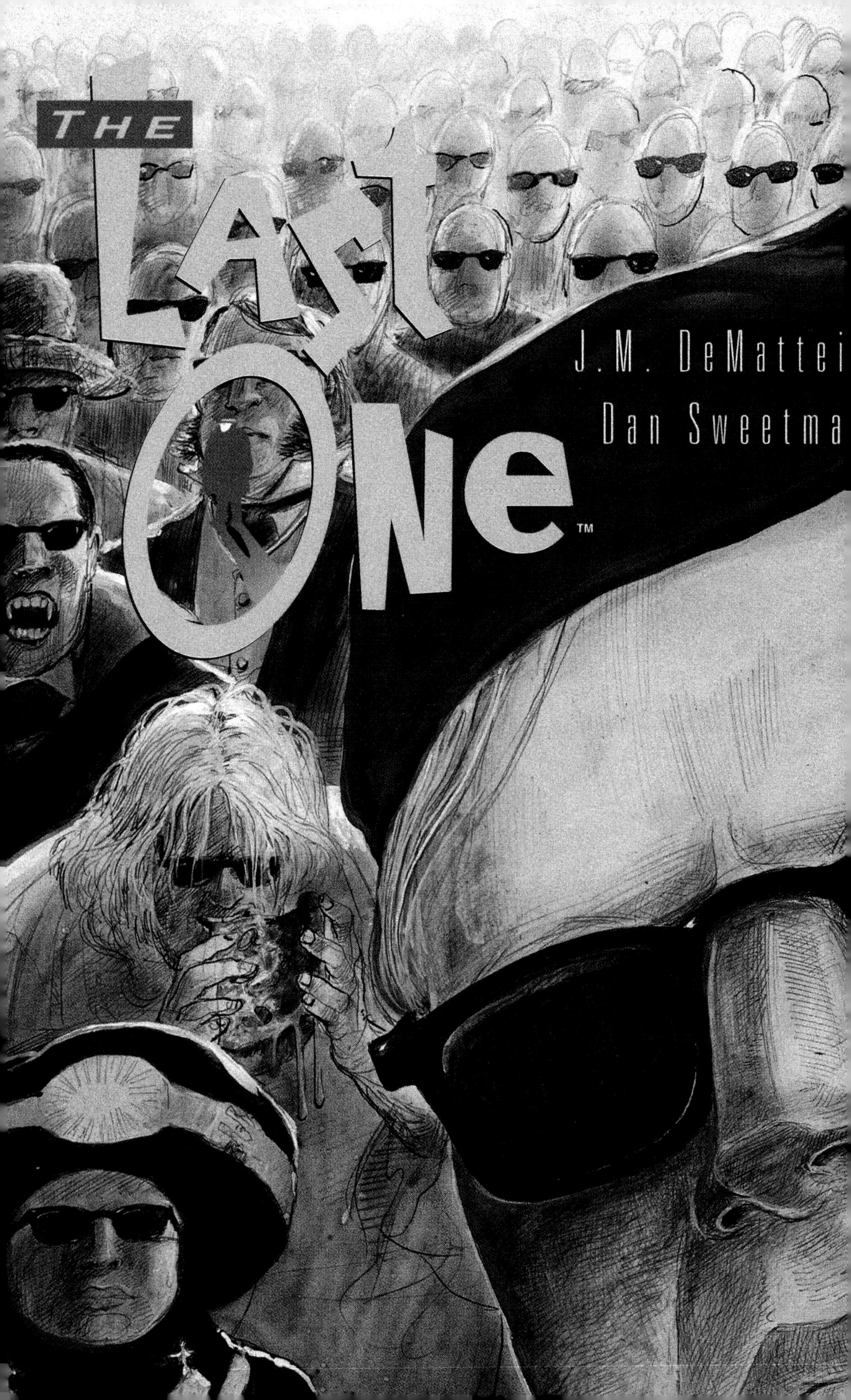
THE
LAST
ONE™
J.M. DeMattei
Dan Sweetma

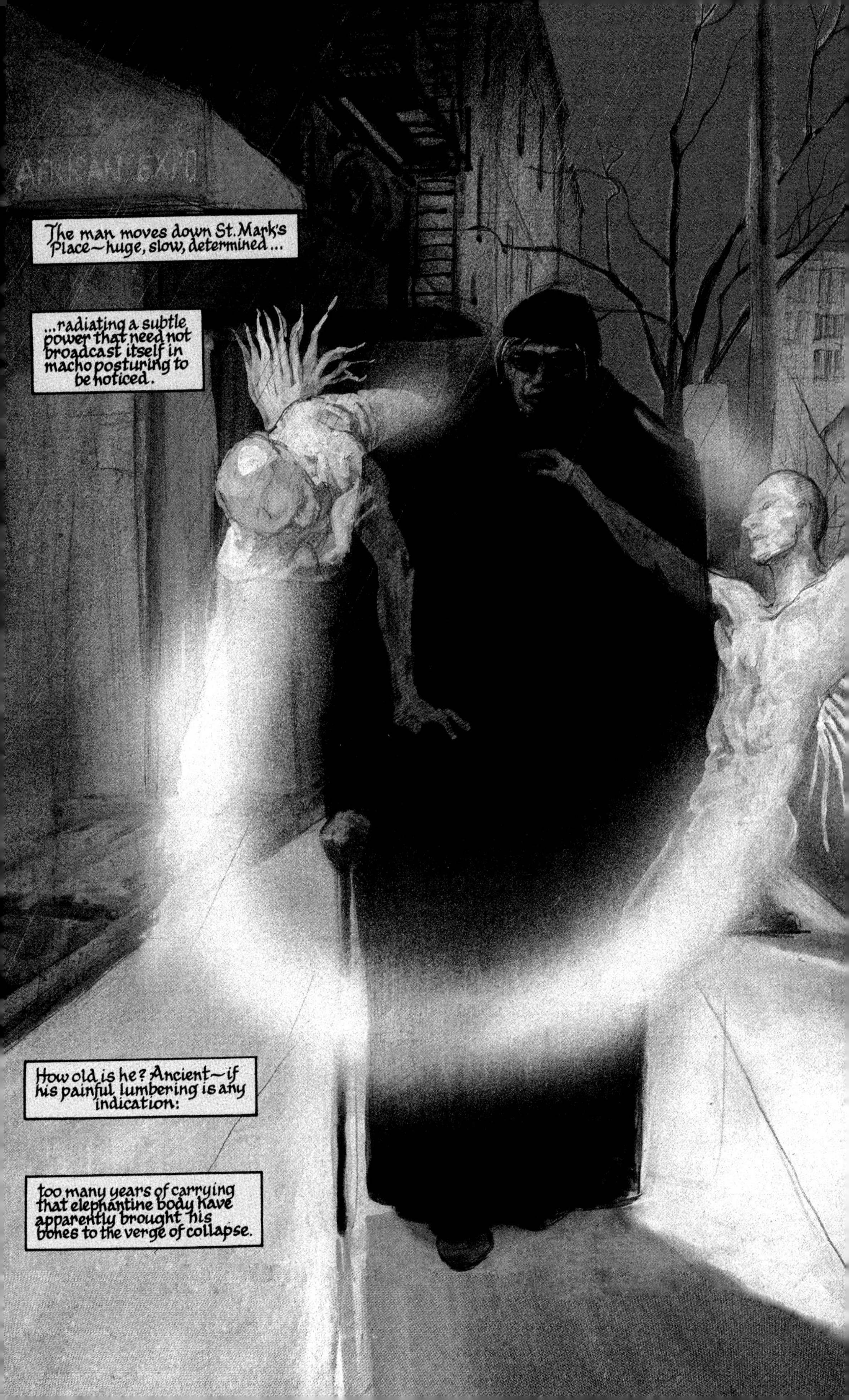

The man moves down St. Mark's Place~huge, slow, determined...
...radiating a subtle power that need not broadcast itself in macho posturing to be noticed.
How old is he? Ancient~if his painful lumbering is any indication:
too many years of carrying that elephantine body have apparently brought his bones to the verge of collapse.

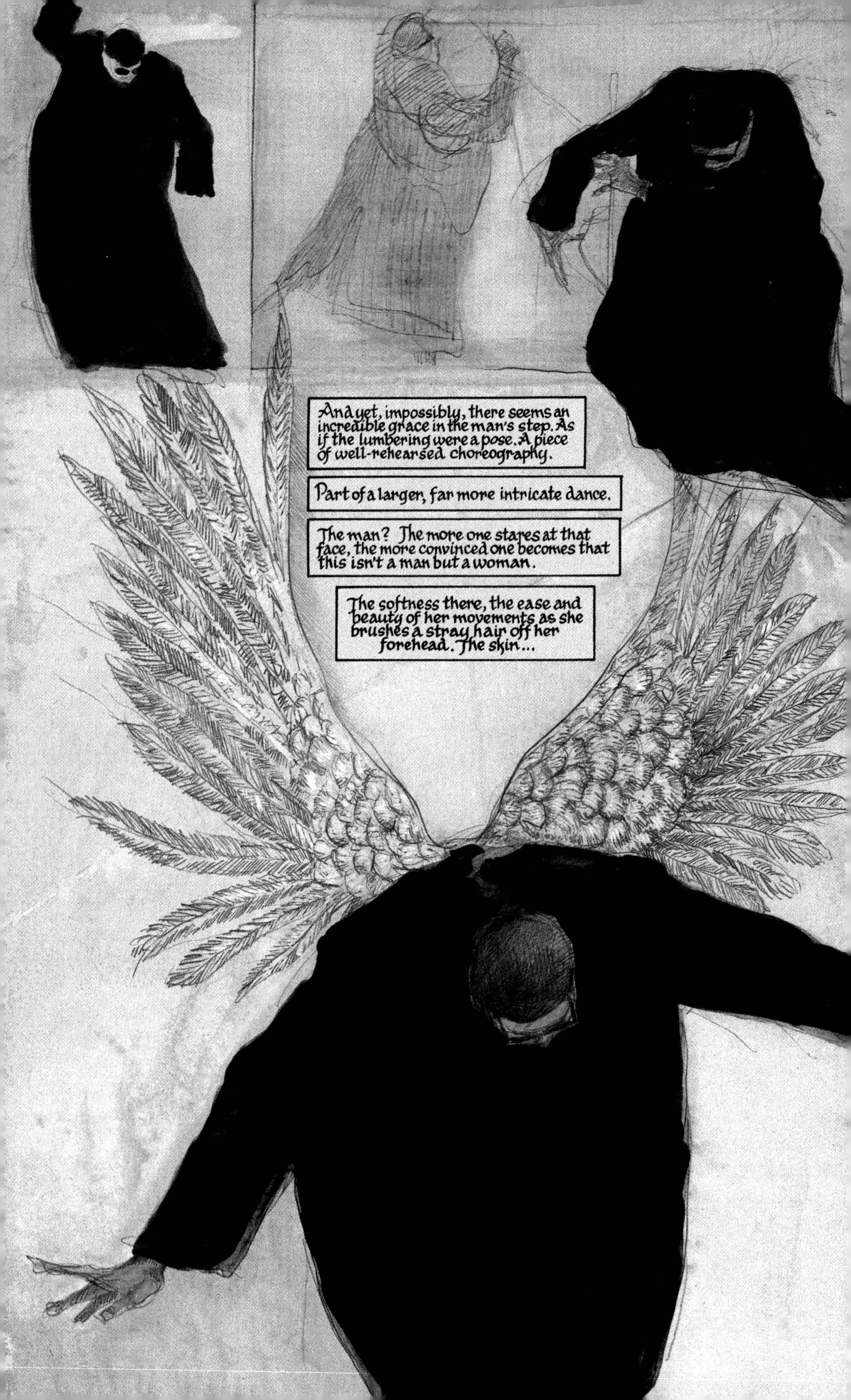
And yet, impossibly, there seems an incredible grace in the man's step. As if the lumbering were a pose. A piece of well-rehearsed choreography.
Part of a larger, far more intricate dance.
The man? The more one stares at that face, the more convinced one becomes that this isn't a man but a woman.
The softness there, the ease and beauty of her movements as she brushes a stray hair off her forehead. The skin...

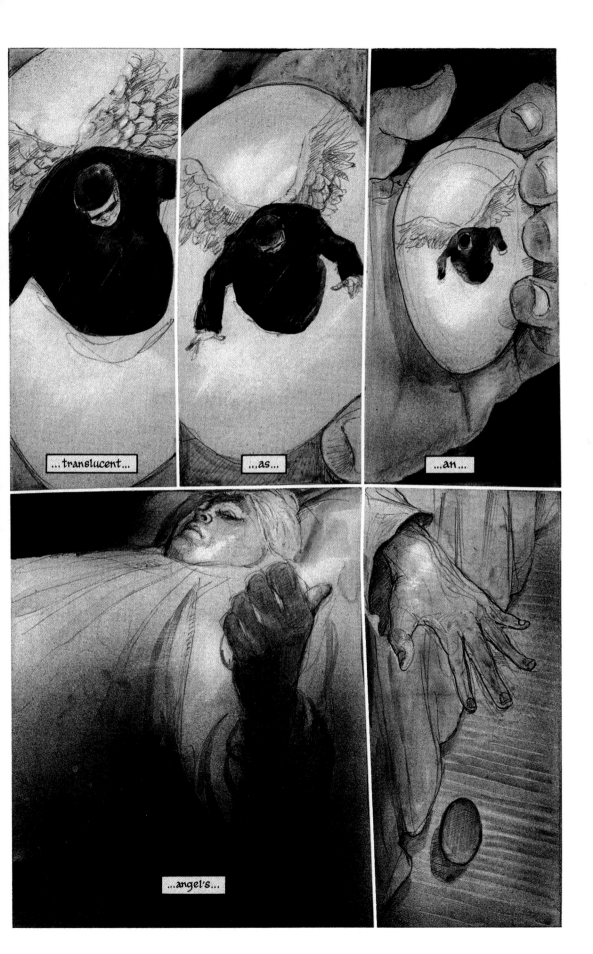

...translucent...

...as...

...an...

...angel's...

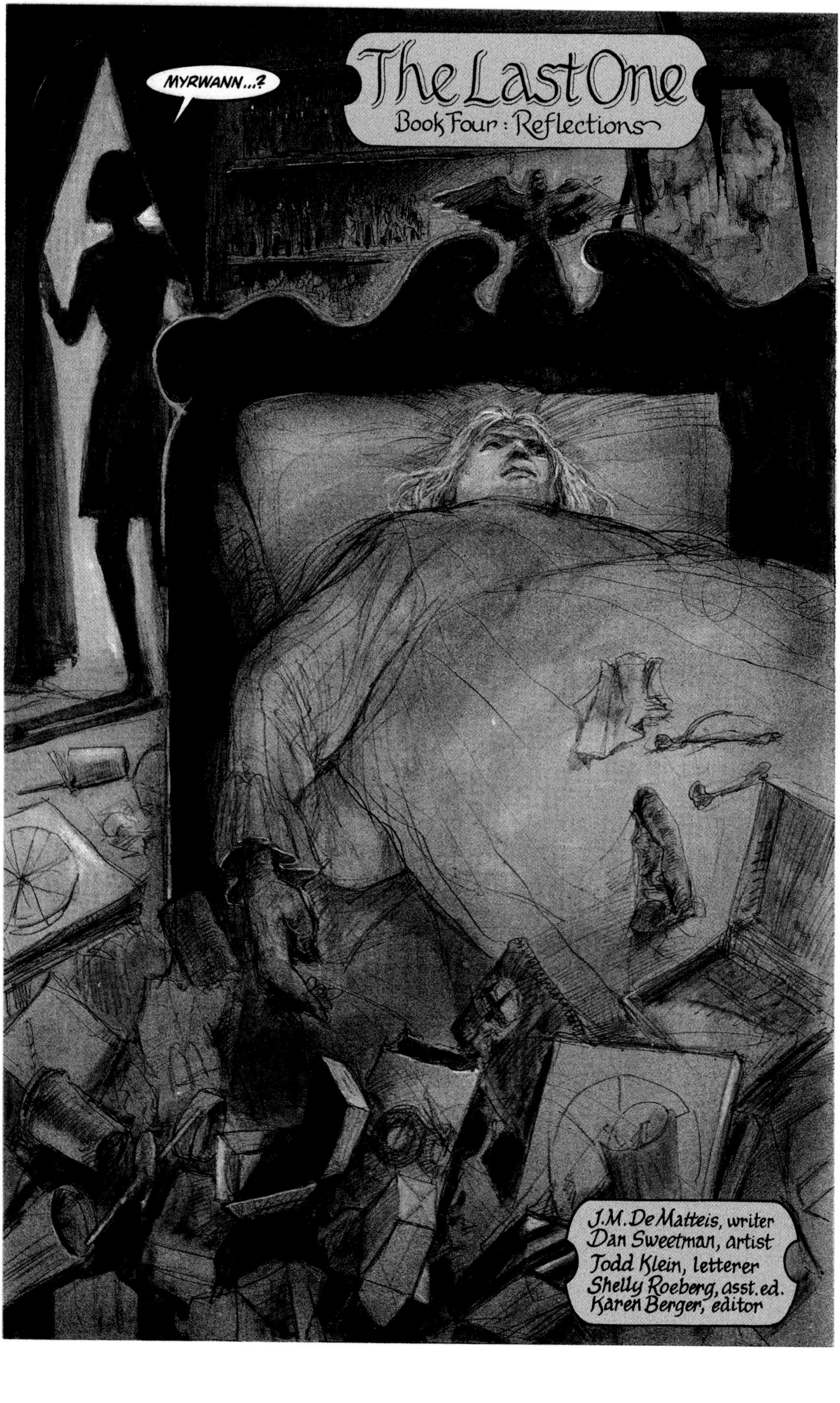
MYRWANN...?
The Last One
Book Four: Reflections
J.M. DeMatteis, writer
Dan Sweetman, artist
Todd Klein, letterer
Shelly Roeberg, asst. ed.
Karen Berger, editor

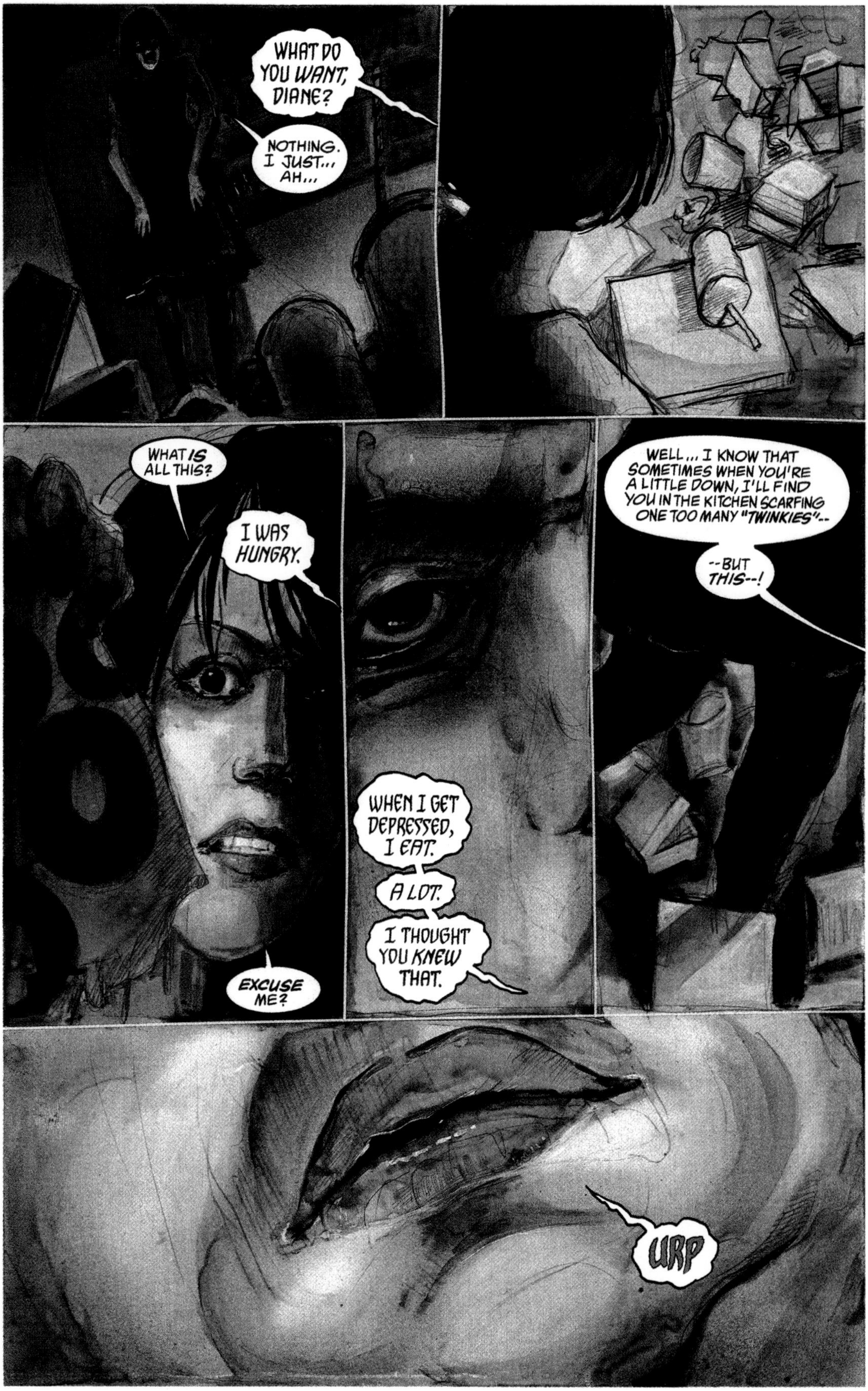
WHAT DO YOU WANT, DIANE?
NOTHING. I JUST..., AH...
WHAT IS ALL THIS?
I WAS HUNGRY.
EXCUSE ME?
WHEN I GET DEPRESSED, I EAT.
A LOT.
I THOUGHT YOU KNEW THAT.
WELL... I KNOW THAT SOMETIMES WHEN YOU'RE A LITTLE DOWN, I'LL FIND YOU IN THE KITCHEN SCARFING ONE TOO MANY "TWINKIES"--
--BUT THIS--!
URP

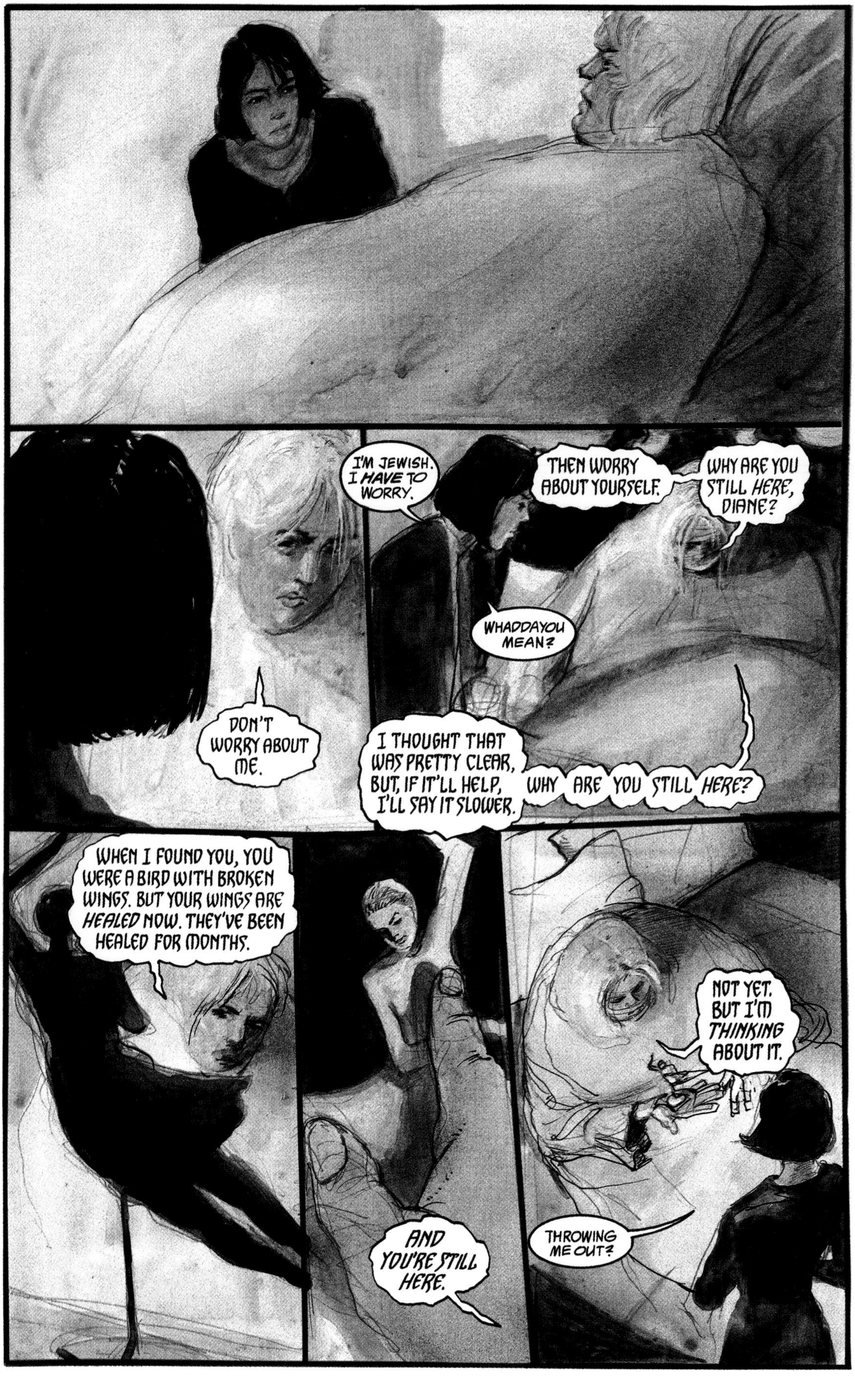
DON'T WORRY ABOUT ME.
I'M JEWISH. I HAVE TO WORRY.
THEN WORRY ABOUT YOURSELF.
WHY ARE YOU STILL HERE, DIANE?
WHADDAYOU MEAN?
I THOUGHT THAT WAS PRETTY CLEAR, BUT, IF IT'LL HELP, I'LL SAY IT SLOWER.
WHY ARE YOU STILL HERE?
WHEN I FOUND YOU, YOU WERE A BIRD WITH BROKEN WINGS. BUT YOUR WINGS ARE HEALED NOW. THEY'VE BEEN HEALED FOR MONTHS.
AND YOU'RE STILL HERE.
THROWING ME OUT?
NOT YET. BUT I'M THINKING ABOUT IT.

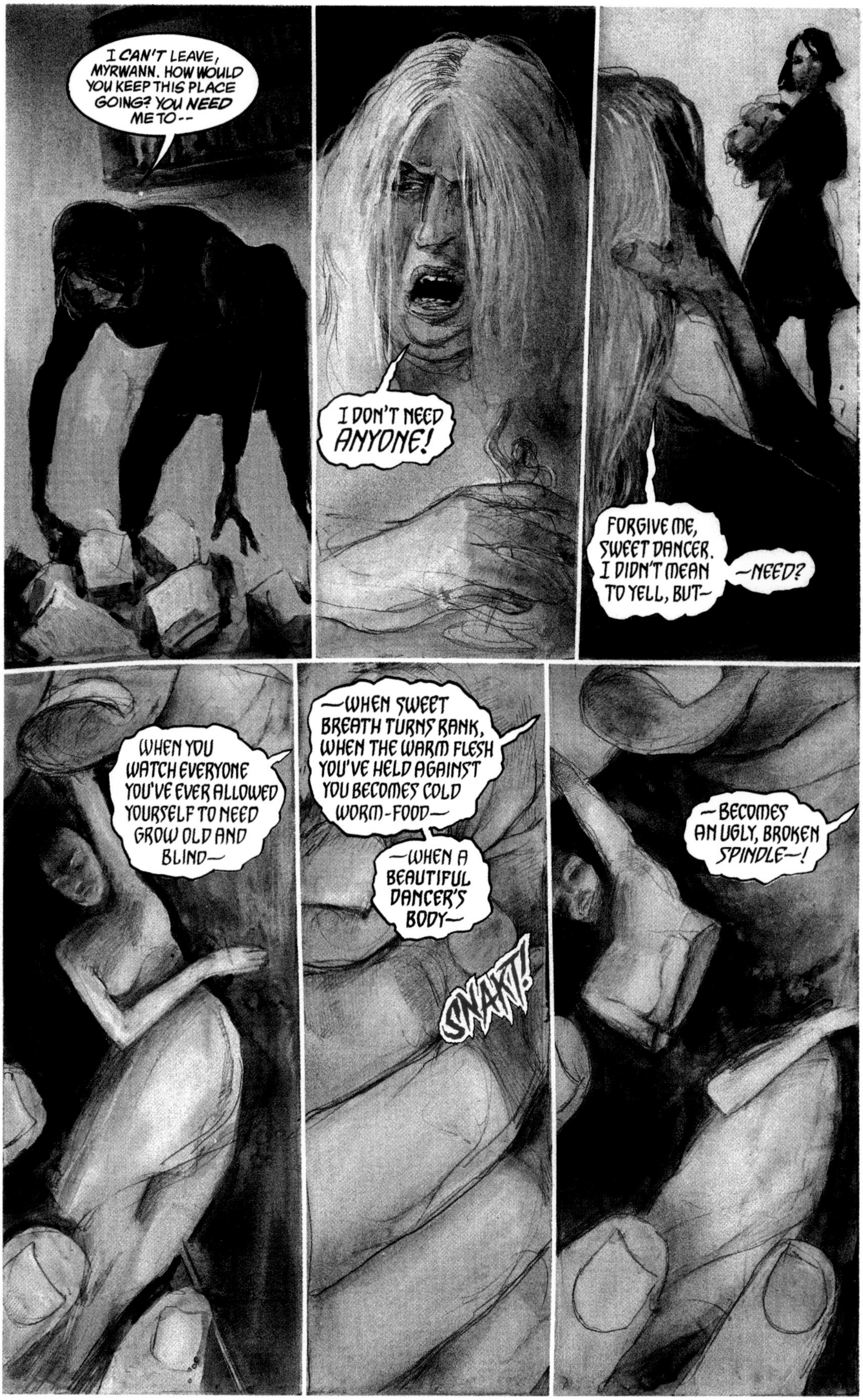
I CAN'T LEAVE, MYRWANN. HOW WOULD YOU KEEP THIS PLACE GOING? YOU NEED ME TO--
I DON'T NEED ANYONE!
FORGIVE ME, SWEET DANCER. I DIDN'T MEAN TO YELL, BUT—
—NEED?
WHEN YOU WATCH EVERYONE YOU'VE EVER ALLOWED YOURSELF TO NEED GROW OLD AND BLIND—
—WHEN SWEET BREATH TURNS RANK, WHEN THE WARM FLESH YOU'VE HELD AGAINST YOU BECOMES COLD WORM-FOOD—
—WHEN A BEAUTIFUL DANCER'S BODY—
SNAKT!
—BECOMES AN UGLY, BROKEN SPINDLE—!

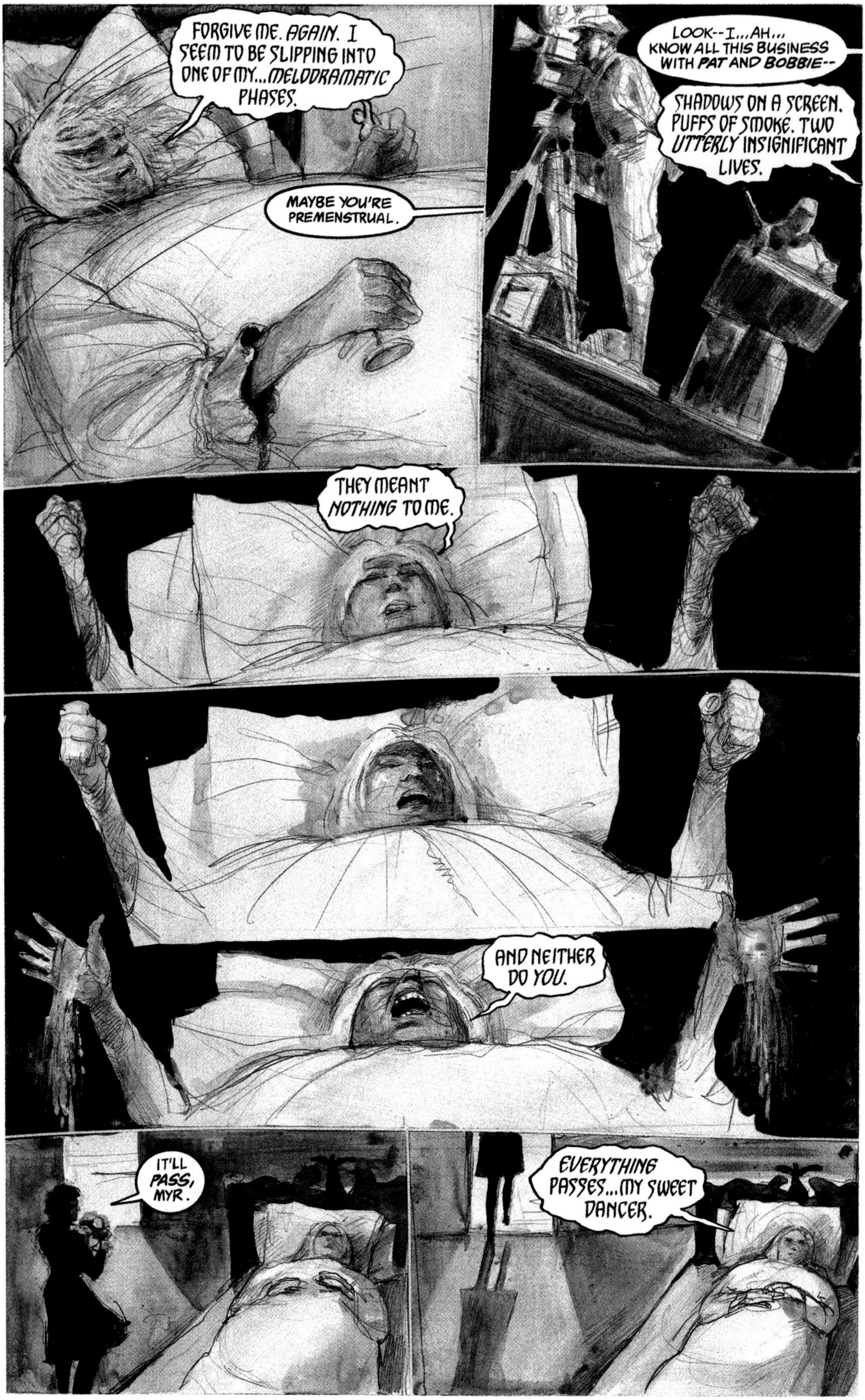
FORGIVE ME. AGAIN. I SEEM TO BE SLIPPING INTO ONE OF MY... MELODRAMATIC PHASES.
MAYBE YOU'RE PREMENSTRUAL.
LOOK--I...AH... KNOW ALL THIS BUSINESS WITH PAT AND BOBBIE--
SHADOWS ON A SCREEN. PUFFS OF SMOKE. TWO UTTERLY INSIGNIFICANT LIVES.
THEY MEANT NOTHING TO ME.
AND NEITHER DO YOU.
IT'LL PASS, MYR.
EVERYTHING PASSES... MY SWEET DANCER.

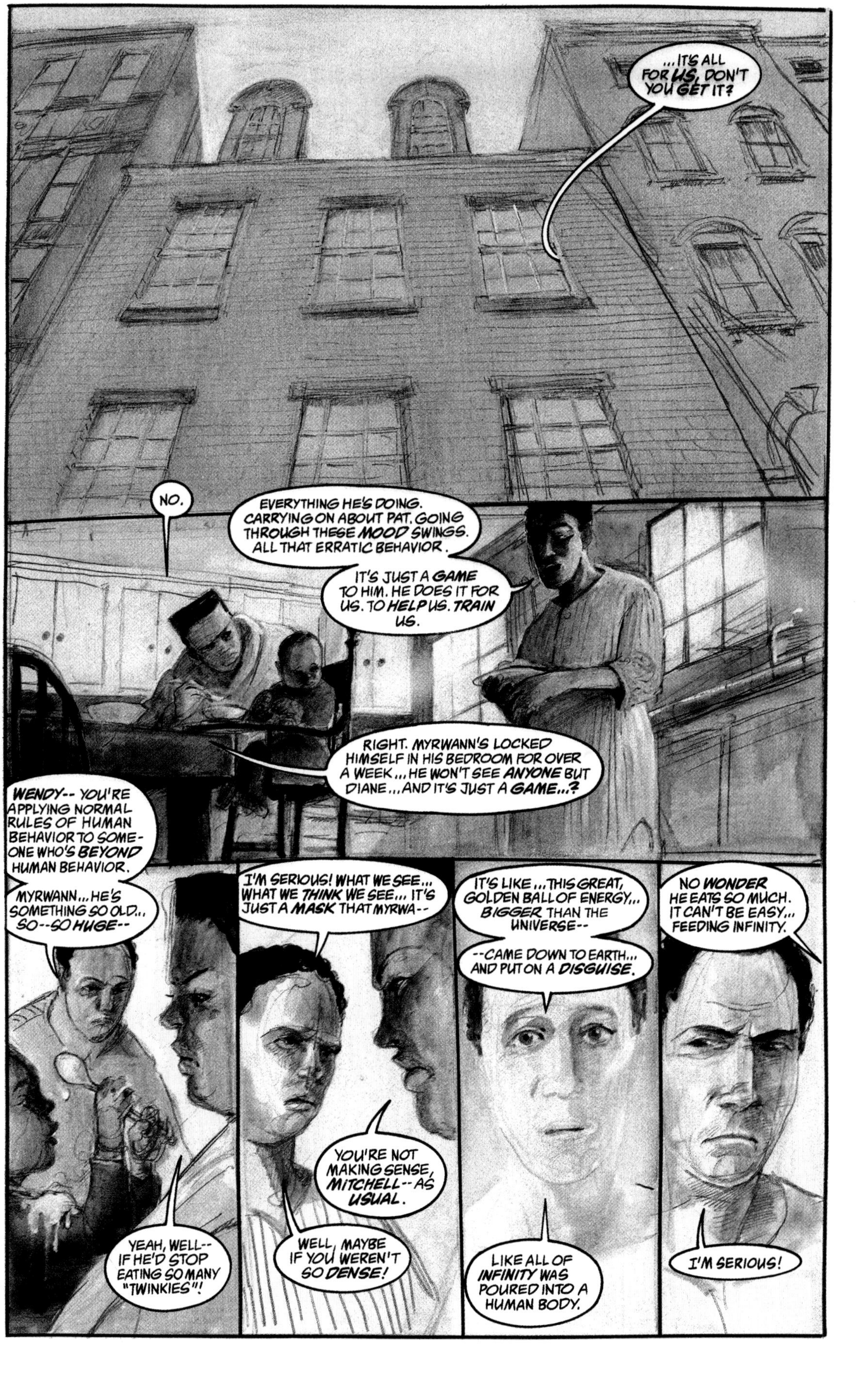
...IT'S ALL FOR US, DON'T YOU GET IT?
NO.
EVERYTHING HE'S DOING. CARRYING ON ABOUT PAT. GOING THROUGH THESE MOOD SWINGS. ALL THAT ERRATIC BEHAVIOR.
IT'S JUST A GAME TO HIM. HE DOES IT FOR US. TO HELP US. TRAIN US.
RIGHT. MYRWANN'S LOCKED HIMSELF IN HIS BEDROOM FOR OVER A WEEK... HE WON'T SEE ANYONE BUT DIANE... AND IT'S JUST A GAME...?
WENDY-- YOU'RE APPLYING NORMAL RULES OF HUMAN BEHAVIOR TO SOMEONE WHO'S BEYOND HUMAN BEHAVIOR.
MYRWANN... HE'S SOMETHING SO OLD... SO--SO HUGE--
YEAH, WELL-- IF HE'D STOP EATING SO MANY "TWINKIES"!
I'M SERIOUS! WHAT WE SEE... WHAT WE THINK WE SEE... IT'S JUST A MASK THAT MYRWA--
YOU'RE NOT MAKING SENSE, MITCHELL-- AS USUAL.
WELL, MAYBE IF YOU WEREN'T SO DENSE!
IT'S LIKE... THIS GREAT, GOLDEN BALL OF ENERGY... BIGGER THAN THE UNIVERSE--
--CAME DOWN TO EARTH... AND PUT ON A DISGUISE.
LIKE ALL OF INFINITY WAS POURED INTO A HUMAN BODY.
NO WONDER HE EATS SO MUCH. IT CAN'T BE EASY... FEEDING INFINITY.
I'M SERIOUS!

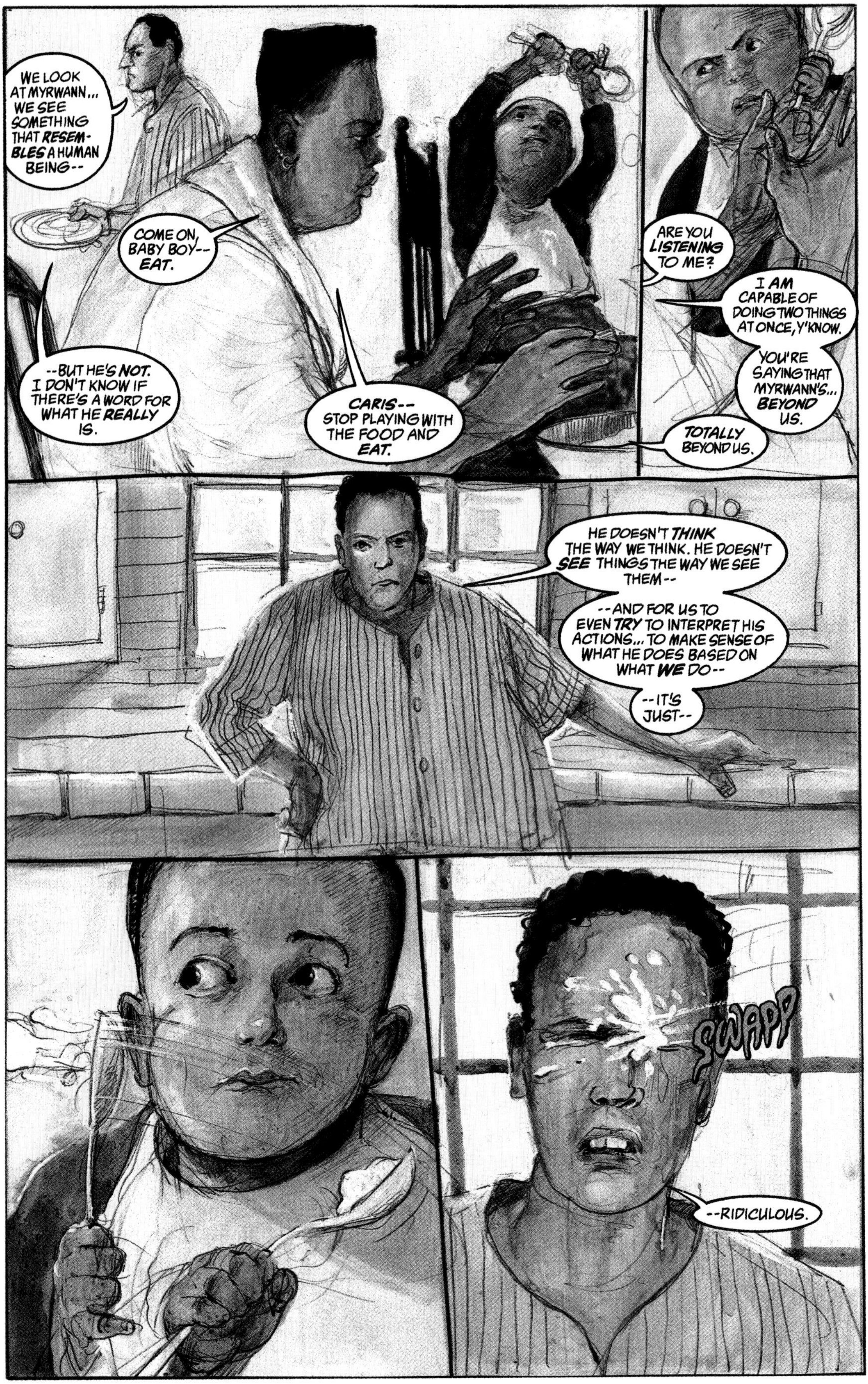
WE LOOK AT MYRWANN... WE SEE SOMETHING THAT RESEMBLES A HUMAN BEING--
COME ON, BABY BOY-- EAT.
--BUT HE'S NOT. I DON'T KNOW IF THERE'S A WORD FOR WHAT HE REALLY IS.
CARIS-- STOP PLAYING WITH THE FOOD AND EAT.
ARE YOU LISTENING TO ME?
I AM CAPABLE OF DOING TWO THINGS AT ONCE, Y'KNOW.
YOU'RE SAYING THAT MYRWANN'S... BEYOND US.
TOTALLY BEYOND US.
HE DOESN'T THINK THE WAY WE THINK. HE DOESN'T SEE THINGS THE WAY WE SEE THEM--
--AND FOR US TO EVEN TRY TO INTERPRET HIS ACTIONS... TO MAKE SENSE OF WHAT HE DOES BASED ON WHAT WE DO--
--IT'S JUST--
SWAPP
--RIDICULOUS.

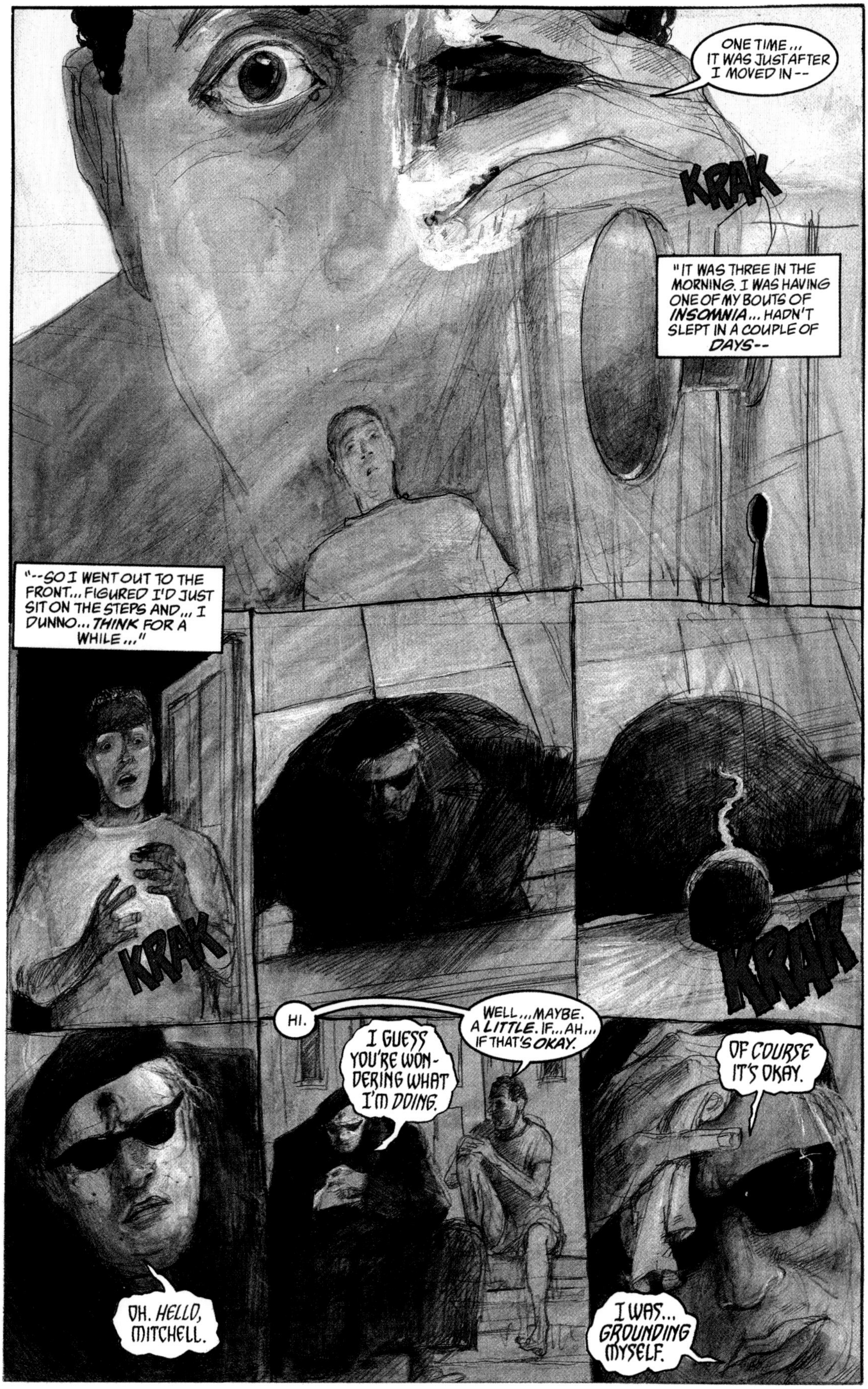

ONE TIME... IT WAS JUST AFTER I MOVED IN--
KRAK
"IT WAS THREE IN THE MORNING. I WAS HAVING ONE OF MY BOUTS OF INSOMNIA... HADN'T SLEPT IN A COUPLE OF DAYS--
"--SO I WENT OUT TO THE FRONT... FIGURED I'D JUST SIT ON THE STEPS AND... I DUNNO... THINK FOR A WHILE..."
KRAK
KRAK
OH. HELLO, MITCHELL.
HI.
I GUESS YOU'RE WONDERING WHAT I'M DOING.
WELL... MAYBE. A LITTLE. IF... AH... IF THAT'S OKAY.
OF COURSE IT'S OKAY.
I WAS... GROUNDING MYSELF.

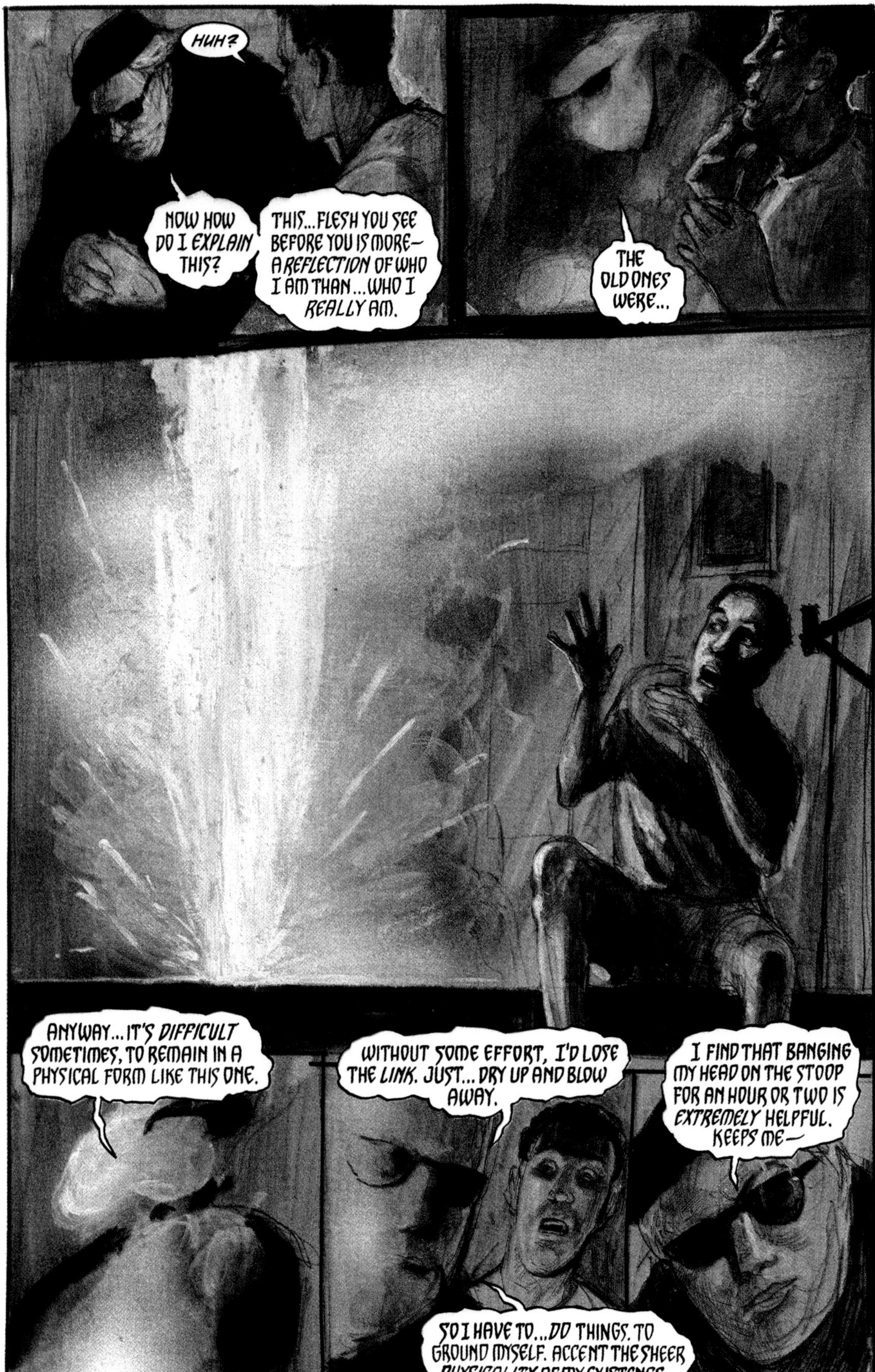
HUH?
NOW HOW DO I *EXPLAIN* THIS?
THIS... FLESH YOU SEE BEFORE YOU IS MORE— A *REFLECTION* OF WHO I AM THAN... WHO I *REALLY* AM.
THE OLD ONES WERE...
ANYWAY... IT'S *DIFFICULT* SOMETIMES, TO REMAIN IN A PHYSICAL FORM LIKE THIS ONE.
WITHOUT SOME EFFORT, I'D LOSE THE *LINK*. JUST... DRY UP AND BLOW AWAY.
SO I HAVE TO... *DO* THINGS. TO GROUND MYSELF. ACCENT THE SHEER *PHYSICALITY* OF MY EXISTENCE.
I FIND THAT BANGING MY HEAD ON THE STOOP FOR AN HOUR OR TWO IS *EXTREMELY* HELPFUL. KEEPS ME—

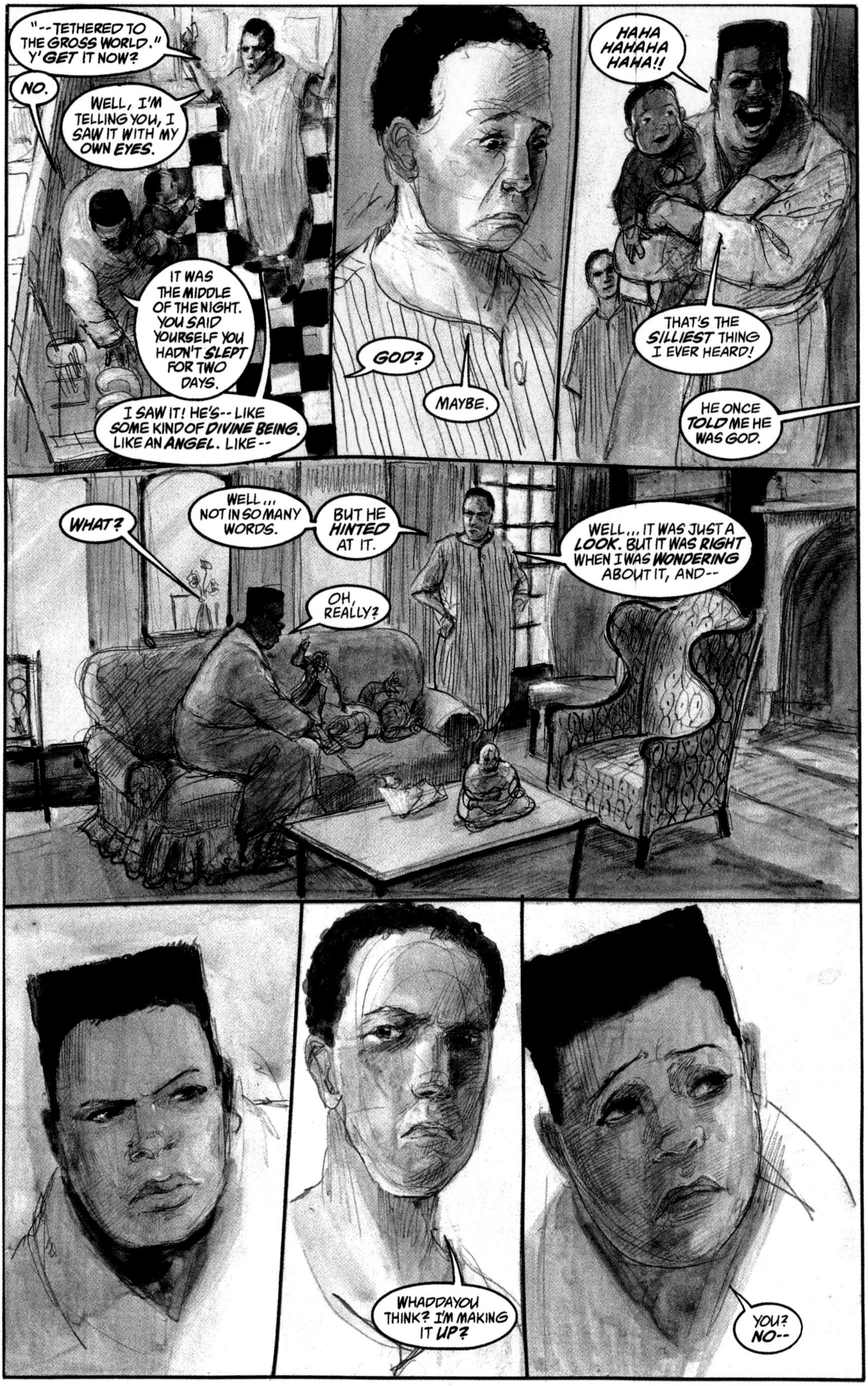
"--TETHERED TO THE GROSS WORLD." Y' GET IT NOW?
NO.
WELL, I'M TELLING YOU, I SAW IT WITH MY OWN EYES.
IT WAS THE MIDDLE OF THE NIGHT. YOU SAID YOURSELF YOU HADN'T SLEPT FOR TWO DAYS.
I SAW IT! HE'S-- LIKE SOME KIND OF DIVINE BEING. LIKE AN ANGEL. LIKE--
GOD?
MAYBE.
HAHA HAHAHA HAHA!!
THAT'S THE SILLIEST THING I EVER HEARD!
HE ONCE TOLD ME HE WAS GOD.
WHAT?
WELL... NOT IN SO MANY WORDS.
BUT HE HINTED AT IT.
OH, REALLY?
WELL... IT WAS JUST A LOOK. BUT IT WAS RIGHT WHEN I WAS WONDERING ABOUT IT, AND--
WHADDAYOU THINK? I'M MAKING IT UP?
YOU? NO--

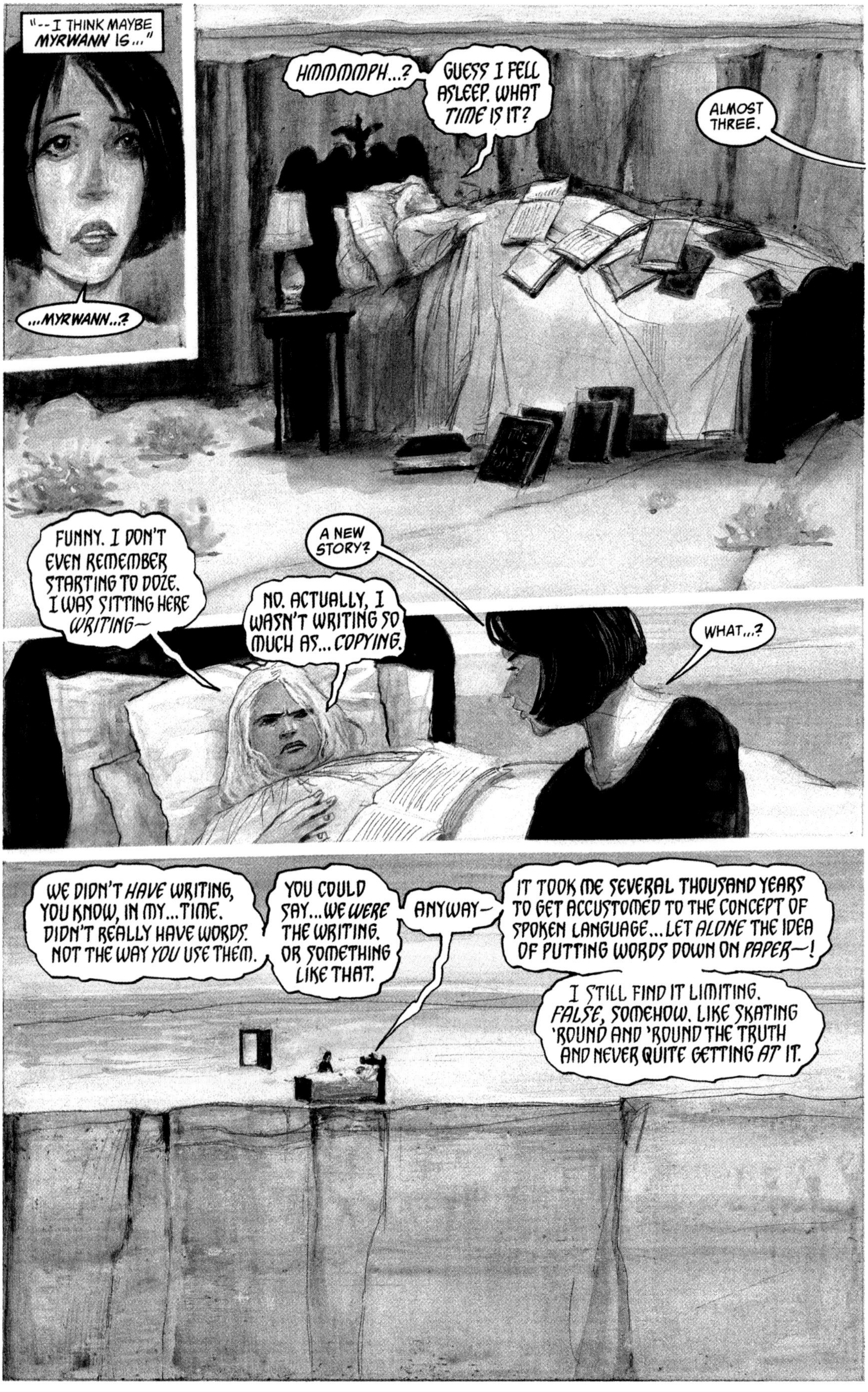
"--I THINK MAYBE MYRWANN IS..."
...MYRWANN...?
HMMMMPH...?
GUESS I FELL ASLEEP. WHAT TIME IS IT?
ALMOST THREE.
FUNNY. I DON'T EVEN REMEMBER STARTING TO DOZE. I WAS SITTING HERE WRITING—
A NEW STORY?
NO. ACTUALLY, I WASN'T WRITING SO MUCH AS... COPYING.
WHAT...?
WE DIDN'T HAVE WRITING, YOU KNOW, IN MY...TIME. DIDN'T REALLY HAVE WORDS. NOT THE WAY YOU USE THEM.
YOU COULD SAY...WE WERE THE WRITING. OR SOMETHING LIKE THAT.
ANYWAY—
IT TOOK ME SEVERAL THOUSAND YEARS TO GET ACCUSTOMED TO THE CONCEPT OF SPOKEN LANGUAGE...LET ALONE THE IDEA OF PUTTING WORDS DOWN ON PAPER—!
I STILL FIND IT LIMITING. FALSE, SOMEHOW. LIKE SKATING 'ROUND AND 'ROUND THE TRUTH AND NEVER QUITE GETTING AT IT.

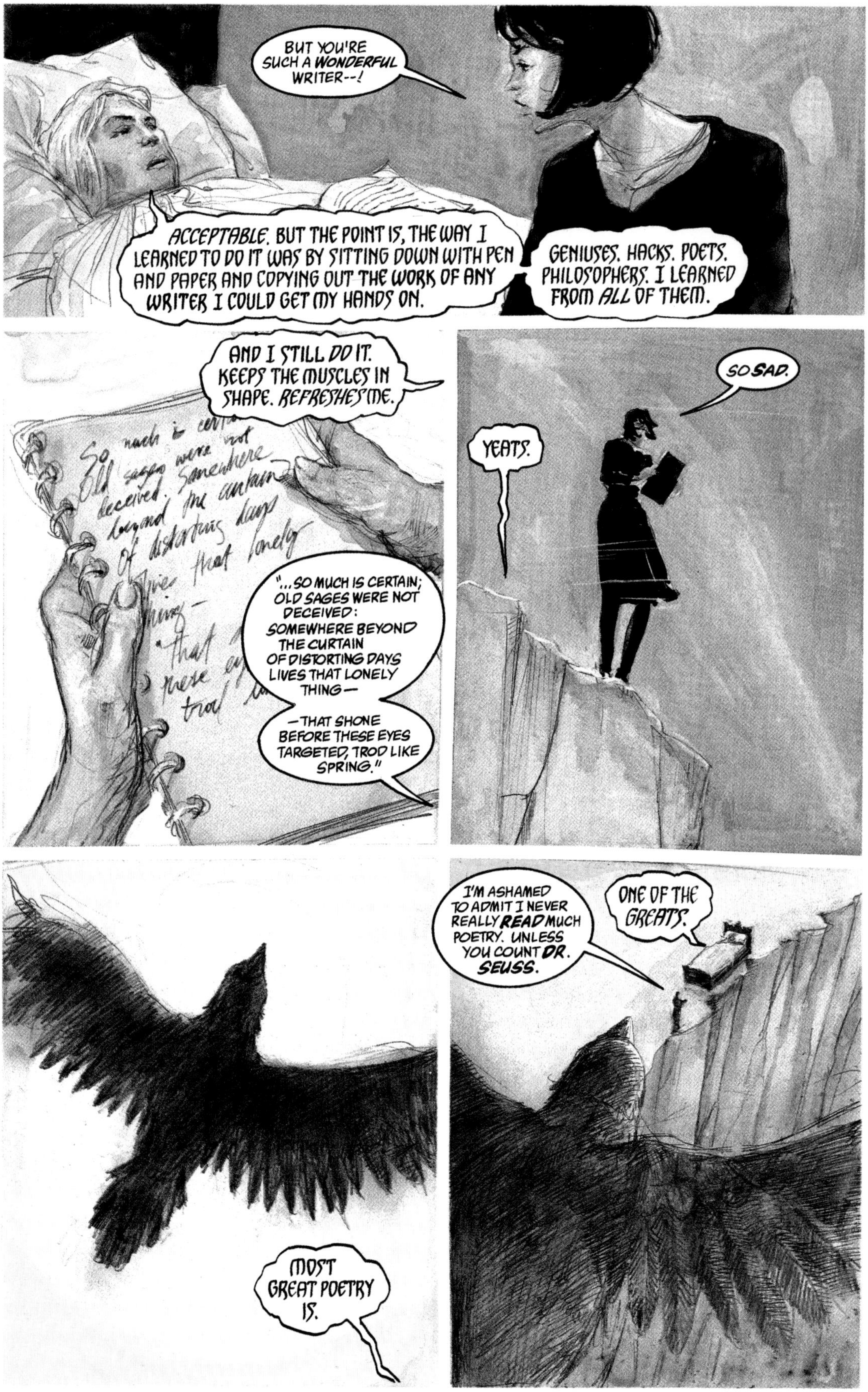
BUT YOU'RE SUCH A WONDERFUL WRITER--!
ACCEPTABLE. BUT THE POINT IS, THE WAY I LEARNED TO DO IT WAS BY SITTING DOWN WITH PEN AND PAPER AND COPYING OUT THE WORK OF ANY WRITER I COULD GET MY HANDS ON.
GENIUSES. HACKS. POETS. PHILOSOPHERS. I LEARNED FROM ALL OF THEM.
AND I STILL DO IT. KEEPS THE MUSCLES IN SHAPE. REFRESHES ME.
"...SO MUCH IS CERTAIN; OLD SAGES WERE NOT DECEIVED: SOMEWHERE BEYOND THE CURTAIN OF DISTORTING DAYS LIVES THAT LONELY THING—
—THAT SHONE BEFORE THESE EYES TARGETED, TROD LIKE SPRING."
SO SAD.
YEATS.
MOST GREAT POETRY IS.
I'M ASHAMED TO ADMIT I NEVER REALLY READ MUCH POETRY. UNLESS YOU COUNT DR. SEUSS.
ONE OF THE GREATS.

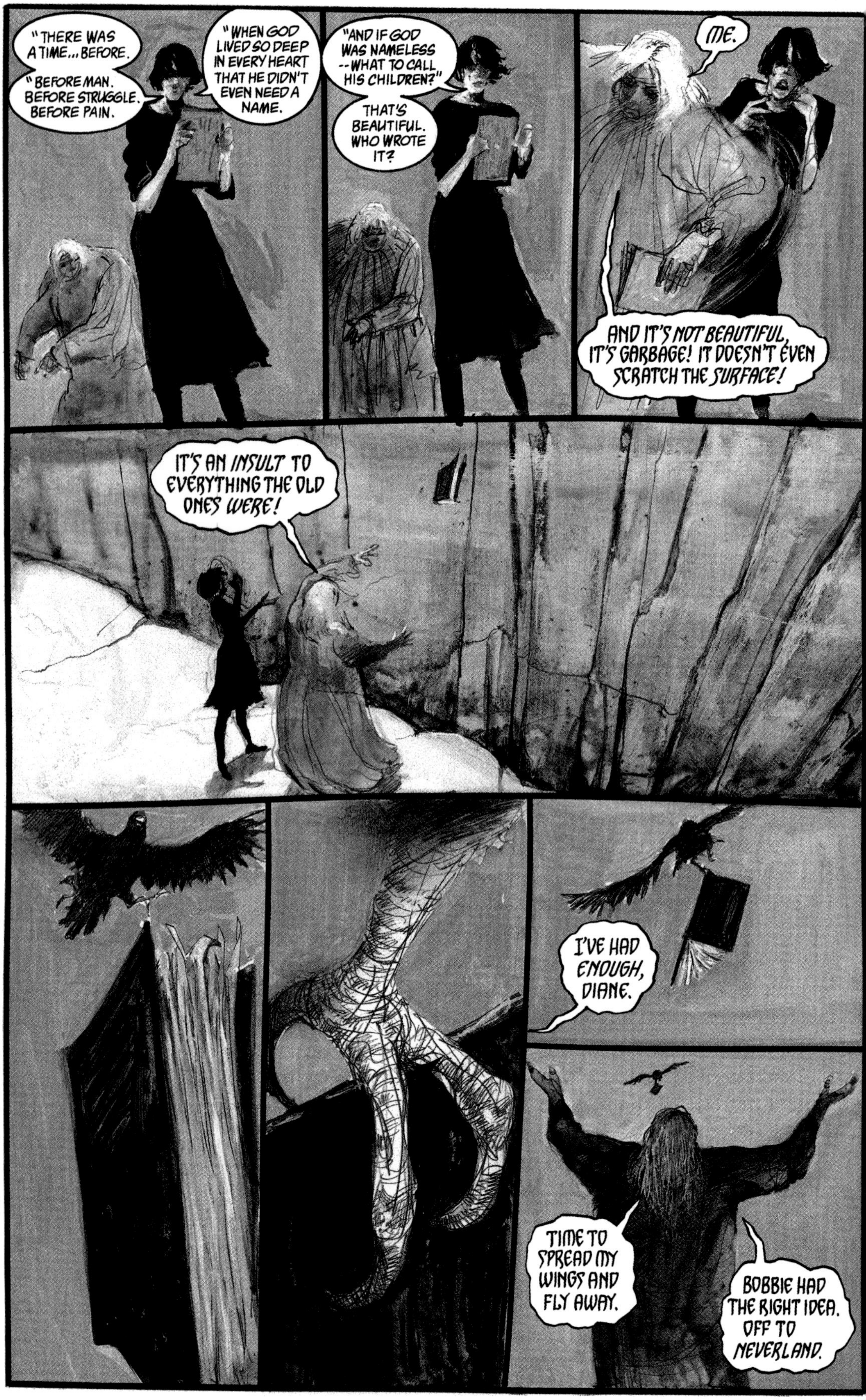
"THERE WAS A TIME... BEFORE.
"BEFORE MAN. BEFORE STRUGGLE. BEFORE PAIN.
"WHEN GOD LIVED SO DEEP IN EVERY HEART THAT HE DIDN'T EVEN NEED A NAME.
"AND IF GOD WAS NAMELESS --WHAT TO CALL HIS CHILDREN?"
THAT'S BEAUTIFUL. WHO WROTE IT?
ME.
AND IT'S NOT BEAUTIFUL, IT'S GARBAGE! IT DOESN'T EVEN SCRATCH THE SURFACE!
IT'S AN INSULT TO EVERYTHING THE OLD ONES WERE!
I'VE HAD ENOUGH, DIANE.
TIME TO SPREAD MY WINGS AND FLY AWAY.
BOBBIE HAD THE RIGHT IDEA. OFF TO NEVERLAND.

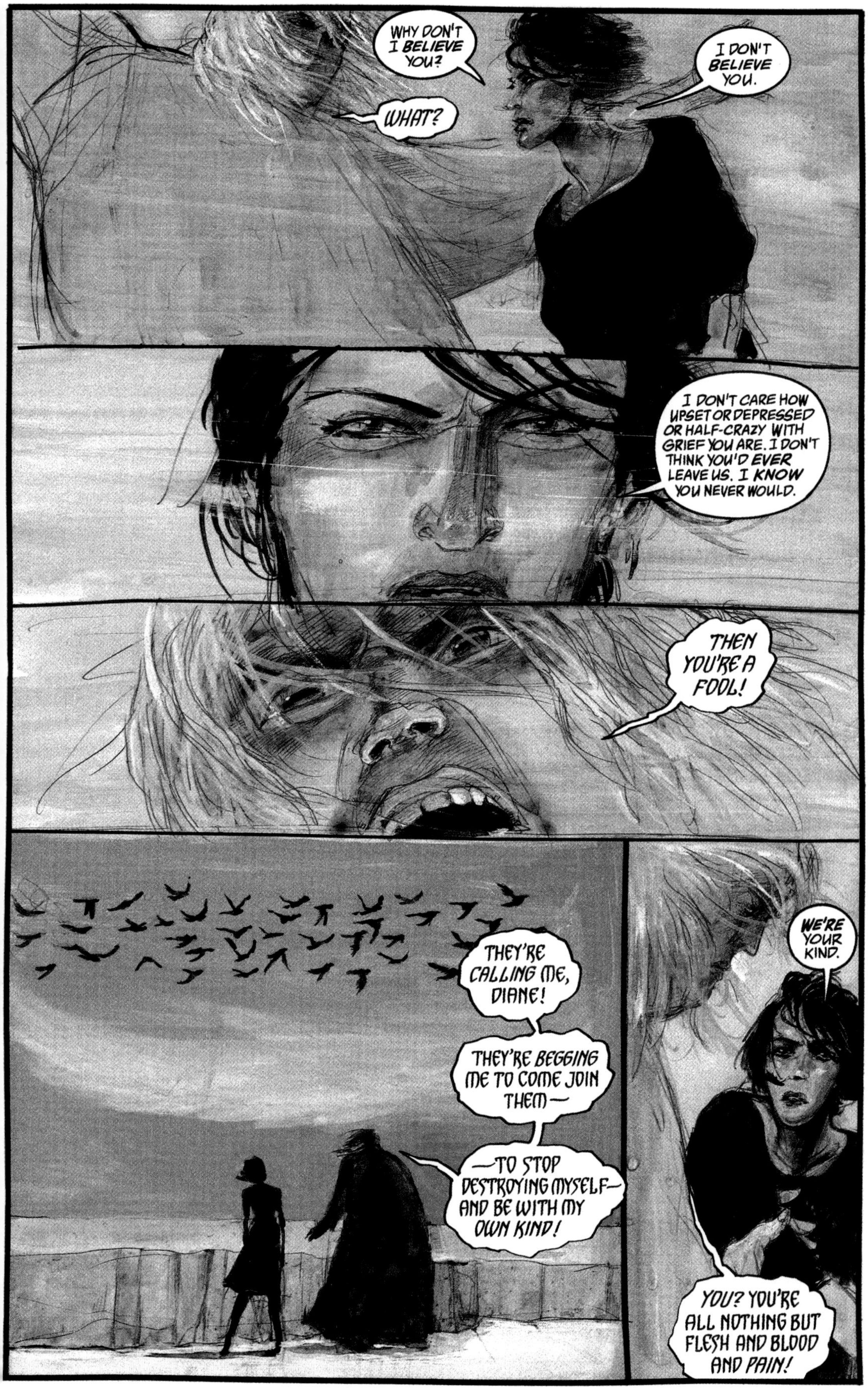
WHY DON'T I BELIEVE YOU?
I DON'T BELIEVE YOU.
WHAT?
I DON'T CARE HOW UPSET OR DEPRESSED OR HALF-CRAZY WITH GRIEF YOU ARE. I DON'T THINK YOU'D EVER LEAVE US. I KNOW YOU NEVER WOULD.
THEN YOU'RE A FOOL!
THEY'RE CALLING ME, DIANE!
THEY'RE BEGGING ME TO COME JOIN THEM—
—TO STOP DESTROYING MYSELF— AND BE WITH MY OWN KIND!
WE'RE YOUR KIND.
YOU? YOU'RE ALL NOTHING BUT FLESH AND BLOOD AND PAIN!

THE MORE TIME I SPEND AMONG YOU NEW ONES...THE MORE OF YOUR PAIN I ABSORB.

IT'S GETTING SO I CAN'T TELL WHERE YOUR PAIN ENDS AND MY OWN BEGINS.

YOU ONCE TOLD ME THAT OUR SUFFERING... IS JUST A PAPER WALL. ALL WE'VE GOTTA DO IS PUSH THROUGH IT AND--

YOU DON'T UNDERSTAND! YOU COULDN'T POSSIBLY UNDERSTAND!

I UNDERSTAND BETTER THAN YOU DO--

GET OUT.

--AND THAT'S WHY I'M NOT LEAVING, EITHER.

GET OUT!!

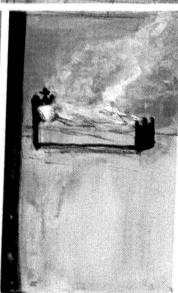

...YOU'RE SAYING THAT MYRWANN'S A LIAR?

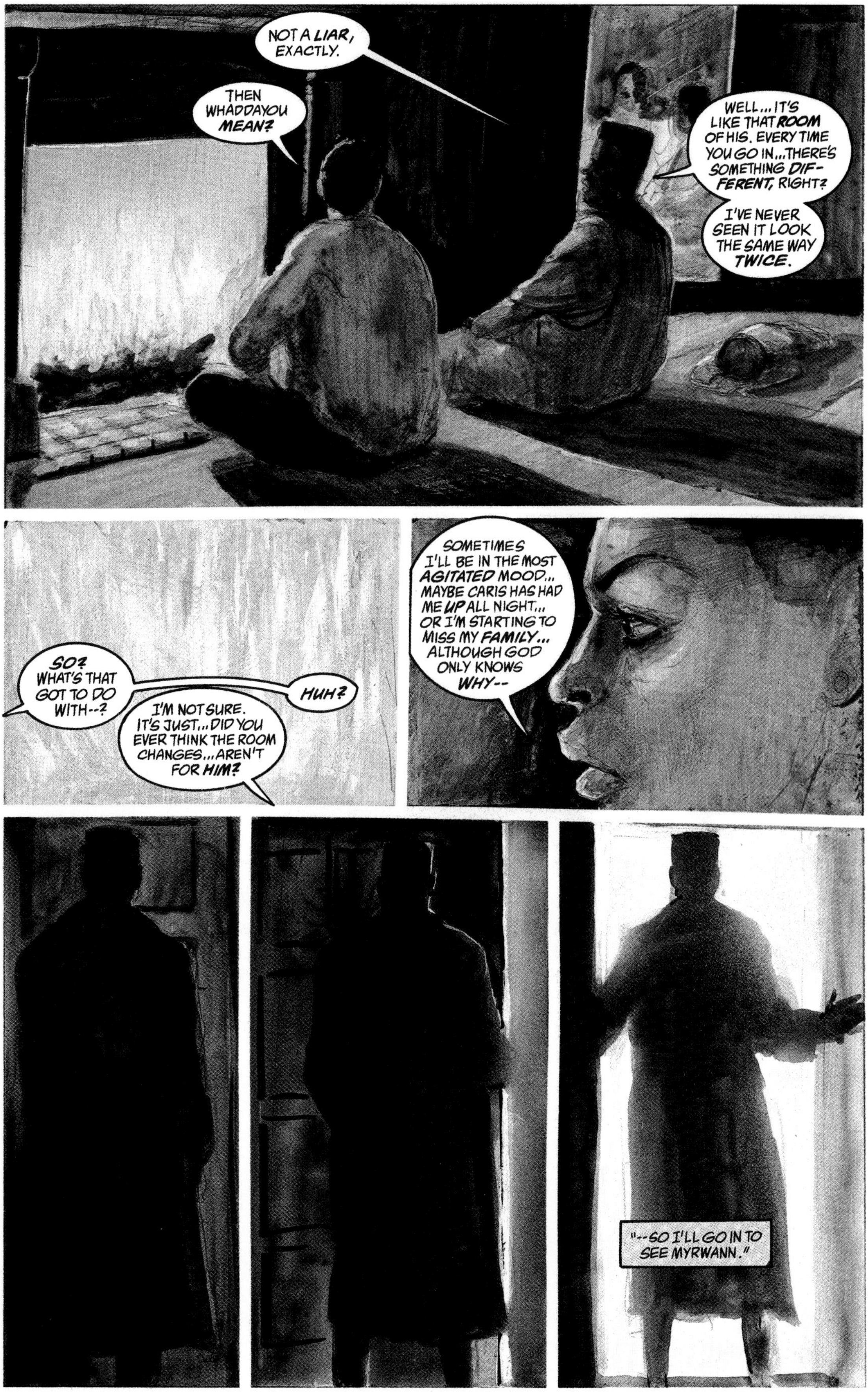

NOT A LIAR, EXACTLY.
THEN WHADDAYOU MEAN?
WELL... IT'S LIKE THAT ROOM OF HIS. EVERY TIME YOU GO IN... THERE'S SOMETHING DIF-FERENT, RIGHT?
I'VE NEVER SEEN IT LOOK THE SAME WAY TWICE.
SOMETIMES I'LL BE IN THE MOST AGITATED MOOD... MAYBE CARIS HAS HAD ME UP ALL NIGHT... OR I'M STARTING TO MISS MY FAMILY... ALTHOUGH GOD ONLY KNOWS WHY--
SO? WHAT'S THAT GOT TO DO WITH--?
HUH?
I'M NOT SURE. IT'S JUST... DID YOU EVER THINK THE ROOM CHANGES... AREN'T FOR HIM?
"--SO I'LL GO IN TO SEE MYRWANN."

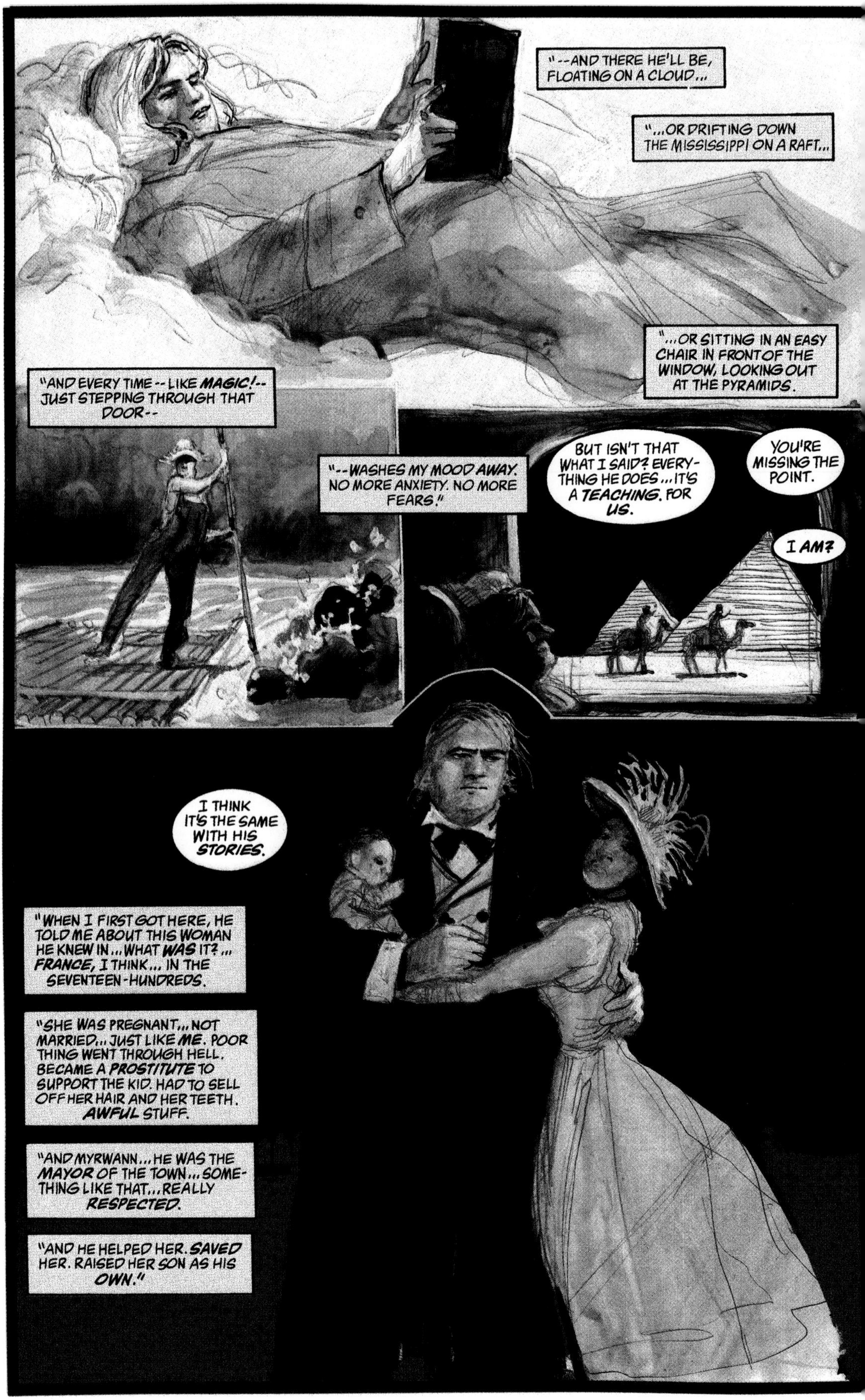
"--AND THERE HE'LL BE, FLOATING ON A CLOUD...
"...OR DRIFTING DOWN THE MISSISSIPPI ON A RAFT...
"...OR SITTING IN AN EASY CHAIR IN FRONT OF THE WINDOW, LOOKING OUT AT THE PYRAMIDS.
"AND EVERY TIME -- LIKE MAGIC! -- JUST STEPPING THROUGH THAT DOOR--
"--WASHES MY MOOD AWAY. NO MORE ANXIETY. NO MORE FEARS."
BUT ISN'T THAT WHAT I SAID? EVERYTHING HE DOES... IT'S A TEACHING. FOR US.
YOU'RE MISSING THE POINT.
I AM?
I THINK IT'S THE SAME WITH HIS STORIES.
"WHEN I FIRST GOT HERE, HE TOLD ME ABOUT THIS WOMAN HE KNEW IN... WHAT WAS IT?... FRANCE, I THINK... IN THE SEVENTEEN-HUNDREDS.
"SHE WAS PREGNANT... NOT MARRIED... JUST LIKE ME. POOR THING WENT THROUGH HELL. BECAME A PROSTITUTE TO SUPPORT THE KID. HAD TO SELL OFF HER HAIR AND HER TEETH. AWFUL STUFF.
"AND MYRWANN... HE WAS THE MAYOR OF THE TOWN... SOMETHING LIKE THAT... REALLY RESPECTED.
"AND HE HELPED HER. SAVED HER. RAISED HER SON AS HIS OWN."

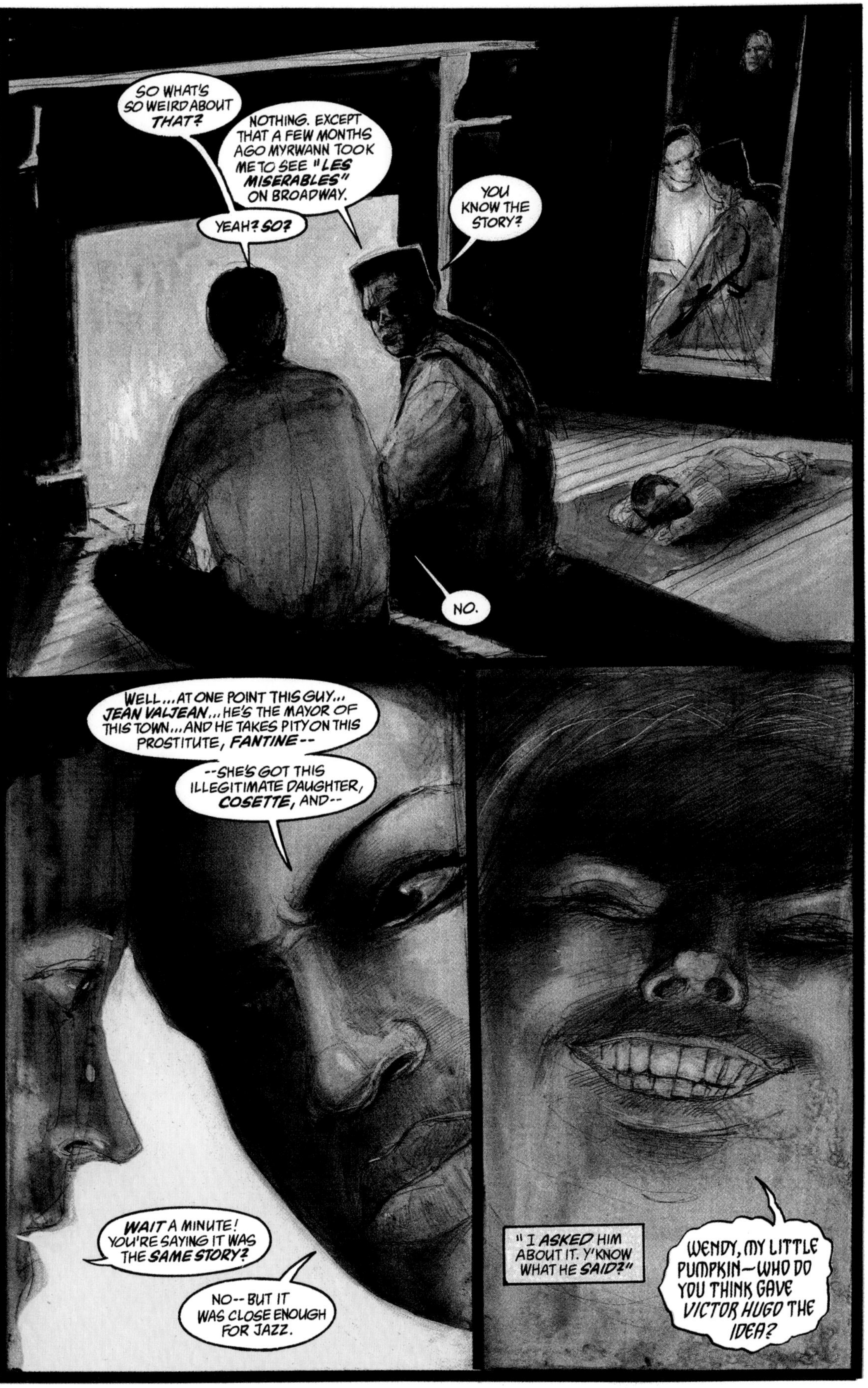
SO WHAT'S SO WEIRD ABOUT THAT?
NOTHING. EXCEPT THAT A FEW MONTHS AGO MYRWANN TOOK ME TO SEE "LES MISERABLES" ON BROADWAY.
YEAH? SO?
YOU KNOW THE STORY?
NO.
WELL... AT ONE POINT THIS GUY... JEAN VALJEAN... HE'S THE MAYOR OF THIS TOWN... AND HE TAKES PITY ON THIS PROSTITUTE, FANTINE--
--SHE'S GOT THIS ILLEGITIMATE DAUGHTER, COSETTE, AND--
WAIT A MINUTE! YOU'RE SAYING IT WAS THE SAME STORY?
NO-- BUT IT WAS CLOSE ENOUGH FOR JAZZ.
"I ASKED HIM ABOUT IT. Y'KNOW WHAT HE SAID?"
WENDY, MY LITTLE PUMPKIN— WHO DO YOU THINK GAVE VICTOR HUGO THE IDEA?

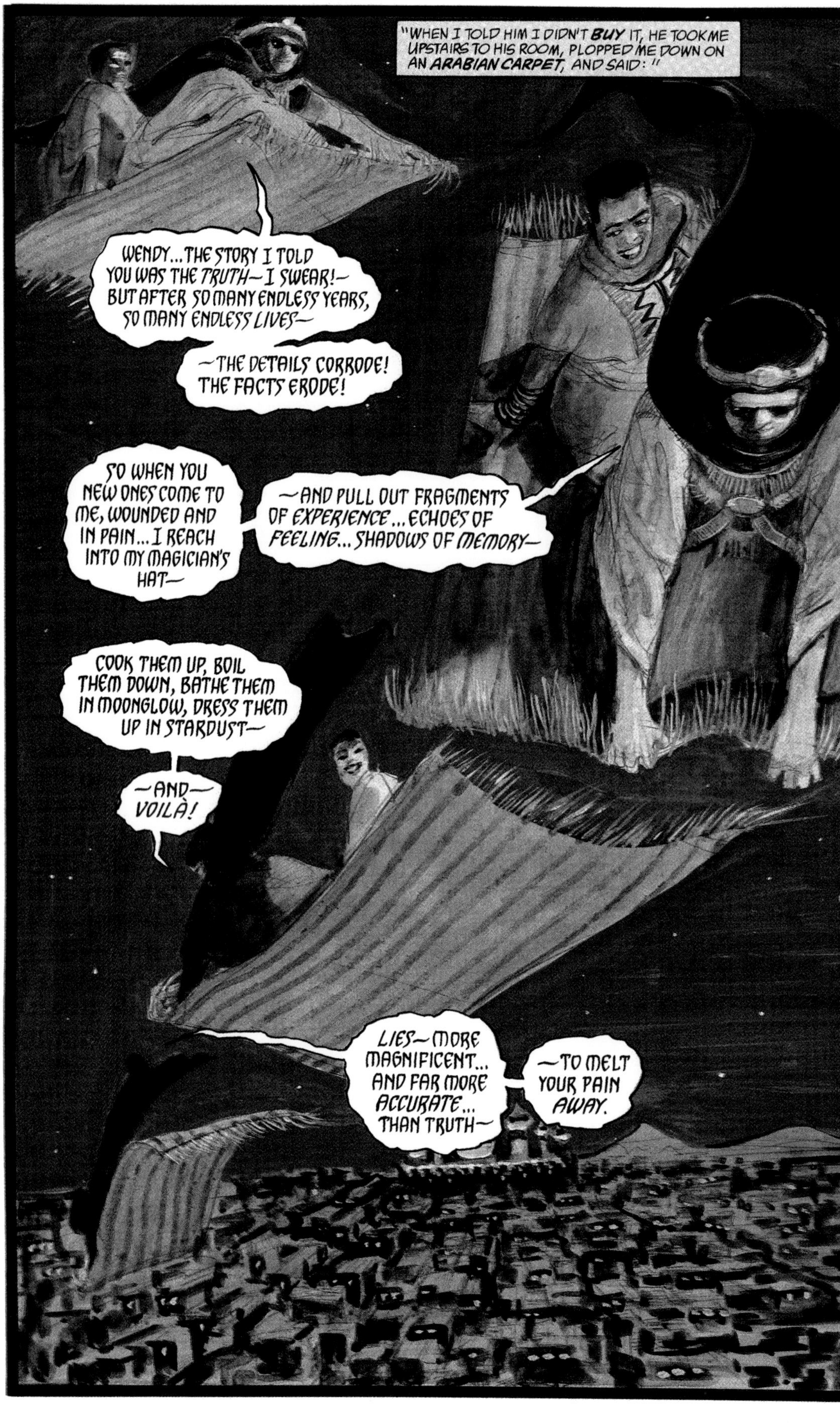
"WHEN I TOLD HIM I DIDN'T BUY IT, HE TOOK ME UPSTAIRS TO HIS ROOM, PLOPPED ME DOWN ON AN ARABIAN CARPET, AND SAID:"
WENDY... THE STORY I TOLD YOU WAS THE TRUTH— I SWEAR!— BUT AFTER SO MANY ENDLESS YEARS, SO MANY ENDLESS LIVES—
—THE DETAILS CORRODE! THE FACTS ERODE!
SO WHEN YOU NEW ONES COME TO ME, WOUNDED AND IN PAIN... I REACH INTO MY MAGICIAN'S HAT—
—AND PULL OUT FRAGMENTS OF EXPERIENCE... ECHOES OF FEELING... SHADOWS OF MEMORY—
COOK THEM UP, BOIL THEM DOWN, BATHE THEM IN MOONGLOW, DRESS THEM UP IN STARDUST—
—AND— VOILÀ!
LIES—MORE MAGNIFICENT... AND FAR MORE ACCURATE... THAN TRUTH—
—TO MELT YOUR PAIN AWAY.

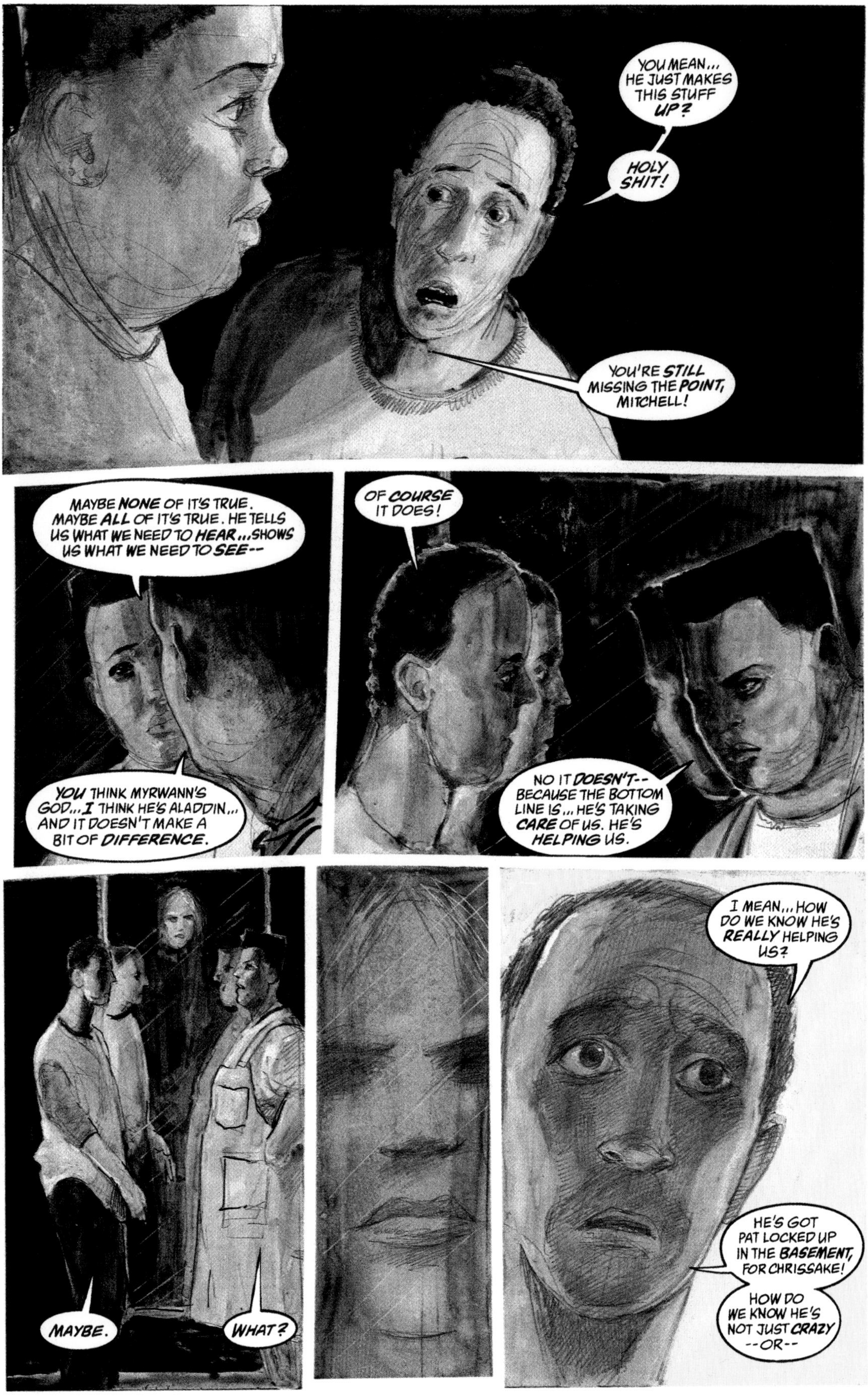
YOU MEAN... HE JUST MAKES THIS STUFF UP?
HOLY SHIT!
YOU'RE STILL MISSING THE POINT, MITCHELL!
MAYBE NONE OF IT'S TRUE. MAYBE ALL OF IT'S TRUE. HE TELLS US WHAT WE NEED TO HEAR... SHOWS US WHAT WE NEED TO SEE--
YOU THINK MYRWANN'S GOD... I THINK HE'S ALADDIN... AND IT DOESN'T MAKE A BIT OF DIFFERENCE.
OF COURSE IT DOES!
NO IT DOESN'T-- BECAUSE THE BOTTOM LINE IS... HE'S TAKING CARE OF US. HE'S HELPING US.
MAYBE.
WHAT?
I MEAN... HOW DO WE KNOW HE'S REALLY HELPING US?
HE'S GOT PAT LOCKED UP IN THE BASEMENT, FOR CHRISSAKE!
HOW DO WE KNOW HE'S NOT JUST CRAZY --OR--

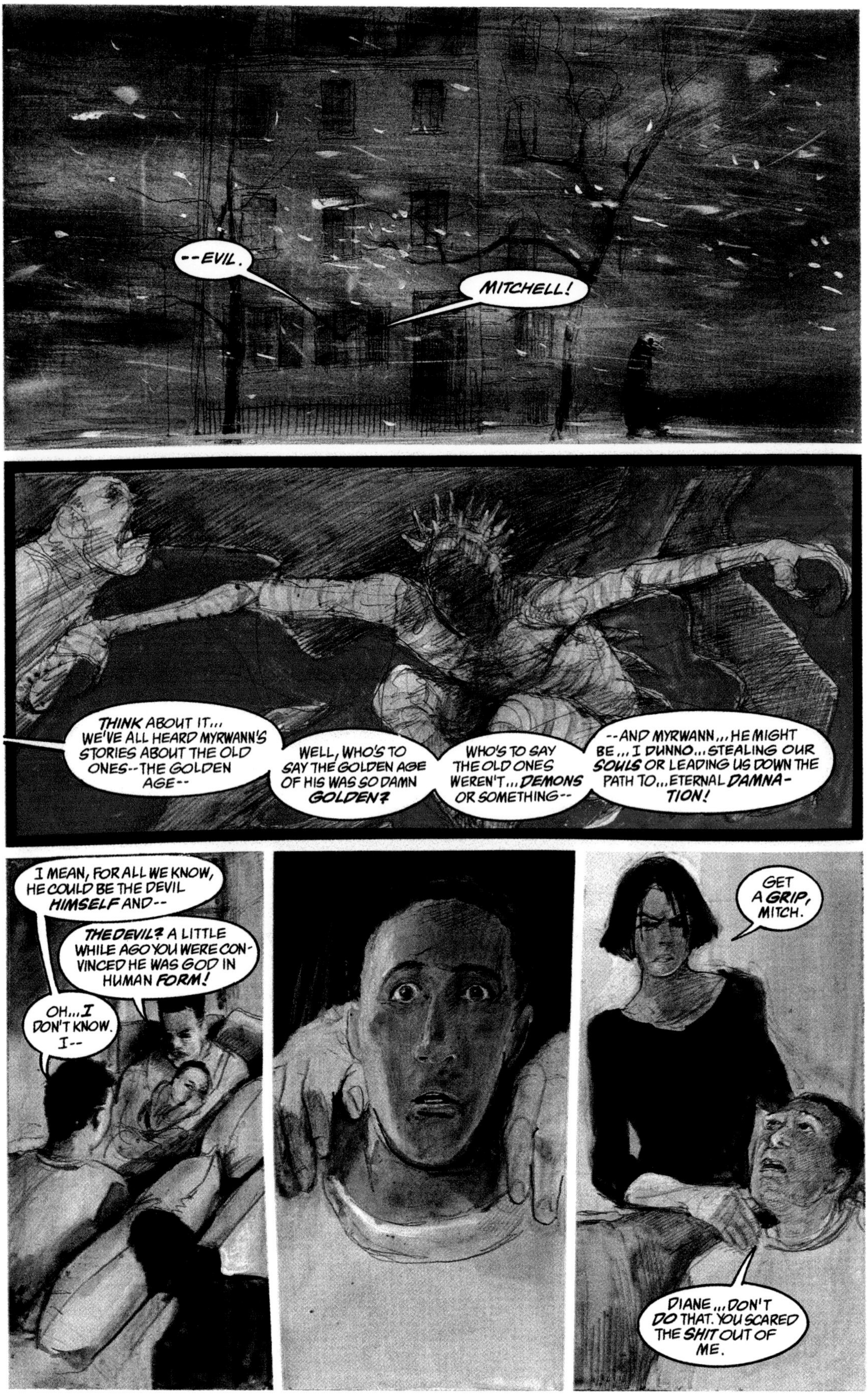
--EVIL.
MITCHELL!
THINK ABOUT IT... WE'VE ALL HEARD MYRWANN'S STORIES ABOUT THE OLD ONES--THE GOLDEN AGE--
WELL, WHO'S TO SAY THE GOLDEN AGE OF HIS WAS SO DAMN GOLDEN?
WHO'S TO SAY THE OLD ONES WEREN'T... DEMONS OR SOMETHING--
--AND MYRWANN... HE MIGHT BE... I DUNNO... STEALING OUR SOULS OR LEADING US DOWN THE PATH TO... ETERNAL DAMNATION!
I MEAN, FOR ALL WE KNOW, HE COULD BE THE DEVIL HIMSELF AND--
THE DEVIL? A LITTLE WHILE AGO YOU WERE CONVINCED HE WAS GOD IN HUMAN FORM!
OH... I DON'T KNOW. I--
GET A GRIP, MITCH.
DIANE... DON'T DO THAT. YOU SCARED THE SHIT OUT OF ME.

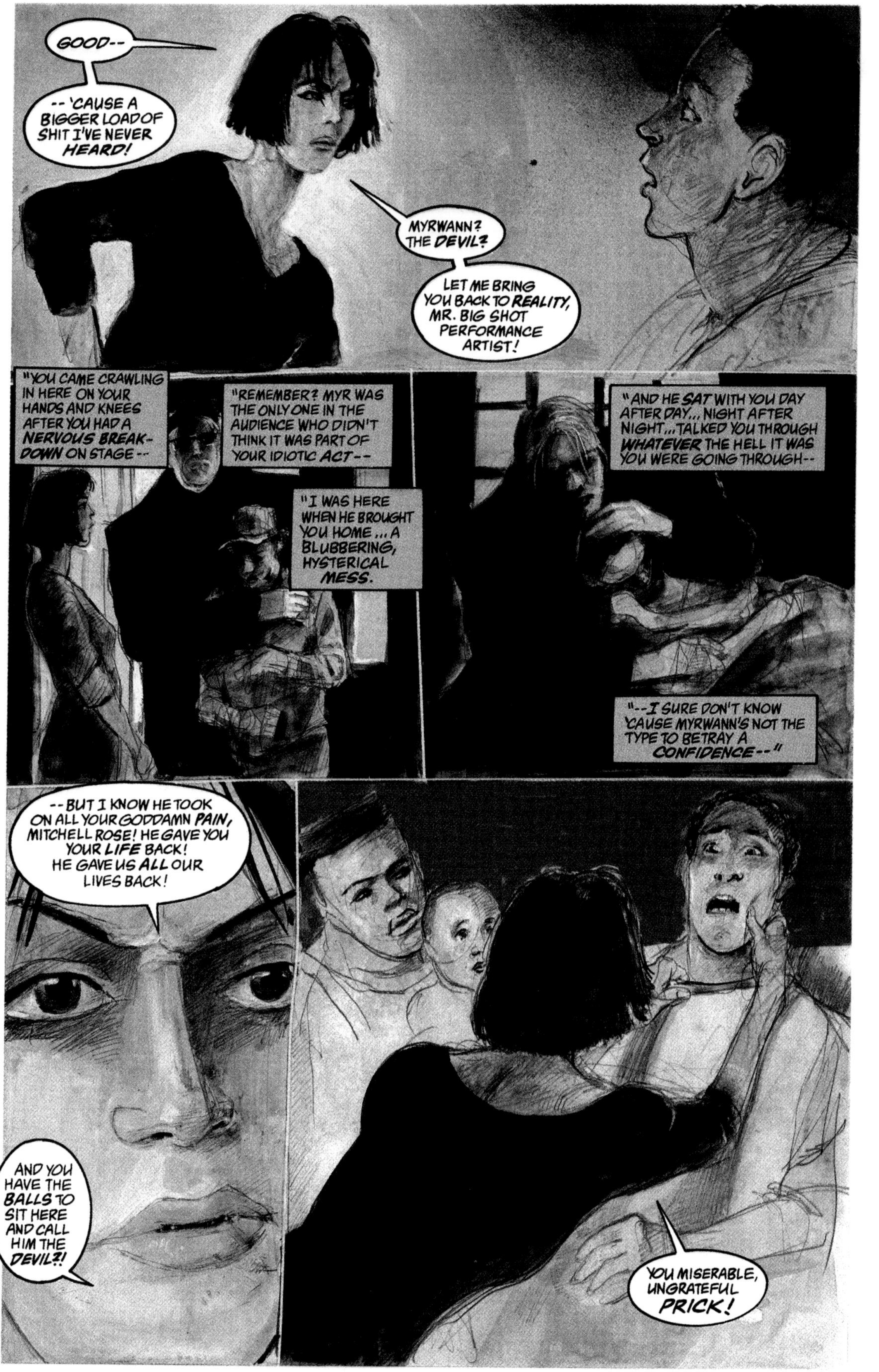
GOOD--
--'CAUSE A BIGGER LOAD OF SHIT I'VE NEVER HEARD!
MYRWANN? THE DEVIL?
LET ME BRING YOU BACK TO REALITY, MR. BIG SHOT PERFORMANCE ARTIST!
"YOU CAME CRAWLING IN HERE ON YOUR HANDS AND KNEES AFTER YOU HAD A NERVOUS BREAK-DOWN ON STAGE--
"REMEMBER? MYR WAS THE ONLY ONE IN THE AUDIENCE WHO DIDN'T THINK IT WAS PART OF YOUR IDIOTIC ACT--
"I WAS HERE WHEN HE BROUGHT YOU HOME... A BLUBBERING, HYSTERICAL MESS.
"AND HE SAT WITH YOU DAY AFTER DAY... NIGHT AFTER NIGHT... TALKED YOU THROUGH WHATEVER THE HELL IT WAS YOU WERE GOING THROUGH--
"--I SURE DON'T KNOW 'CAUSE MYRWANN'S NOT THE TYPE TO BETRAY A CONFIDENCE--"
--BUT I KNOW HE TOOK ON ALL YOUR GODDAMN PAIN, MITCHELL ROSE! HE GAVE YOU YOUR LIFE BACK! HE GAVE US ALL OUR LIVES BACK!
AND YOU HAVE THE BALLS TO SIT HERE AND CALL HIM THE DEVIL?!
YOU MISERABLE, UNGRATEFUL PRICK!

DIANE ... TAKE IT *EASY!* MITCHELL AND I--WE WERE JUST... *THINKING OUT LOUD*--

YOU KNOW HOW IT IS...LATE AT NIGHT... WHEN YOU GET TO TALKING--

YOUR IMAGINATION STARTS GOING...YOU SAY THINGS YOU NORMALLY *WOULDN'T*...

HELL, I'VE THOUGHT THE SAME THINGS AS MITCH.

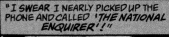

"FIRST MYRWANN'S GOD, THEN HE'S LUCIFER. ONE TIME I WAS *SURE* HE WAS ELVIS--

"I SWEAR I NEARLY PICKED UP THE PHONE AND CALLED *'THE NATIONAL ENQUIRER'!*"

THERE WAS THIS NIGHT... COUPLE WEEKS AFTER I FIRST MOVED IN. I WAS HOME *ALONE* WITH HER...

...AND MY MIND STARTS RACING. I TOTALLY CON-VINCE MYSELF THAT--

--GOD, THIS IS EMBARRASSING--

"--THAT SHE'S A *VAMPIRE.*

"I'M *SURE* SHE'S GONNA BUST INTO MY ROOM AND SUCK OUT EVERY LAST DROP OF MY *BLOOD.*"

I'M SO *WORRIED* ABOUT HER.

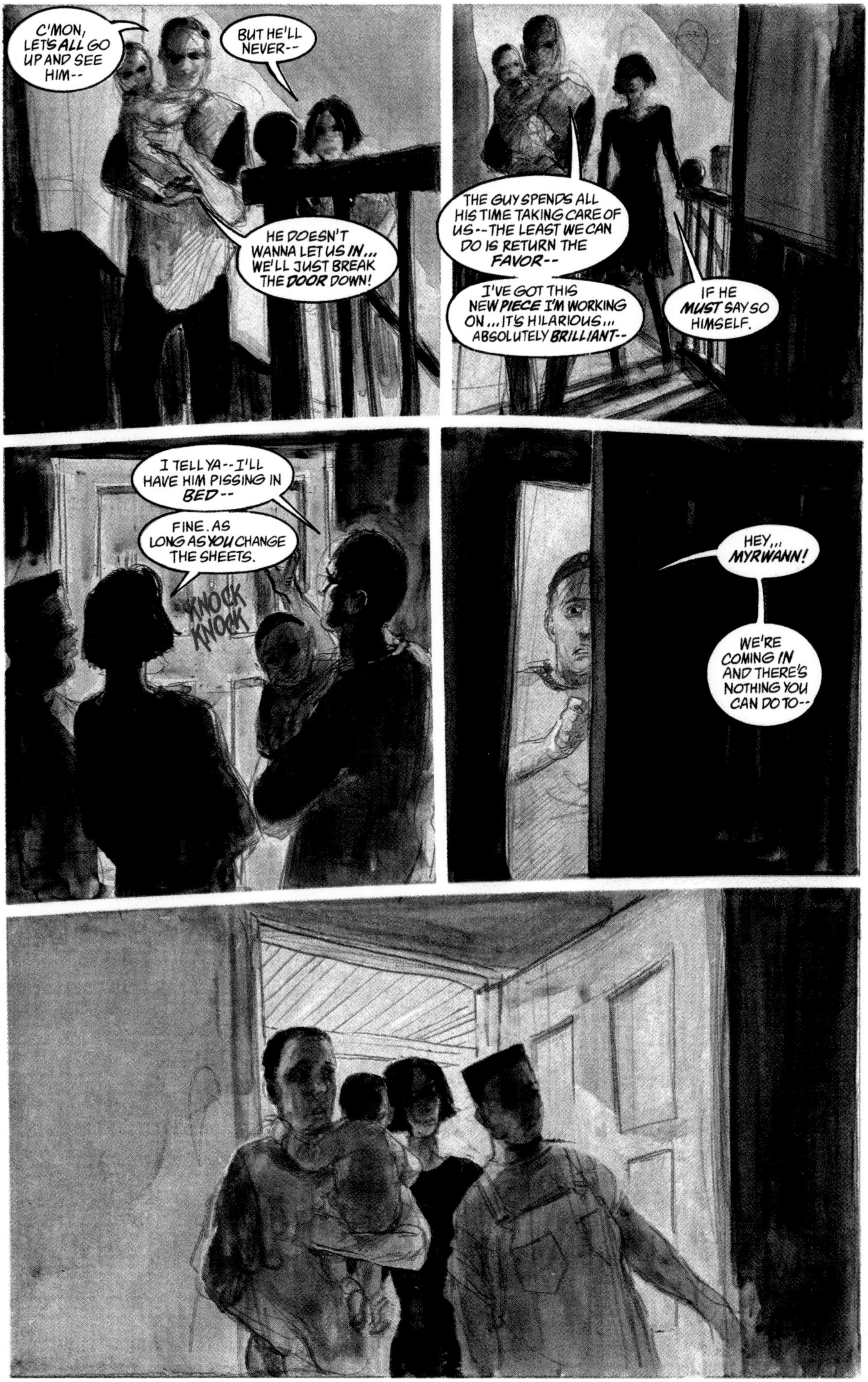
C'MON, LET'S ALL GO UP AND SEE HIM--
BUT HE'LL NEVER--
HE DOESN'T WANNA LET US IN... WE'LL JUST BREAK THE DOOR DOWN!
THE GUY SPENDS ALL HIS TIME TAKING CARE OF US--THE LEAST WE CAN DO IS RETURN THE FAVOR--
I'VE GOT THIS NEW PIECE I'M WORKING ON... IT'S HILARIOUS... ABSOLUTELY BRILLIANT--
IF HE MUST SAY SO HIMSELF.
I TELL YA--I'LL HAVE HIM PISSING IN BED--
FINE. AS LONG AS YOU CHANGE THE SHEETS.
KNOCK KNOCK
HEY... MYRWANN!
WE'RE COMING IN AND THERE'S NOTHING YOU CAN DO TO--

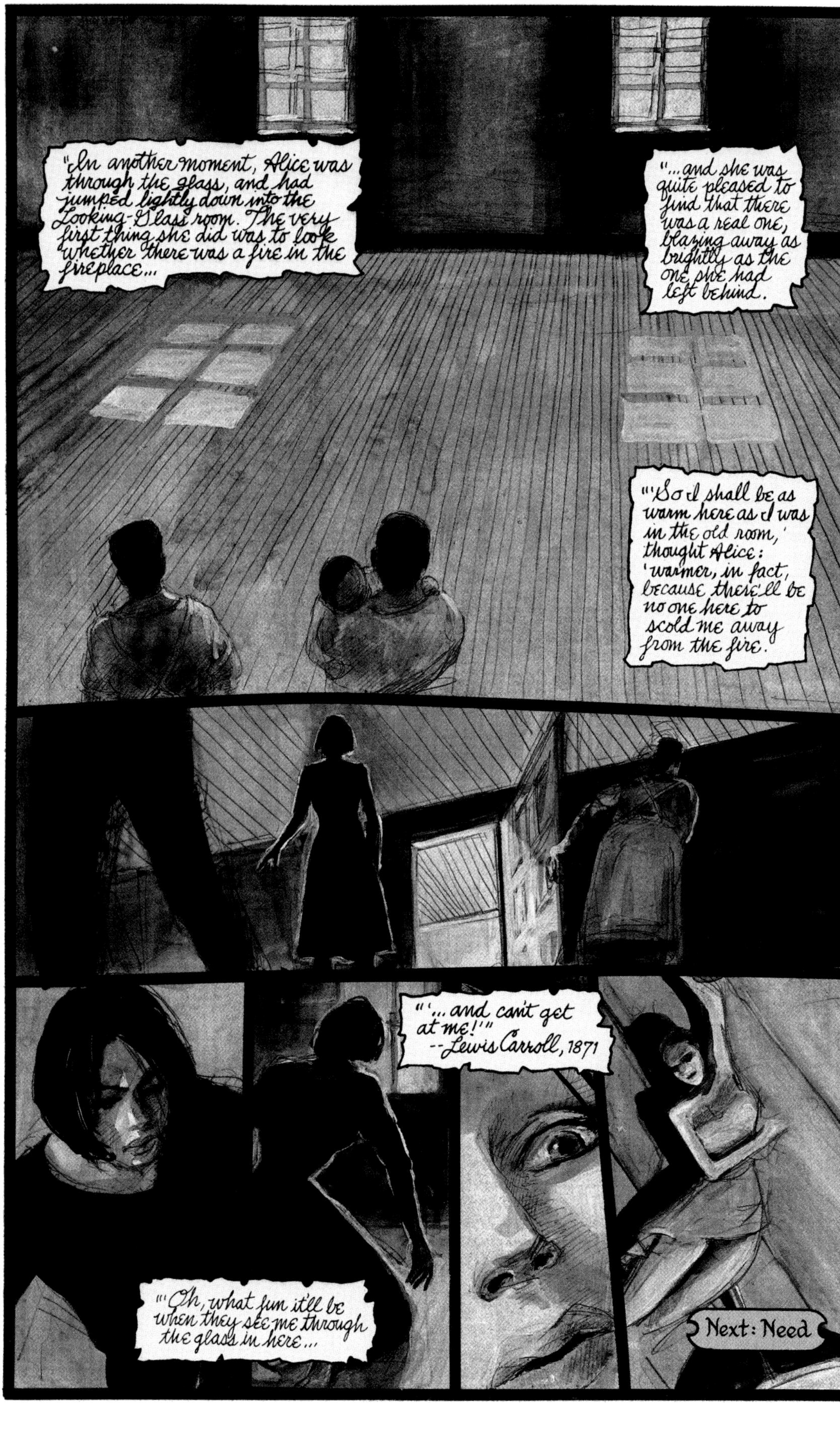
"In another moment, Alice was through the glass, and had jumped lightly down into the Looking-Glass room. The very first thing she did was to look whether there was a fire in the fireplace...
"...and she was quite pleased to find that there was a real one, blazing away as brightly as the one she had left behind.
"'So I shall be as warm here as I was in the old room,' thought Alice: 'warmer, in fact, because there'll be no one here to scold me away from the fire.
"'Oh, what fun it'll be when they see me through the glass in here...
"'...and can't get at me!'"
--Lewis Carroll, 1871
Next: Need

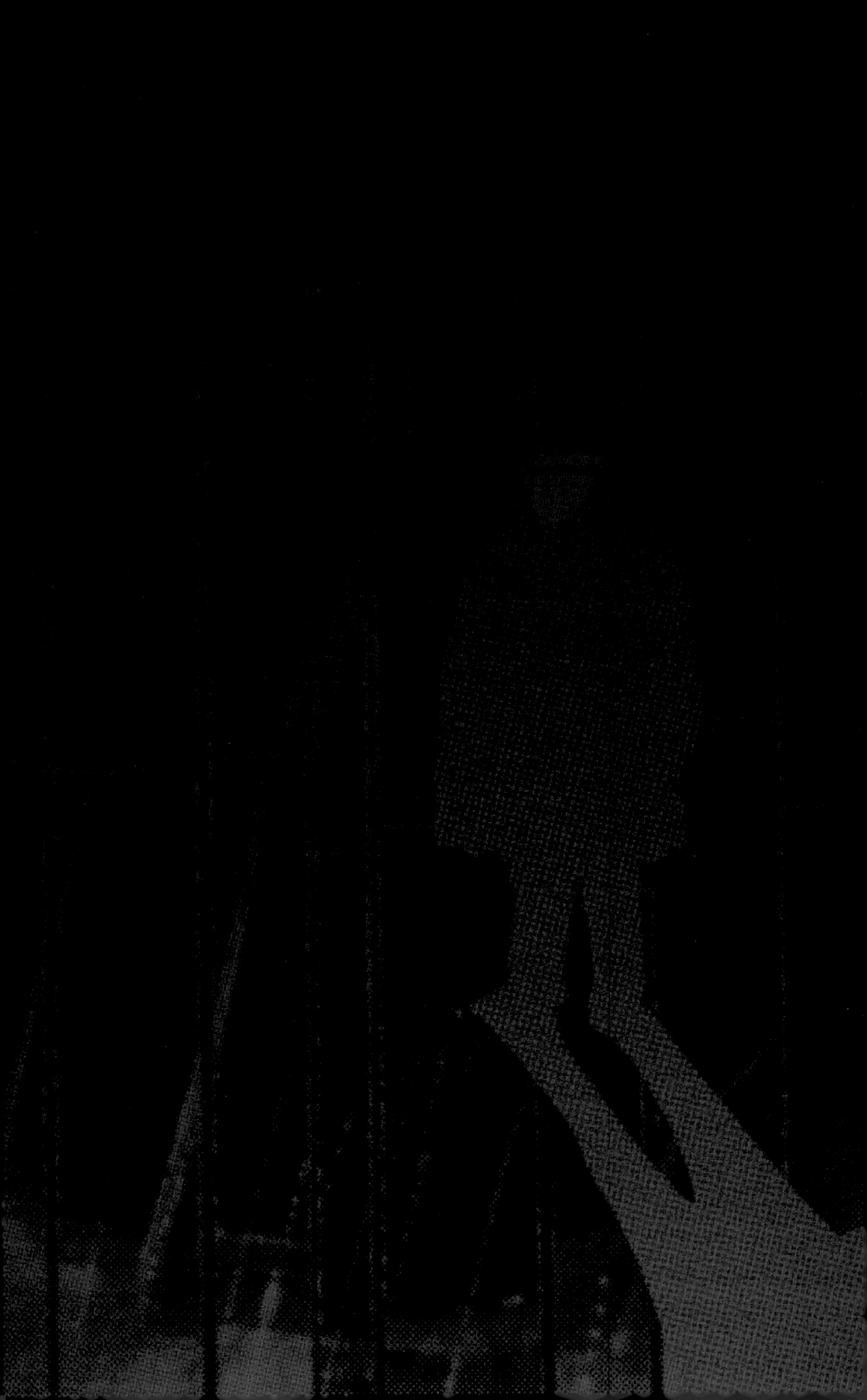

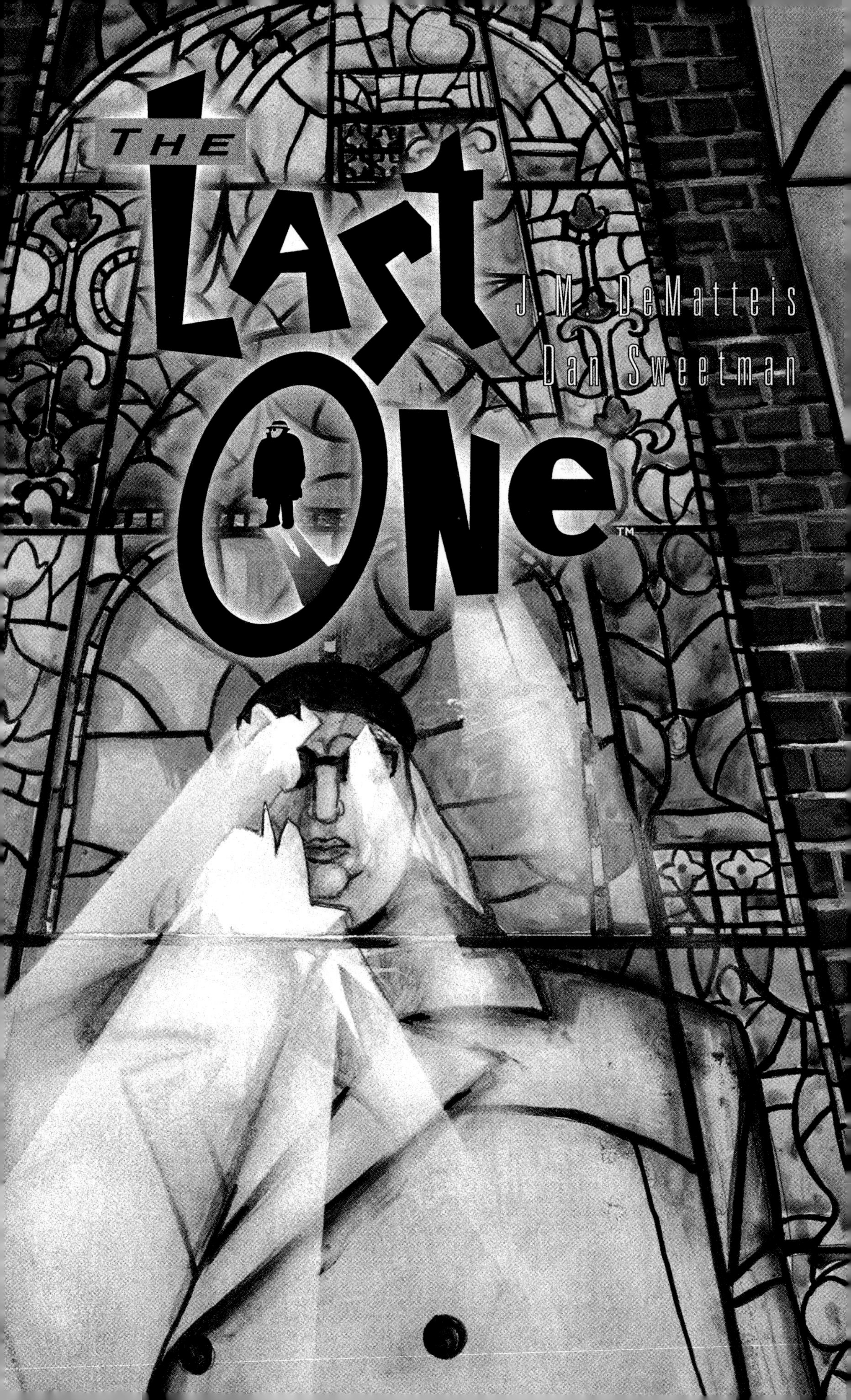
THE
Last
One™
J.M. DeMatteis
Dan Sweetman

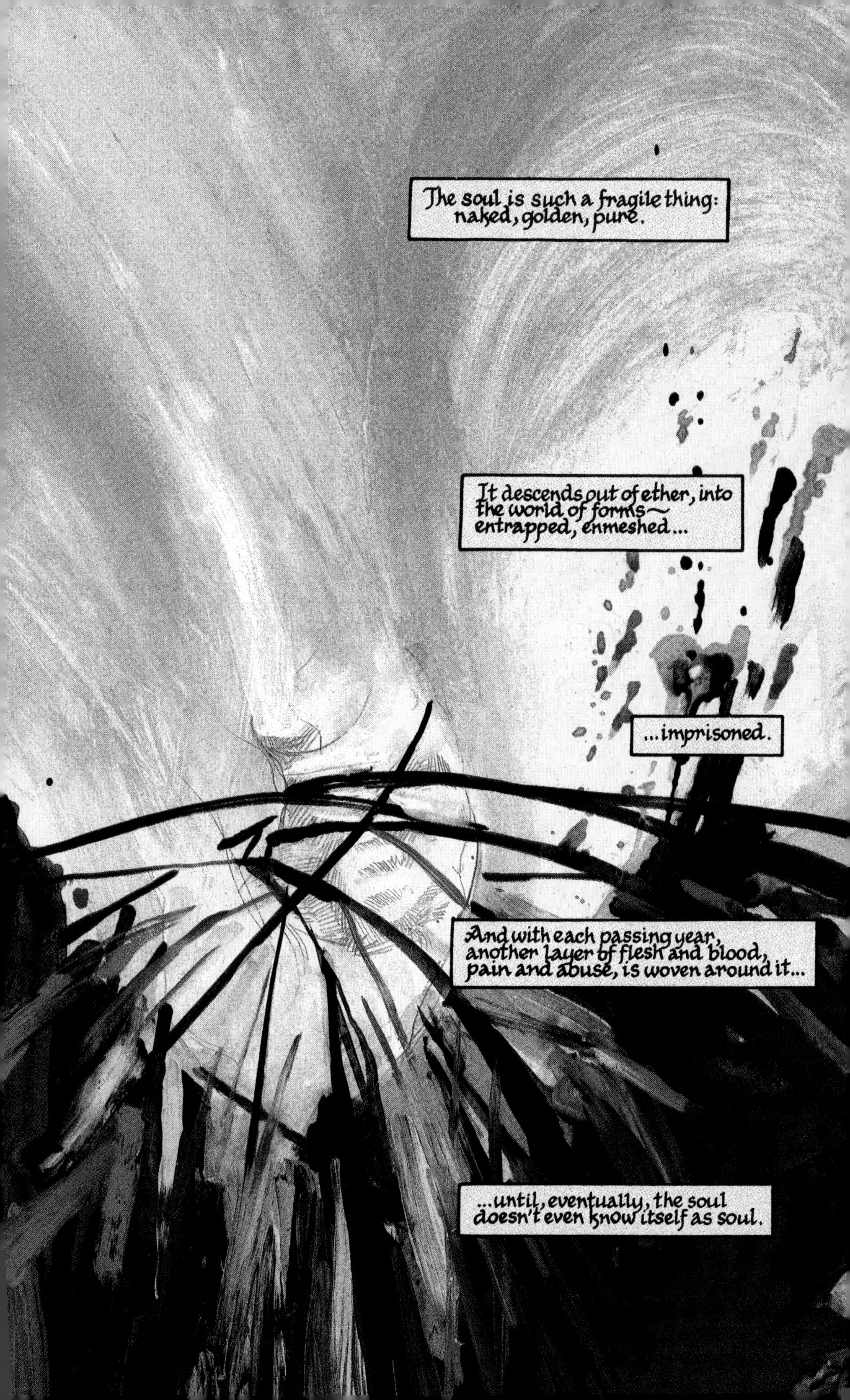
The soul is such a fragile thing: naked, golden, pure.
It descends out of ether, into the world of forms~ entrapped, enmeshed...
...imprisoned.
And with each passing year, another layer of flesh and blood, pain and abuse, is woven around it...
...until, eventually, the soul doesn't even know itself as soul.

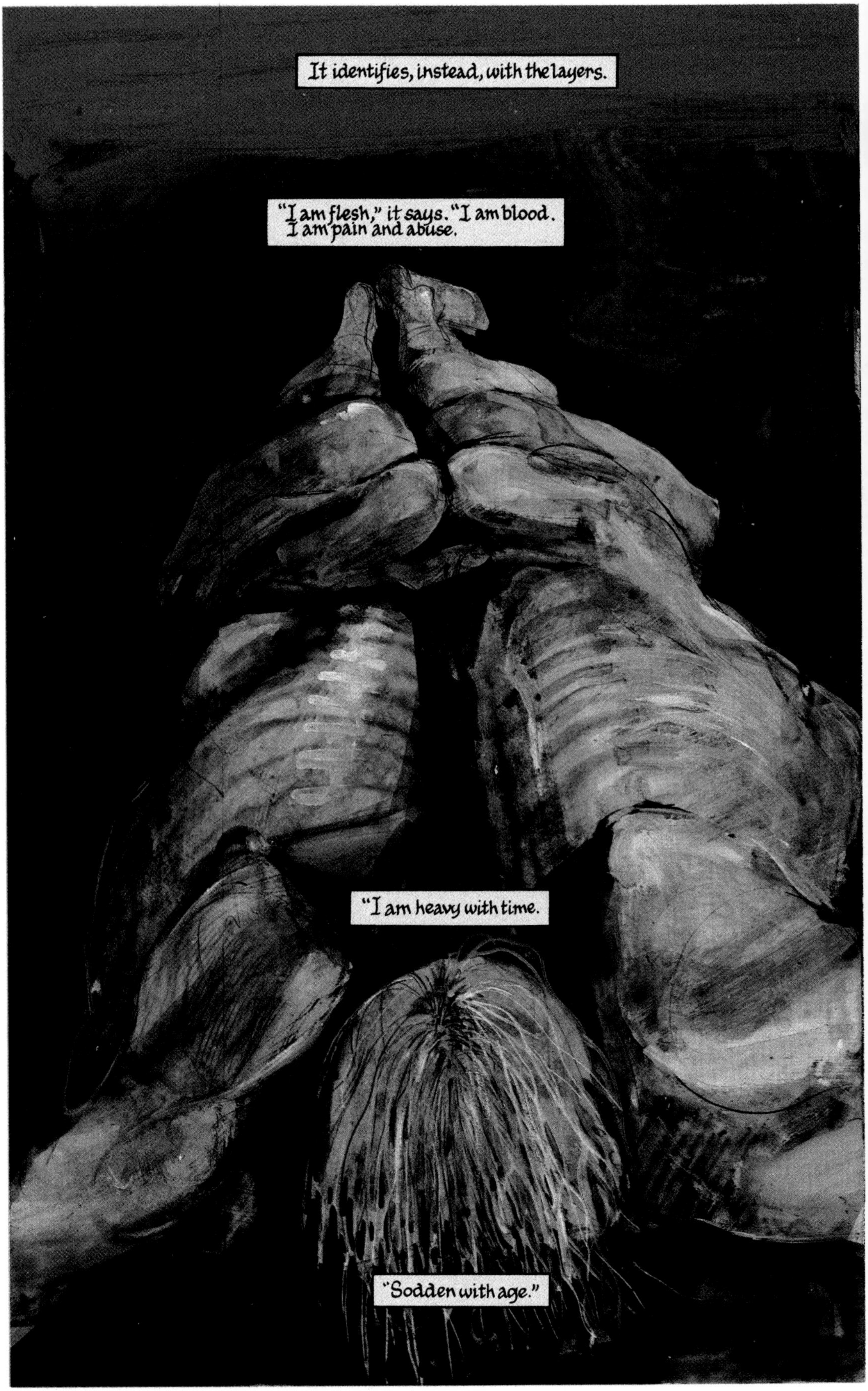
It identifies, instead, with the layers.
"I am flesh," it says. "I am blood. I am pain and abuse.
"I am heavy with time.
"Sodden with age."

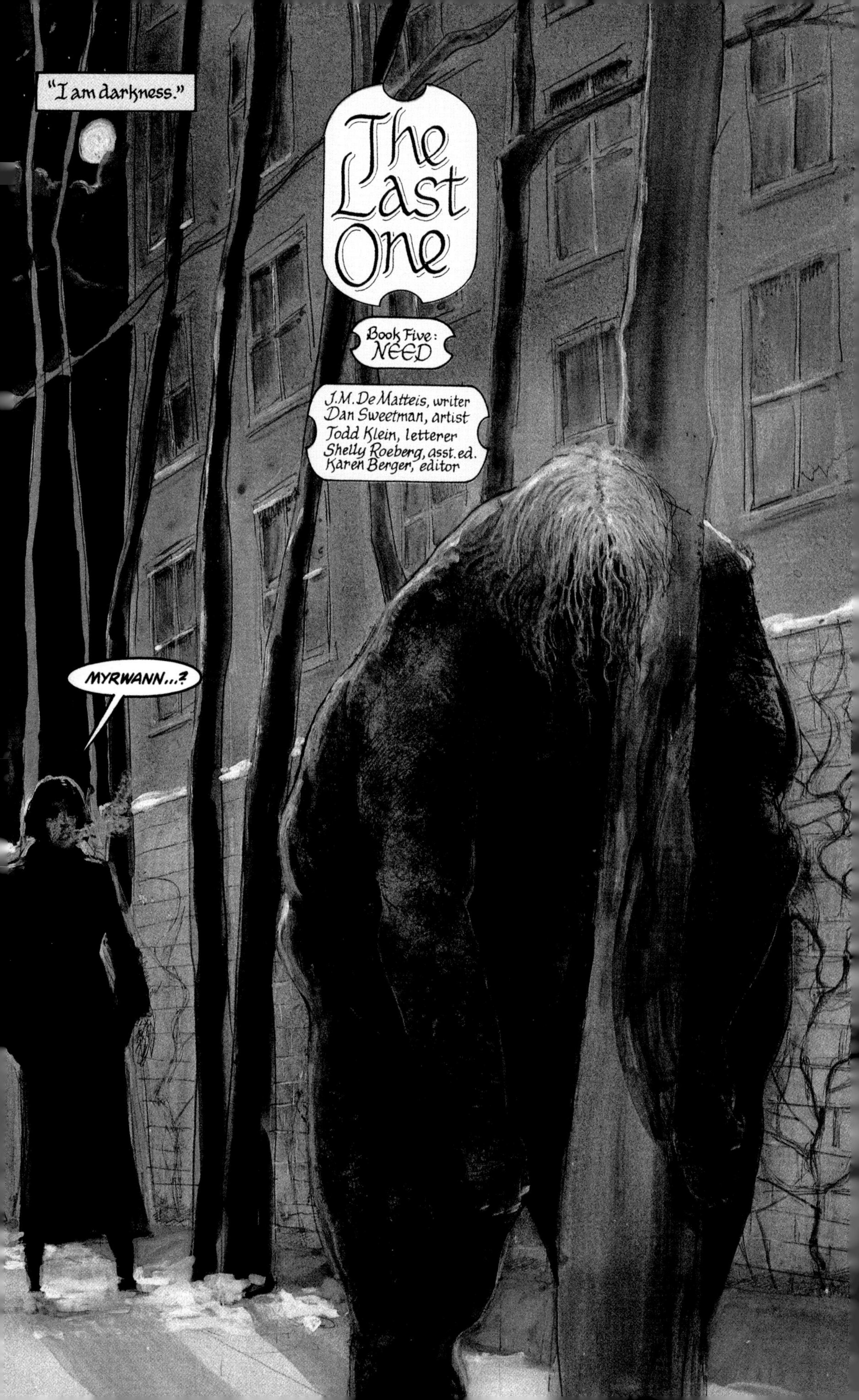
"I am darkness."
The Last One
Book Five: NEED
J.M. De Matteis, writer
Dan Sweetman, artist
Todd Klein, letterer
Shelly Roeberg, asst. ed.
Karen Berger, editor
MYRWANN...?

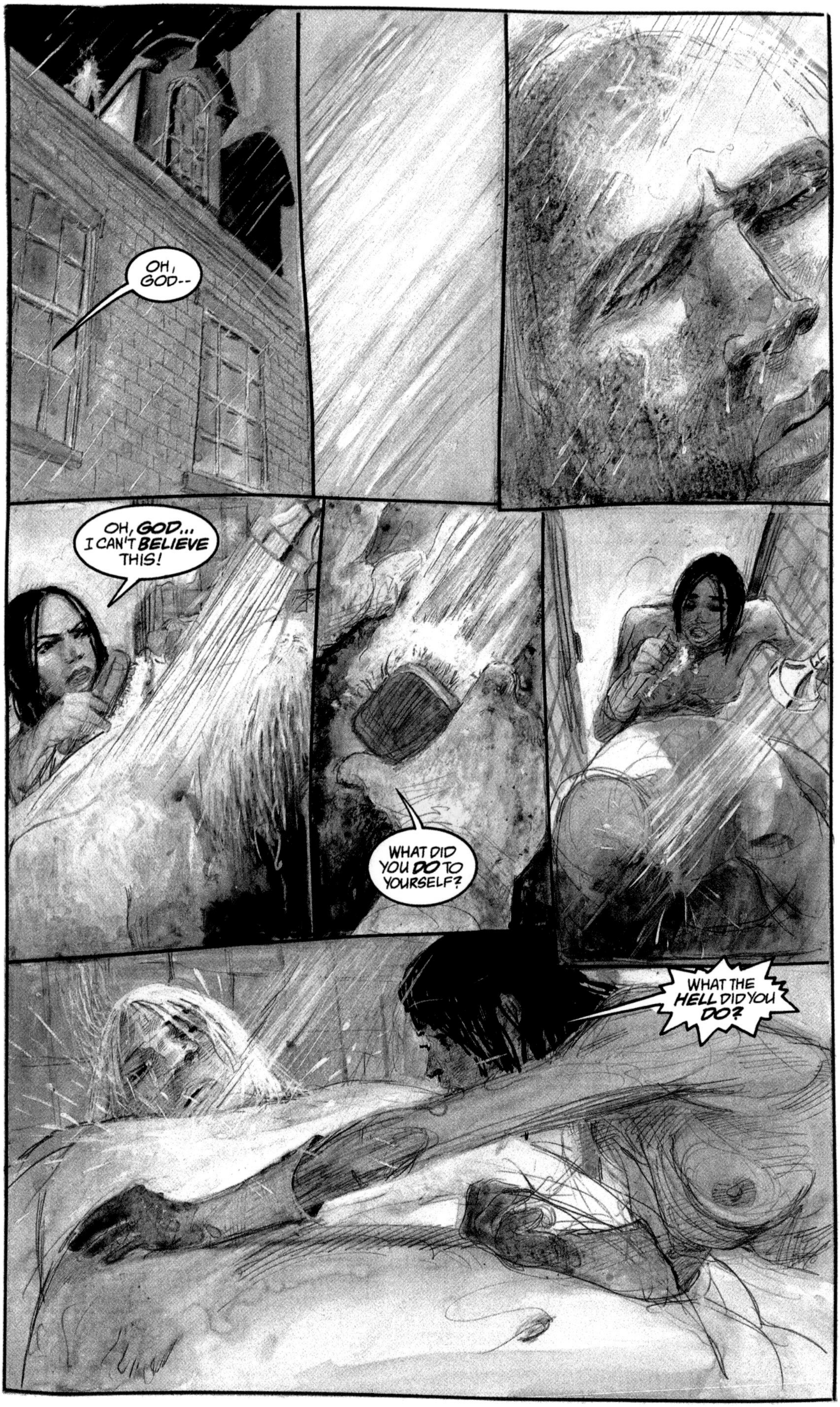
OH, GOD--
OH, GOD... I CAN'T BELIEVE THIS!
WHAT DID YOU DO TO YOURSELF?
WHAT THE HELL DID YOU DO?

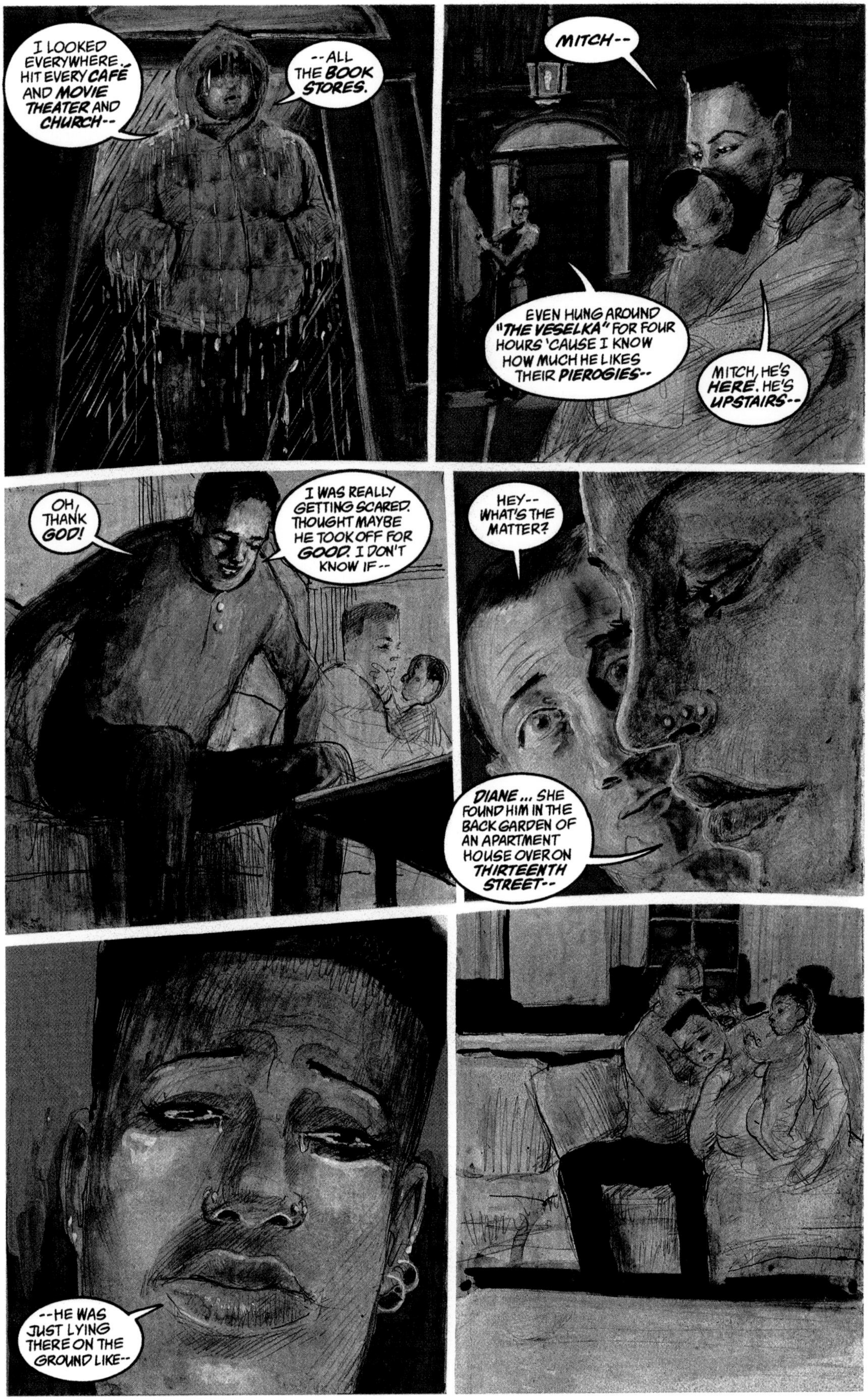

I LOOKED EVERYWHERE. HIT EVERY CAFÉ AND MOVIE THEATER AND CHURCH--
--ALL THE BOOK STORES.
MITCH--
EVEN HUNG AROUND "THE VESELKA" FOR FOUR HOURS 'CAUSE I KNOW HOW MUCH HE LIKES THEIR PIEROGIES--
MITCH, HE'S HERE. HE'S UPSTAIRS--
OH, THANK GOD!
I WAS REALLY GETTING SCARED. THOUGHT MAYBE HE TOOK OFF FOR GOOD. I DON'T KNOW IF--
HEY-- WHAT'S THE MATTER?
DIANE... SHE FOUND HIM IN THE BACK GARDEN OF AN APARTMENT HOUSE OVER ON THIRTEENTH STREET--
--HE WAS JUST LYING THERE ON THE GROUND LIKE--

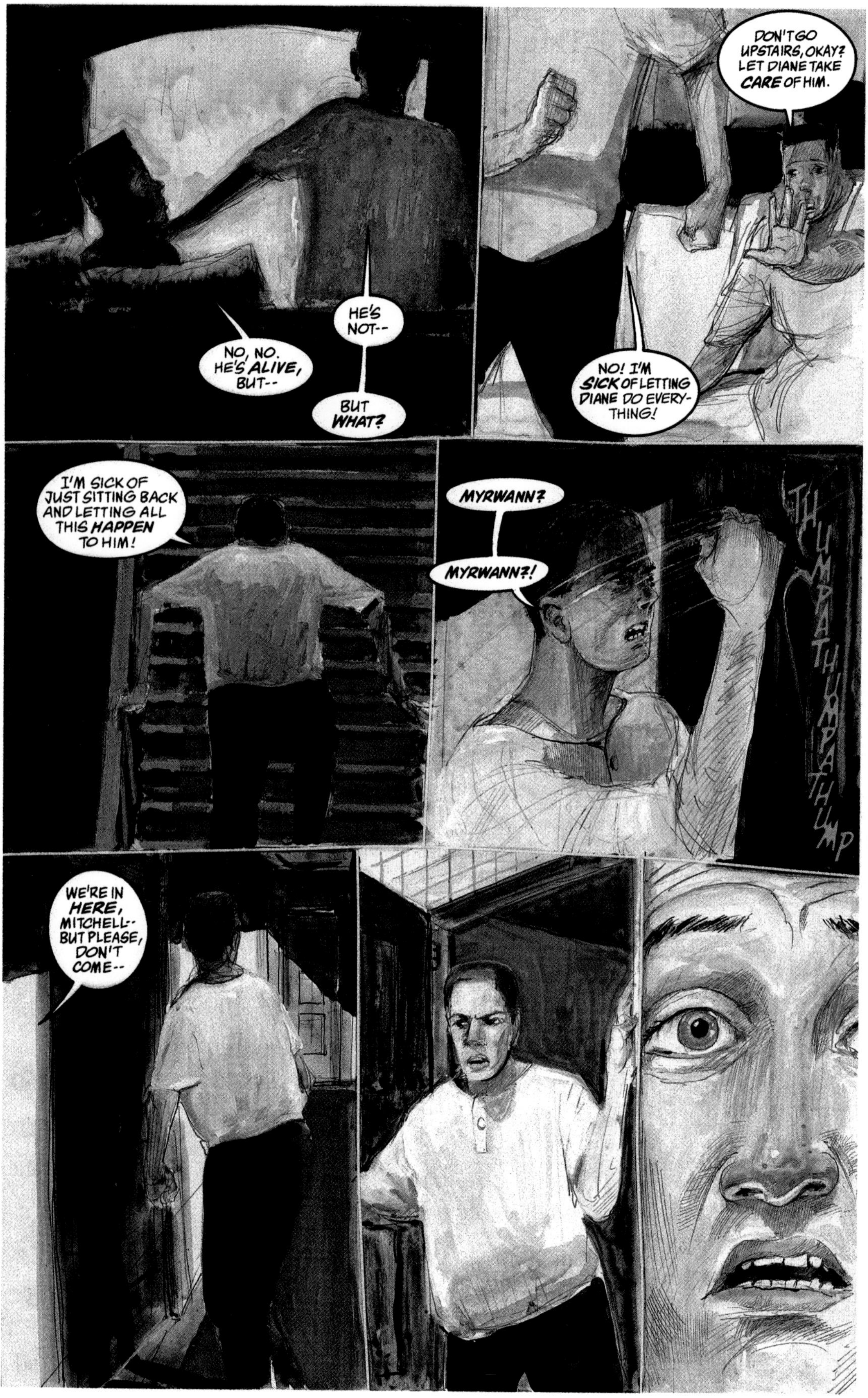
HE'S NOT--
NO, NO. HE'S ALIVE, BUT--
BUT WHAT?
DON'T GO UPSTAIRS, OKAY? LET DIANE TAKE CARE OF HIM.
NO! I'M SICK OF LETTING DIANE DO EVERY-THING!
I'M SICK OF JUST SITTING BACK AND LETTING ALL THIS HAPPEN TO HIM!
MYRWANN?
MYRWANN?!
THUMPATHUMPATHUMPATHUMP
WE'RE IN HERE, MITCHELL-- BUT PLEASE, DON'T COME--

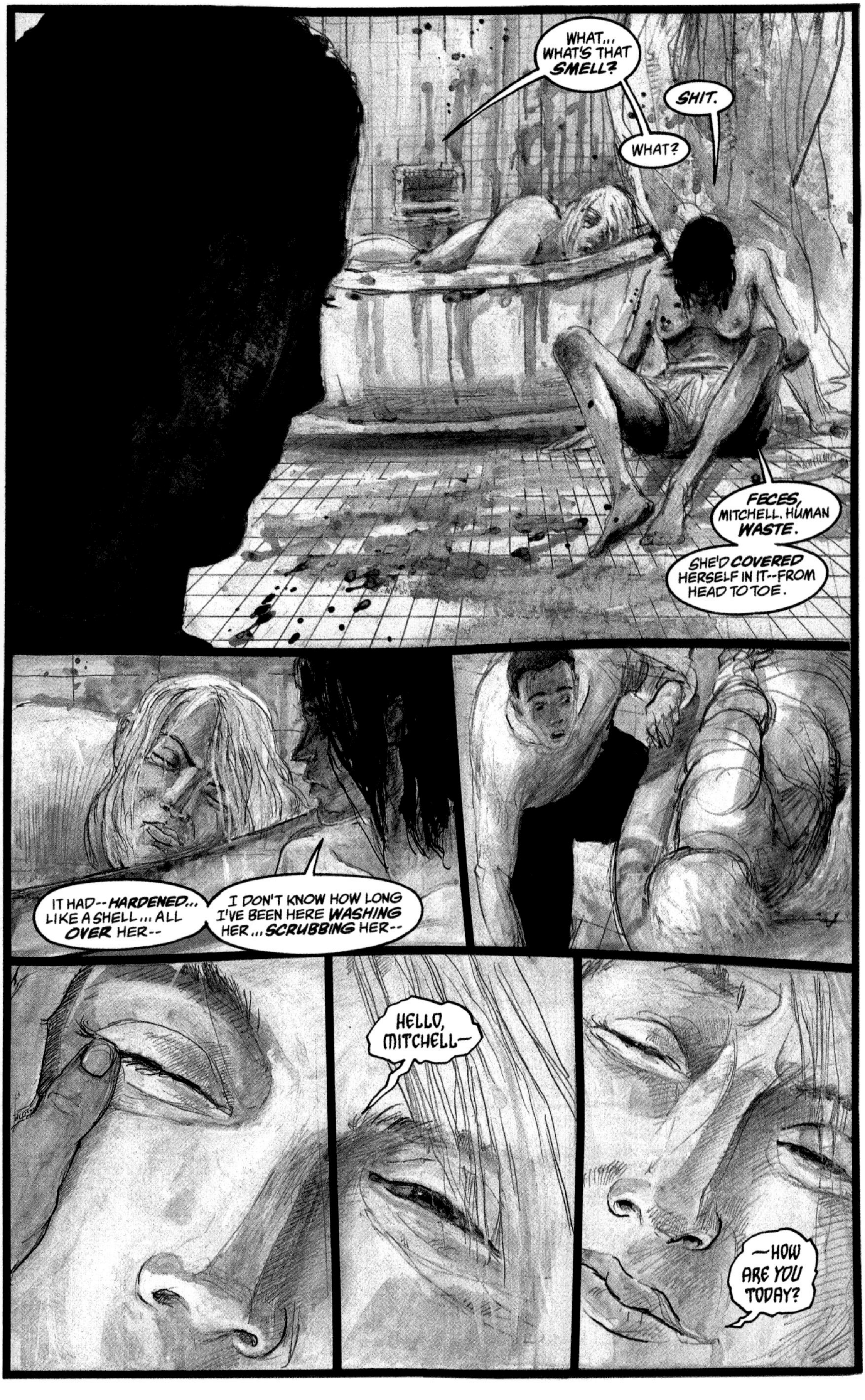
WHAT... WHAT'S THAT SMELL?
SHIT.
WHAT?
FECES, MITCHELL. HUMAN WASTE.
SHE'D COVERED HERSELF IN IT--FROM HEAD TO TOE.
IT HAD--HARDENED... LIKE A SHELL... ALL OVER HER--
I DON'T KNOW HOW LONG I'VE BEEN HERE WASHING HER... SCRUBBING HER--
HELLO, MITCHELL--
--HOW ARE YOU TODAY?

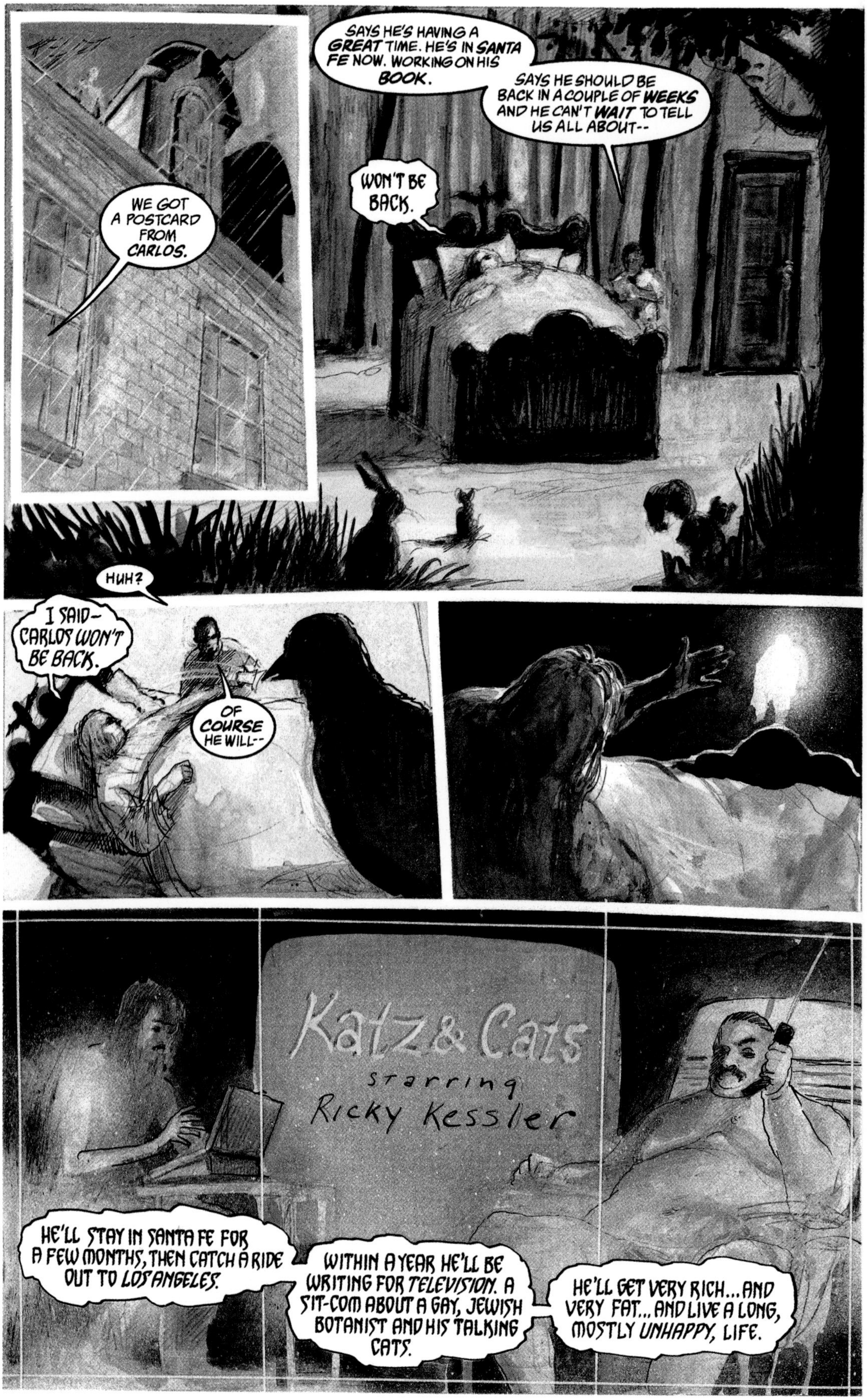
WE GOT A POSTCARD FROM CARLOS.
SAYS HE'S HAVING A GREAT TIME. HE'S IN SANTA FE NOW. WORKING ON HIS BOOK.
SAYS HE SHOULD BE BACK IN A COUPLE OF WEEKS AND HE CAN'T WAIT TO TELL US ALL ABOUT--
WON'T BE BACK.
HUH?
I SAID-CARLOS WON'T BE BACK.
OF COURSE HE WILL--
Katz & Cats
starring
Ricky Kessler
HE'LL STAY IN SANTA FE FOR A FEW MONTHS, THEN CATCH A RIDE OUT TO LOS ANGELES.
WITHIN A YEAR HE'LL BE WRITING FOR TELEVISION. A SIT-COM ABOUT A GAY, JEWISH BOTANIST AND HIS TALKING CATS.
HE'LL GET VERY RICH... AND VERY FAT... AND LIVE A LONG, MOSTLY UNHAPPY, LIFE.

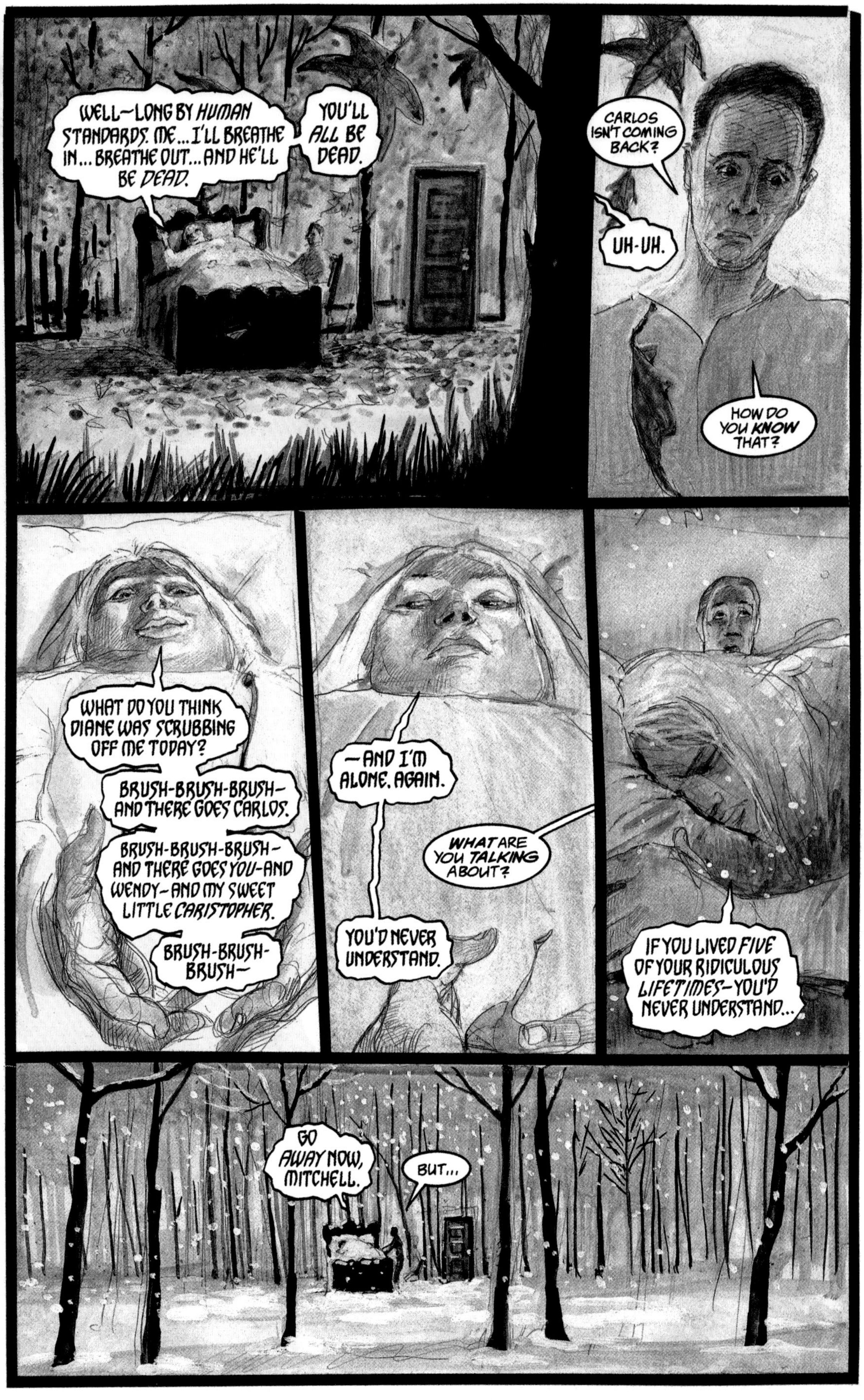
WELL—LONG BY HUMAN STANDARDS. ME... I'LL BREATHE IN... BREATHE OUT... AND HE'LL BE DEAD.
YOU'LL ALL BE DEAD.
CARLOS ISN'T COMING BACK?
UH-UH.
HOW DO YOU KNOW THAT?
WHAT DO YOU THINK DIANE WAS SCRUBBING OFF ME TODAY?
BRUSH-BRUSH-BRUSH—AND THERE GOES CARLOS.
BRUSH-BRUSH-BRUSH—AND THERE GOES YOU—AND WENDY—AND MY SWEET LITTLE CHRISTOPHER.
BRUSH-BRUSH-BRUSH—
—AND I'M ALONE. AGAIN.
WHAT ARE YOU TALKING ABOUT?
YOU'D NEVER UNDERSTAND.
IF YOU LIVED FIVE OF YOUR RIDICULOUS LIFETIMES—YOU'D NEVER UNDERSTAND...
GO AWAY NOW, MITCHELL.
BUT...

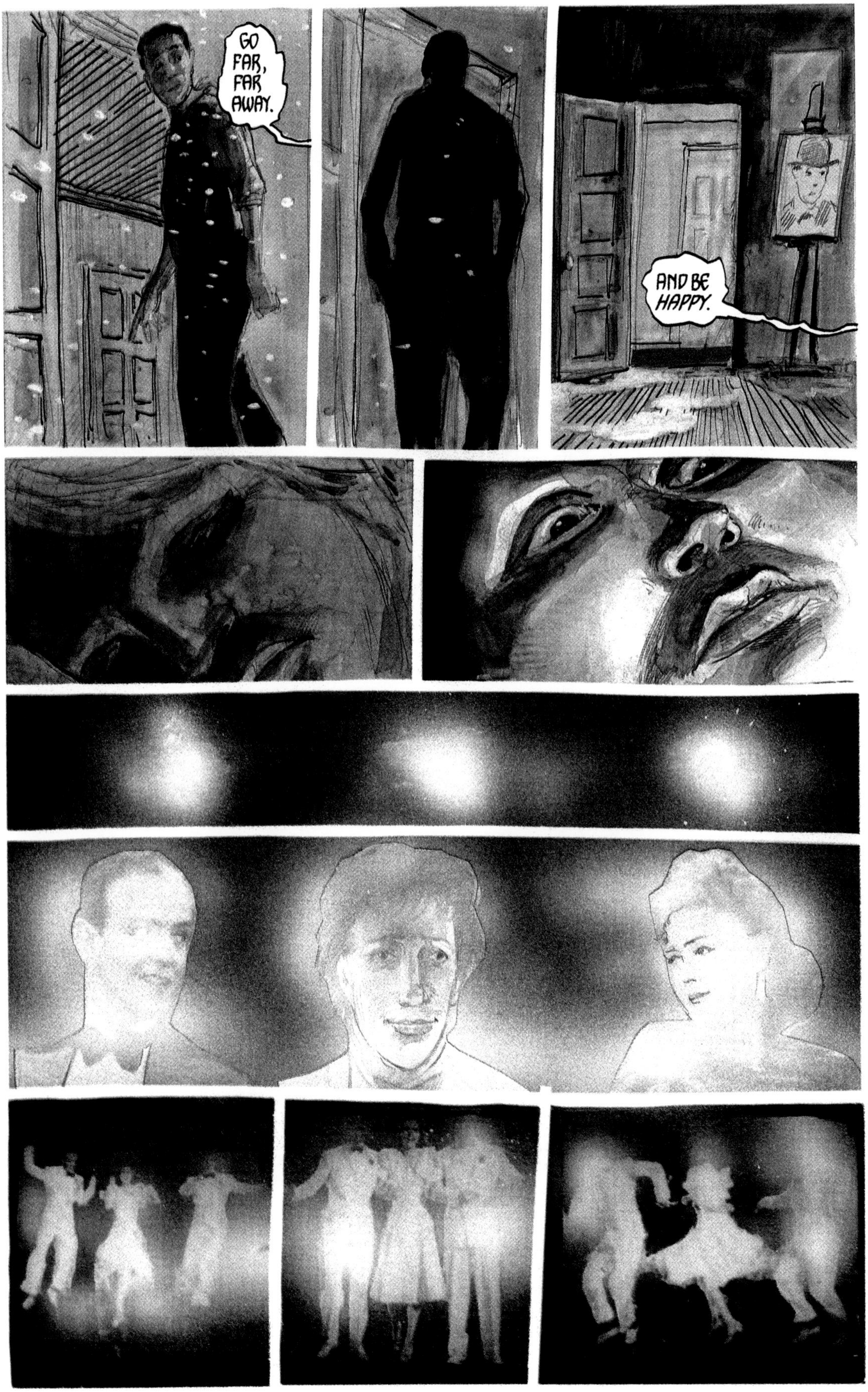
GO FAR, FAR AWAY.
AND BE HAPPY.

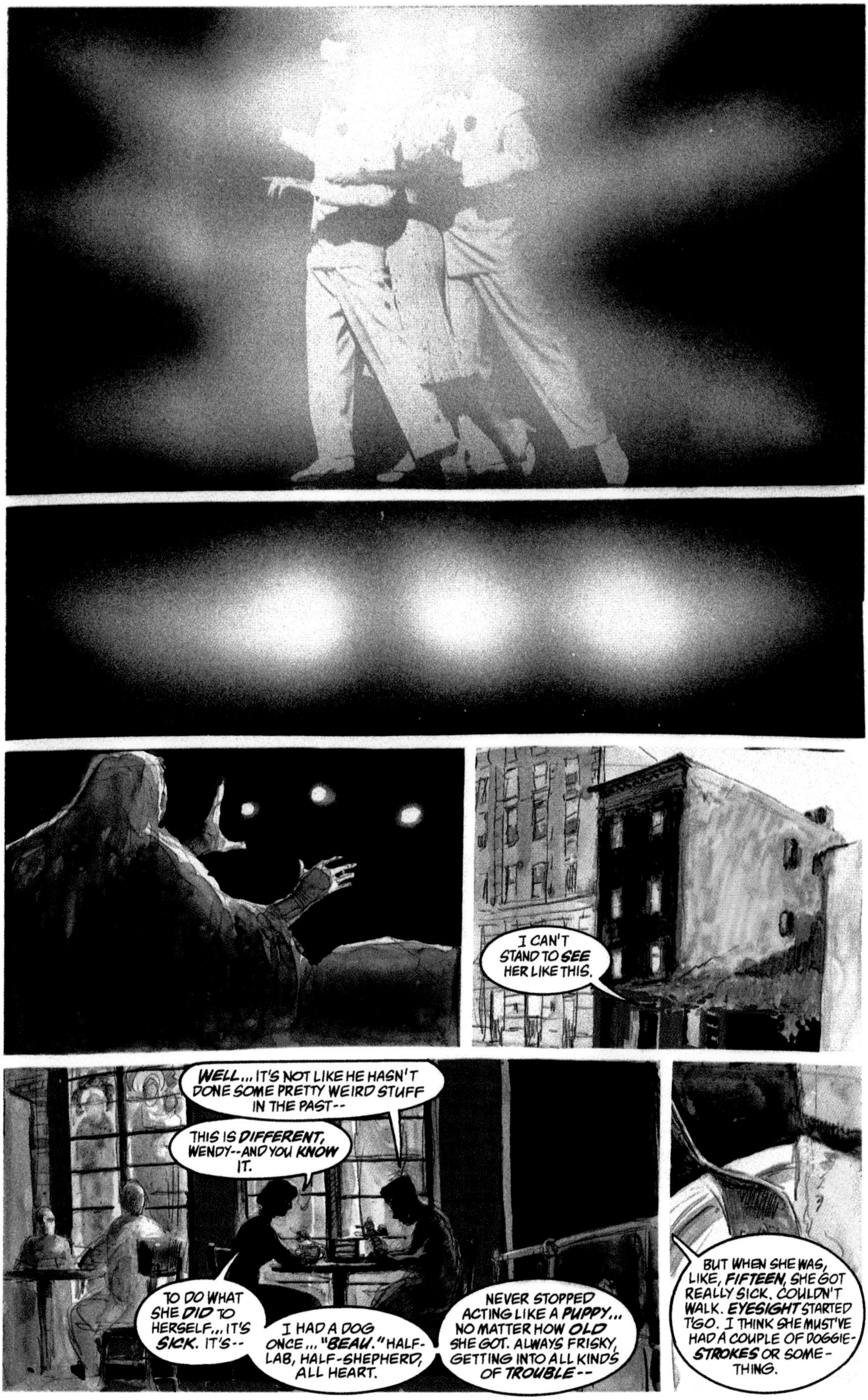
I CAN'T STAND TO SEE HER LIKE THIS.
WELL... IT'S NOT LIKE HE HASN'T DONE SOME PRETTY WEIRD STUFF IN THE PAST--
THIS IS DIFFERENT, WENDY--AND YOU KNOW IT.
TO DO WHAT SHE DID TO HERSELF... IT'S SICK. IT'S--
I HAD A DOG ONCE... "BEAU." HALF-LAB, HALF-SHEPHERD, ALL HEART.
NEVER STOPPED ACTING LIKE A PUPPY... NO MATTER HOW OLD SHE GOT. ALWAYS FRISKY, GETTING INTO ALL KINDS OF TROUBLE--
BUT WHEN SHE WAS, LIKE, FIFTEEN, SHE GOT REALLY SICK. COULDN'T WALK. EYESIGHT STARTED T'GO. I THINK SHE MUST'VE HAD A COUPLE OF DOGGIE-STROKES OR SOME-THING.

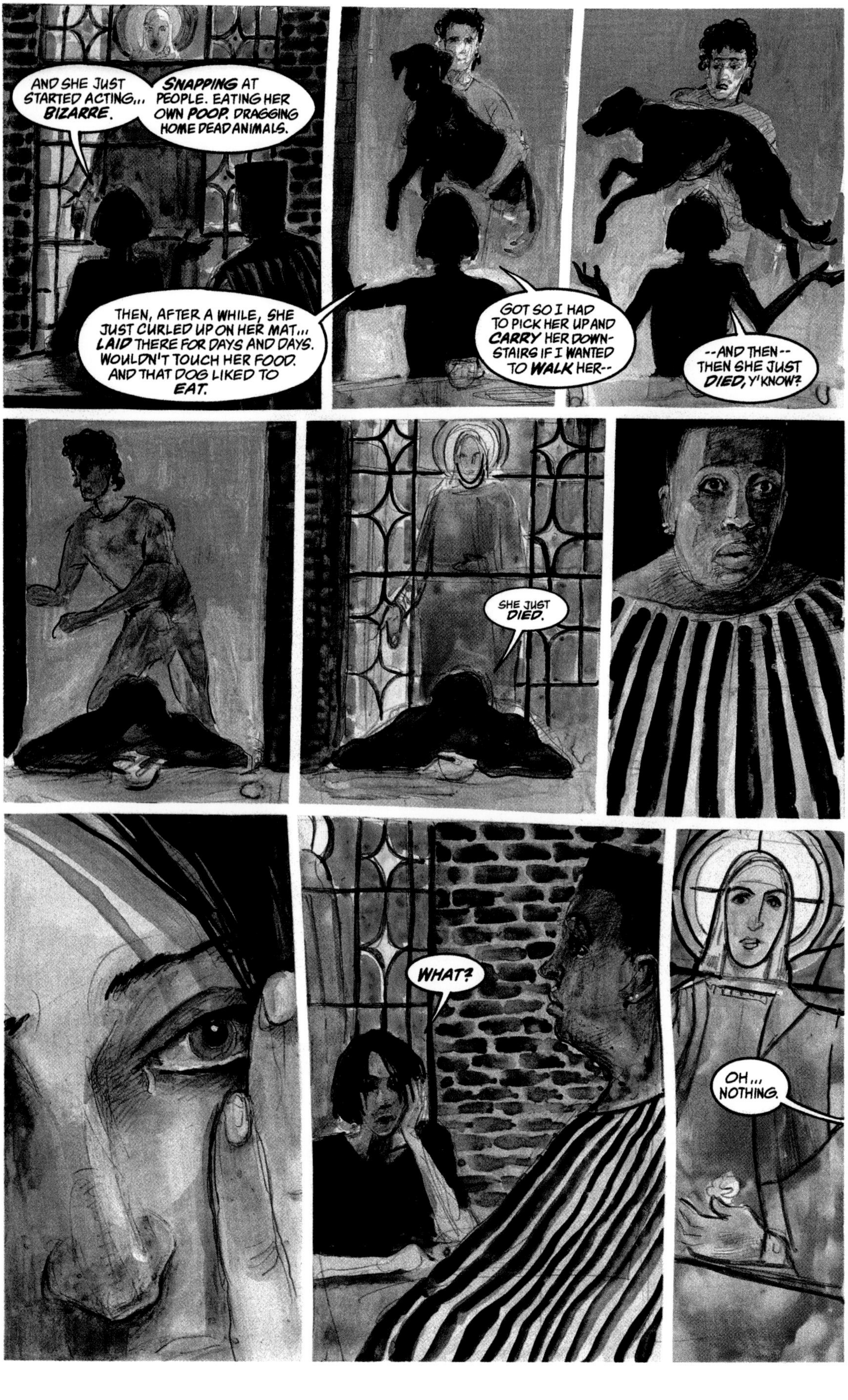
AND SHE JUST STARTED ACTING... BIZARRE.
SNAPPING AT PEOPLE. EATING HER OWN POOP. DRAGGING HOME DEAD ANIMALS.
THEN, AFTER A WHILE, SHE JUST CURLED UP ON HER MAT... LAID THERE FOR DAYS AND DAYS. WOULDN'T TOUCH HER FOOD. AND THAT DOG LIKED TO EAT.
GOT SO I HAD TO PICK HER UP AND CARRY HER DOWN-STAIRS IF I WANTED TO WALK HER--
--AND THEN-- THEN SHE JUST DIED, Y'KNOW?
SHE JUST DIED.
WHAT?
OH... NOTHING.

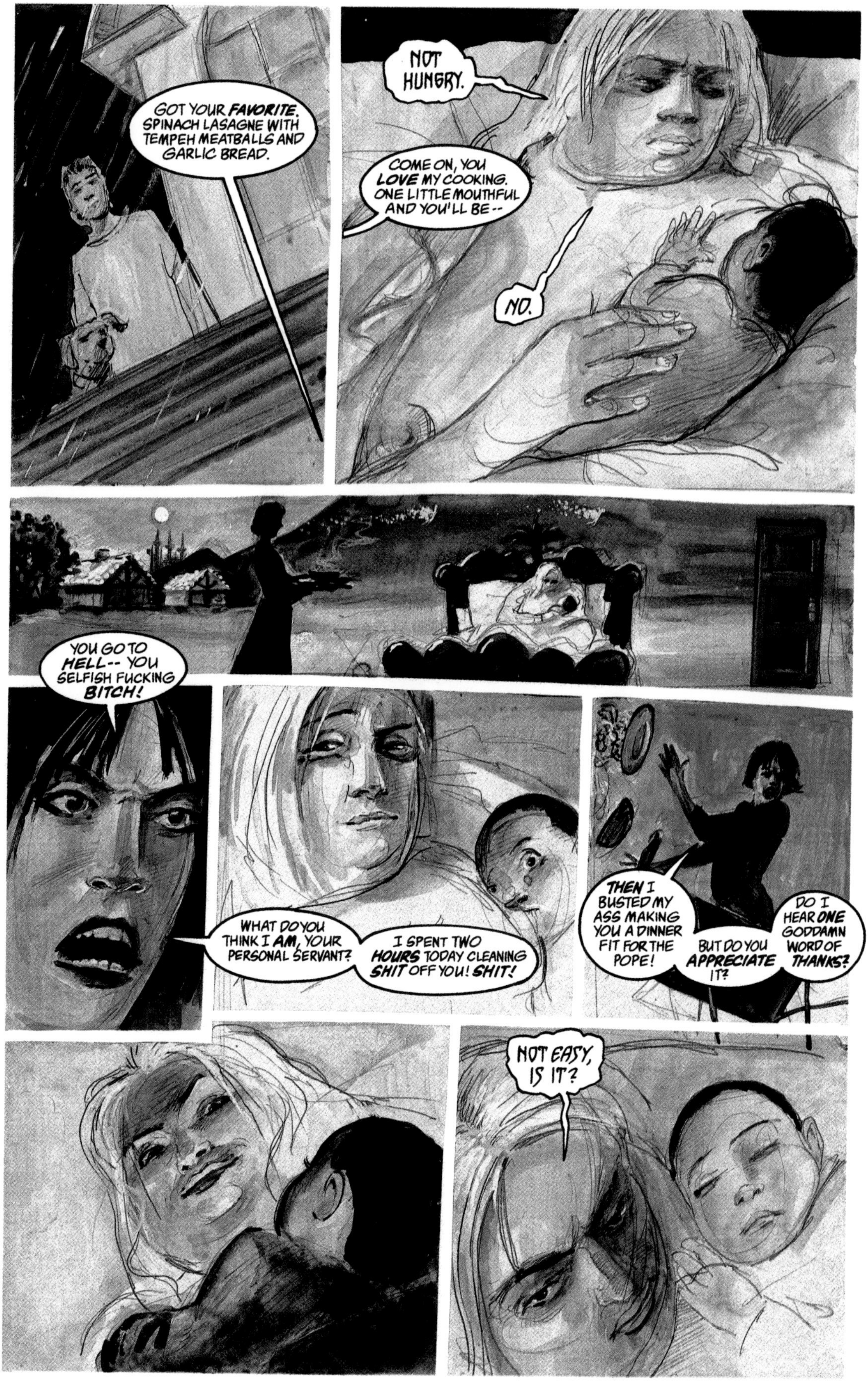
GOT YOUR **FAVORITE.** SPINACH LASAGNE WITH TEMPEH MEATBALLS AND GARLIC BREAD.
NOT HUNGRY.
COME ON, YOU **LOVE** MY COOKING. ONE LITTLE MOUTHFUL AND YOU'LL BE --
NO.
YOU GO TO **HELL**-- YOU SELFISH FUCKING **BITCH!**
WHAT DO YOU THINK I **AM**, YOUR PERSONAL SERVANT?
I SPENT TWO **HOURS** TODAY CLEANING **SHIT** OFF YOU! **SHIT!**
THEN I BUSTED MY ASS MAKING YOU A DINNER FIT FOR THE POPE!
BUT DO YOU **APPRECIATE** IT?
DO I HEAR **ONE** GODDAMN WORD OF **THANKS?**
NOT EASY, IS IT?

YOU GIVE AND YOU GIVE AND YOU GIVE—
—UNTIL ONE DAY... YOU JUST CAN'T DO IT ANYMORE.
IT'S LIKE THE WELL HAS JUST...RUN DRY. YOU LOOK FOR SOMETHING—
—THE TINIEST DROP OF LOVE... COMPASSION... BUT—
—NOTHING.
YOU'RE JUST TIRED. A LITTLE REST--
A LONG REST.
ONCE THE LOVE IS GONE, DIANE... ONCE THE HEART IS EMPTY—
—THERE'S NO POINT.

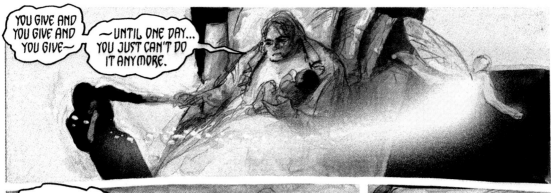

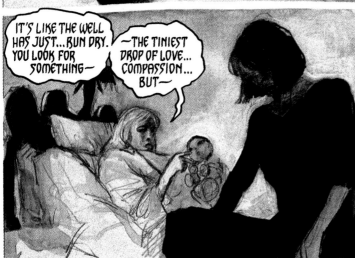

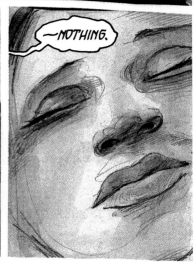

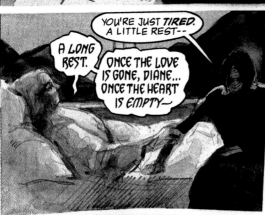

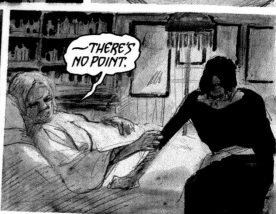

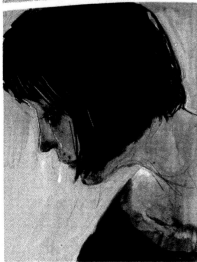

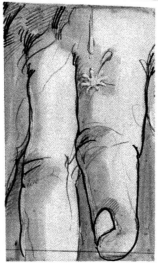

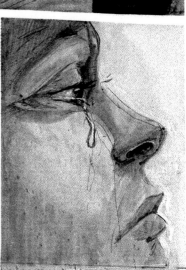

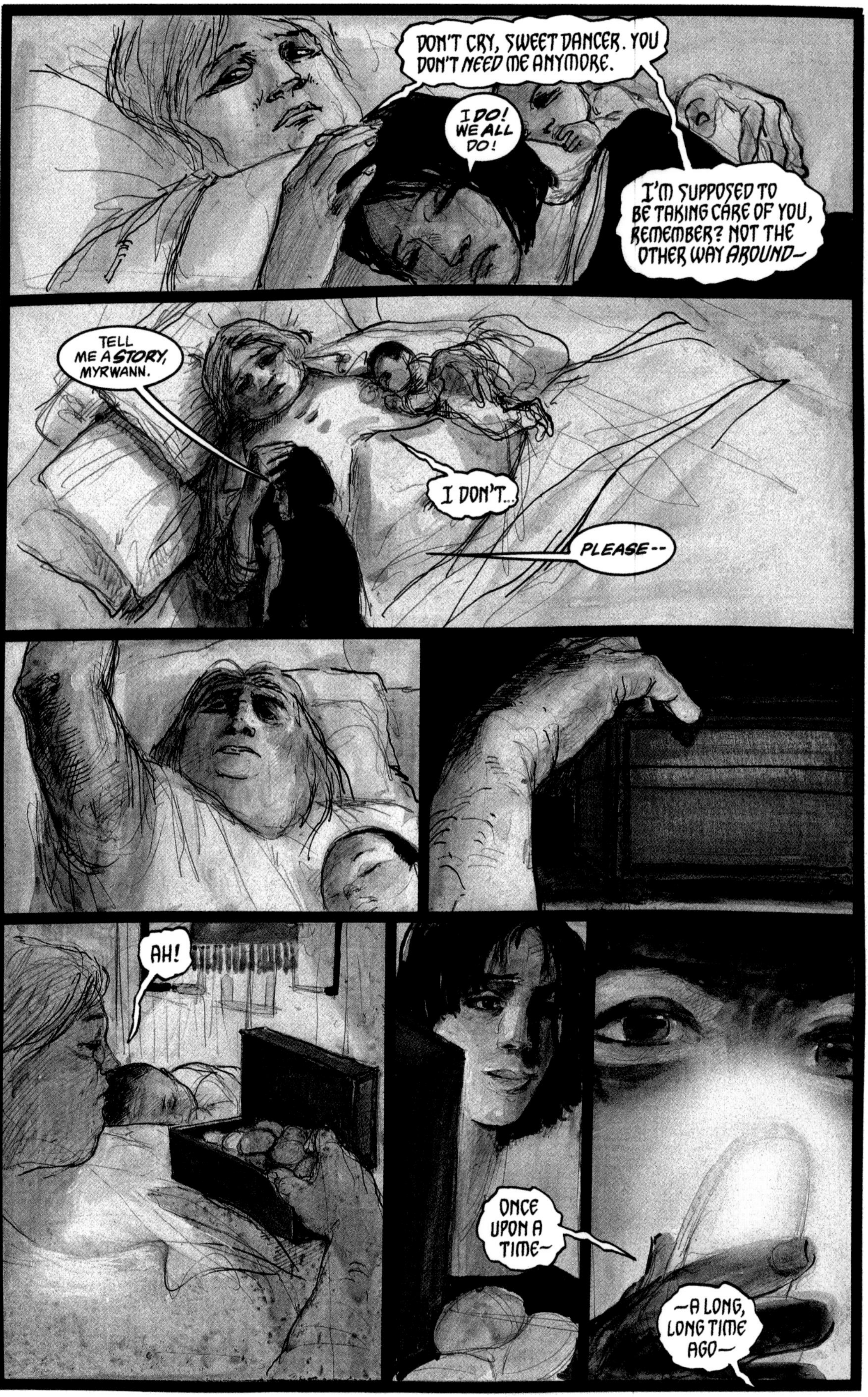
DON'T CRY, SWEET DANCER. YOU DON'T NEED ME ANYMORE.
I DO! WE ALL DO!
I'M SUPPOSED TO BE TAKING CARE OF YOU, REMEMBER? NOT THE OTHER WAY AROUND—
TELL ME A STORY, MYRWANN.
I DON'T...
PLEASE--
AH!
ONCE UPON A TIME—
—A LONG, LONG TIME AGO—

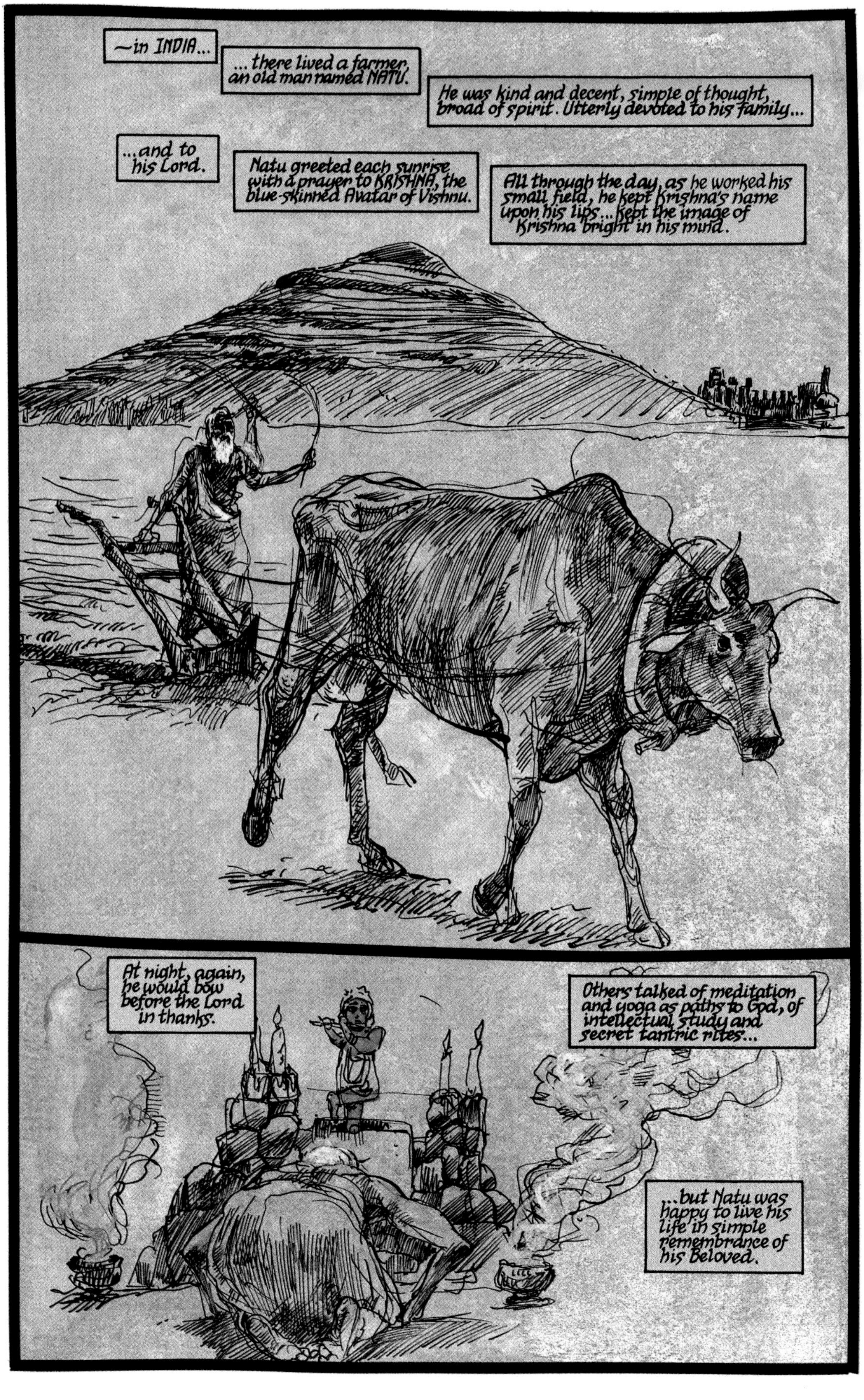
~in INDIA...
... there lived a farmer, an old man named NATU.
He was kind and decent, simple of thought, broad of spirit. Utterly devoted to his family...
...and to his Lord.
Natu greeted each sunrise with a prayer to KRISHNA, the blue-skinned Avatar of Vishnu.
All through the day, as he worked his small field, he kept Krishna's name upon his lips... kept the image of Krishna bright in his mind.
At night, again, he would bow before the Lord in thanks.
Others talked of meditation and yoga as paths to God, of intellectual study and secret tantric rites...
...but Natu was happy to live his life in simple remembrance of his Beloved.

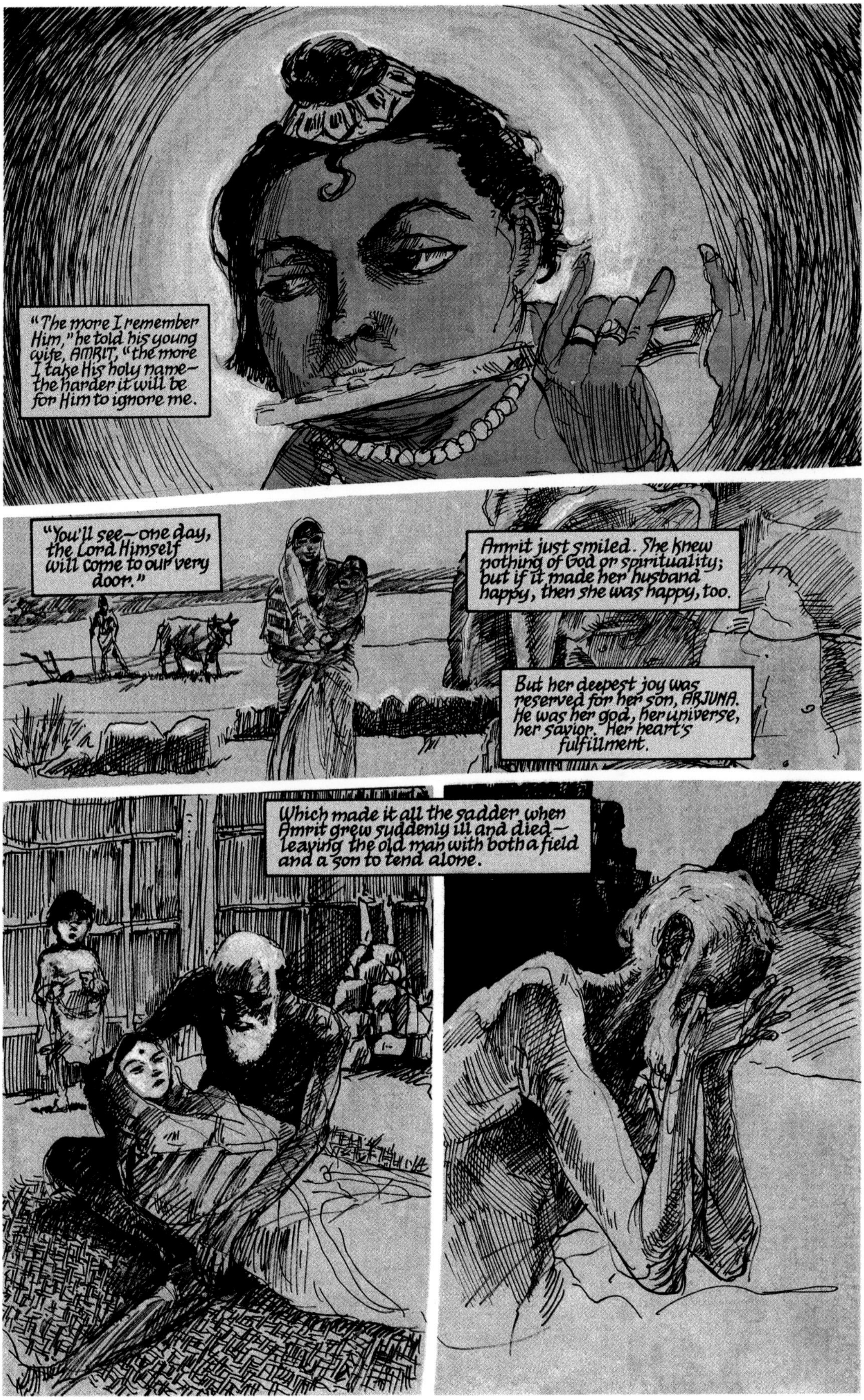
"The more I remember Him," he told his young wife, AMRIT, "the more I take His holy name— the harder it will be for Him to ignore me.
"You'll see—one day, the Lord Himself will come to our very door."
Amrit just smiled. She knew nothing of God or spirituality; but if it made her husband happy, then she was happy, too.
But her deepest joy was reserved for her son, ARJUNA. He was her god, her universe, her savior. Her heart's fulfillment.
Which made it all the sadder when Amrit grew suddenly ill and died— leaving the old man with both a field and a son to tend alone.

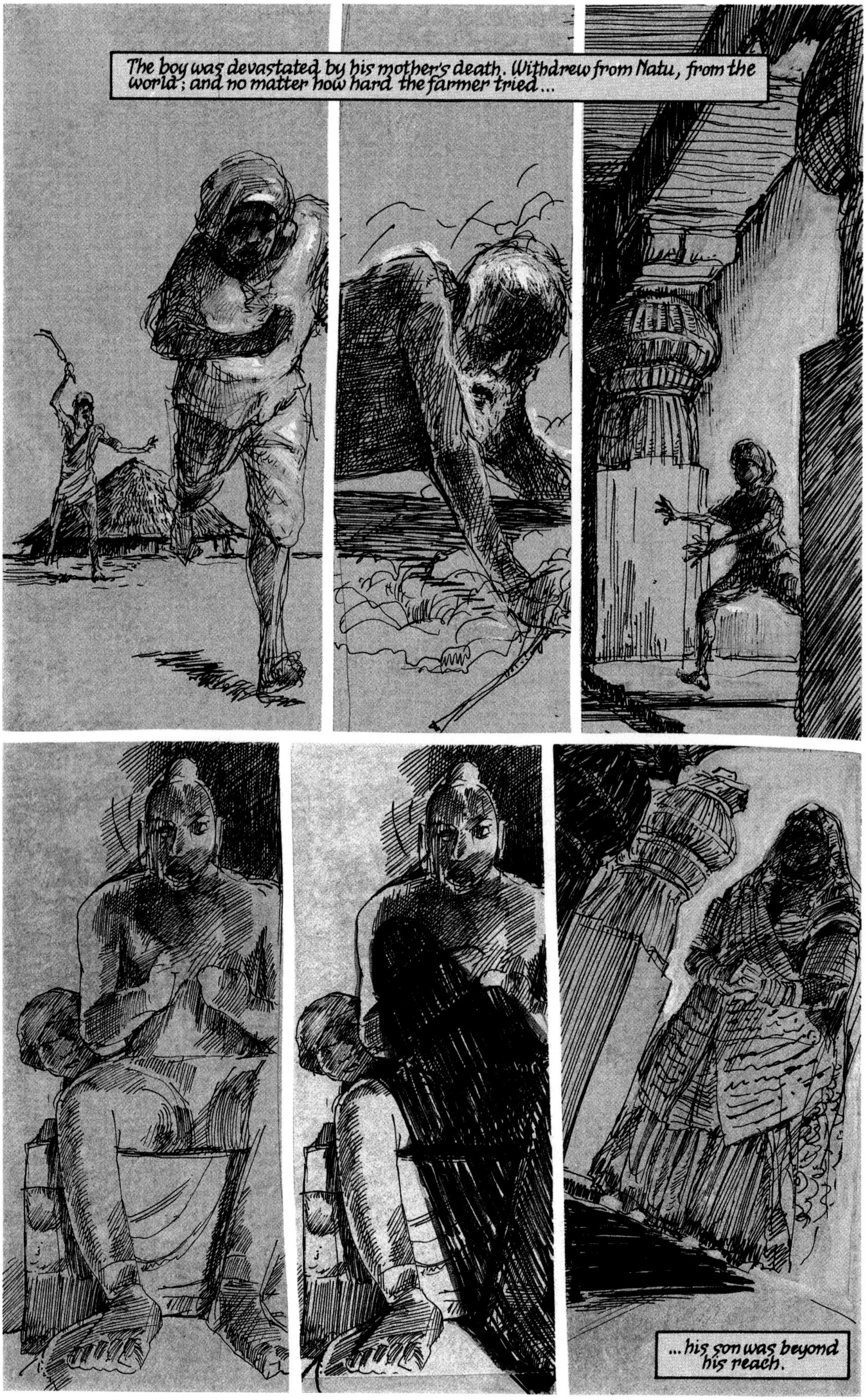
The boy was devastated by his mother's death. Withdrew from Natu, from the world; and no matter how hard the farmer tried...
...his son was beyond his reach.

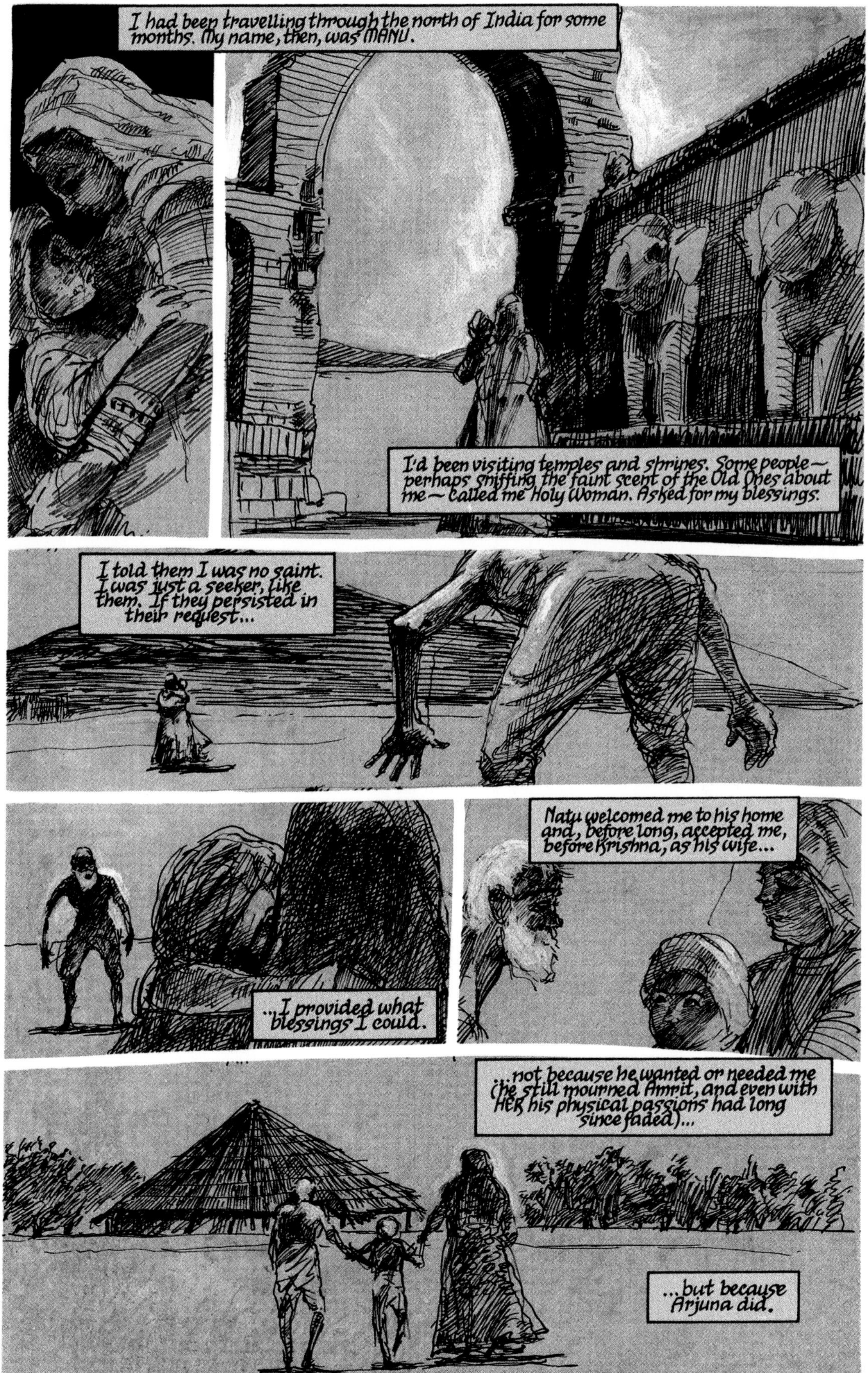
I had been travelling through the north of India for some months. My name, then, was MANU.
I'd been visiting temples and shrines. Some people—perhaps sniffing the faint scent of the Old Ones about me—called me Holy Woman. Asked for my blessings.
I told them I was no saint. I was just a seeker, like them. If they persisted in their request...
...I provided what blessings I could.
Natu welcomed me to his home and, before long, accepted me, before Krishna, as his wife...
...not because he wanted or needed me (he still mourned Amrit, and even with HER his physical passions had long since faded)...
...but because Arjuna did.

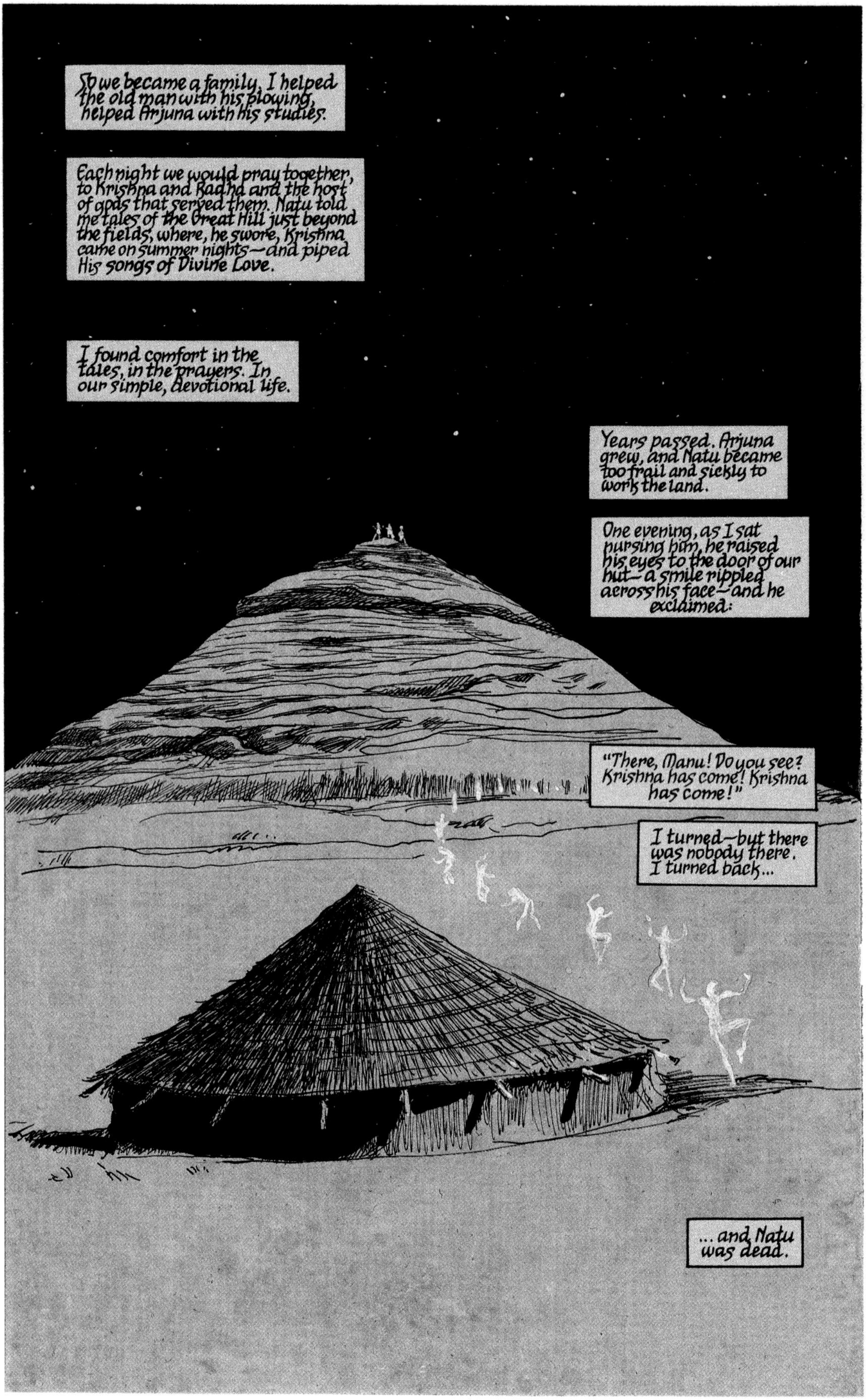
So we became a family. I helped the old man with his plowing, helped Arjuna with his studies.
Each night we would pray together, to Krishna and Radha and the host of gods that served them. Natu told me tales of the Great Hill just beyond the fields, where, he swore, Krishna came on summer nights—and piped His songs of Divine Love.
I found comfort in the tales, in the prayers. In our simple, devotional life.
Years passed. Arjuna grew, and Natu became too frail and sickly to work the land.
One evening, as I sat nursing him, he raised his eyes to the door of our hut—a smile rippled across his face—and he exclaimed:
"There, Manu! Do you see? Krishna has come! Krishna has come!"
I turned—but there was nobody there. I turned back...
...and Natu was dead.

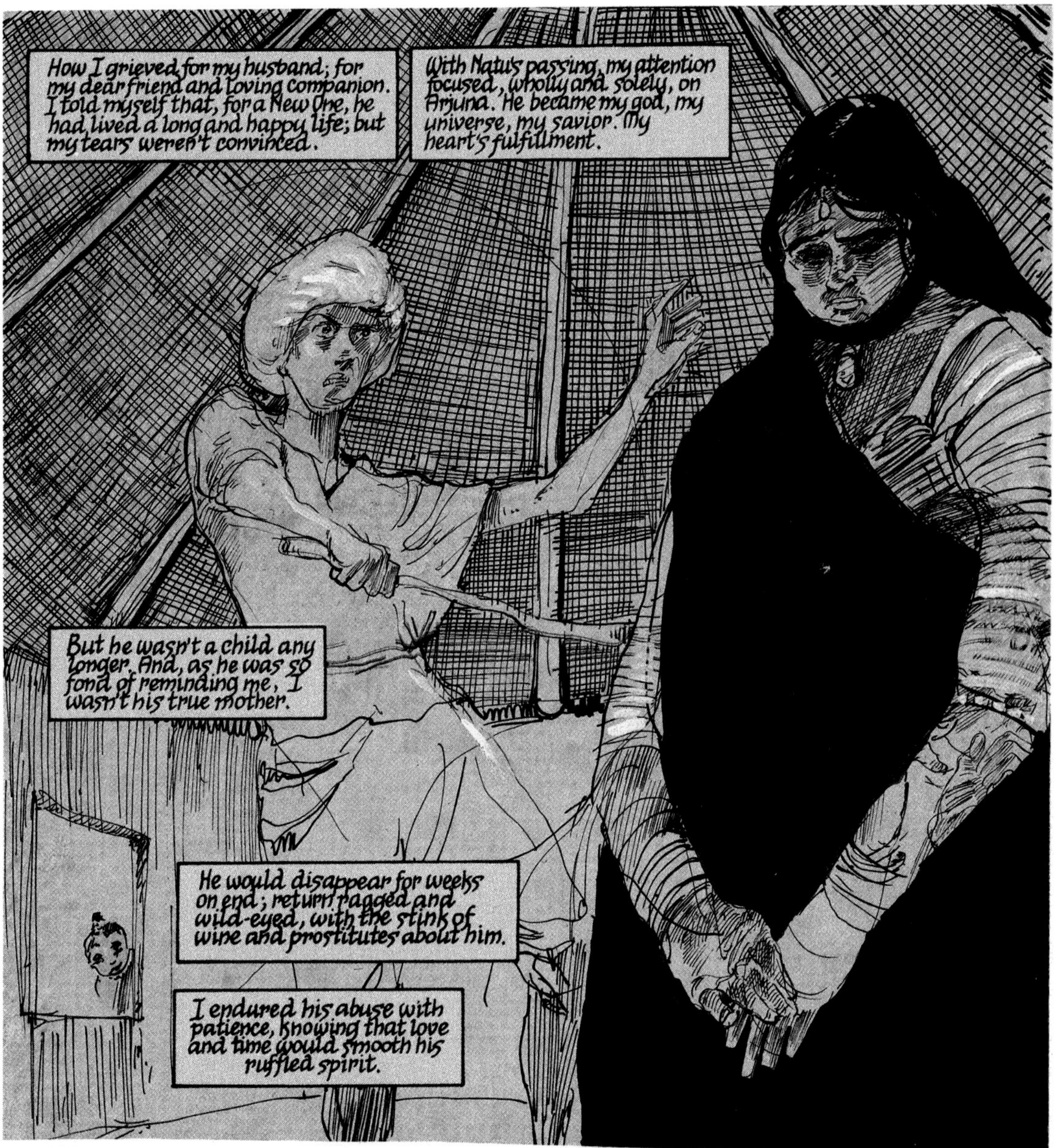
How I grieved for my husband; for my dear friend and loving companion. I told myself that, for a New One, he had lived a long and happy life; but my tears weren't convinced.
With Natu's passing, my attention focused, wholly and solely, on Arjuna. He became my god, my universe, my savior. My heart's fulfillment.
But he wasn't a child any longer. And, as he was so fond of reminding me, I wasn't his true mother.
He would disappear for weeks on end; return ragged and wild-eyed, with the stink of wine and prostitutes about him.
I endured his abuse with patience, knowing that love and time would smooth his ruffled spirit.

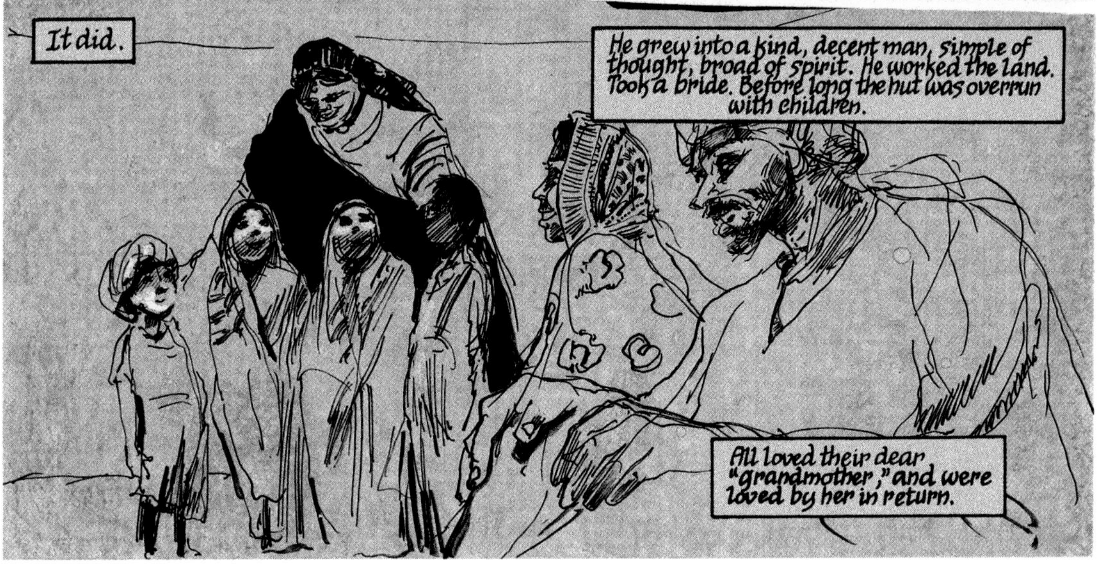
It did.
He grew into a kind, decent man, simple of thought, broad of spirit. He worked the land. Took a bride. Before long the hut was overrun with children.
All loved their dear "grandmother," and were loved by her in return.

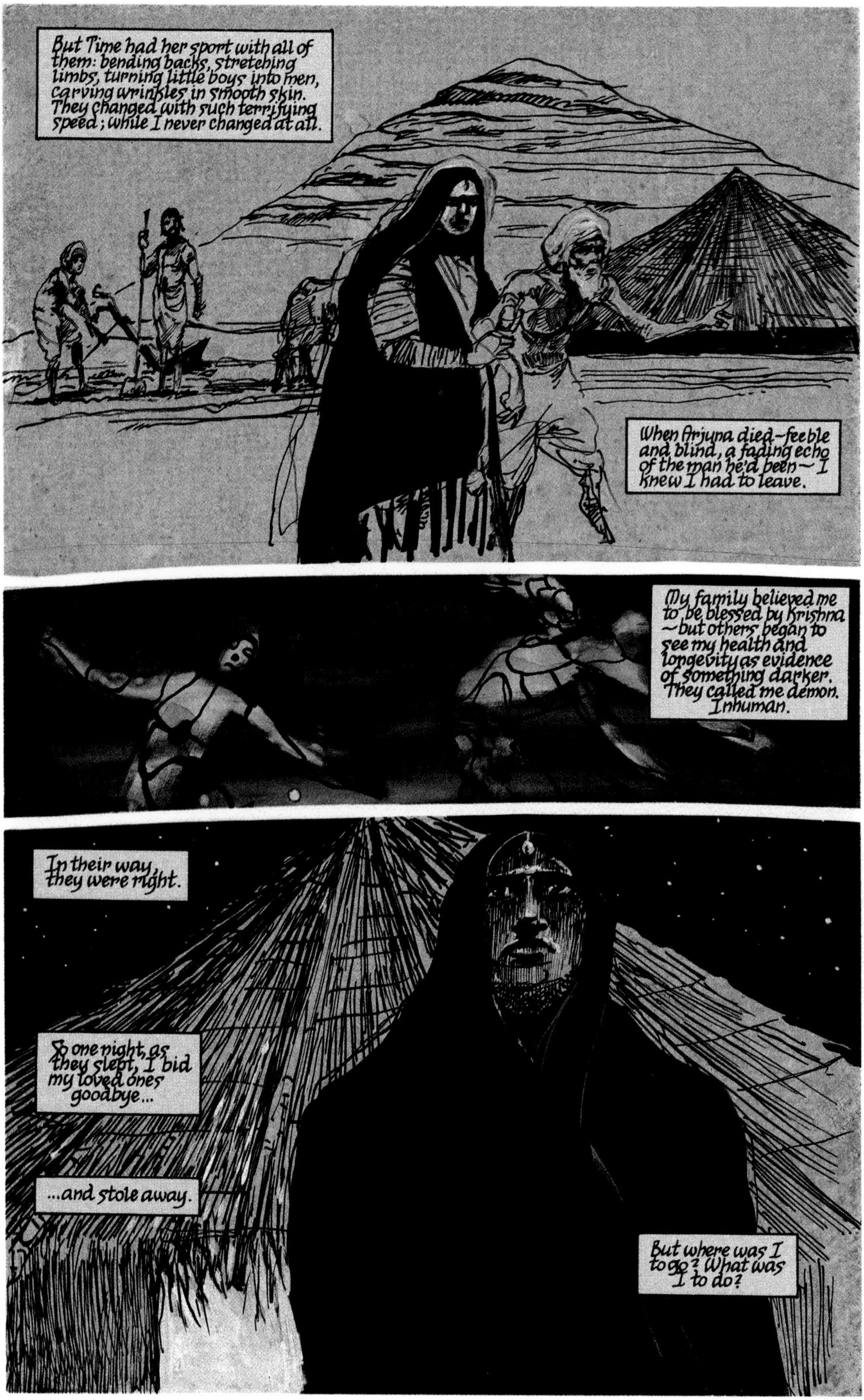

But Time had her sport with all of them: bending backs, stretching limbs, turning little boys into men, carving wrinkles in smooth skin. They changed with such terrifying speed; while I never changed at all.
When Arjuna died—feeble and blind, a fading echo of the man he'd been—I knew I had to leave.
My family believed me to be blessed by Krishna—but others began to see my health and longevity as evidence of something darker. They called me demon. Inhuman.
In their way, they were right.
So one night, as they slept, I bid my loved ones goodbye...
...and stole away.
But where was I to go? What was I to do?

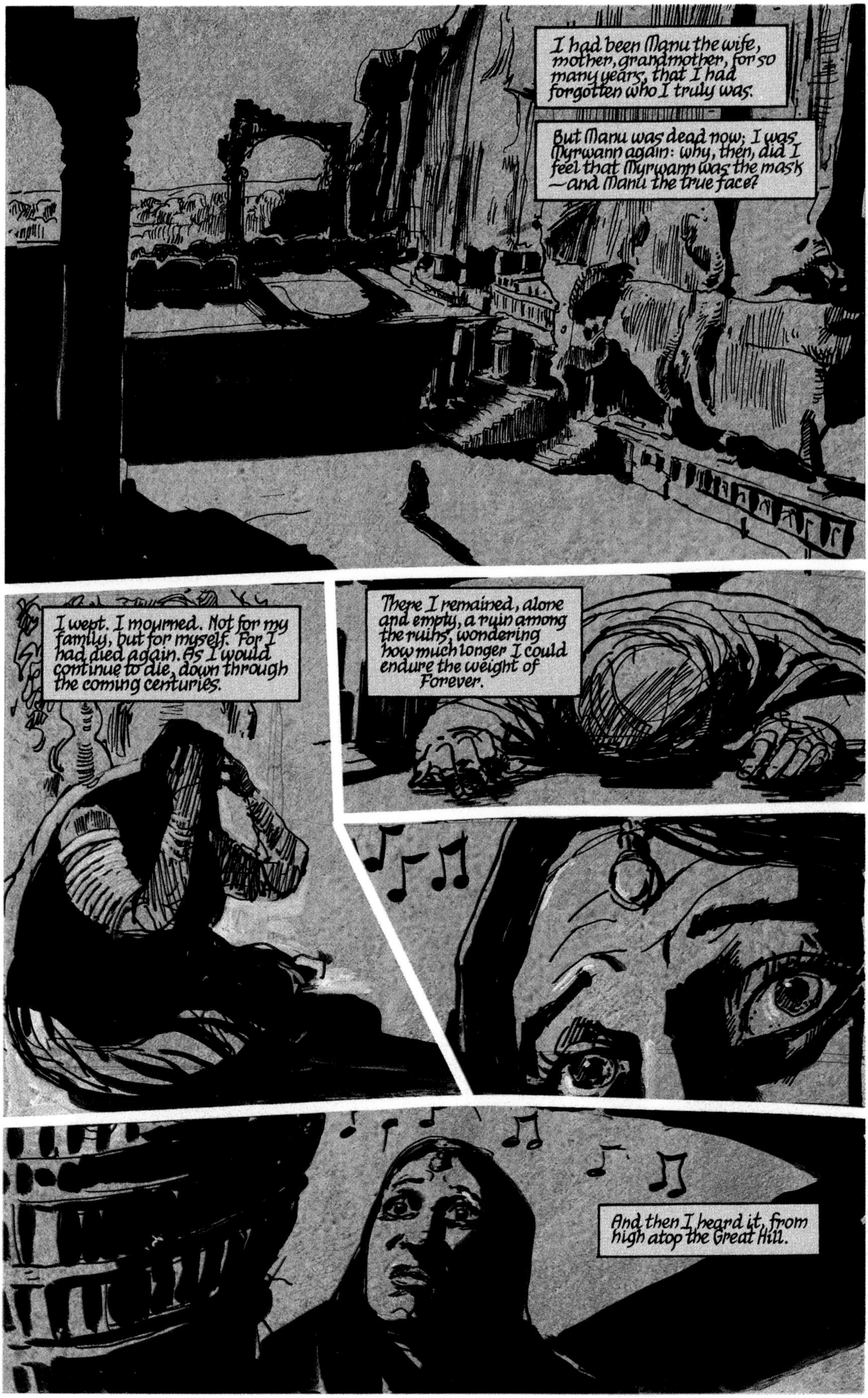
I had been Manu the wife, mother, grandmother, for so many years, that I had forgotten who I truly was.
But Manu was dead now; I was Myrwann again: why, then, did I feel that Myrwann was the mask —and Manu the true face?
I wept. I mourned. Not for my family, but for myself. For I had died again. As I would continue to die, down through the coming centuries.
There I remained, alone and empty, a ruin among the ruins, wondering how much longer I could endure the weight of Forever.
And then I heard it, from high atop the Great Hill.

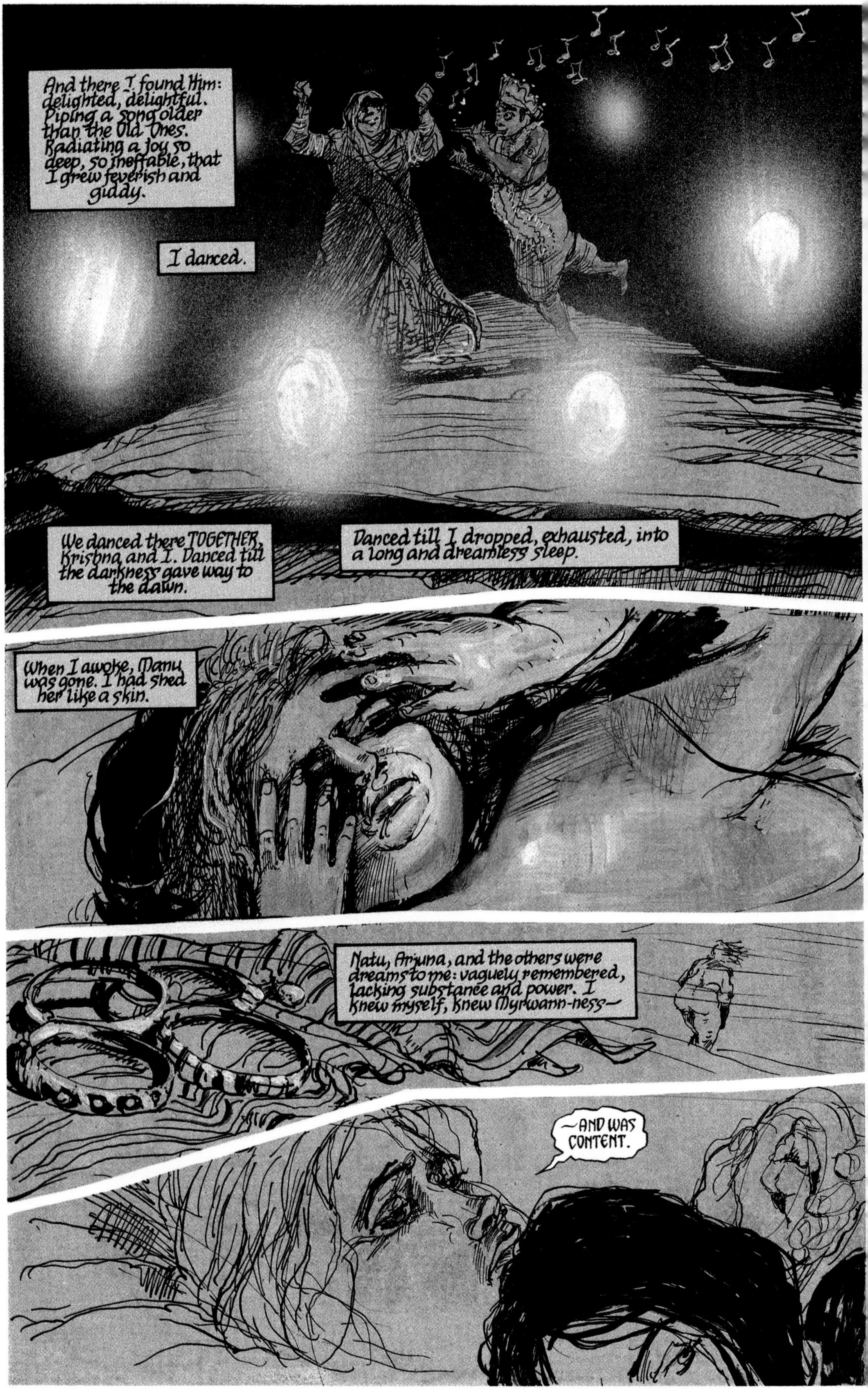
And there I found Him: delighted, delightful. Piping a song older than the Old Ones. Radiating a joy so deep, so ineffable, that I grew feverish and giddy.
I danced.
We danced there TOGETHER, Krishna and I. Danced till the darkness gave way to the dawn.
Danced till I dropped, exhausted, into a long and dreamless sleep.
When I awoke, Manu was gone. I had shed her like a skin.
Natu, Arjuna, and the others were dreams to me: vaguely remembered, lacking substance and power. I knew myself, knew Myrwann-ness—
—AND WAS CONTENT.

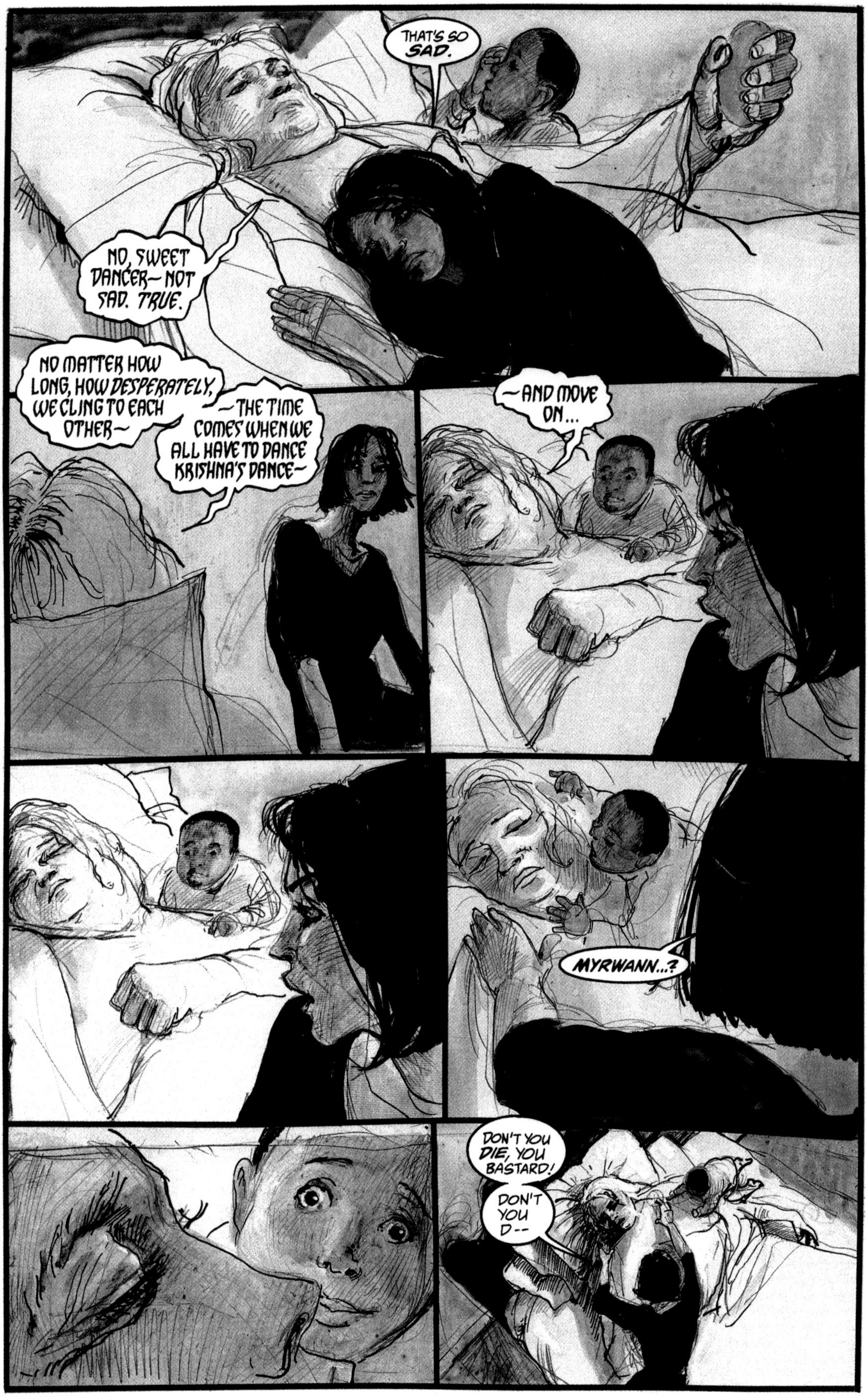
THAT'S SO SAD.
NO, SWEET DANCER— NOT SAD. TRUE.
NO MATTER HOW LONG, HOW DESPERATELY, WE CLING TO EACH OTHER~
~THE TIME COMES WHEN WE ALL HAVE TO DANCE KRISHNA'S DANCE~
~AND MOVE ON...
MYRWANN...?
DON'T YOU DIE, YOU BASTARD!
DON'T YOU D--

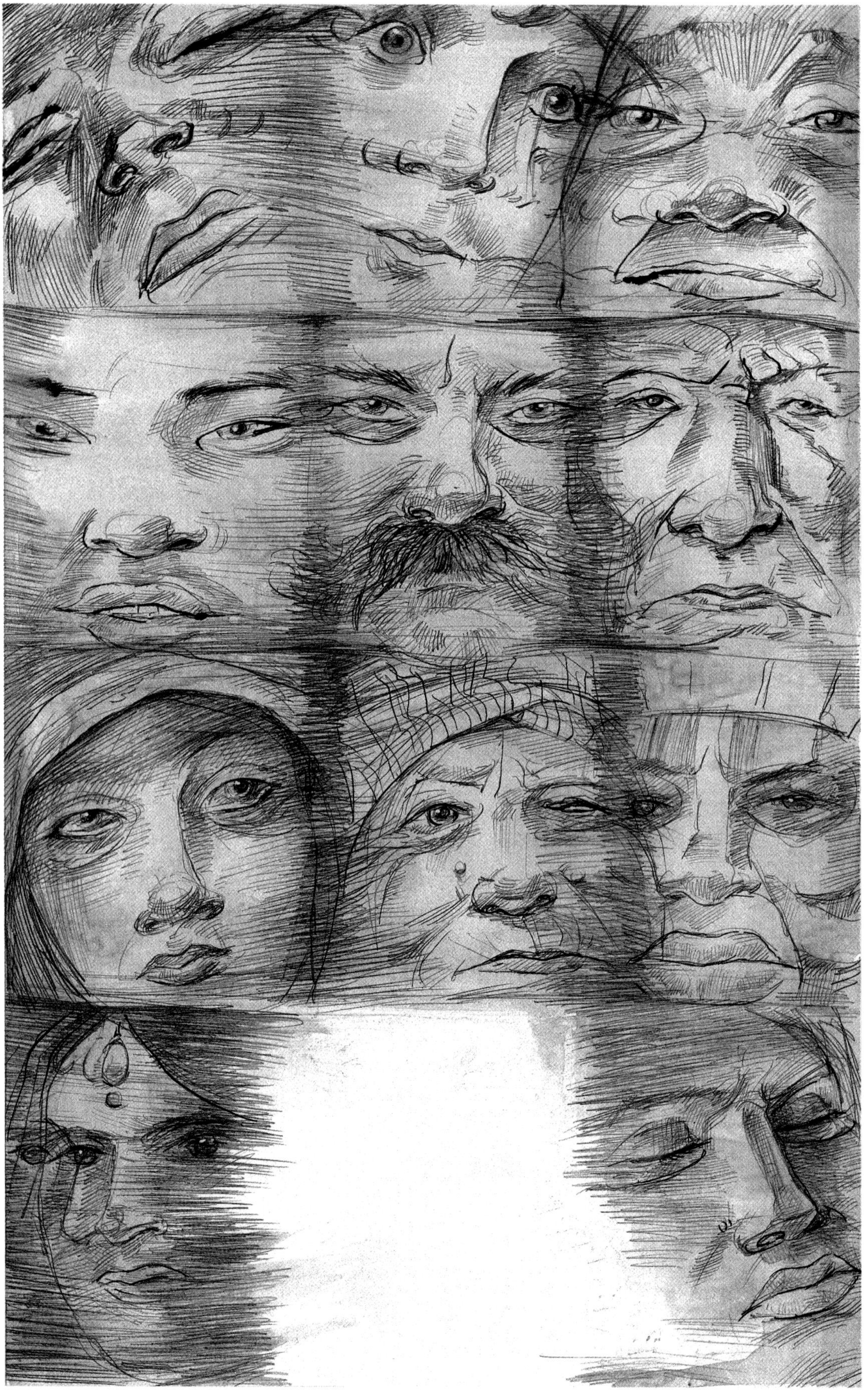

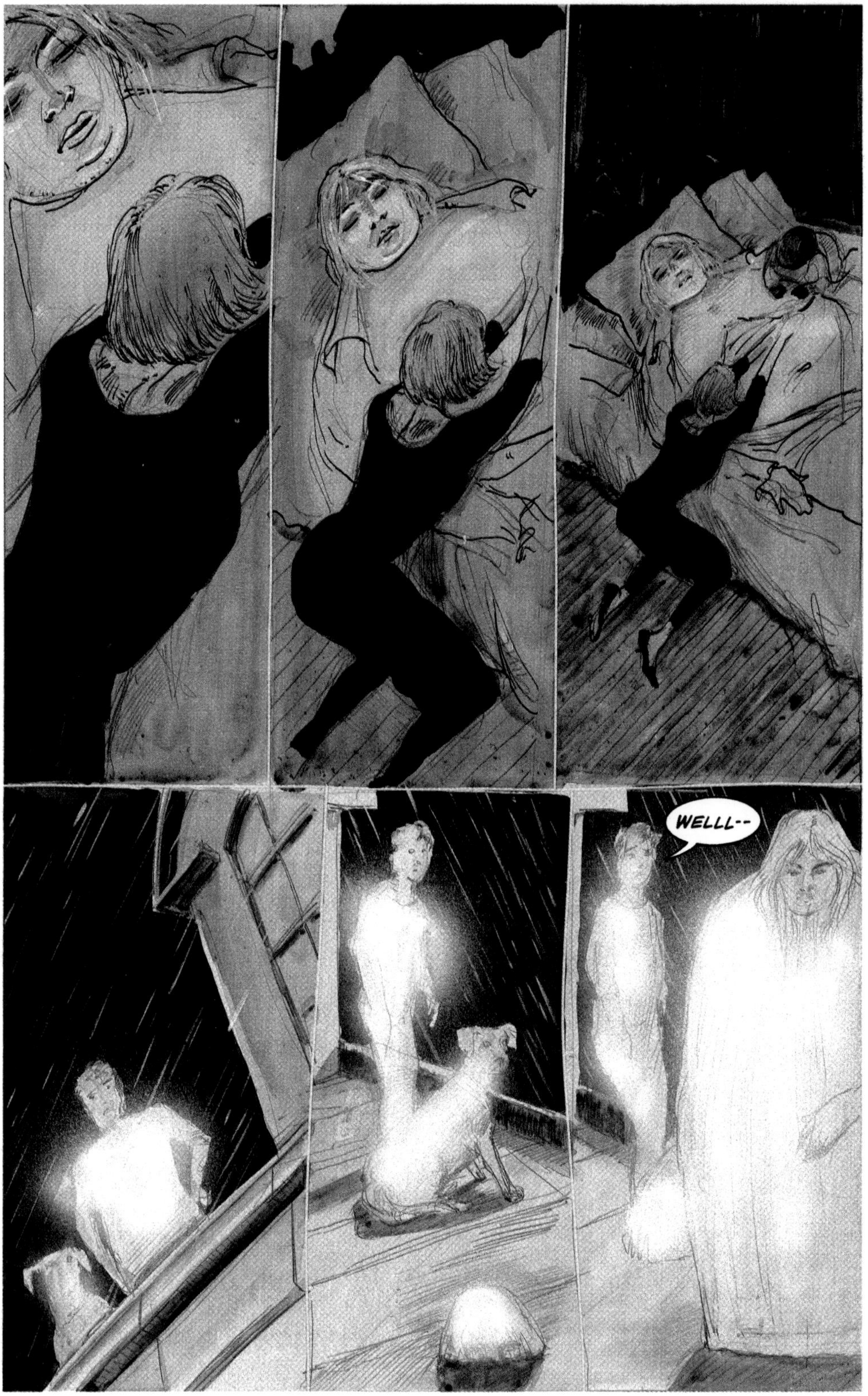
WELLL--

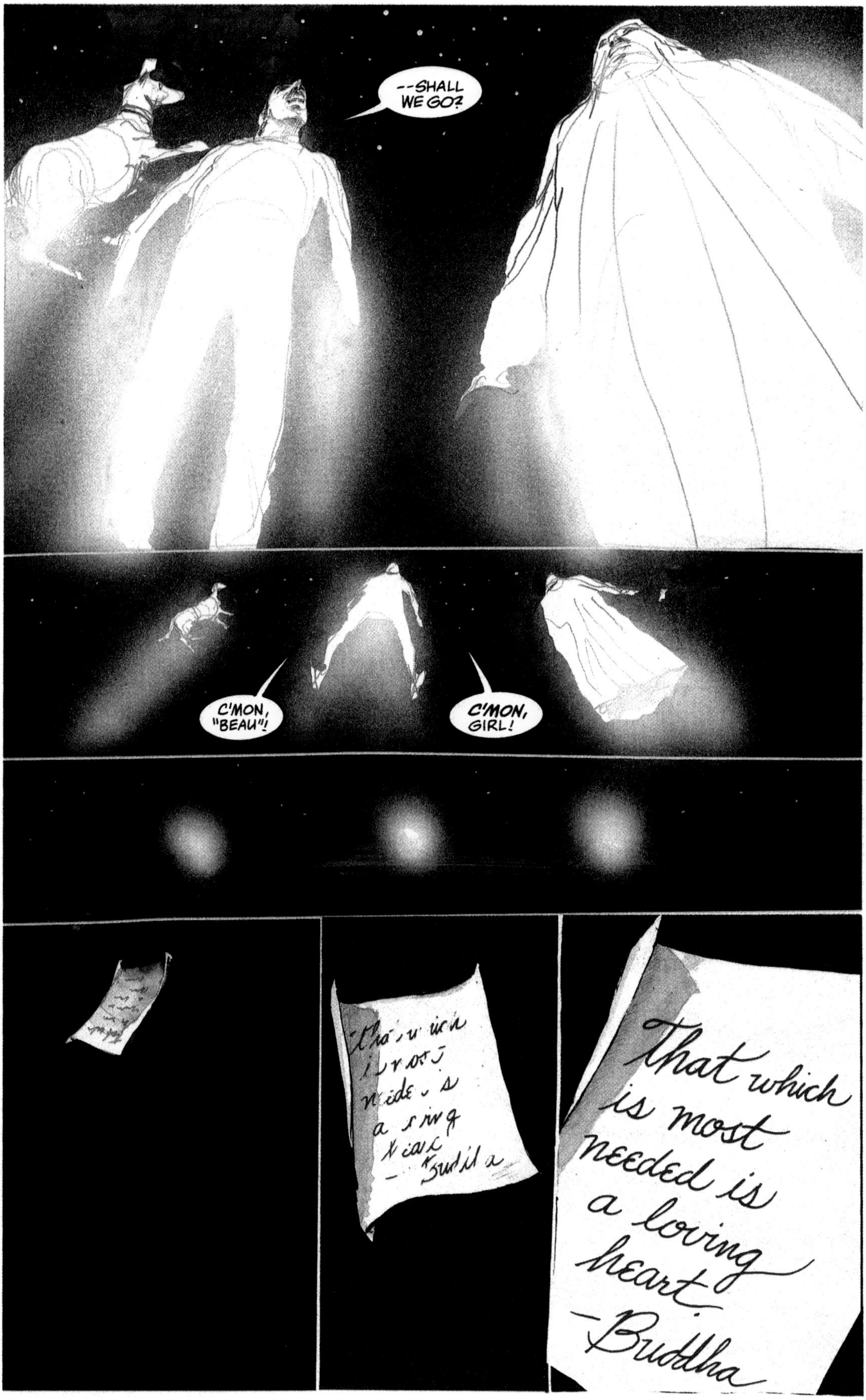
--SHALL WE GO?
C'MON, "BEAU"!
C'MON, GIRL!
That which is most needed is a loving heart. -Buddha

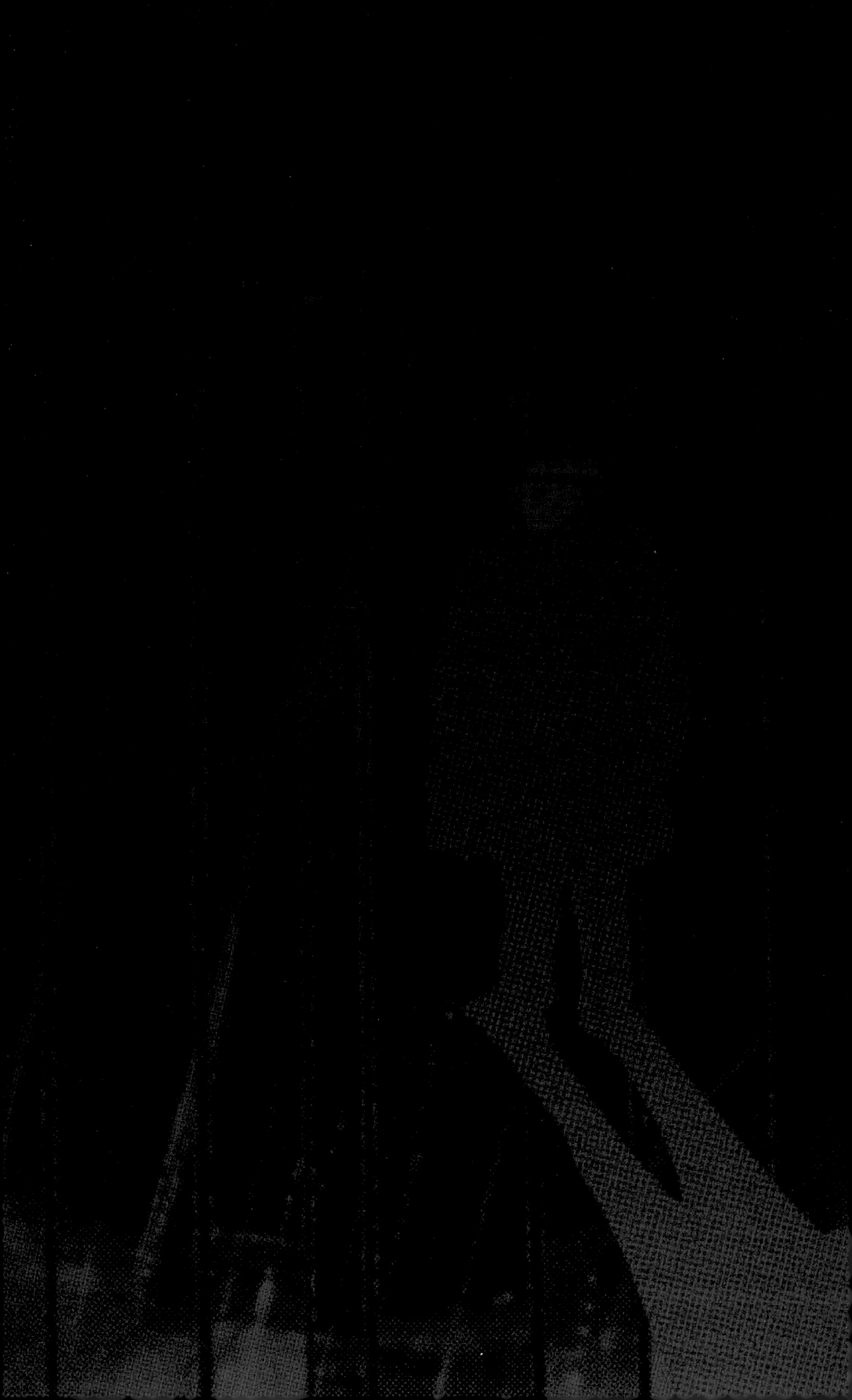

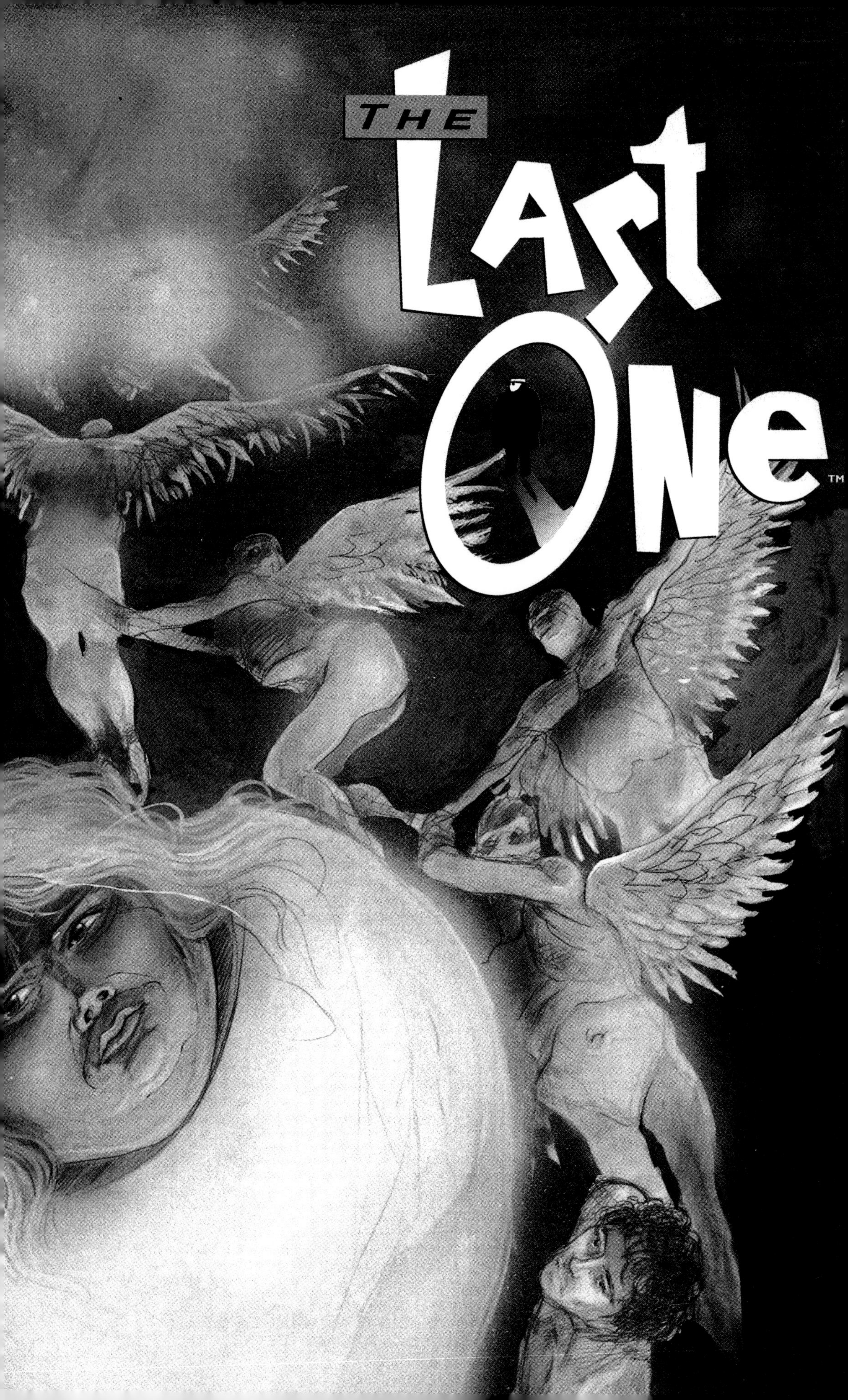
THE
LAST
ONE™

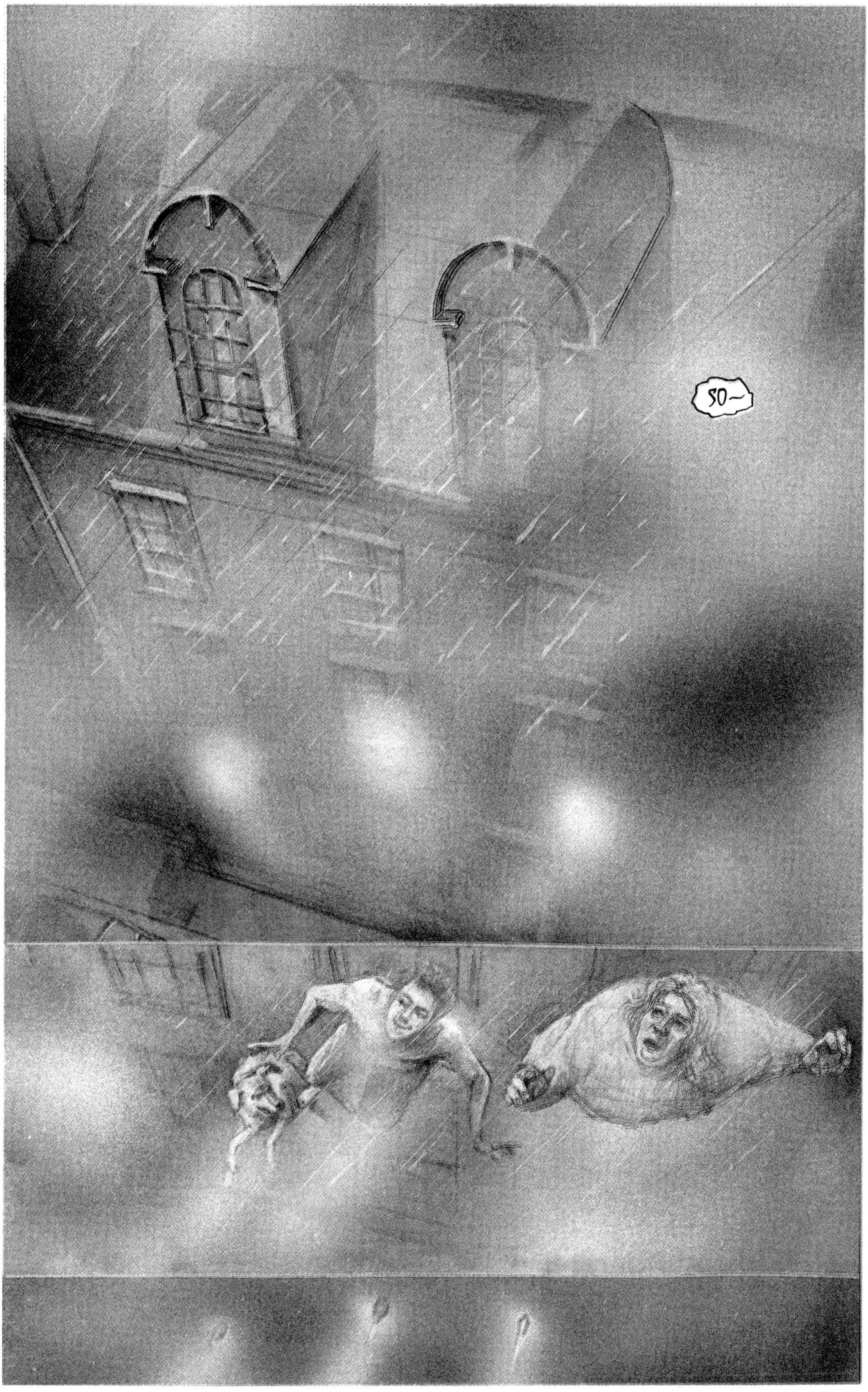
SO~

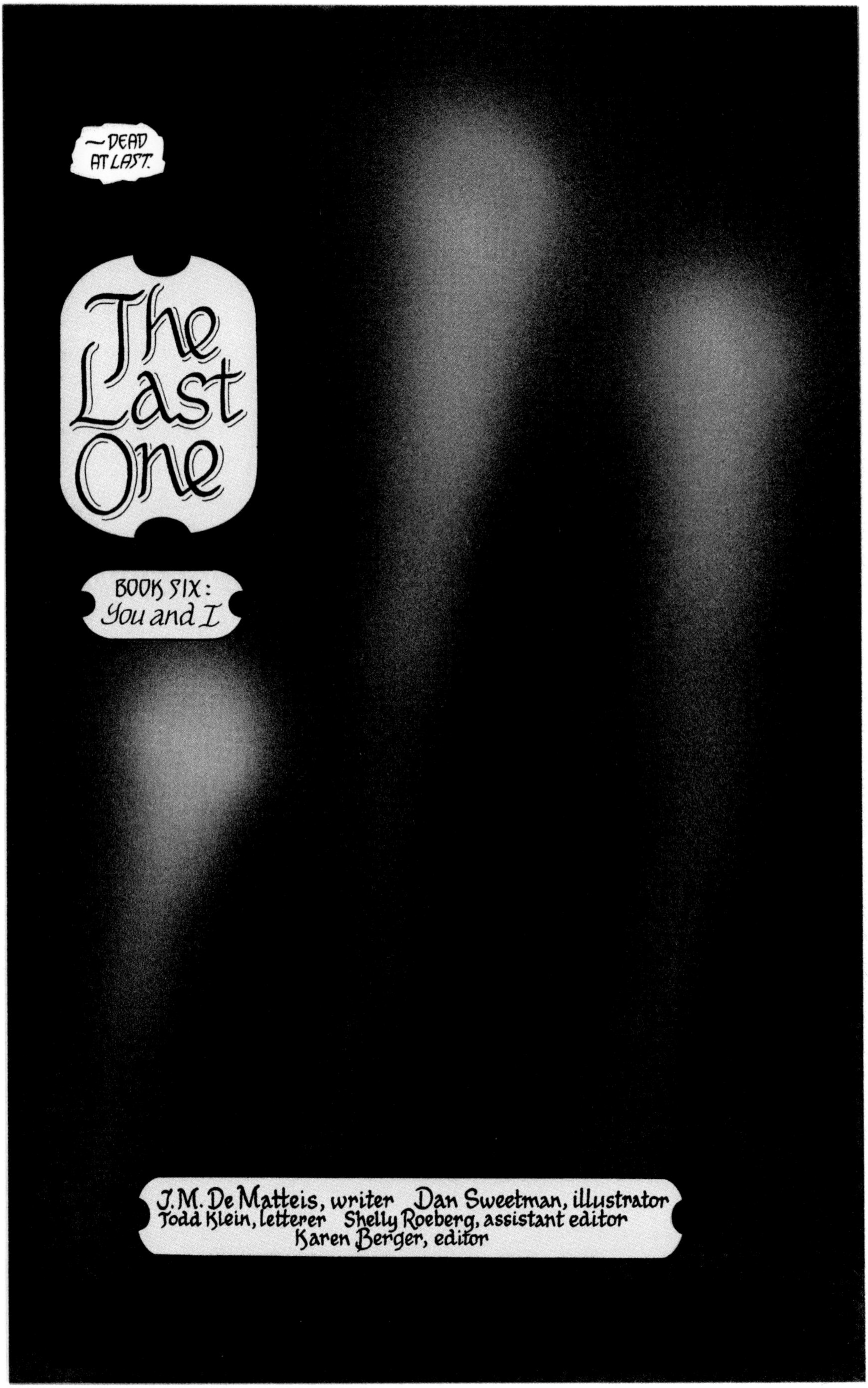

—DEAD AT LAST.
The Last One
BOOK SIX: You and I
J.M. De Matteis, writer Dan Sweetman, illustrator
Todd Klein, letterer Shelly Roeberg, assistant editor
Karen Berger, editor

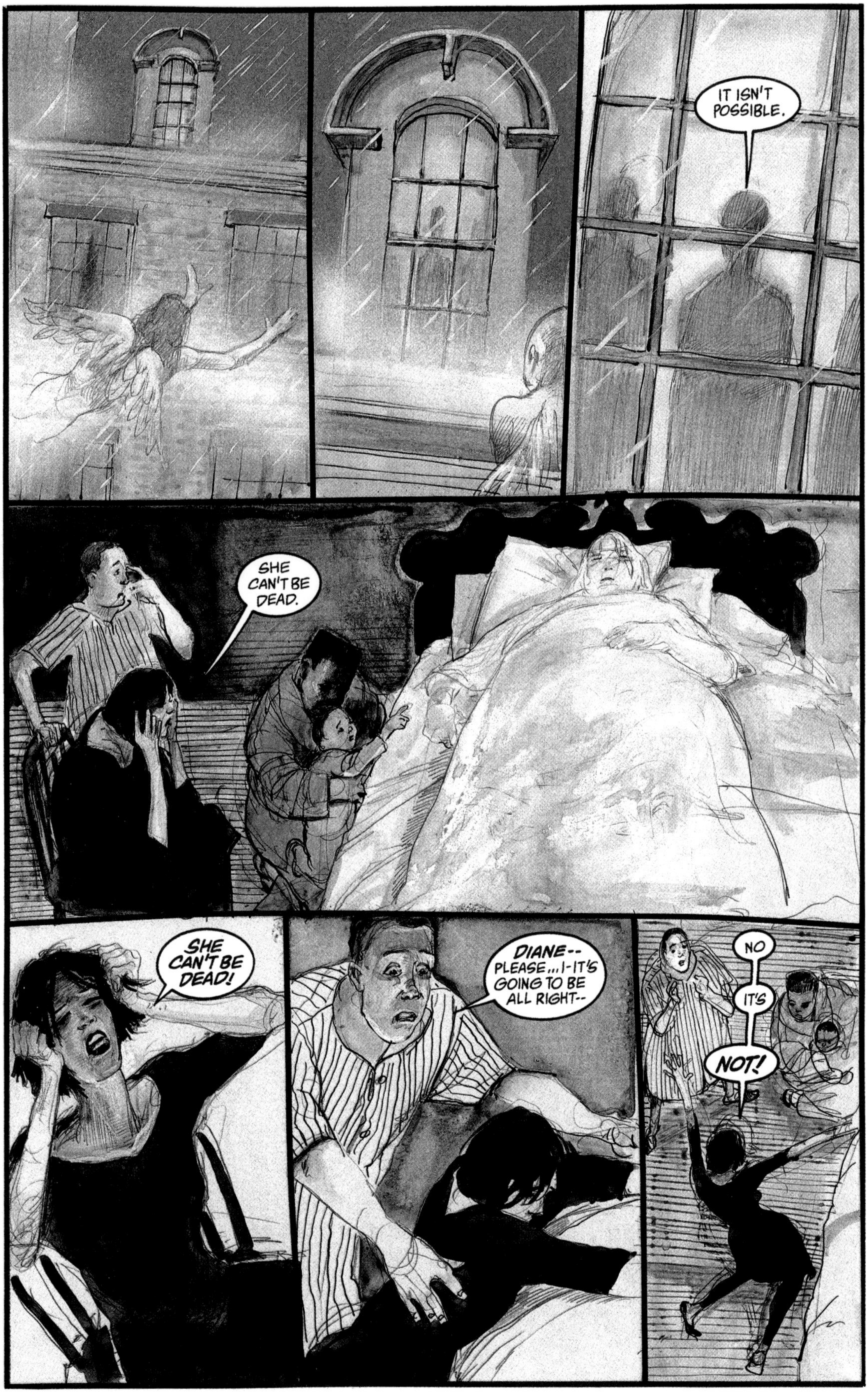
IT ISN'T POSSIBLE.
SHE CAN'T BE DEAD.
SHE CAN'T BE DEAD!
DIANE-- PLEASE... I-IT'S GOING TO BE ALL RIGHT--
NO
IT'S
NOT!

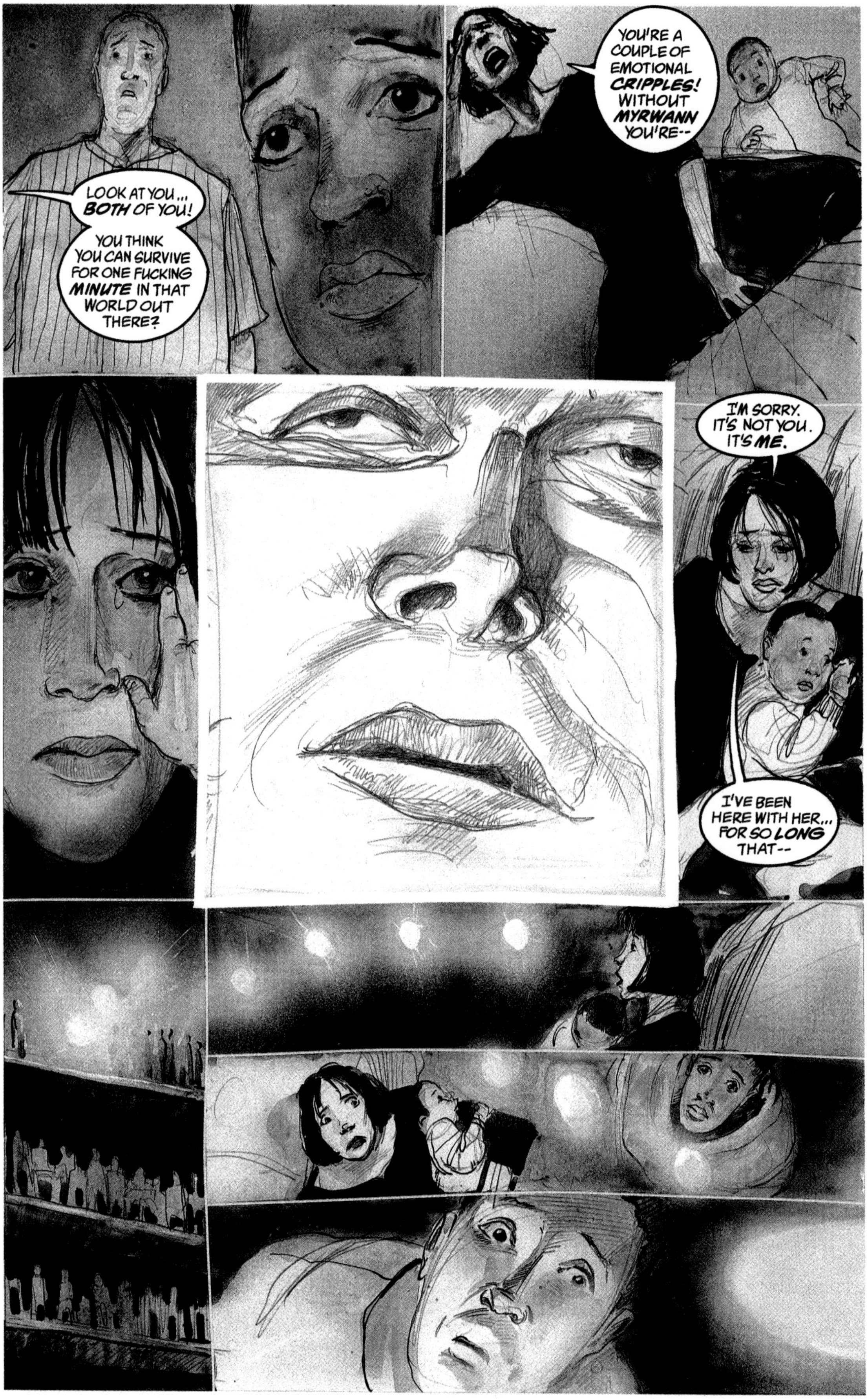
LOOK AT YOU... BOTH OF YOU!
YOU THINK YOU CAN SURVIVE FOR ONE FUCKING MINUTE IN THAT WORLD OUT THERE?
YOU'RE A COUPLE OF EMOTIONAL CRIPPLES! WITHOUT MYRWANN YOU'RE--
I'M SORRY. IT'S NOT YOU. IT'S ME.
I'VE BEEN HERE WITH HER... FOR SO LONG THAT--

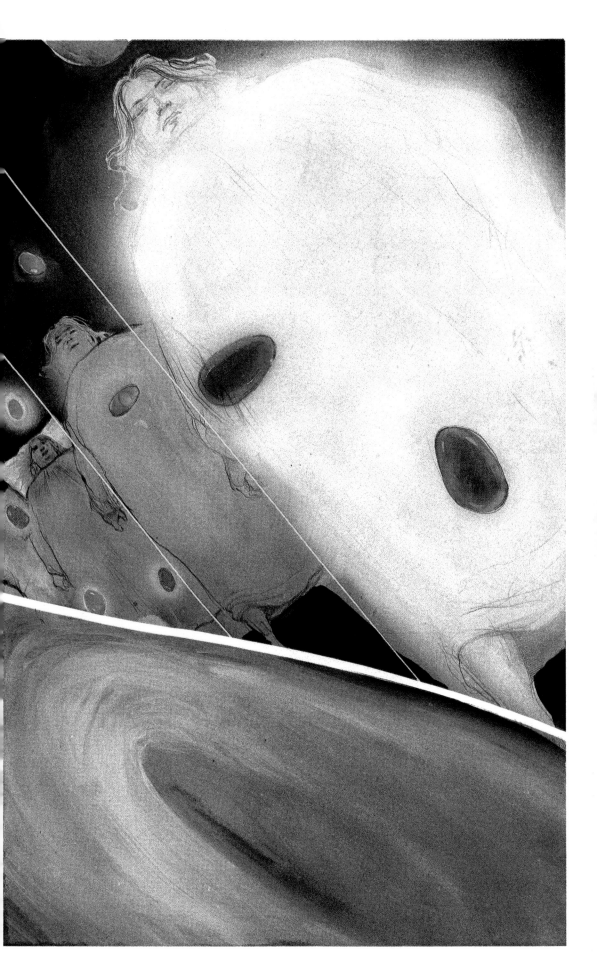

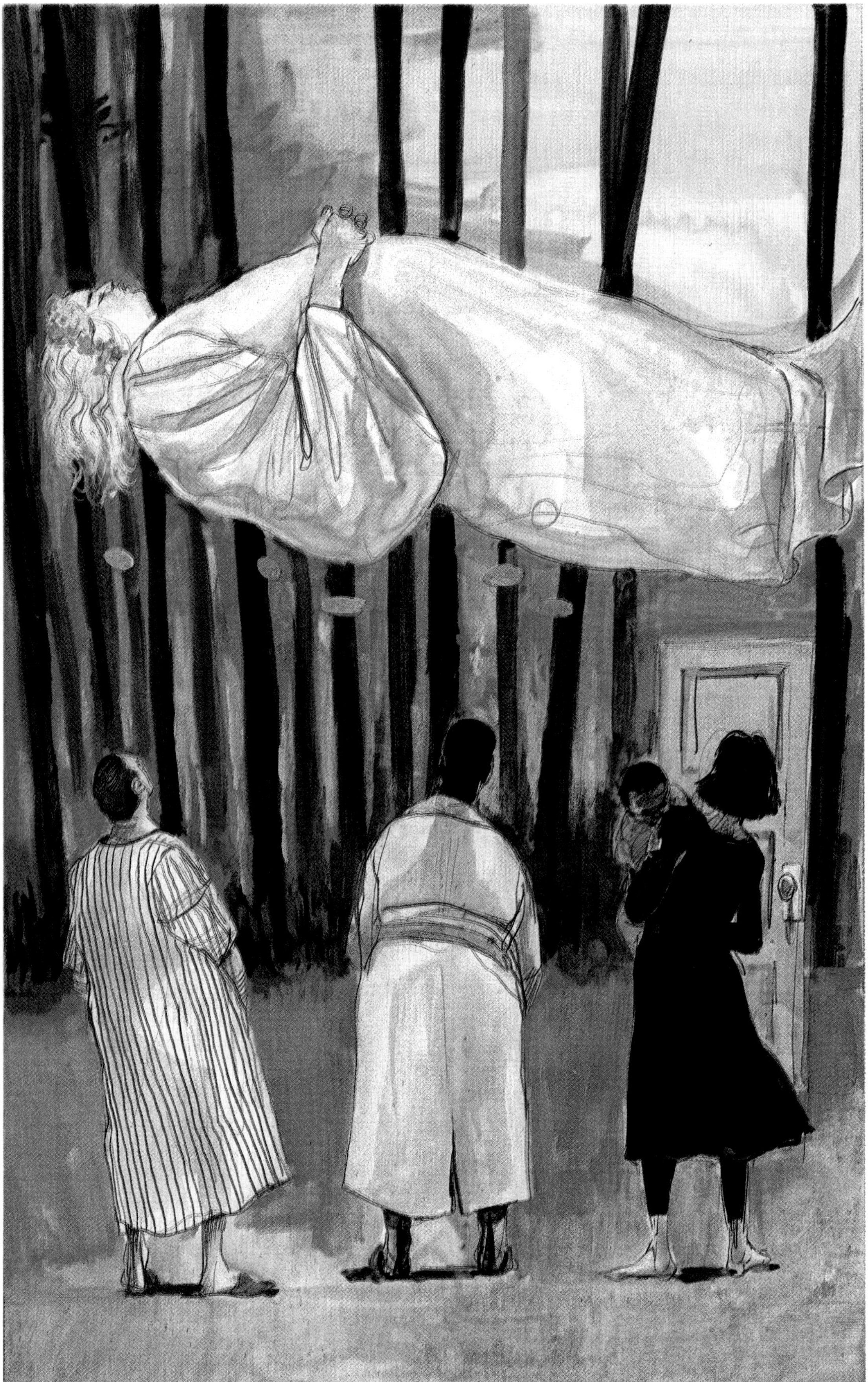

I'M GONNA MAKE A FEW CALLS.

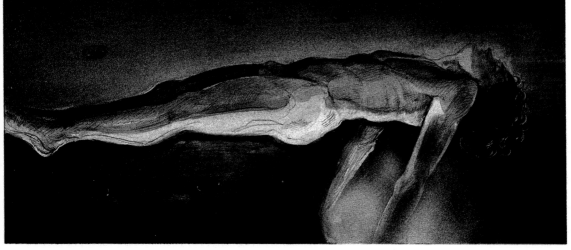

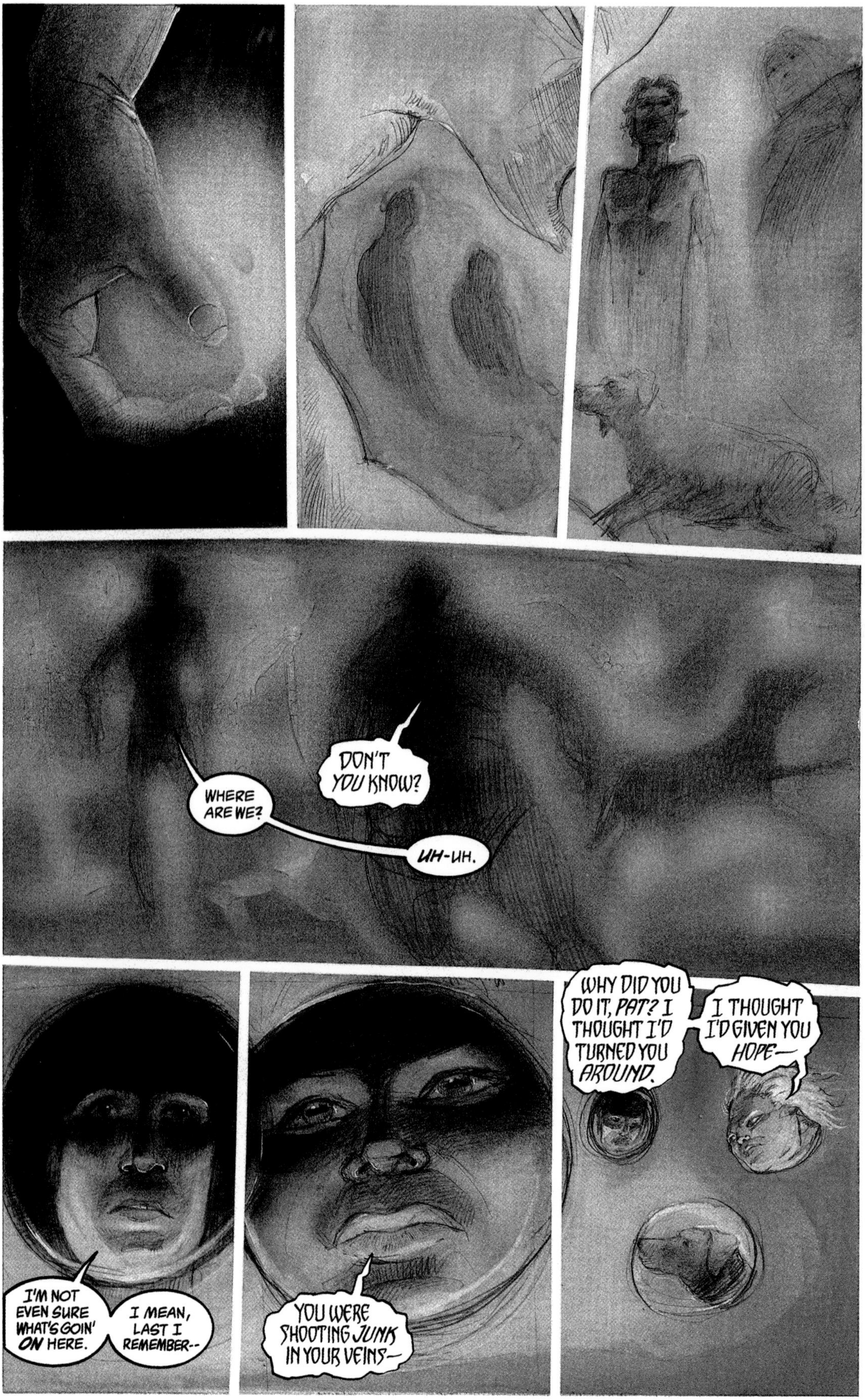
WHERE ARE WE?
DON'T YOU KNOW?
UH-UH.
I'M NOT EVEN SURE WHAT'S GOIN' ON HERE.
I MEAN, LAST I REMEMBER--
YOU WERE SHOOTING JUNK IN YOUR VEINS—
WHY DID YOU DO IT, PAT? I THOUGHT I'D TURNED YOU AROUND.
I THOUGHT I'D GIVEN YOU HOPE—

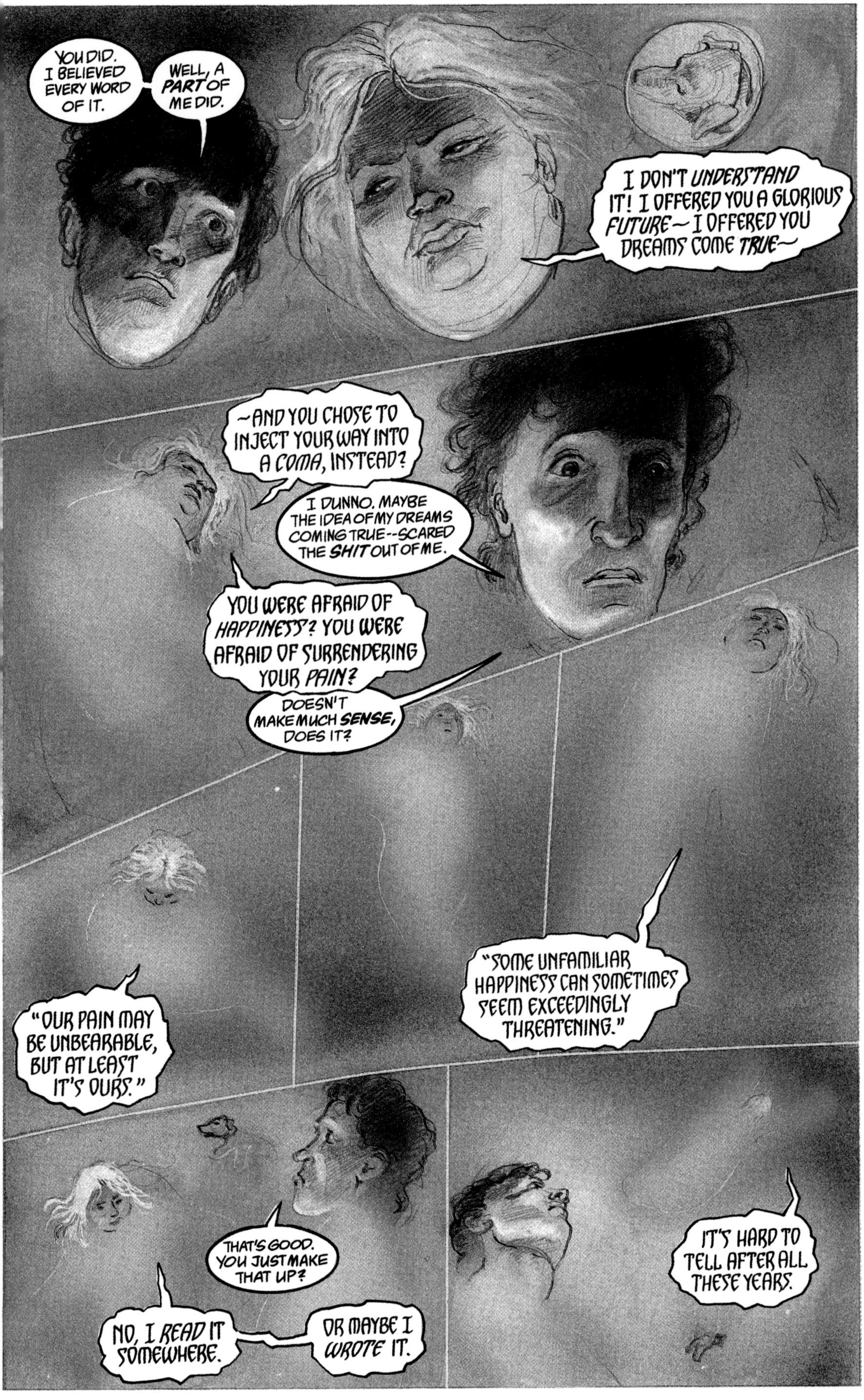
YOU DID. I BELIEVED EVERY WORD OF IT.
WELL, A PART OF ME DID.
I DON'T UNDERSTAND IT! I OFFERED YOU A GLORIOUS FUTURE~ I OFFERED YOU DREAMS COME TRUE~
~AND YOU CHOSE TO INJECT YOUR WAY INTO A COMA, INSTEAD?
I DUNNO. MAYBE THE IDEA OF MY DREAMS COMING TRUE--SCARED THE SHIT OUT OF ME.
YOU WERE AFRAID OF HAPPINESS? YOU WERE AFRAID OF SURRENDERING YOUR PAIN?
DOESN'T MAKE MUCH SENSE, DOES IT?
"SOME UNFAMILIAR HAPPINESS CAN SOMETIMES SEEM EXCEEDINGLY THREATENING."
"OUR PAIN MAY BE UNBEARABLE, BUT AT LEAST IT'S OURS."
THAT'S GOOD. YOU JUST MAKE THAT UP?
NO, I READ IT SOMEWHERE.
OR MAYBE I WROTE IT.
IT'S HARD TO TELL AFTER ALL THESE YEARS.

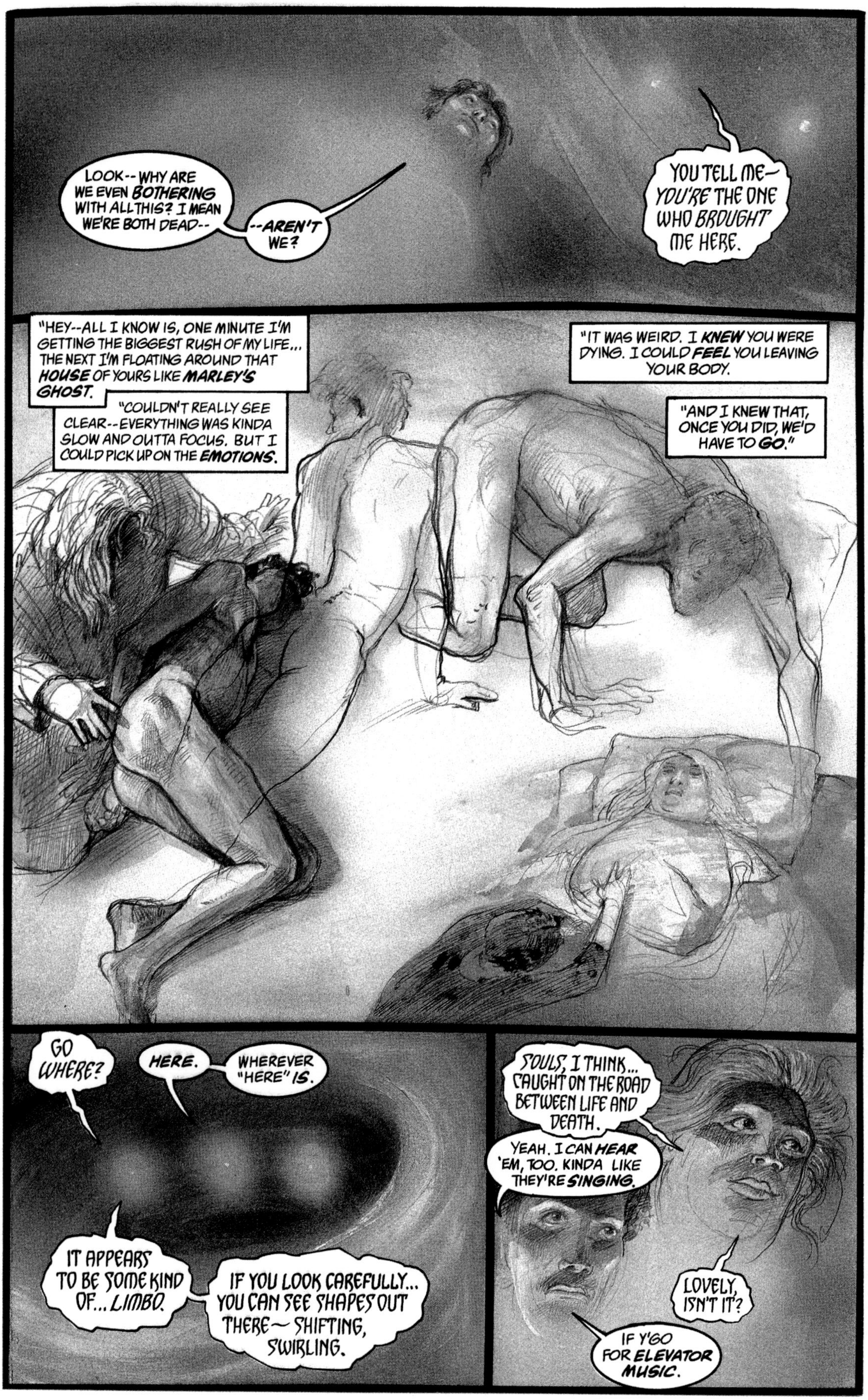

LOOK-- WHY ARE WE EVEN BOTHERING WITH ALL THIS? I MEAN WE'RE BOTH DEAD--
--AREN'T WE?
YOU TELL ME-- YOU'RE THE ONE WHO BROUGHT ME HERE.
"HEY--ALL I KNOW IS, ONE MINUTE I'M GETTING THE BIGGEST RUSH OF MY LIFE... THE NEXT I'M FLOATING AROUND THAT HOUSE OF YOURS LIKE MARLEY'S GHOST.
"COULDN'T REALLY SEE CLEAR--EVERYTHING WAS KINDA SLOW AND OUTTA FOCUS. BUT I COULD PICK UP ON THE EMOTIONS.
"IT WAS WEIRD. I KNEW YOU WERE DYING. I COULD FEEL YOU LEAVING YOUR BODY.
"AND I KNEW THAT, ONCE YOU DID, WE'D HAVE TO GO."
GO WHERE?
HERE.
WHEREVER "HERE" IS.
IT APPEARS TO BE SOME KIND OF... LIMBO.
IF YOU LOOK CAREFULLY... YOU CAN SEE SHAPES OUT THERE-- SHIFTING, SWIRLING.
SOULS, I THINK... CAUGHT ON THE ROAD BETWEEN LIFE AND DEATH.
YEAH. I CAN HEAR 'EM, TOO. KINDA LIKE THEY'RE SINGING.
LOVELY, ISN'T IT?
IF Y'GO FOR ELEVATOR MUSIC.

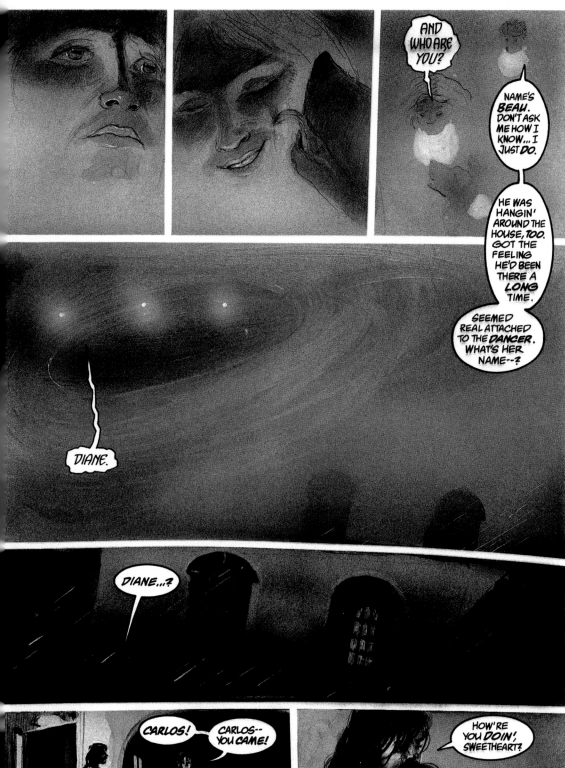

AND WHO ARE YOU?

NAME'S *BEAU*. DON'T ASK ME HOW I KNOW... I JUST *DO*.

HE WAS HANGIN' AROUND THE HOUSE, *TOO*. GOT THE FEELING HE'D BEEN THERE A *LONG* TIME.

SEEMED REAL ATTACHED TO THE *DANCER*. WHAT'S HER NAME--?

DIANE.

DIANE...?

CARLOS!

CARLOS-- YOU *CAME*!

HOW COULD I *NOT*?

SOON AS MITCHELL CALLED, I GOT MY ASS ON THE FIRST PLANE *BACK*.

HOW'RE YOU *DOIN'*, SWEETHEART?

I...I DON'T KNOW HOW I'M DOING, I JUST... IT DOESN'T MAKE ANY *SENSE*-- IT--

C'MON... LET'S GO *UPSTAIRS*.

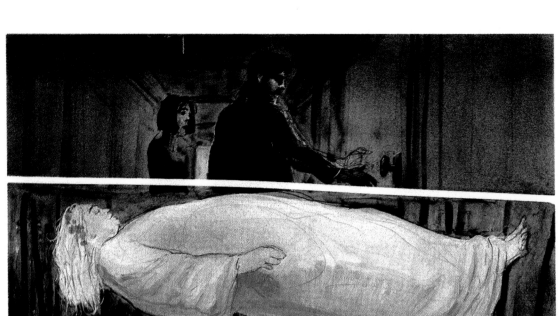

I GUESS I SHOULD SAY SOMETHING-- --ALTHOUGH I'M NOT SURE WHAT. MOST OF YOU KNOW IT ALL, ANYWAY.

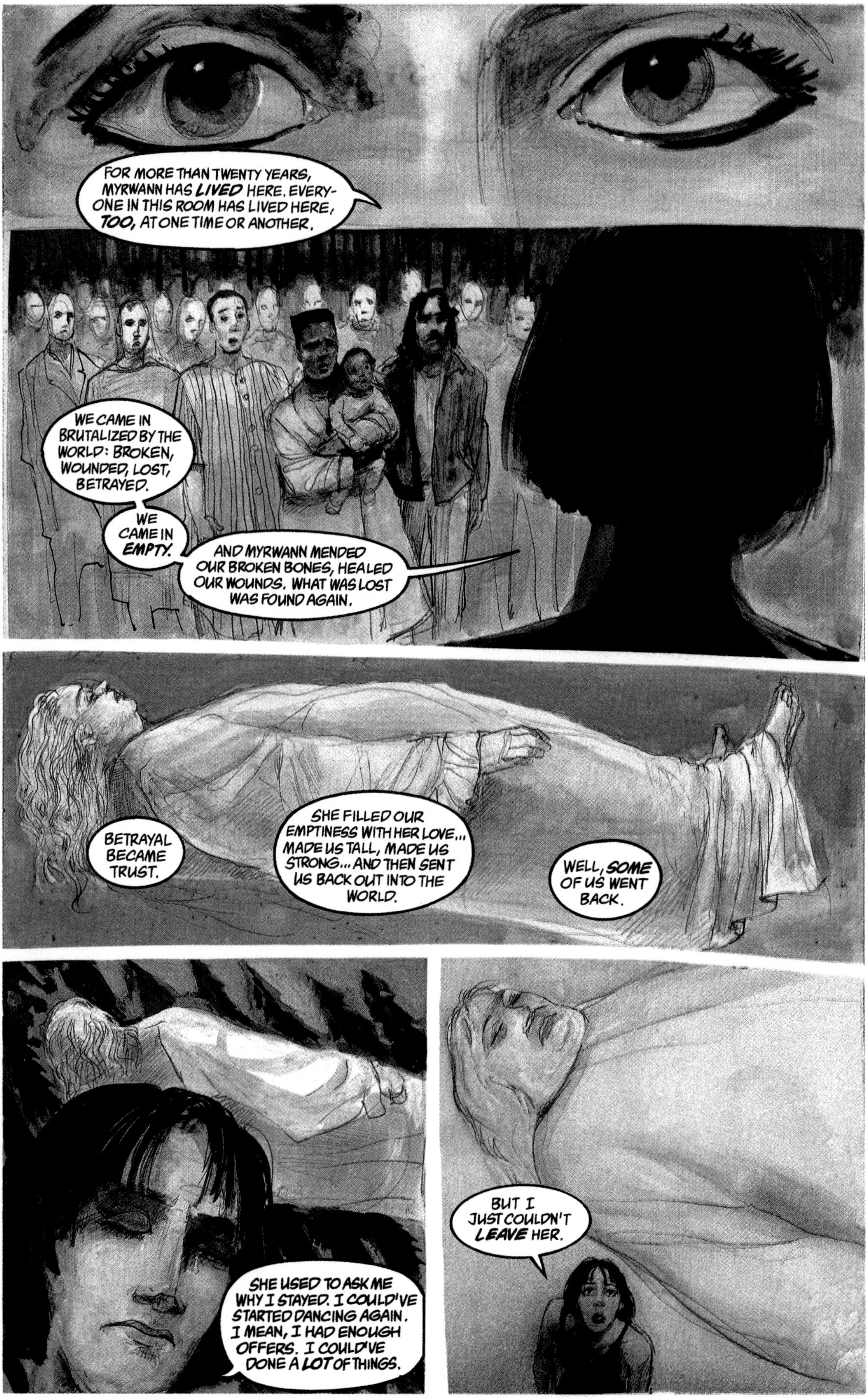
FOR MORE THAN TWENTY YEARS, MYRWANN HAS LIVED HERE. EVERY-ONE IN THIS ROOM HAS LIVED HERE, TOO, AT ONE TIME OR ANOTHER.
WE CAME IN BRUTALIZED BY THE WORLD: BROKEN, WOUNDED, LOST, BETRAYED.
WE CAME IN EMPTY.
AND MYRWANN MENDED OUR BROKEN BONES, HEALED OUR WOUNDS. WHAT WAS LOST WAS FOUND AGAIN.
BETRAYAL BECAME TRUST.
SHE FILLED OUR EMPTINESS WITH HER LOVE... MADE US TALL, MADE US STRONG... AND THEN SENT US BACK OUT INTO THE WORLD.
WELL, SOME OF US WENT BACK.
SHE USED TO ASK ME WHY I STAYED. I COULD'VE STARTED DANCING AGAIN. I MEAN, I HAD ENOUGH OFFERS. I COULD'VE DONE A LOT OF THINGS.
BUT I JUST COULDN'T LEAVE HER.

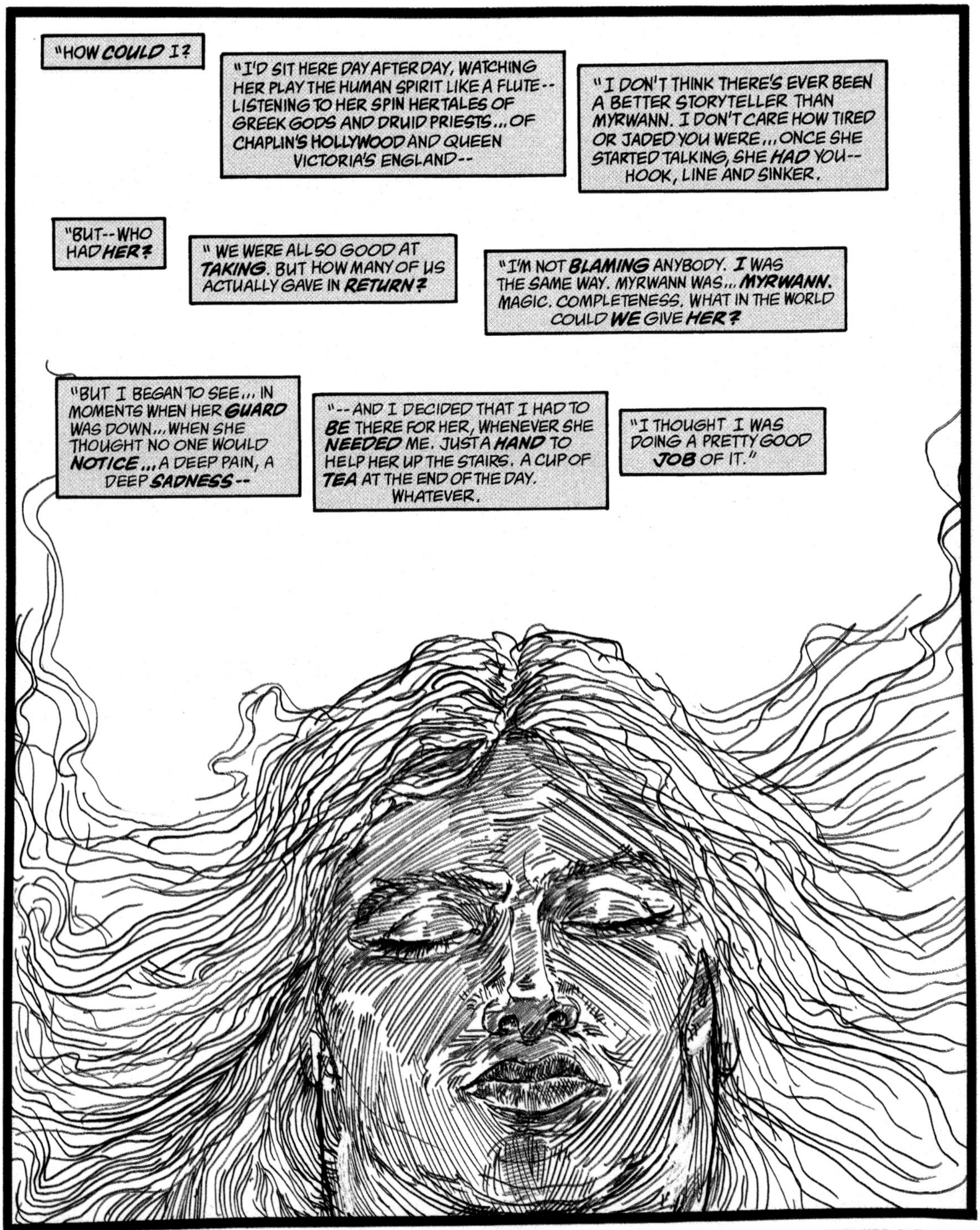
"HOW COULD I?
"I'D SIT HERE DAY AFTER DAY, WATCHING HER PLAY THE HUMAN SPIRIT LIKE A FLUTE -- LISTENING TO HER SPIN HER TALES OF GREEK GODS AND DRUID PRIESTS ... OF CHAPLIN'S HOLLYWOOD AND QUEEN VICTORIA'S ENGLAND --
"I DON'T THINK THERE'S EVER BEEN A BETTER STORYTELLER THAN MYRWANN. I DON'T CARE HOW TIRED OR JADED YOU WERE ... ONCE SHE STARTED TALKING, SHE HAD YOU -- HOOK, LINE AND SINKER.
"BUT -- WHO HAD HER?
"WE WERE ALL SO GOOD AT TAKING. BUT HOW MANY OF US ACTUALLY GAVE IN RETURN?
"I'M NOT BLAMING ANYBODY. I WAS THE SAME WAY. MYRWANN WAS ... MYRWANN. MAGIC. COMPLETENESS. WHAT IN THE WORLD COULD WE GIVE HER?
"BUT I BEGAN TO SEE ... IN MOMENTS WHEN HER GUARD WAS DOWN ... WHEN SHE THOUGHT NO ONE WOULD NOTICE ... A DEEP PAIN, A DEEP SADNESS --
"-- AND I DECIDED THAT I HAD TO BE THERE FOR HER, WHENEVER SHE NEEDED ME. JUST A HAND TO HELP HER UP THE STAIRS. A CUP OF TEA AT THE END OF THE DAY. WHATEVER.
"I THOUGHT I WAS DOING A PRETTY GOOD JOB OF IT."

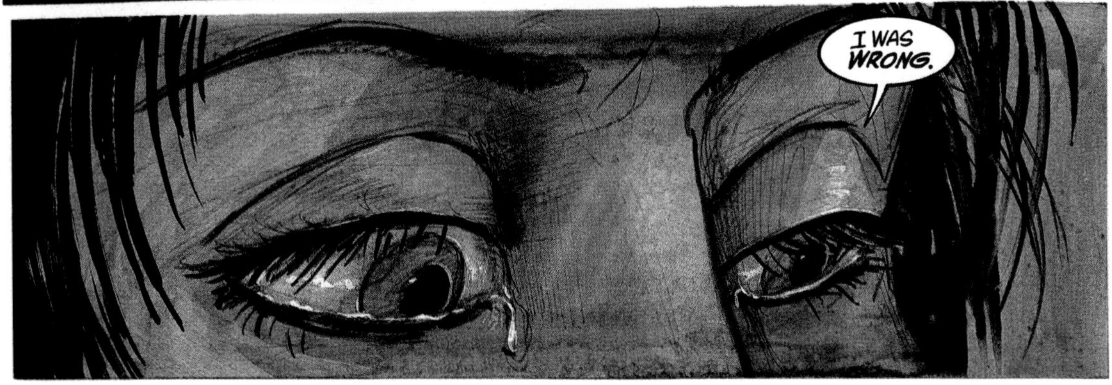
I WAS WRONG.

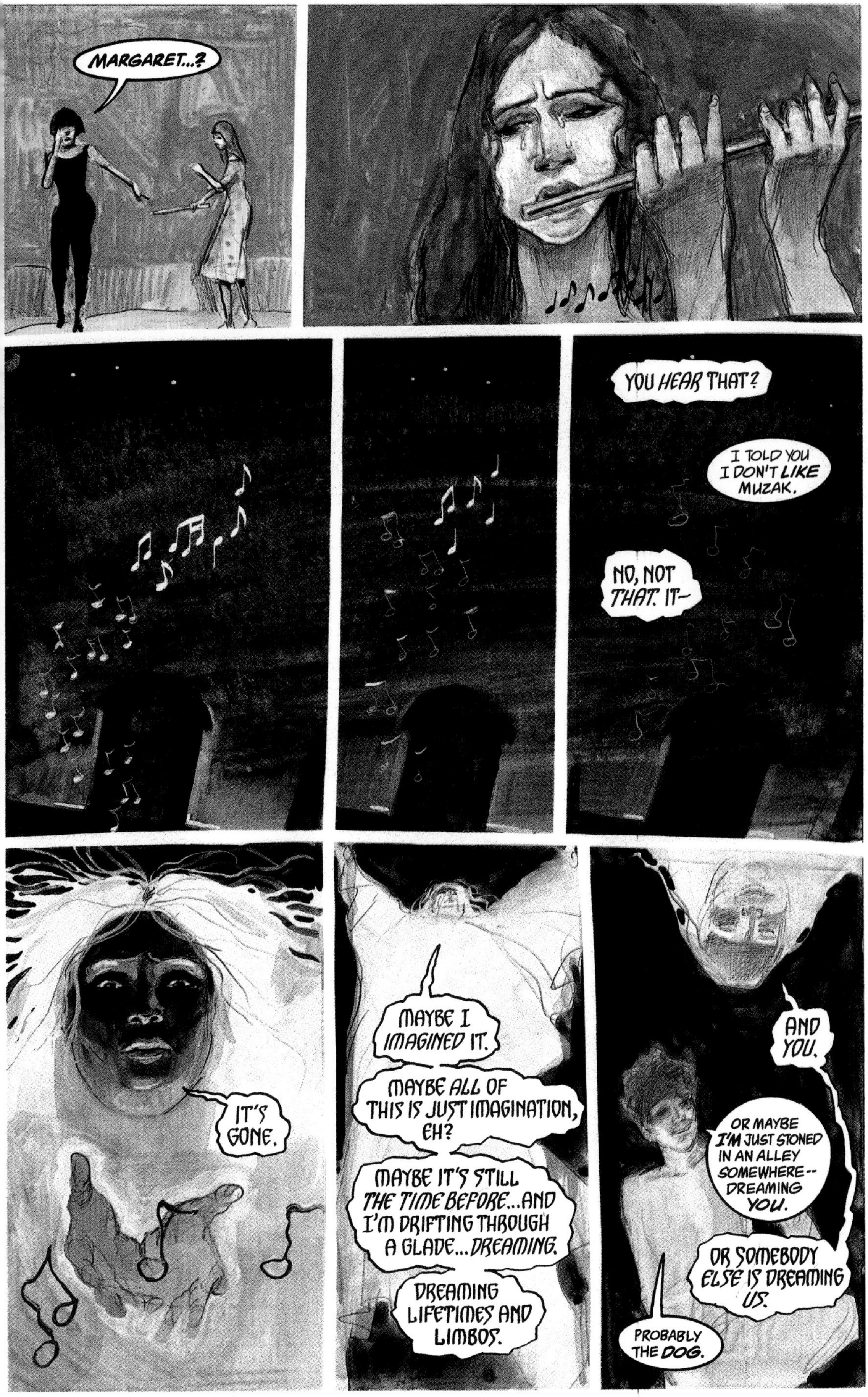
MARGARET...?
YOU HEAR THAT?
I TOLD YOU I DON'T LIKE MUZAK.
NO, NOT THAT. IT—
IT'S GONE.
MAYBE I IMAGINED IT.
MAYBE ALL OF THIS IS JUST IMAGINATION, EH?
MAYBE IT'S STILL THE TIME BEFORE...AND I'M DRIFTING THROUGH A GLADE...DREAMING.
DREAMING LIFETIMES AND LIMBOS.
AND YOU.
OR MAYBE I'M JUST STONED IN AN ALLEY SOMEWHERE--DREAMING YOU.
OR SOMEBODY ELSE IS DREAMING US.
PROBABLY THE DOG.

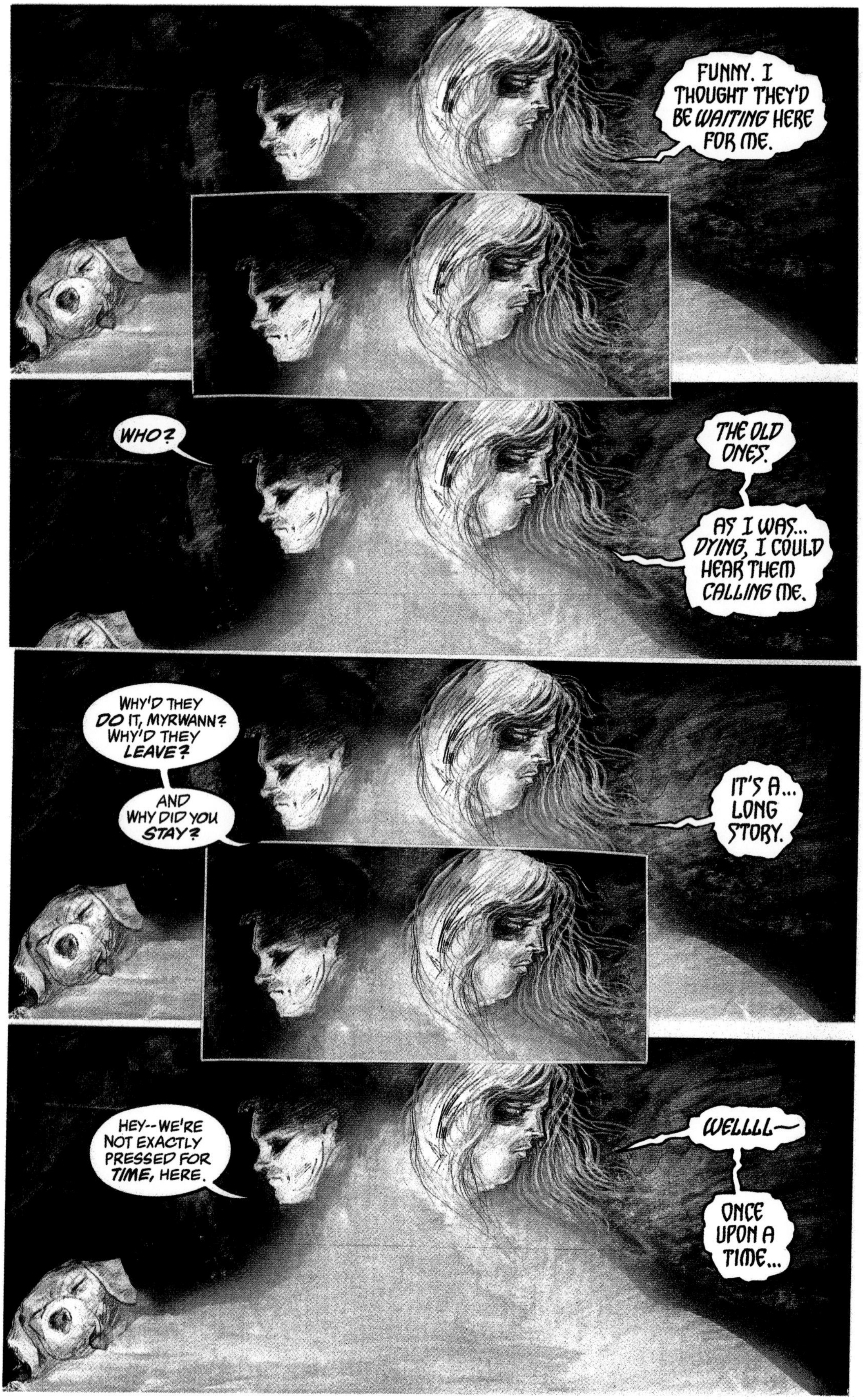
FUNNY. I THOUGHT THEY'D BE *WAITING* HERE FOR ME.
WHO?
THE OLD ONES.
AS I WAS... *DYING*, I COULD HEAR THEM CALLING ME.
WHY'D THEY *DO* IT, MYRWANN? WHY'D THEY *LEAVE*?
AND WHY DID YOU *STAY*?
IT'S A... LONG STORY.
HEY--WE'RE NOT EXACTLY PRESSED FOR *TIME*, HERE.
WELLLL--
ONCE UPON A TIME...

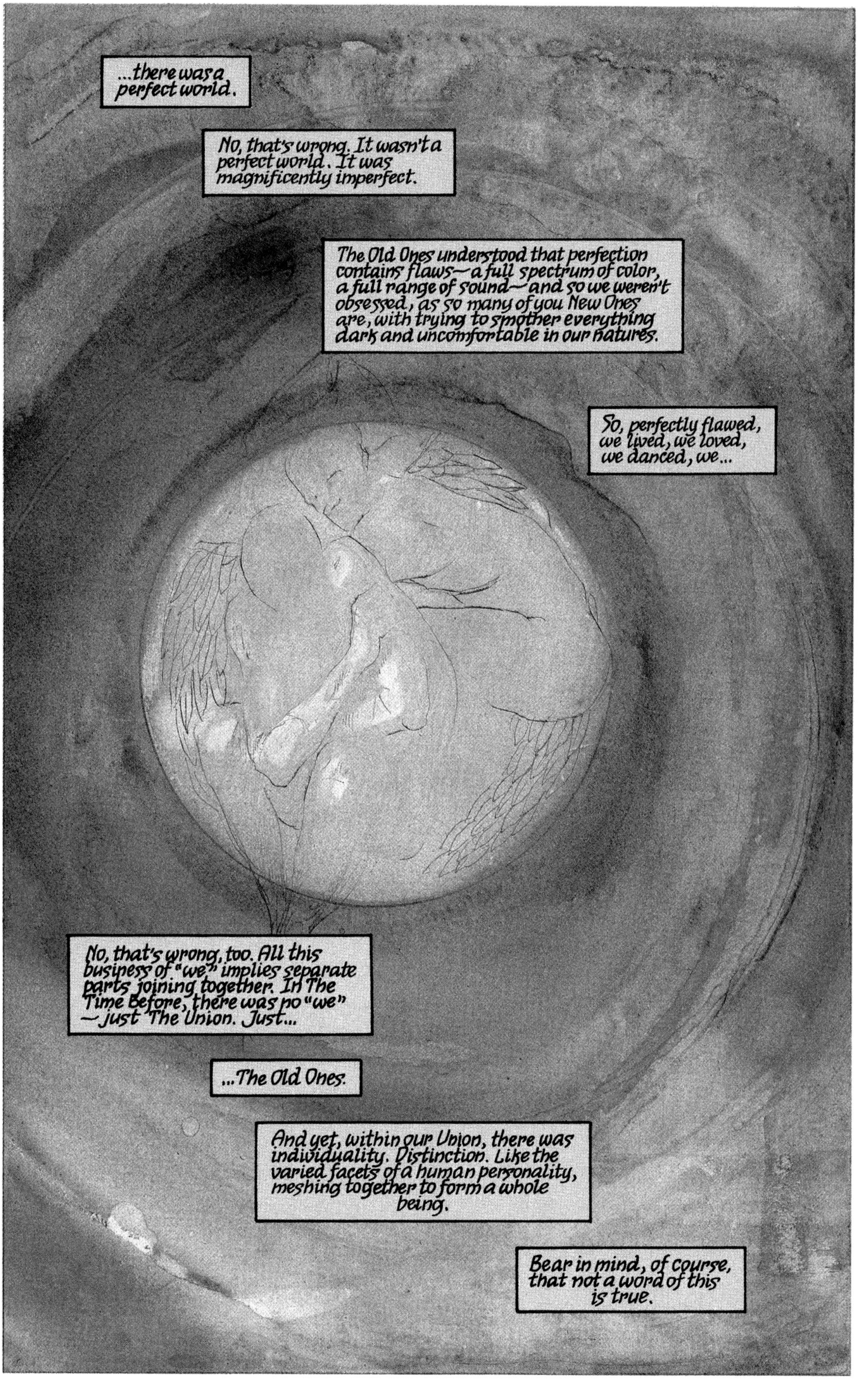
...there was a perfect world.
No, that's wrong. It wasn't a perfect world. It was magnificently imperfect.
The Old Ones understood that perfection contains flaws— a full spectrum of color, a full range of sound— and so we weren't obsessed, as so many of you New Ones are, with trying to smother everything dark and uncomfortable in our natures.
So, perfectly flawed, we lived, we loved, we danced, we...
No, that's wrong, too. All this business of "we" implies separate parts joining together. In The Time Before, there was no "we" —just The Union. Just...
...The Old Ones.
And yet, within our Union, there was individuality. Distinction. Like the varied facets of a human personality, meshing together to form a whole being.
Bear in mind, of course, that not a word of this is true.

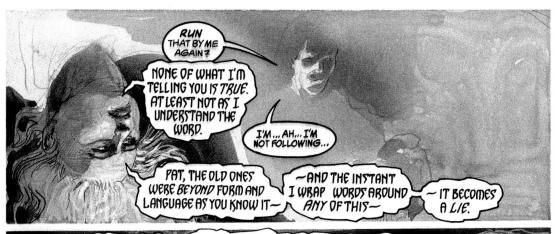

RUN THAT BY ME AGAIN?

NONE OF WHAT I'M TELLING YOU IS *TRUE*. AT LEAST NOT AS I UNDERSTAND THE WORD.

I'M... AH... I'M NOT FOLLOWING...

PAT, THE OLD ONES WERE *BEYOND* FORM AND LANGUAGE AS YOU KNOW IT—

—AND THE INSTANT I WRAP *WORDS* AROUND *ANY* OF THIS—

—IT BECOMES A *LIE*.

I CAN'T EVEN TRUST MY OWN *MEMORY* ANY- MORE!

I'VE BEEN BOUND UP BY FLESH AND THOUGHT AND SPEECH SO LONG THAT MY PERCEPTION OF WHAT WE WERE HAS BECOME TOTALLY *DISTORTED*—

—I'VE GONE... *SENILE!*

GO ON WITH THE STORY.

PLEASE?

THE ARRIVAL OF THE NEW—

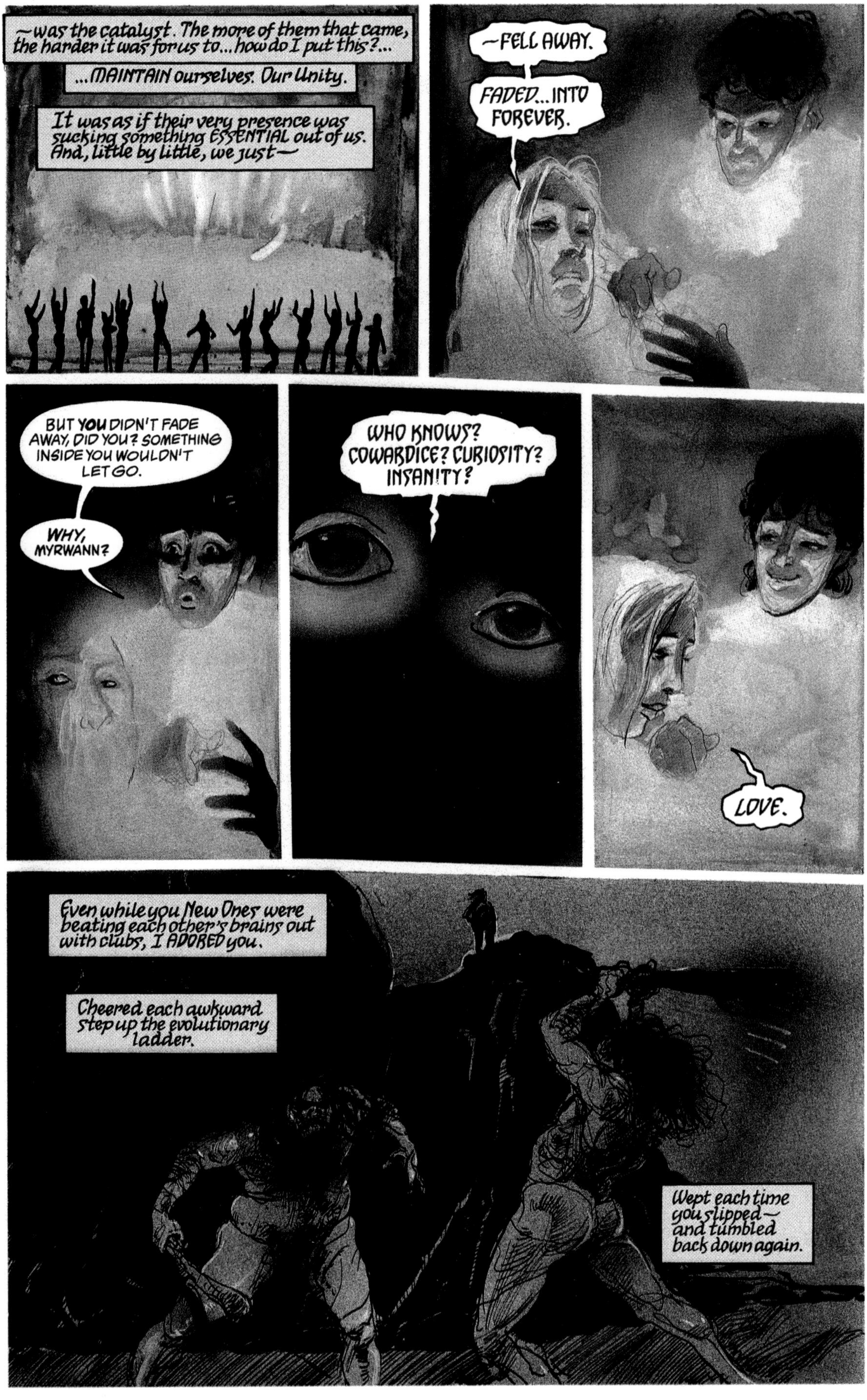
~was the catalyst. The more of them that came, the harder it was for us to... how do I put this?...
...MAINTAIN ourselves. Our Unity.
It was as if their very presence was sucking something ESSENTIAL out of us. And, little by little, we just—
~FELL AWAY.
FADED...INTO FOREVER.
BUT YOU DIDN'T FADE AWAY, DID YOU? SOMETHING INSIDE YOU WOULDN'T LET GO.
WHY, MYRWANN?
WHO KNOWS? COWARDICE? CURIOSITY? INSANITY?
LOVE.
Even while you New Ones were beating each other's brains out with clubs, I ADORED you.
Cheered each awkward step up the evolutionary ladder.
Wept each time you slipped— and tumbled back down again.

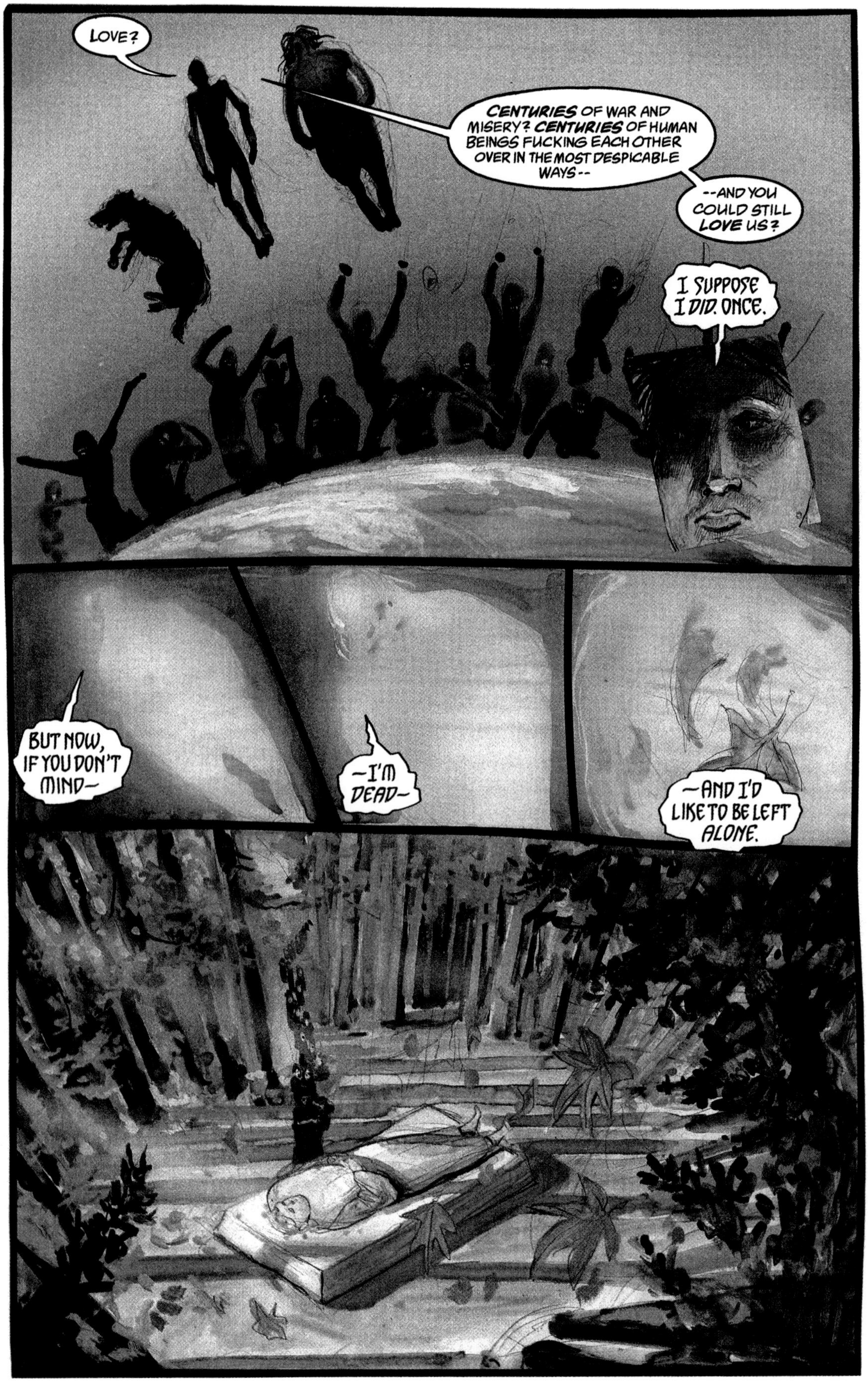
LOVE?
CENTURIES OF WAR AND MISERY? CENTURIES OF HUMAN BEINGS FUCKING EACH OTHER OVER IN THE MOST DESPICABLE WAYS--
--AND YOU COULD STILL LOVE US?
I SUPPOSE I DID. ONCE.
BUT NOW, IF YOU DON'T MIND—
—I'M DEAD—
—AND I'D LIKE TO BE LEFT ALONE.

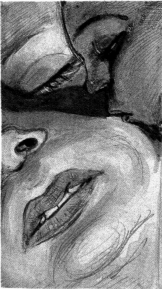

HEY... MYRWANN?

MYRWANN?

HMMM?

I WAS JUST THINKING.

I'M VERY HAPPY FOR YOU.

NO, NO--I'M SERIOUS.

YOU SAW THE WORST IN US, DIDN'T YOU?

PAT, PLEASE—

DIDN'T YOU?

YES. YES, I DID.

BUT FOR ALL THAT-- YOU NEVER STOPPED LOVING US?
WHAT'S NOT TO LOVE?
PERFECTION INCLUDES IMPERFECTION, RIGHT?
A FULL SPECTRUM OF COLOR?
A FULL RANGE OF SOUND.
NOW WOULD YOU MIND TELLING ME WHAT—
OH.
A LITTLE HOME-SICK, ARE WE?
WELL, LET ME REMIND YOU THAT YOU HATED THAT WORLD SO MUCH, YOU TRIED EVERY WAY YOU COULD TO ESCAPE IT. AND, CONGRATULATIONS—
—YOU SUCCEEDED.
HEY... YOU'RE DEAD, TOO, Y'KNOW.
NOT BY MY OWN HAND! AND NOT AFTER A PITIFUL NINETEEN YEARS!
I'VE LIVED, PAT— AS FULL AND RICH A LIFE AS ANY SOUL IN CREATION HAS EVER KNOWN! BUT, YOU—
AH... WHAT'S THE POINT OF EVEN TALKING ABOUT IT? IT'S NOT LIKE I CAN JUST TURN AROUND AND GO BACK--
WHO SAYS YOU CAN'T?
THAT'S NOT FUNNY.
I'M NOT JOKING.

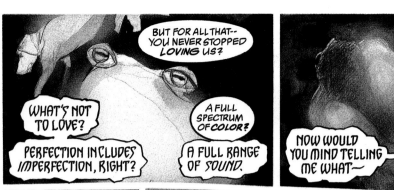

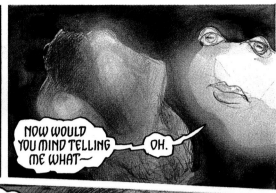

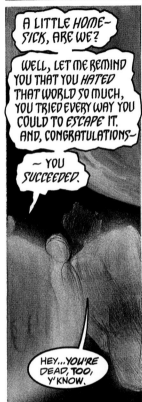

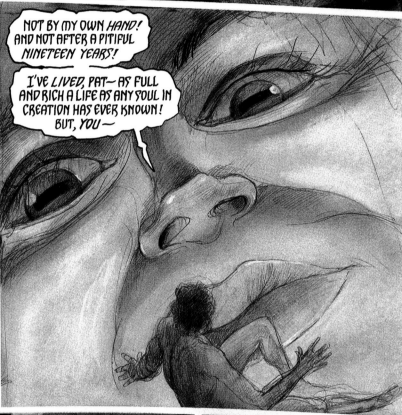

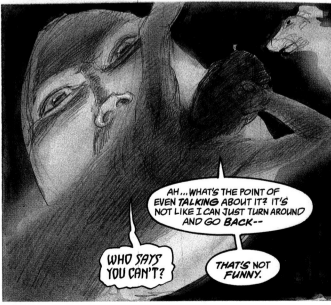

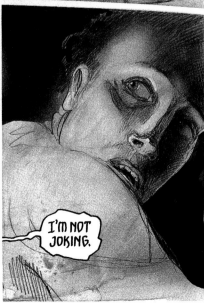

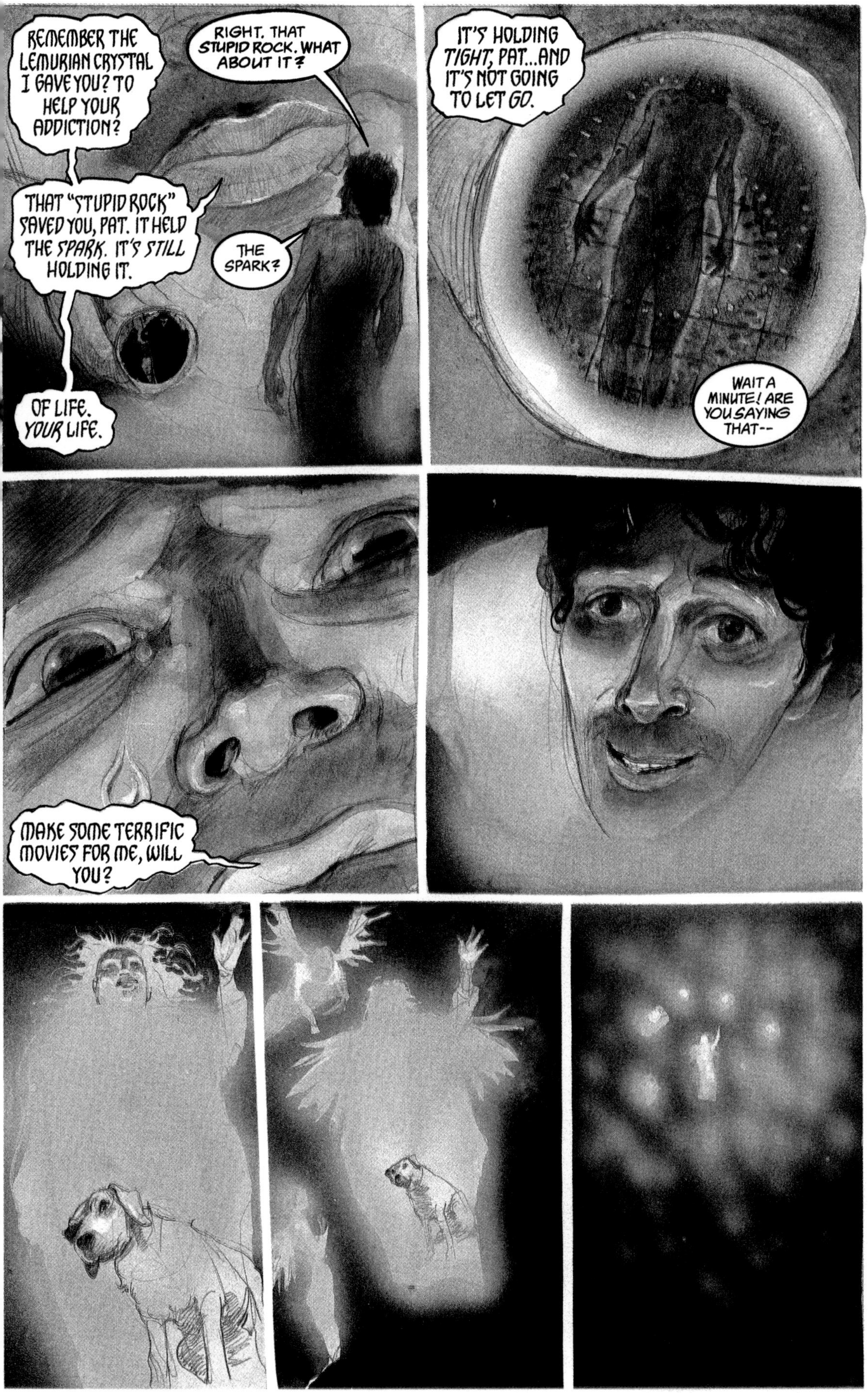
REMEMBER THE LEMURIAN CRYSTAL I GAVE YOU? TO HELP YOUR ADDICTION?
RIGHT. THAT STUPID ROCK. WHAT ABOUT IT?
THAT "STUPID ROCK" SAVED YOU, PAT. IT HELD THE *SPARK*. IT'S *STILL* HOLDING IT.
THE SPARK?
OF LIFE. *YOUR* LIFE.
IT'S HOLDING *TIGHT*, PAT...AND IT'S NOT GOING TO LET *GO*.
WAIT A MINUTE! ARE YOU SAYING THAT--
MAKE SOME TERRIFIC MOVIES FOR ME, WILL YOU?

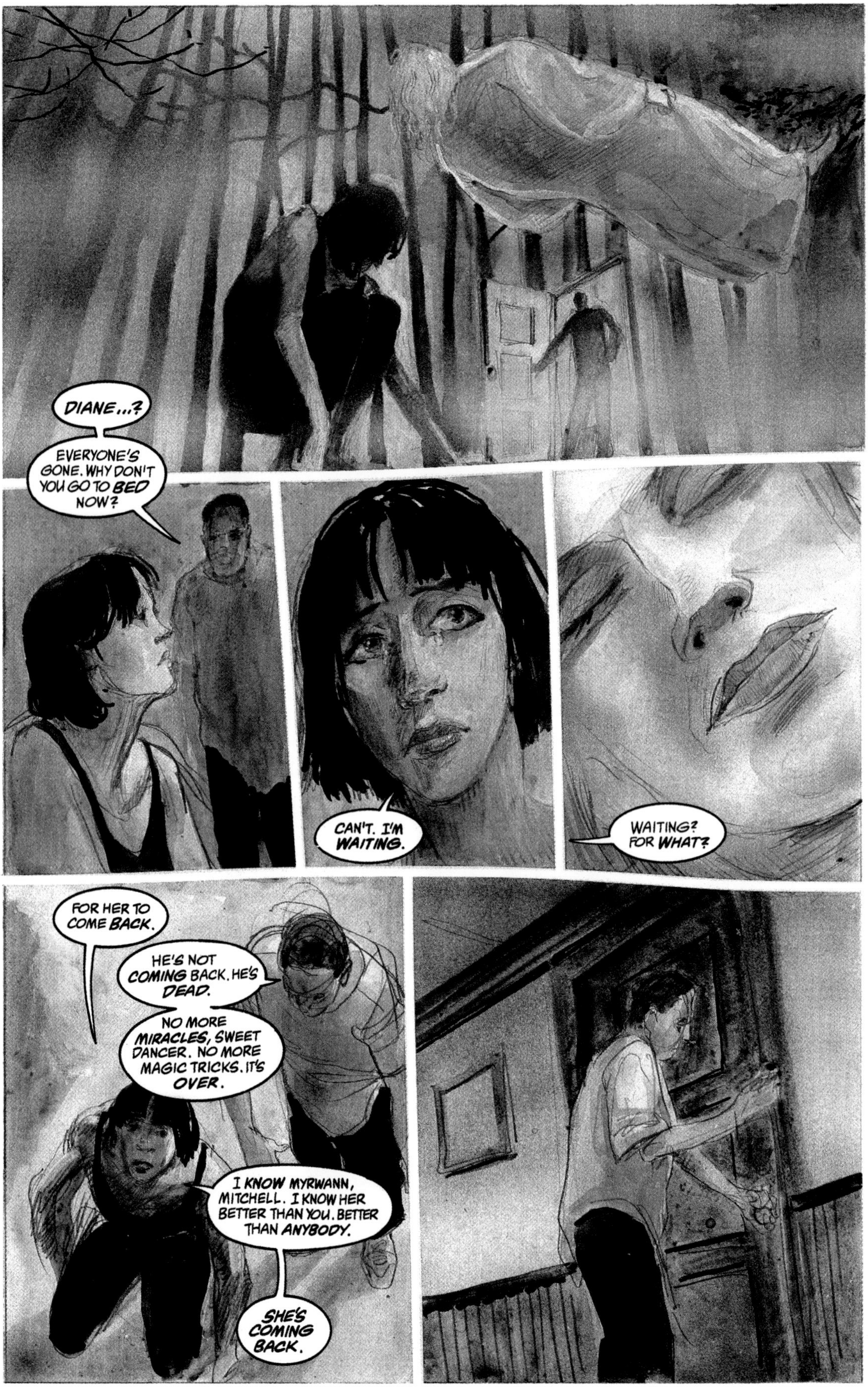
DIANE...?
EVERYONE'S GONE. WHY DON'T YOU GO TO BED NOW?
CAN'T. I'M WAITING.
WAITING? FOR WHAT?
FOR HER TO COME BACK.
HE'S NOT COMING BACK. HE'S DEAD.
NO MORE MIRACLES, SWEET DANCER. NO MORE MAGIC TRICKS. IT'S OVER.
I KNOW MYRWANN, MITCHELL. I KNOW HER BETTER THAN YOU. BETTER THAN ANYBODY.
SHE'S COMING BACK.

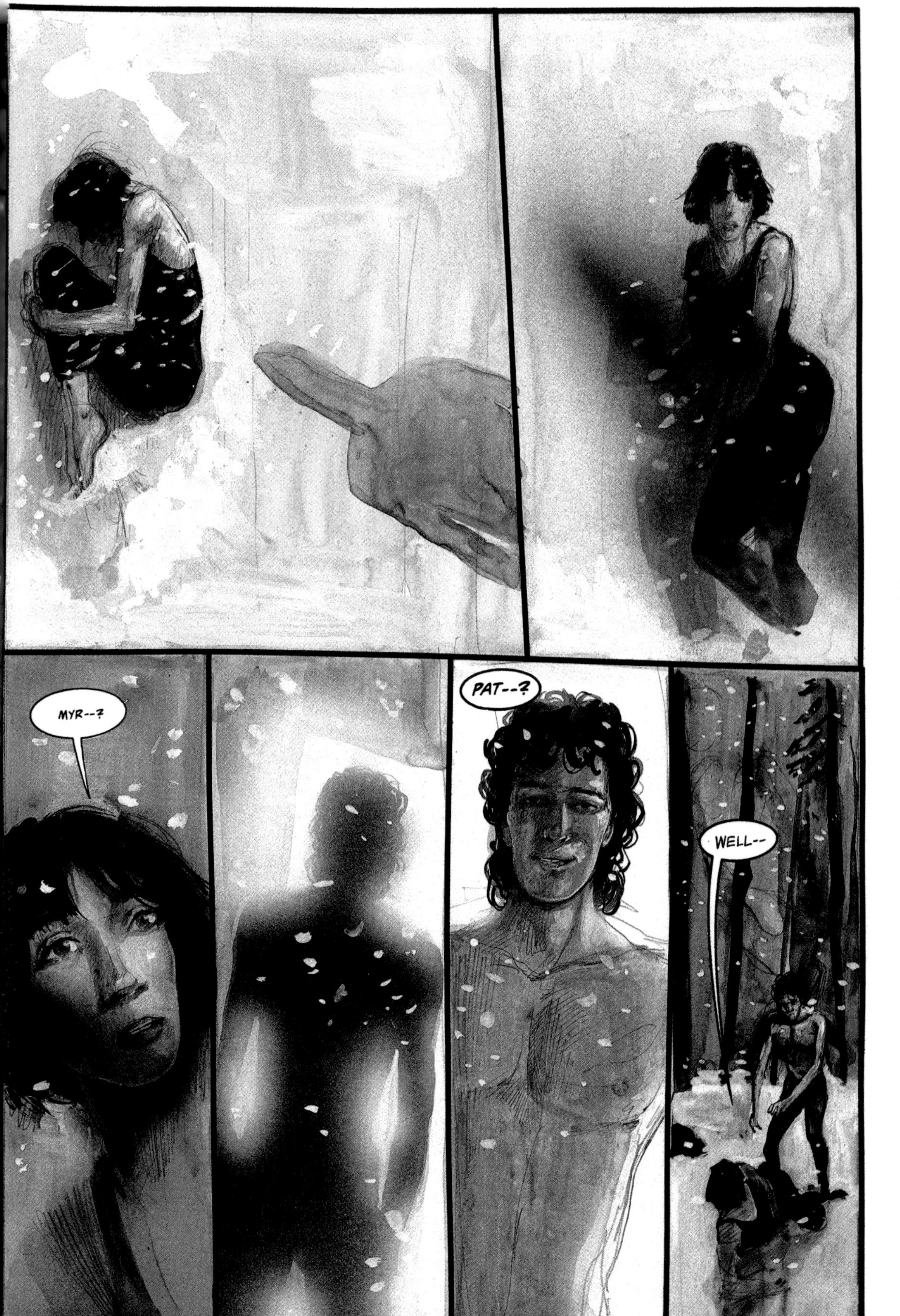
MYR--?
PAT--?
WELL--

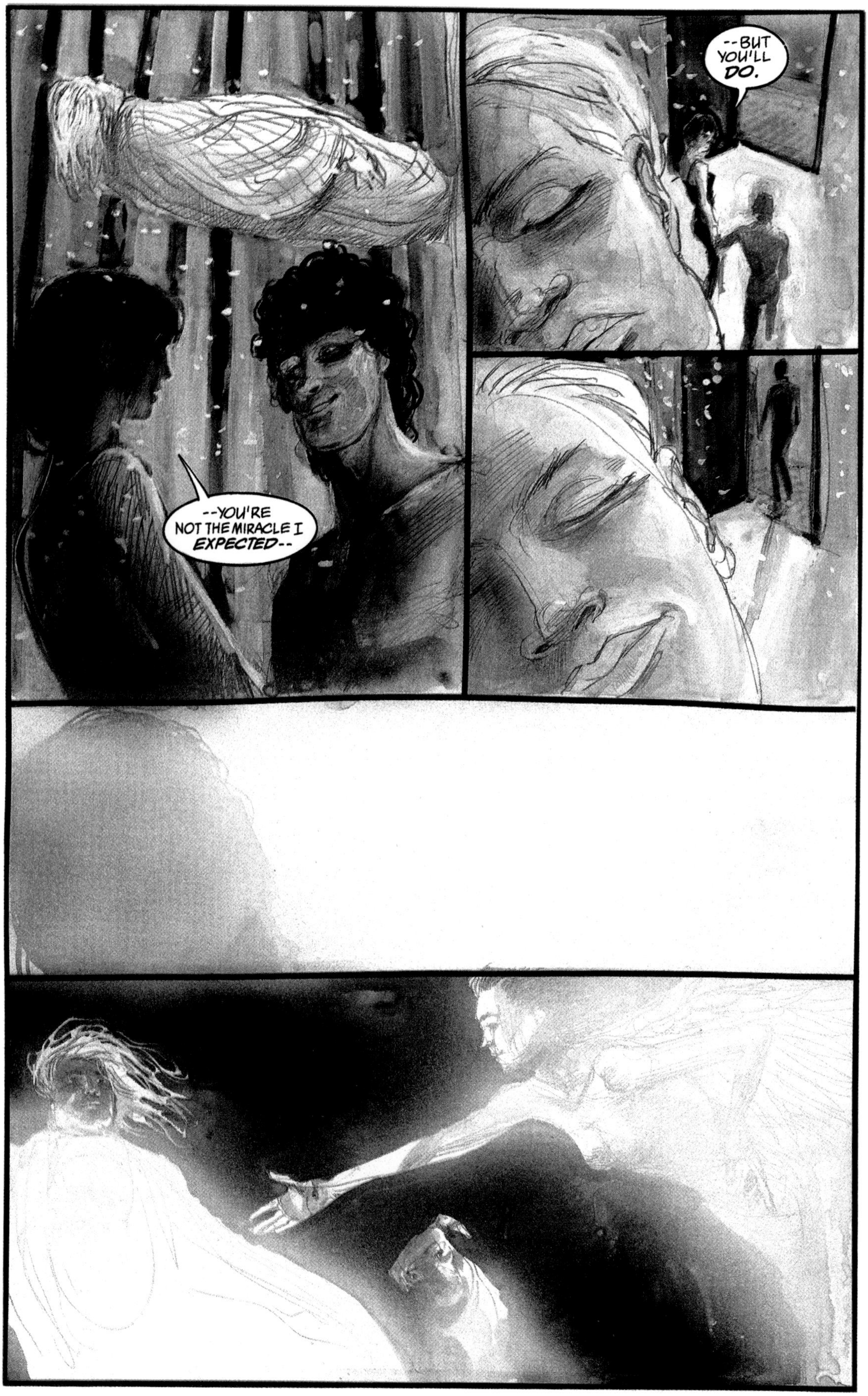
--YOU'RE NOT THE MIRACLE I EXPECTED--
--BUT YOU'LL DO.

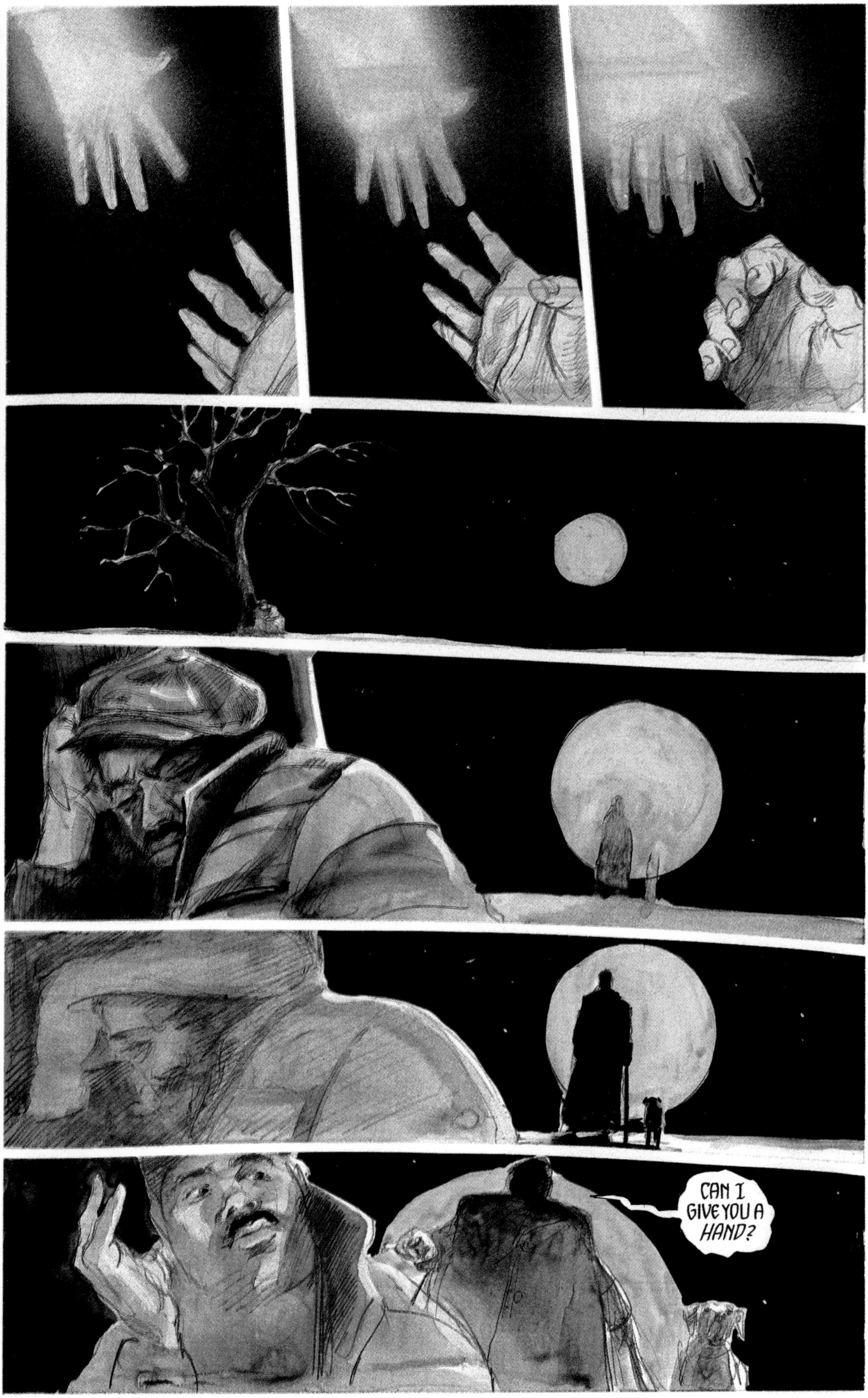
CAN I GIVE YOU A HAND?

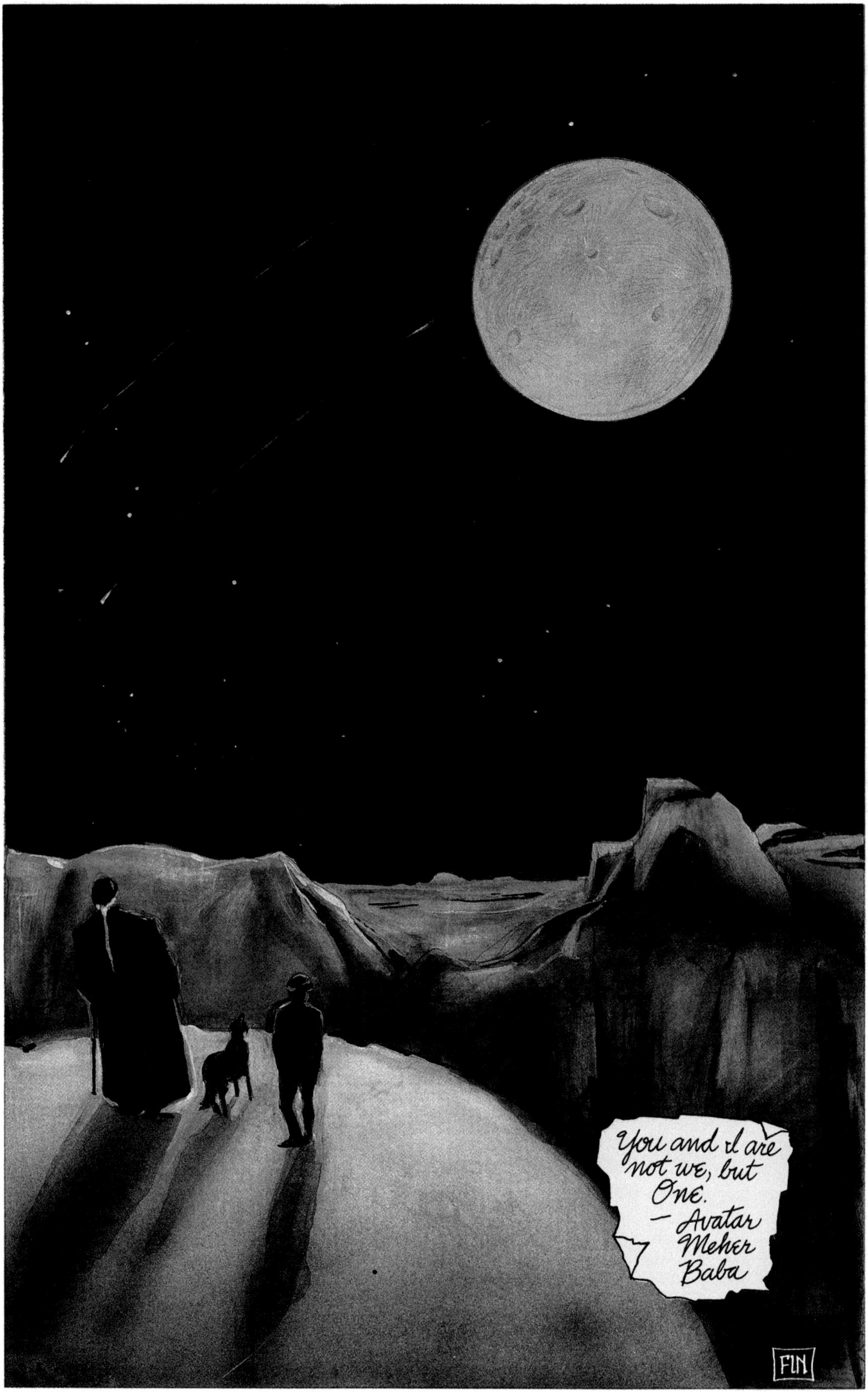
You and I are not we, but One.
— Avatar Meher Baba
FIN

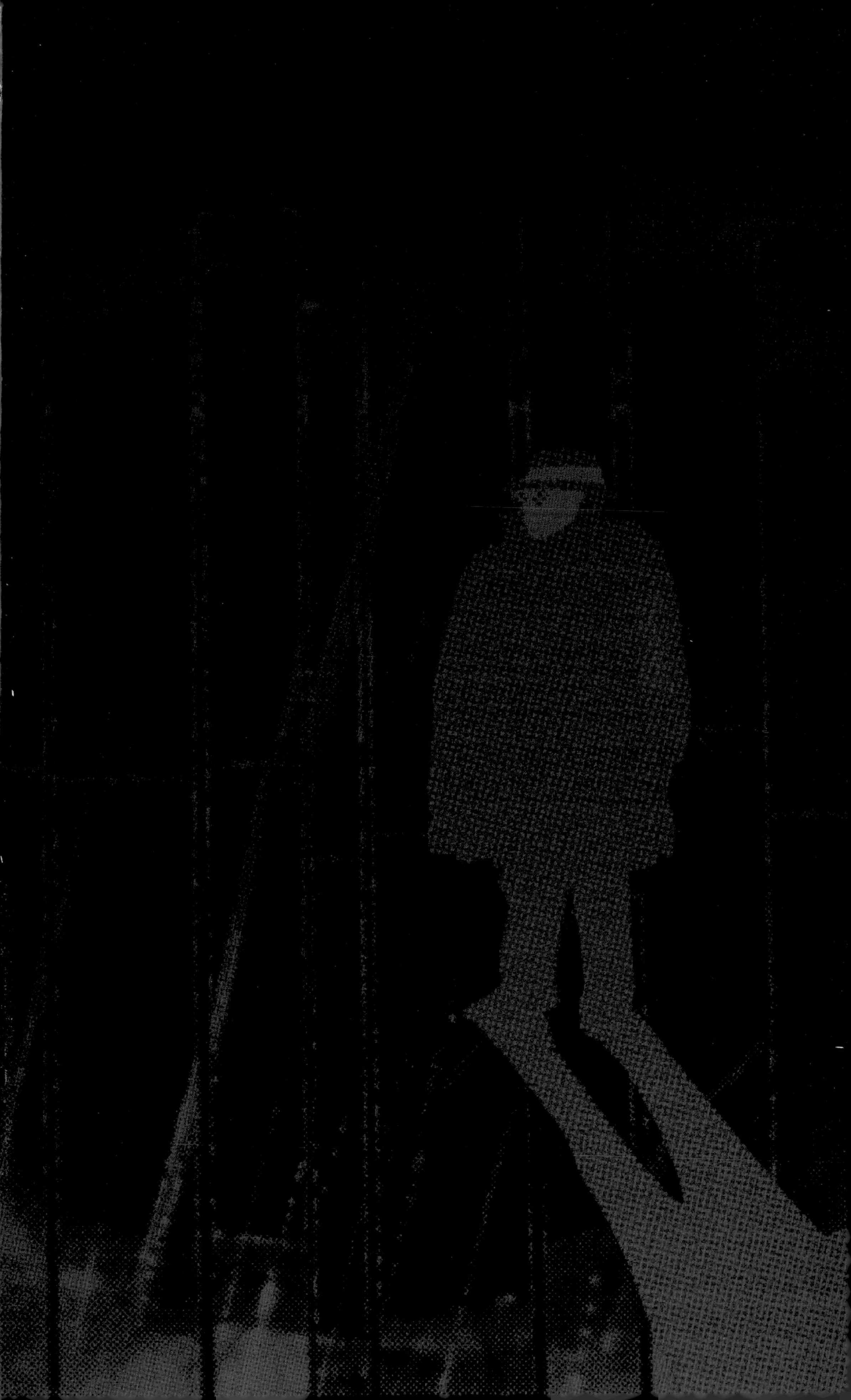